WE SHALL BE MASTERS

WE SHALL BE MASTERS

Russian Pivots to East Asia from

Peter the Great to Putin

CHRIS MILLER

HARVARD UNIVERSITY PRESS

CAMBRIDGE, MASSACHUSETTS

LONDON, ENGLAND

2021

LIBRARY OF CONGRESS CATALOGING-IN-PUBLICATION DATA

Names: Miller, Chris (Research fellow), author.
Title: We shall be masters : Russian pivots to East Asia
from Peter the Great to Putin / Chris Miller.
Description: Cambridge, Massachusetts : Harvard University
Press, 2021. | Includes bibliographical references and index.
Identifiers: LCCN 2020043291 | ISBN 9780674916449 (cloth)
Subjects: LCSH: Russia—Territorial expansion—History. |
Russia—Relations—Asia. | Asia—Relations—Russia. | Soviet
Union—Relations—Asia. | Asia—Relations—Soviet Union. |
Russia (Federation)—Relations—Asia. | Asia—Relations—
Russia (Federation). | Russia—Colonies—America.
Classification: LCC DS33.4.R8 M56 2021 | DDC 947—dc23
LC record available at https://lccn.loc.gov/2020043291

To Liya

In Europe we were hangers-on and slaves,
while in Asia we shall be masters.

In Europe we were Tatars, while in Asia we are the Europeans.

—FYODOR DOSTOYEVSKY, *A Writer's Diary*

CONTENTS

CONTENTS

Conclusion: "Heir to the Empire of Genghis Khan"
Vladimir Putin's Pivot to Asia

WE SHALL BE MASTERS

Contemporary Russia

"ONLY A SHORT DISTANCE AWAY"

Russia's Arrival on the Pacific Coast

FORT ANADYRSK was a strange place to find a Greek. The icy outpost on the Icha River was about as far from Athens as one could get. There were scarcely several dozen Russians in the entire Kamchatka Peninsula, on the Far Eastern frontier of Tsar Peter the Great's vast empire, just across the straits from Alaska. Vladimir Atlasov, a Russian explorer, had traveled to Kamchatka and arrived at Fort Anadyrsk to chart the region's rivers and coasts, opening it to navigation, to fur trapping, and to Tsar Peter's control. Atlasov's expedition confirmed that Eurasia was separated from North America by icy waters, not connected by a land bridge. He mapped Kamchatka, recording that it was "an impassable . . . peninsula that extends into the sea." The Russian explorers were accustomed to cold seas and snowy winters, but this land of smoking volcanoes and thick fogs was as strange as any they had seen. Atlasov's most unexpected discovery, however, was a man named Dembei.[1]

When the local Kamchadal people reported that they had a Russian in their custody, Atlasov ordered that he be handed over immediately. When the prisoner arrived, he had fair skin and black hair, and spoke not a word of Russian. Atlasov first thought that he must be a Greek. How a Greek could have ended up on the Kamchatkan coast, none could say. Greeks were usually Christians, but the prisoner knew nothing of Christ. By 1697, when Dembei was transferred into Atlasov's custody, Russians had been exploring Asia for many decades and had been interacting with it for centuries. Russia had signed trade treaties with China, and the two empires shared a sparsely populated borderland along their Central Asian and Siberian frontiers. Camel caravans plodded to and from China, across the Mongolian deserts, into Russian Siberia, bringing the Russians occasional news of Chinese affairs.

The Russians knew enough about China to deduce that Dembei was not Chinese. While in custody, Dembei had learned some of the language of the local Kamchadal people, so the Russians asked him the name of his country's capital city. "Edo," he said, referring to the ancient name for Tokyo, a city of which the Russians had never heard. "India!" the Russians concluded, puzzling over how an Indian had washed up on the shores of Kamchatka. Atlasov decided to send his Indian captive across Siberia to Moscow, a journey of several thousand miles. Dembei's trek across the Russian Empire would take three or four years.

Dembei was not the only person in Russia on a great journey that year. Tsar Peter the Great had set off for Europe in March 1697, seeking technology for Russia's navy and allies in his wars against the Ottoman Empire. He traveled under the name of "Peter Mikhailov," ostensibly incognito, though European newspapers reported that the visitor named Peter was actually the tsar.[2] Some foreign diplomats, knowing the young tsar's reputation for drunken revelry, assumed that the trip was "merely a cloak to allow the Tsar to get out of his country and travel in freedom." Yet Peter's purpose was far more serious. He traveled first to Riga, on the Baltic Sea, then to Konigsberg, where he met with Fredrick, Elector of Brandenberg and Duke of Prussia. Then Peter set off for Amsterdam and London, the commercial and maritime capitals of Europe. He met with Dutch and English diplomats, discussing his relations with the Ottomans, the French, and the Poles as he crafted his foreign policy. He investigated Western culture, attending Protestant church services and Quaker meetings. He studied Western technology, too—above all, the shipbuilding expertise that made England and the Netherlands great trading nations and naval powers.[3]

Peter's main interest was to bolster the foundations of Russian power so that he could wage war on his rivals. Sweden was still a major power in the Baltic Sea, and the Ottoman Empire controlled much of the Black Sea. Peter wanted to defeat both of them, seizing their territory and opening space for Russian expansion. Wars on Russia's western front were to be expected. It was along the European borderland where Russia faced its most dangerous adversaries. Europe was the source of Russia's most advanced technology, including Peter's beloved ships. And it was Europe with which Russia conducted the bulk of its trade, including in new luxuries like tobacco, which the English supplied and of which Peter was notoriously fond. Yet even though Peter's greatest wars aimed to expand Russia's borders to the west, his explorers on the edge of Siberia were continuously pushing Russia's frontier to the east. The two efforts were connected because, with the exception of China, with which Russia had contact from the caravan trade across the Mongolian plains, much of Russia's knowledge of Asia came via Dutch merchants and English frigates, from Europe.[4]

Just as Vladimir Atlasov was being introduced to Dembei along the Kamchatkan coast, on the opposite end of Eurasia, Peter the Great was befriending Amsterdam mayor Nicolaes Witsen. A famed geographer, Witsen had studied the voyages of the Dutch navigators who had sailed to Asia. The Dutch had visited the Japanese coast as far north as Hokkaido, sailed to the shores of the long island of Sakhalin, and even reached the Kuril Islands, the archipelago that dangles off Kamchatka's southern coast, not far from where Atlasov had taken control of Dembei, the Indian prisoner.

Witsen was an expert cartographer, publishing maps and collecting knowledge of the diverse lands of the East, from Siberia to Suriname, Java to Japan. His knowledge of Japan was unique. The Dutch were, at the time, the only Europeans with permission to trade with Japan, having promised that they wouldn't proselytize and would limit their activities to a single island in Nagasaki Harbor. Granted a monopoly over Europe's trade with Japan, the Dutch happily complied. When Tsar Peter arrived in Amsterdam, the city was not only a center of shipbuilding technology. It was also Europe's center of expertise about Japan.[5] Witsen and Peter struck a lasting friendship, with Witsen sharing knowledge of the Netherlands' Asian explorations.[6]

Peter returned to Moscow in summer 1698, as Dembei was just beginning his long journey across Siberia. The tsar was busy with an ambitious agenda: suppressing his rebellious *streltsy* soldiers, banishing his hated wife to a convent and replacing her with an illiterate peasant, and taxing the Russian noblemen who refused his demand that they shave their beards in the European fashion. On top of this he launched the Great Northern War, trying to overturn Swedish dominance in the Baltic Sea. Peter believed that he would only succeed if he modernized Russia by importing new technology and culture. This set up a clash with the most powerful groups in Russian society: the nobility, the church, even his own soldiers. Yet Peter was confident that Westernization—adopting Dutch and English naval technology, European fashions, and absolutist rule—was the key to success at home and abroad.[7]

In late 1701 or early 1702, as the Great Northern War raged along the shores of the Baltic Sea and Peter struggled to force Moscow's disputatious nobility to shave their beards and behave like Europeans, the mysterious captive Dembei arrived in Moscow. The learned experts of Moscow were assembled to determine the origins of the strange Indian and to ascertain how he had ended up in Kamchatka. They soon realized Atlasov's mistake. With the help of a German picture book depicting scenes of life in Japan, the mysterious prisoner from the land of Edo was properly identified: he was neither Greek nor Indian, but Japanese.

Dembei had set sail from Osaka in 1695, bound for Edo, through waters that the Dutch cartographers only vaguely knew. His ship was a normal trading vessel, stocked with rice and sake. Hit by a typhoon, it was driven a thousand miles to the north, heavily damaged, only barely reaching the Kamchatkan shores. Then Dembei's ship was set upon by the local Kamchadal people, who attacked with axes and arrows, took him captive, and later handed him over to Atlasov. From Osaka to Kamchatka, then from Fort Anadyrsk to Moscow, Dembei became the first Japanese known to have set foot in Russia's capital.[8]

Peter was plenty busy managing diplomacy with the royal houses of Europe and the religious leaders of Christendom. Yet he took time away from matters of state to meet the Japanese castaway. On January 8, 1702, Peter held an audience with Dembei at his country house. The estate itself was a reflection of Peter's personality, drawing on Western architectural traditions and incorporating the latest European technology, such as streetlights, as well as a small citadel purpose-built for Peter's personal war games. It was fitting that Peter welcomed Dembei into a residence defined by the tsar's two distinguishing characteristics: a fascination with European technology and a love of war. Dembei himself represented a third facet of Peter's rule that is usually ignored: interest in the lands far off in the east.

Records do not report what Peter and Dembei discussed. Yet the castaway appears to have been well received for, after his audience, the tsar granted him a stipend for food and clothes, ordering him to teach Russians to read and write Japanese. What grand designs Peter had for these Japanese language lessons, the sources do not say. We do know, however, that Peter met Dembei at least one other time, in 1710. Peter continued to support Russia's exploration of the North Pacific coast. Russians at the time looked jealously on Dutch, English, French, and Portuguese merchants' trade with China. They worried about the Dutch, in particular, fearing that Dutch traders, already trading with Japan, might establish a settlement on the Asian mainland.[9] Peter's diplomats, meanwhile, negotiated with China to delineate the two countries' border and to expand and regulate the caravan trade between Siberia and Beijing.[10]

Today, Peter is not remembered for his knowledge of Asia or his interest in Japan. He is known instead for his Westernization of Russian culture, his autocratic politics, his love of ships, and his wars on the European front. In foreign policy, his military machine was kept busy fighting Sweden and the Ottoman Empire. Peter's crowning achievement was the founding of St. Petersburg, a port on the Baltic Sea that he envisioned as Russia's "window to the West." Yet as he lay on his deathbed in December 1724, Peter fixated not on the West, which he jealously admired, but on Asia. "I have been thinking over the matter," he wrote one of his admirals just before his death, of "finding a passage to China and India through the Arctic Sea."[11]

A EUROPEAN POWER?

The image of Peter the Great laying on his deathbed dreaming of India and China is not how we usually think of Russia's foreign policy priorities. The contradiction posed by Peter—a Westernizer constantly at war with his Western neighbors—has provided fertile ground for generations of historians to psychoanalyze Russians and their leaders' relations with Europe. Peter was a pupil of European learning, a jealous imitator of European fashions and culture, and yet also an invader of Europe, a would-be conqueror of the continent. On the European front, Russia's alliances have fluctuated over time, of course, and its borders have moved back and forth with the shifting geopolitical winds. Periods of Russian expansion have induced other powers to try to contain Russia, while containment has produced feelings of anger and humiliation that incite the Russian government to build vast armies and devote enormous resources to breaking out. From Peter's Great Northern War to Alexander I's crushing of Napoleon's armies to Nicholas I's defeat by the British and French in the Crimean War, through Stalin and the Soviet period, cycles of expansion and containment in Europe have continued apace.[12]

Russia is seen primarily via this European lens—if not exactly part of Europe, then at least deeply interlinked with it. This perspective is as common in Russia as it is in the country's neighbors. And there is good reason for it. The children of the tsars intermarried with the European nobility while the Bolsheviks imported a philosophy, Marxism, developed by Germans who lived in London. The trade of preindustrial Russia—exporting grain and importing industrial goods and luxury products—was conducted primarily with Europe, just as today most of Russia's oil and gas is shipped to European markets. Russia's great novelists, such as Leo Tolstoy and Fyodor Dostoyevsky, are read alongside other European classics. Today, as under the tsars, Russia's ruling class vacations along the French Riviera and in the Swiss Alps. Is Russia "European"? The question is impossible to answer because the concept of Europe is itself something that has shifted over time. Is Turkey part of Europe? Are the Balkans? Is Italy? There is no immutable answer to these questions, just as there is no unchanging definition of Russia's relationship with Europe. But Russia's complicated European orientation has been the starting point of most attempts to understand the country's foreign policy for centuries.[13]

In terms of foreign policy, the centrality of Europe to the history of Russian diplomacy is rarely questioned. Most histories of Russia's wars and of Russian diplomacy are centered on the country's relations with Europe, its drive toward European seas, its appetite for European territory, and its complicated relationship with European culture and civilization. In Russia, the wars with Napoleon in the early 1800s and the struggle with Hitler during World War II—both conflicts fought almost entirely on the country's European borderlands—shaped Russians' perception of their identity as a great power in European politics.

It is true that Russia has waged devastating wars over the approaches to St. Petersburg, the forests and steppe of Poland and Ukraine, and the borderlands with the Ottoman Empire. In the 300 years since Tsar Peter's reign, the greatest of all Russia's geopolitical contests have been over Eastern Europe. This was the territory over which Napoleon's Grande Armée marched in 1812. Russian, Austro-Hungarian, and German troops fought over these territories in the bloody battles of World War I. And it was across Eastern Europe that Hitler's forces drove during Operation Barbarossa. It makes sense that Russians have focused more on threats from the West: it is far easier to march across the thousand miles that separate Berlin from Moscow than it is to reach Russia's capital from Beijing, which is well over three times as distant.

Yet none of the rulers involved in these great struggles—neither Peter the Great, nor Alexander I, nor Stalin—viewed their foreign policies solely through a European lens. For all the destructive wars over the bloodlands of Eastern Europe, Asia has, at certain times, attracted as much Russian attention as Europe. Ever since Peter the Great, the famed Westernizer, took time off from his campaigns against Sweden to meet Dembei and to study Japan, the promise of opportunity in the East has piqued the interest of even Russia's most devoted Westernizers. It was Peter the Great's explorers, after all, who established Fort Anadyrsk on the distant Kamchatkan coast, many years before Russians founded St. Petersburg. Fort Anadyrsk was an icy outpost rather than a warm-water port, but the prospect of new lands and rich discoveries inspired further exploration of Asia. Moreover, Peter was not the first tsar to have ordered expeditions eastward. As early as the 1500s, Ivan the Terrible sent forces deep into Siberia to acquire new lands for the tsar.

What began a half millennium ago has continued, in an on-and-off fashion, into the present. Over the centuries, Russia established a chain of settlements across Siberia, from Irkutsk, on the shores of Lake Baikal, to Yakutsk, on the Lena River in Russia's far northeast where winter temperatures regularly touch −40°F, to Okhotsk, a small spit of land jutting out into the cold seas of the North Pacific, not far from where Atlasov first encountered Dembei. This activity in Asia has brought interaction with Asia's great powers. Alliances and clashes with China, Japan, and other powers in the Pacific have been recurring features of Russian diplomatic history, even under Russia's most Westernizing leaders, like Peter.

"WHAT IS ASIA TO US?"

After Peter returned to Moscow from Amsterdam at the end of his great journey, Mayor Nicolaes Witsen sent the tsar a new drawing of the Eurasian landmass. "A New Map," it was titled, "of the North and East Part of Asia and Europe." Marking rivers and coastlines, forests and peaks, the map presented the cutting edge of cartographical science. Witsen based his knowledge of Siberia and the Arctic on accounts from the Russian explorers, while he drew details of China's geography from Chinese mapmakers and Jesuits based in Beijing. Arabic, Japanese, and Spanish maps were used to fill in gaps along the Pacific Coast and in Central Asia. The result was "Columbus-like" in opening new lands to European knowledge, one British admirer wrote to Witsen after receiving a copy.[14]

What did Peter the Great see upon unfurling Witsen's map? Russia appeared part of a vast Eurasian continent stretching all the way to the Pacific, to lands that Peter's explorers and fur trappers only vaguely knew. At the top of the map was the long island of Novaya Zemlya, stretching for 200 miles through the Arctic Sea, in the icy waters to the northwest of the port of Archangelsk. Then the map traced Russia's Arctic coast, illustrating the great Siberian rivers, the Ob, Irtysh, and Lena, which gathered waters from the center of Eurasia before reaching the Arctic Sea in the far north. In the upper right corner of the map was Kamchatka, the peninsula where Atlasov had just become acquainted with Dembei, which was so poorly understood that it barely features on the map. From Kamchatka the map cut southward down the Pacific Coast, across the still mysterious delta where the Amur River emptied into the sea before reaching the peninsula of Korea. The bottom edge of the map turned back westward, illustrating the geography of northern China and the lands of the Mongols; through the mountains and steppes inhabited by Kyrgyz, Kazakhs, and Kalmyks; eventually reaching the Caspian Sea and the far eastern border of the Ottoman Empire. These lands, Witsen's map declared, constituted the "North and East Part of Asia and Europe."

Peter the Great had a clear conception of Europe: the lands to his West. Among the European countries, Peter thought of Sweden, which then dominated the Baltic Sea, and the Kingdom of Prussia, just beginning its rise to dominance over the German lands. He thought of the Hapsburg Empire, ruling most of Central Europe, and France, then at the peak of its power under Louis XIV, the Sun King. On the far coast of Europe were the Netherlands and Britain, the maritime powers that Peter most admired. These were the lands that defined European culture, the economies that drove technological innovation, the geopolitical heavyweights that shaped the balance of power on Peter's western frontier. The great powers of Europe were models for Peter, and the continent's absolutist monarchs provided a template as the tsar sought to strengthen his own power.

Maps like Witsen's made visible what Peter intuitively knew: Russia stood astride vast territories and bordered many lands, of which Europe was only one. But what were these other lands? Could they, like Europe, be grouped together as a single unit? Many Russians referred to the countries stretching from the Ottoman Empire through Central Asia to China and the Pacific as "Asia" or often as "the East." The definition of these territories in Russian thinking shifted over time. When the Russian Foreign Ministry established an "Asiatic Department" in 1819, it had two subdivisions. The first managed relations with the Ottoman Empire, Persia, the Georgians, and the peoples of the Caucasus Mountains, not yet then fully under Russian rule. The second managed affairs with the peoples of the steppe, stretching north and east of the Caspian Sea all the way to the lands of the Kazakhs. Relations with China, meanwhile, were controlled not by the Foreign Ministry, but by an embassy of the Russian Orthodox Church in Beijing.[15] In the mind of Witsen the mapmaker, Asia stretched almost the entire length his 1697 map, from the southern edge of Europe, in the Balkans and the coast of the Black Sea, all the way to the Pacific. Peter, who learned his geography from the Dutch masters, had a similar view.

"What is Asia to us?" Dostoyevsky asked in a famous essay in 1881, over 150 years after Peter's reign.[16] Answering that question first required ascertaining which lands "Asia" referred to. Witsen's definition of Asia as nearly the entire Eurasian landmass illustrated Russia's connections with many non-European lands. In the nineteenth century it was common to contrast "European Russia," referring to the country's Western core, around Moscow and St. Petersburg, with "Asian Russia," which referred to almost everything else. A related Russian concept is that of *Vostok*—"the East" or "the Orient," which sounds less archaic in contemporary Russian usage than it does in English. In the nineteenth century, "the East" was used to refer to lands as diverse as Croatia and Korea, stretching from the Ottoman borderlands to the Pacific Ocean and encompassing everything in between. In today's Russia, it would sound strange to refer to one of the countries in the Balkans—situated southwest of Moscow—as "Eastern." Yet "the East" is still a vast territory in contemporary Russia usage. Today the Moscow-based Institut Vostokove-deniia (Institute of Oriental Studies) has scholars specializing in topics from Israel to Mongolia.

Though the terminology can be tricky, Russians have approached the various lands they referred to as "the East" in different ways. Russia's relations with the Balkans differed from its ties with the Caucasus; its approach to the Caspian Sea can be distinguished from the drivers of its policy toward East Asia and the Pacific Ocean. Peter the Great might not have considered the Ottoman Empire part of Europe, but it was a central player in the European international system, forging alliances with different European powers even as it traded extensively with them, exchanging goods, fashions, and ideas. The countries of the Caucasus, too, were deeply intertwined with Russia from as early as the 1700s and were an integral part of the Russian Empire from the 1800s. The steppe lands that stretch from Kalmykia on the northern shores of the Caspian Sea all the way to the oases of Central Asia had long been subject to Russian settlement.

When Russians looked at world maps, China and the Pacific coast were almost always seen as a different part of "the East" from the Balkans, the Middle East, or Central Asia. By Peter's time Russians had for several decades conducted regular caravan trade with China, having even signed a treaty delineating the Russia-China border during the 1600s. But the realities of distance in an era of travel on horse or by foot meant that China and the Pacific Coast were much farther away than the other territories that Russians lumped together under the concept of "the East." Exchanges of goods and ideas with East Asia were more limited than with lands located closer to the Russian heartland. From the perspective of Moscow or St. Petersburg, Japan, Korea, and the lands across the Pacific were even farther away and more unknown. Despite the dreams of Peter the Great and some of his successors, it was not until the time of Alexander I (1801–1825) that Russia began thinking seriously about East Asia and the Pacific Ocean as a space of territorial enlargement, commercial expansion, or geopolitical competition. From Japan and Korea to China and its vast borderlands, to the thousands of miles of the Pacific Ocean's coast, the dynamics governing Russia's relations with these lands were different from those motivating Russian policy in other parts of the vast continent that Russians referred to as "the East."

"IN ASIA WE SHALL BE MASTERS"

Why would Russia involve itself in East Asia, in lands far from its core interests, thousands of miles from its main cities or most of its population? Many historians of Russian diplomacy have interpreted Russia's engagement in Asia as driven by enduring interests, whether a need for warm-water ports, a deep-set desire for superiority over China and Japan, a craving for control of valuable trade routes, or a fear that other great powers—the British Empire in the nineteenth century or the Americans in the twentieth—might set upon Russia from the East. The thesis that Russian diplomacy is driven by "continuous policy" and an "overarching vision" has deep roots in Western historians' thinking about Russia—and in Russia's thinking about itself. Amid the last major wave of American research on the history of Russian foreign policy during the early Cold War, historians identified deep factors such as an "urge to the sea" that supposedly drove Russia's expansion from the forests of Eastern Europe, across Eurasia's great rivers, to outlets on the ocean as distant from Moscow as the Far Eastern port of Vladivostok.[17]

The argument that Russia has enduring interests dictated by geography dates back at least 200 years. In the nineteenth century, discussion focused on Russia's supposed fixation on accessing warm-water ports and controlling maritime chokepoints. "It is abundantly clear," declared the famed American naval strategist Alfred Thayer Mahan in 1900, "that Russia can never be satisfied with the imperfect, and politically dependent, access to the sea afforded her by the Baltic and the Black Sea." Russia, Mahan argued, needs "access to the sea as extensive and as free as possible: on the east by the Chinese seaboard."[18]

Geography does create enduring realities. And culture, social structures, and political organizations change only slowly, creating patterns that persist over time. "Just let people begin to understand," Dostoyevsky exclaimed in 1881, "that our outlet is in the Asia of the future; that our riches are there; that our ocean is there." These were ostensibly enduring interests: the location of the Pacific Ocean wouldn't change, nor would the existence of Asian markets, though their attractiveness fluctuated over time. Dostoyevsky perceived another supposedly enduring reality of Russia's relations with Asia: it need not suffer from the inferiority complex that had beguiled Russian relations with Europe since at least the time of Peter the Great. "In Europe we were hangers-on and slaves, while in Asia we shall be masters," Dostoyevsky declared to his readers. "In Europe we were Tatars, while in Asia we are the Europeans."[19]

Yet the argument that enduring factors—whether geography, commerce, or identity—are the best guide to understanding Russian engagement with Asia fits poorly with the historical evidence. Rather than enduring, Russia's level of interest in Asia has fluctuated wildly over time. Geography, culture, and society may change slowly, but their interaction with politics can shift rapidly when conditions change. Russia's foreign policy in Asia has been episodic and erratic. The Kremlin's definitions of its core interests have shifted frequently, along with its willingness to devote resources to achieve them.

At times, Russia has devoted enormous attention to China, Japan, Korea, and the Pacific Ocean's other military powers, including the British Empire and the United States. Certain tsars, at certain times, saw opportunity in Asia. Others saw only risk. Some saw danger and believed that the best defense was to expand Russia's role. Others wanted only to batten down the hatches and defend what Russia had. Others still barely thought of Asia at all, even if writers like Dostoyevsky promised that "we shall be masters." Along the shores of the Pacific, Russia has sometimes been a decisive player, driven by spasms of intense activity. But at other times it has ignored Asia and has been all but irrelevant. How can this be explained?

"THE RUGGED RUSSIAN BEAR"

For centuries, analysts of Russian diplomacy have advanced theories to explain why "the rugged Russian bear . . . has crawl'd out of his lair," as a nineteenth-century British ditty put it. But Russia's cycles of interest and disinterest in Asia follow no obvious schematic, nor are they mostly explainable by external events. One might expect that the emergence of a power vacuum in Asia would pique Russian interest, but Russian leaders have just as frequently focused on the region when it was a zone of intense competition as when it was a strategic backwater. At times, Russia has devoted energy to eastward expansion when it was locked out of European politics and looking for other outlets. At other times, however, Russia has paid attention to Asia when it sensed not opportunity but danger in the rising influence of

Pacific Ocean powers. The unifying factor behind Russia's periodic pivots to Asia is the bubbling up from within Russian society and politics of a new optimism about what can be accomplished, a new hope for diplomatic partners and for trade, and a new assessment of Russia's military might, coupled with a belief that force can be deployed to win influence abroad.

This optimism has often been misplaced. Russia's periodic spasms of attention on Asia have rarely been matched by commensurate shifts in Russian resources in the country's Far East. The focus of Russia's leaders can change rapidly; the country's infrastructure, its trade links, and its military emplacements do not. There is an enduring gap between Russia's periodic bursts of enthusiasm about Asia and the reality that its interests and its capabilities are anchored in the West. This creates a persistent dilemma for every Russian strategist looking to play a bigger role in Asia. It also produces a pattern of pullback from Asia when exuberant dreams about Russia's future role in Asia are punctured; when leaders realize that projecting power in Asia requires costly investments; and when the realities of Russia's limited infrastructure in Siberia and its Far East make asserting an expansive role in Asia difficult or impossible. Russia's interest in Asia fluctuates, but its limitations are enduring.

In 1928, historian Andrei Lobanov-Rostovsky published an essay titled "Russia at the Crossroads: Europe or Asia."[20] Born in Japan to the child of a Russian diplomat, Lobanov-Rostovsky had left Russia after the 1917 revolution, spending time at universities in Paris and London.[21] The Bolsheviks who chased his family out of Russia, he believed, marked a new era in Russian history—an era in which Russia might be more closely linked to Asia than to Europe. Lobanov-Rostovsky saw this as a return to a historical trend, with the Bolsheviks evidence of a shift toward the "Asiatic stage." "If we follow the course of Russian history," he declared, "we shall find a perpetual swinging of the pendulum between two poles of attraction, Europe and Asia."[22]

The pendulum metaphor gets some things right about Russia's foreign policy orientation, such as the episodic nature of Russia's involvement in Asia. It correctly highlights the extent to which, at least on this question, history has repeated itself many times over. The subsequent chapters will trace multiple "pendulum swings" set off by a surge of optimism that soon dissipated as hopeful bubbles were burst by logistical realities, domestic disagreement, and military defeat. Yet the image of a pendulum swinging between Europe and Asia understates the extent to which, even during the times in which Russia has focused on Asia, the realities of geography have made it impossible to disengage with Europe. The sinews of trade, political interlinkages, and geography bind Europe and Russia too tightly. Even when Russia has been its most engaged in Asia—whether fighting the Russo-Japanese War, spreading communism to China, or inciting the Korean War—it has been motivated in no small part by its relationship with Western powers, struggling for influence in Asia in the hope that this will enhance Russia's bargaining position in Europe. Even in Asia, Russia is a Eurocentric power.

There are two explanations for why this European orientation has persisted. The geopolitical factor is straightforward: for several centuries, the world's great powers have been located on Russia's western borders, in Europe. This was true when the relevant powers were the Swedes and the Ottomans in the seventeenth century or the British and German Empires in the nineteenth. It is true now, when the power in question is the United States, which borders Russia on the Pacific Ocean and the Arctic, but whose standoff with Russia, which dates to the earliest days of the Cold War, has focused on Europe. The rise of China today shifts this dynamic somewhat, but no more so than the rise of the Sino-Soviet antagonism in the 1960s, nor the start of the Russo-Japanese War in 1904. Asia has often had powerful countries, and Russians have often believed that Asian powers were rising in importance. But Russia has always perceived the more important great powers to be in Europe. Since the Mongol armies of Genghis Khan's heirs subjugated Russia in the 1200s, all the existential threats faced by Russia, whether from the Swedes, the Poles, the Habsburgs, Napoleon, or Hitler, have come from the West.

In economic terms, too, Asia has always been relatively unimportant for Russia. On a regular basis over the past several centuries, many Russians have expected this to change, pointing toward Asia's massive markets, vast populations, and rapid growth rates. But no level of Asian economic growth in the past has ever succeeded in reorienting Russia's economy to the East— neither Japan's industrialization after the 1868 Meiji Restoration, nor the entry of China into the global economy in the late nineteenth century, nor Japan's post-1945 economic boom, nor China's extraordinary economic ascent in recent decades. Russia's economic linkages with Asia have undulated over time, rolling upward and downward like the hills over which camel caravans plodded as they marched from Siberia to Beijing. But then, as now, most of Russia's trade and investment was with Europe. Russia has regularly been seized by dreams of new riches and by claims that the world economy's future is in Asia. Over the past several centuries, it has commonly been asserted that the possibilities of Asian trade are just about to be finally realized. Thus far, these hopes have always disappointed.

This is why the "enduring interests" thesis so poorly explains Russian foreign policy in Asia. Geography has persisted, social and cultural institutions have changed only slowly, but the level of attention Russia devotes to Asia has fluctuated wildly. Diplomatic energy, military power, and economic leverage in Asia has been deployed in spasms, driven at times by new power balances or economic opportunities, but more often by subjective factors: hopes and dreams of what might be accomplished in Asia; perceptions of opportunities, some real, many imagined. When these overoptimistic expectations are dashed, claims that Russia has a unique Asian role are promptly rolled back or abandoned.

The only "enduring" feature that unites Russia's various Asian pivots is the role of excessive optimism in launching them. At different times, Russians have hoped that they might find warm-water ports, rich farmland, vast Asian markets, new lands open for conquest, riches, and glory. Only a small fraction of these hopes materialized, usually at far greater cost than initially expected. Many were naive from the outset; others were based on a profound misreading either of Asian opportunities or Russian capabilities. Rather than enduring interests, Russian foreign policy in Asia has been built on a foundation of fantasies, on dreams and delusions.

This has limited the durability and duration of Russia's great "turns to the East," but it has not deterred the next generation of Russians from waiting a few decades and trying again. There is always a new technology, a new ideology, a new distribution of power that can be construed as providing an opportunity for gold or glory in Asia. Hence Peter the Great's deathbed dream of Arctic sea routes to Asia has today been resurrected in many Russians' hopes that the melting of Arctic ice caps will open a highway for trade between Asia and the West. Such hopes and dreams fit the historical pattern. Since the days of Dembei, the Kamchatkan castaway, Russia's diplomats and strategists have been on constant lookout for Asian opportunities. The explorer Vladimir Atlasov was confused about how an Indian could have washed up on the Kamchatkan coastline in 1697, given the thousands of miles that separated Russia's North Pacific coastline from the warm waters of the Indian Ocean. Yet scarcely two decades later, in the final years of Peter the Great's reign, a different Russian officer advised the tsar to use Kamchatka as a springboard to dominion in the East—to Japan, China, even India, which, this officer assured the tsar, was "only a short distance away."[23]

1

LORD OF ALASKA

Tsar Alexander I's Transpacific Empire

"RUSSIAN RIGHTS on the most remote islands in Russian possessions should be strengthened at once," read the orders. Aleksandr Baranov was to demonstrate Russian control by displaying crests every time he made landfall as he sailed from Russia's Pacific coast toward Kamchatka, then up the Aleutian Islands, before finally reaching Alaska. "You will do all in your power to carry out these instructions, making it your goal to extend the boundaries of the Russian Empire," the orders continued. "You will regard it as your sacred duty . . . to extend the glory and benefits of the Empire and the welfare of her subjects in the most remote regions now and in the future."[1]

Born in the 1740s to a family of merchants in a small town northeast of St. Petersburg, Aleksandr Baranov's life mapped the rise and fall of Russia's dreams of empire in the North Pacific. Tsar Alexander I, who ruled Russia from 1801 to 1825, wanted to build an empire on the Pacific—at least for a time. Russia's settlement of Alaska had its roots in the decades before Alexander took the throne. Explorers like Vladimir Atlasov mapped Kamchatka; seafarers such as Vitus Bering charted the North Pacific coastline in the 1720s and 1730s; Russian fur trappers established a Russian presence on the shores of the Pacific. But until Alexander I's reign began in 1801, Russia's rulers mostly ignored the North Pacific colonies. Alexander's predecessors occasionally approved initiatives to explore Alaska, but devoted little attention to the scarcely understood waters of the North Pacific.

During the first decade of the 1800s however, Russians began to see new opportunities in the region. The Napoleonic Wars—a period in which Russia fought a series of devastating conflicts in Europe—might not have seemed like an auspicious time for expansion. But Russians began to perceive the Pacific Ocean as field in which they could outcompete their rivals, claiming new territories, establishing new trade routes, and founding new bases from which to project Russian power. Over the first half of Alexander I's reign, Russia's ambitions in the region ballooned. The tsar and his advisers imagined an empire centered on Alaska, spreading toward Japan, California, and even Hawaii. Aleksandr Baranov, appointed to govern Russian America, was tasked with making this vision a reality.[2]

THE ORIGINS OF RUSSIAN AMERICA

Aleksandr Baranov volunteered for service in Alaska to redeem a failed business career. He had moved to Irkutsk, one of Siberia's biggest cities, in 1781, seeking riches on Russia's frontier. He invested in a variety of businesses, including one to ship vodka from three distilleries to frozen Siberian outposts. Baranov took out large loans yet his sales stagnated, and he struggled to repay his debts. By the end of the 1780s, these ventures failing, Baranov signed up to work for Grigory Shelikhov, one of Siberia's leading fur traders, who had grand plans to expand not only throughout the Kuril Islands off Russia's Pacific coast, but even across the Pacific Ocean. Shelikhov had been born in 1748 in Rylsk, a small town on the far western frontier of the Russian Empire, near the present-day border with Ukraine. In 1772, his father, a merchant, sent him eastward to Siberia, in part to develop the family business, in part to avoid a plague that was then ravaging the country. Upon arriving in Siberia, Shelikhov struck up a partnership with another merchant who had fur trading interests that stretched all the way to the Pacific Ocean port of Okhotsk, from where Russian ships could sail to Alaska's Aleutian Islands. In 1775, Shelikhov married Natalia Kozhevina, who managed his growing business empire.[3]

In 1790, Baranov accepted a five-year contract to build Shelikhov's business in Alaska. Did Baranov have what it would take? "He was not burdened with religion, was loose in morals, sometimes drunk, and would lie officially without scruple," one of his biographers reported. For an empire builder on the rough Alaskan frontier, these were useful qualities. So, too, were his "energetic" character and his "shrewd yet coarse" personality, as he sought to transform a hostile wilderness into a factory of furs.[4]

By the time of Baranov's appointment, Russians had been exploring and hunting along Alaska's islands and coasts for almost half a century. They were pulled ever eastward, hopping up the Aleutian Island chain and toward the Alaskan mainland, driven above all by a need for new hunting grounds. Native Alaskans had long coexisted with the region's sea creatures, killing only small numbers for fur and food. When Russian hunters entered Alaskan waters, they were spurred on by the global fur trade stretching from Europe to China. They hunted so aggressively that the population of maritime mammals along the shores of Russia's new territories plummeted.

In the fifteen years after Vitus Bering, who discovered Alaska for Russia, died of scurvy and starvation on an island off the Kamchatkan coast, the Russians hunted the animals on that island toward extinction. So Russian hunters moved eastward along the Aleutian Islands to new hunting grounds, coercing native Aleut and Alutiiq peoples, who were skilled hunters, to collect furs for them in vast quantities. By 1750, just a decade after Bering's death, Russians began large-scale hunting in the upper Aleutian Islands. Soon there were few otters left on the entire Aleutian chain. By the early 1780s, Russians began pushing yet farther eastward in search of new furs.[5]

Russian explorers had known of Kodiak, Alaska's largest island, since 1763. Shelikhov, the Siberian fur magnate, believed that Kodiak could serve as Russia's next rich source of fur. He organized his first expedition to the island in 1783. Upon making landfall he fought with the island's inhabitants, killing perhaps several hundred with guns while losing six of his own men to his opponents' arrows. Having seized the island for Russia, Shelikhov established a settlement at Three Saints Bay and hunkered down for the winter. By the time spring arrived, eleven of his sixty-eight men had died, nine of them from scurvy.[6]

When the ice began to melt, Shelikhov found an island rich in plants and animals—the type of island where, he believed, Russians could live. "There are also good lands suitable for agriculture, which was confirmed by my own experiments having planted barley, millet, peas, beans, pumpkins, carrots, mustard, beetroot, potatoes, turnips and rhubarb," Shelikhov reported.

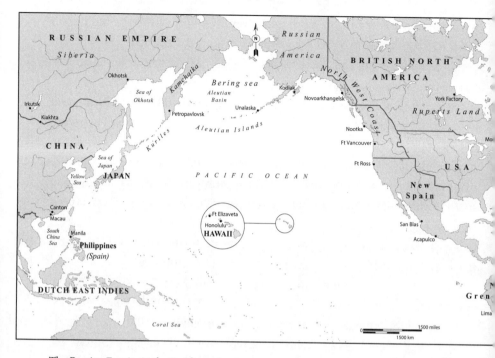

The Russian Empire in the Pacific, early 1800s

"Everything came up very well . . . there are meadows suitable for making hay, and many types of grass, and in places cattle can subsist through the whole winter." And "berries are plentiful: raspberry, blueberry, blackberry, cloudberry, partridgeberry, guelder rose, cranberry and brambleberry."[7] With a little work, Shelikhov promised, the island would prove a suitable base for the expansion of Russian fur hunters across Alaska's southern coast.

The prospects for Russian hunters seemed rich indeed. "Sea animals include: sea otter, sea lion, whales, seal," Shelikhov reported. And on land: "beavers, otters . . . foxes, wolves, bears, ermine, deer, sable, hare, wolverine, lynx, marmot." The island was also replete with native inhabitants who could be hired or coerced to serve as hunters. Kodiak's residents live in dugout huts, "have no conception of divinity," and "are extremely fond of steam baths," Shelikhov wrote, leading "lives very little different from those of cattle."[8] This presented no problem to Shelikhov so long as they could be put to work like cattle, too. Upon returning to mainland Russia in 1786, Shelikhov set off organizing new expeditions to expand his hunting business in Alaska. He hired Aleksandr Baranov to be his deputy.

"IT IS ONE THING TO TRADE, AND QUITE ANOTHER TO CAPTURE"

Shelikhov's vision of expanding Russia's fur hunting grounds across Alaska's southern coast was not solely a commercial proposition. He believed that an Alaskan empire would make his country rich and bolster its power on the world stage. Yet though he repeatedly turned to the central government for help, in the late 1700s, officials in St. Petersburg were uninterested in the North Pacific. At the time, only several hundred Russians were in Alaska, but the territory was already being contested by the world's greatest empires. Spain controlled the largest stretch of Pacific Coast, from the southern tip of South America through present-day California. In 1775, Spanish explorer Juan Francisco de la Bodega y Quadra even reached Alaska, near present-day Sitka, spurred northward by a desire to lay claim to territory before Russia could first. A decade later, in 1789, the Spanish navy established a fort on Vancouver Island in today's British Columbia, nearly sparking a war with Britain, which also claimed the British Columbian coastline.[9]

Despite its expansive claims, Spain was a declining power in the Pacific. It withdrew from its only North Pacific fort after only several years, leaving it with no outposts north of San Francisco. Britain posed a greater threat to Russian interests. In 1778, the famed British explorer, Captain James Cook, reached Alaska on his third and final voyage in the Pacific, mapping the shores of North America as far north as the Bering Strait. Some in St. Petersburg worried that Cook's voyage presaged an expanded British presence in the region and feared for the safety of Russia's control of the Alaskan islands. Empress Catherine the Great ordered Cook's published journal translated into Russian so that Russian explorers could take advantage of his findings. Before Cook, Russians believed that their geography gave them an advantage in the North Pacific. Russia could "trade with the peoples of Asia without harmful competition on the part of other nations," one of Catherine's officials had argued. Cook's arrival in Alaska changed this. "The most recent discoveries by Cook" meant that Russia's "hunting posts on the Eastern Sea, which until now have been in [our] hands alone," were no longer free from danger.[10]

Yet throughout the eighteenth century, St. Petersburg was unwilling to devote substantial resources to the Pacific. Shelikhov hoped to tap into Russia's fear of competition in America to extract government support for his fur business. He had received orders from the government that when exploring Alaska his employees should bury in the ground iron tablets "with the image of a copper cross superimposed and the following words in copper letters: 'Land under Russian Domain.'" Shelikhov declared that his voyage to America had discovered "islands . . . which had not been reached even by the renowned English navigator Cook." And he proposed the creation of a new corporation under the auspices of the governor-general of Irkutsk that would funnel state funds support to Shelikhov's Alaskan ventures.[11]

The vision of state support for company-led expansion in the Pacific fit Shelikhov's aims perfectly: his firm would not only make money trading furs, it would expand Russia's territory, stave off the country's enemies, and bring glory to the tsar. Yet Catherine the Great was unconvinced of the merits of a state-backed company to explore Alaska. In February 1788, Shelikhov petitioned Catherine to create a company with a monopoly on fur hunting in Russian America. Catherine rejected the idea. She was skeptical of monopolies in general and was waging one of her many wars on the Ottoman Empire, which left few resources for expansion on the Pacific. The root problem, though, was that she was unconvinced of the merits of expansion in the Pacific. "Spreading into the Pacific will not bring firm advantages," she argued. "It is one thing to trade, and quite another to capture."[12]

BARANOV AND THE BOSTONIANS

Royal support or not, Shelikhov was dedicated to expanding his foothold in Alaska, and Baranov was committed to redeeming his failed business career by succeeding in Russian America. In August 1790, Baranov set sail for America, where he would spend the subsequent three decades in cold, foggy outposts on the Alaskan shores. His journey to Alaska was traumatic. A violent storm overturned his ship, which split apart on the rocks, leaving him and his crew marooned on Unalaska Island in the upper Aleutians. After wintering on the island, Baranov's expedition managed to continue onward in three smaller boats, hopping up the Aleutian Islands, trading with native settlements and occasionally Russian fur hunters, before finally reaching Kodiak Island in June 1791 and joining the settlers whom Shelikhov had left behind after his visit to the island five years earlier. Baranov would never again set foot in Russia.[13]

Enlarging Russia's domains in Alaska proved no easy task. In 1799, Baranov established a settlement of around 200 Russians and Aleuts near present-day Sitka, an ice-free harbor 600 miles due east of Kodiak. He built a wooden fort and named the settlement Novo-Arkhangelsk, "novo" meaning "new," and Arkhangelsk referring to Russia's greatest Arctic Ocean port, the main outlet for foreign trade near Baranov's hometown in northeastern Russia. Novo-Arkhangelsk was the farthest eastward that Russians had settled. It was their first major outpost on the islands that stretch southeast from the Alaskan mainland along the North American coast. The waters proved as rich in otters as Shelikhov had imagined. In 1803 alone, nearly 300,000 otter and seal pelts were shipped from Alaska to the Russian mainland, and then onward to China. And warehouses in Russia's Alaskan colonies held perhaps half a million more pelts yet to be transported.[14]

Despite the rich hunting, Alaska's eastern coast proved far from the fertile paradise or the land of vegetables and berries that Shelikhov had promised. Transportation from mainland Russia to Kodiak was perilous, as Baranov had discovered. The outpost at Novo-Arkhangelsk was even farther from mainland Russia, making it impossible to guarantee a steady stream of supplies. Nor was the territory around Novo-Arkhangelsk particularly hospitable. Unlike in the Aleutian Islands and around Kodiak, where Russians had subdued or co-opted the Aleut and Alutiiq inhabitants, the waters around Novo-Arkhangelsk were full of warlike tribes: not only the native Tlingit, but also a rapidly multiplying group of seafarers whom Baranov's men called "the Bostonians."[15]

The problem of supply was straightforward. Baranov had been promised a bountiful land, but Kodiak Island was bleak and the Russian settlement struggled to feed itself. Kodiak was entirely dependent on imports for any metal or manufactured goods. When in 1799 the Russian ship *Feniks* sank while sailing from Kamchatka to Kodiak, the Alaska colonies faced shortages for two years. The next year, the crew of the ship *Sv. Arkhistratii Mikhail* had to dump a third of its cargo overboard to survive a violent storm. When a third ship arrived in Alaska, hungry residents found that during its voyage the crew had eaten most of the supplies they were supposed to deliver.[16]

Geography and weather were the two main obstacles to supplying the several hundred Russian employees in Alaskan colonies. In the early 1800s, Russia had two key ports on the Pacific Ocean: Okhotsk, on Russia's far eastern seaboard; and Petropavlovsk, a vast natural harbor on Kamchatka's eastern shore. The port in Petropavlovsk provided excellent shelter for Russian ships, but Kamchatka was no easier to feed and supply than Alaska. Even today, Kamchatka is not connected to the rest of Russia by roads, and in the early 1800s it had to be supplied via Okhotsk, traversing icy winters and treacherous fogs. Okhotsk itself was scarcely better equipped. True, it was possible to travel from Okhotsk overland to Irkutsk, which took a month, and then onward to Moscow and St. Petersburg, which took several more months. In spring and fall Siberian roads turned to mud; the journey, one Russian lieutenant groaned, was "terrible," and the cost of delivering foodstuffs across Siberia was uneconomic.[17]

Moreover, the harbor in Okhotsk was mediocre: it was not protected from gales and was blocked by ice in winter. "Even at high tide," one Russian naval official complained, "the mouth of the Okhota River, which ships have to cross, is no more than 12 feet deep . . . frequently banks and shallows will appear where previously there had been adequate depth." Getting supplies to Okhotsk was difficult, while transporting them onward to Alaska was at times nearly impossible. The price of grain was regularly five times higher in Okhotsk than in Irkutsk; in Russian America it was ten or even twenty times higher than in Moscow or St. Petersburg.[18]

The only way to survive, Baranov concluded, was to find another source of food. The good news was that Baranov had the option of purchasing foodstuffs and other goods from British and, increasingly, American ships visiting Alaska. But this entailed risks, both that Baranov's trading partners would win a stake in the fur market, which provided his sole source of income, and that as foreign traders' presence in Alaskan waters grew, they would evict the Russians entirely.

Britain was no longer the main concern. When Captain Cook had arrived in Alaska in 1778, some Russians feared British meddling in their North Pacific colonies. Yet by the time that Baranov first arrived in Alaska in 1790, the United States had just ratified its constitution. The Americans were already aspiring to power in the Pacific Ocean. In 1784, the year after America won its independence, Philadelphia merchants outfitted a ship named *Empress of China*, which became the first American ship to reach China, returning home "laden with teas, silks, and porcelains" and having made a handsome profit. Soon dozens of American ships were crossing the Pacific Ocean, whaling, hunting, trading, establishing an American presence in ports from Peru to Oahu—even in Alaska. The arrival of the *Enterprise*, off the waters of Kodiak at first seemed like a blessing to Baranov, because Americans came with plentiful supplies and were eager to trade. The *Enterprise* saved some of Alaska's colonists from hunger by exchanging food and supplies for 12,000 rubles worth of seal and otter pelts.[19] If the Alaskan colonies couldn't be reliably supplied from Okhotsk, perhaps the Americans could provide the goods Baranov needed?

But Russian settlers were not the only Alaskans who desired to trade with Yankee merchants. The Tlingit, who had inhabited the islands around Novo-Arkhangelsk long before either Baranov or the Americans arrived, established an active commerce with the Bostonians, who in exchange for furs supplied the Tlingit with guns, liquor, and other goods. In 1802—armed with guns, ammunition, and powder from the Bostonians—Tlingit groups attacked a group of Russians near Yakutat Bay, killing several. Later that year, the Tlingit ransacked Baranov's fort, setting it afire and forcing Baranov to retreat from Novo-Arkhangelsk.[20] He would not return for two years.

The Russians blamed American traders for the Tlingit attack, and Baranov ordered that "no new efforts should be made there [in Novo-Arkhangelsk] until we have strengthened our possessions." But strengthening Russia's possessions was only possible with supplies—and supplies continued to arrive in Alaska more frequently on American ships than on Russian ones. A year after the Tlingit defeated the Russians at Novo-Arkhangelsk using American firearms, Baranov bartered 37,000 rubles worth of goods and supplies, including two cannons, from American ships visiting Kodiak. When the Americans proposed regular trade with Russia's colonies, Baranov gave them a list of the goods he needed. Meanwhile the Russians continued to lose to storms and to navigation errors the ships needed to supply Alaska. In 1803, the newly built *Sv. Dmitrii* was lost off Umnak Island, and its cargo had to be abandoned, leaving the Russians with only three working ships. The number of Bostonian ships, meanwhile, kept growing. In 1805, Russians bought an entire ship, the *Juno,* as well as all its cargo, from the Bostonian captain D'Wolf for 109,821 rubles. In 1806, Baranov signed a contract with American captain Jonathan Winship for delivery of additional supplies.[21]

The Americans soon realized that the business of supplying the Russian colonies could be coupled with an even more lucrative trading partner: China. The Chinese were the world's most eager consumers of fur. Per a treaty signed in 1727, Russian merchants were allowed to exchange furs for Chinese tea only in the city of Kiakhta, a desolate Mongolian outpost a thousand miles from any Pacific port. Alaskan furs, therefore, had to be gathered in the waters of North America, shipped to Okhotsk, then transported overland in a months-long journey before they could be sold to the Chinese. American and British merchants, by contrast, were allowed to sail directly to the port of Canton (now Guangzhou) from which Chinese law banned Russian traders. The American merchant Joseph O'Cain, therefore, struck a deal with Baranov to ship to Asia furs worth 300,000 rubles.[22] Baranov knew that reliance on the Americans posed a dilemma: If Bostonian captains became Alaska's main source of supply, and if they came to dominate the fur trade from the Alaskan coast to Canton, what would stop them from cutting the Russians out of the fur business entirely?

TSAR ALEXANDER'S ALASKAN AMBITION

Tsar Alexander I, who ascended to the throne in 1801, faced a choice: whether to abandon Russia's American empire or to grow it. Alexander's grandmother, Catherine the Great, had expanded Russia's territory in Europe, but was uninterested in the Pacific. China was a source of art in her royal gardens, not a focus of geopolitical competition.[23] Some of her officials in Siberia had designs on Chinese territory, but these were never popular in St. Petersburg.[24] Catherine had vast territorial ambitions, after all. But they were focused not on the Pacific coastline or the Far Eastern frontier, but in lands held by the Ottoman Empire, along the shores of the Black Sea. She refused to build up Russia's military strength in the Pacific or to subsidize Russian ventures in Alaska.

Tsar Alexander I took a different tack. Skeptical about Russia's old ways of government, he wanted to leave his mark on Russian statecraft. As a child, he had been tutored by a radical Swiss intellectual. Upon taking power, he gathered a group of young, liberal-minded friends who he hoped could help him implement major reforms. He and his advisers hatched plans to streamline Russia's bureaucracy, reform the country's system of serfdom, even to give Russia a constitution. Alexander inherited a vast military that had been forged by Catherine the Great, yet he faced great challenges on the global stage. Europe was roiled by the turmoil of the French Revolution and the Napoleonic Wars. The shifting coalitions of European powers—Napoleon's France, Britain, Prussia, Austria-Hungary, and Russia, plus minor Italian and German states and the Ottoman Empire—fought in every corner of the globe. England and France clashed from the West Indies to the South China Sea. Trade with North America was disrupted, meanwhile, and the rule of the Spanish and Portuguese Empires over the New World was undermined.

In an era of global war, Russia needed a global strategy. This was the argument made by Nikolai Rezanov, an ambitious and well-connected nobleman who had married the daughter of the fur magnate Grigory Shelikhov and inherited his commercial empire when the old merchant died. Rezanov had an ally in Count Nikolai Rumyantsev, the minister of commerce, and later also foreign minister, to Tsar Alexander I. Rumyantsev believed that to survive competition with worldwide empires such as Britain and France, Alexander needed to compete in Asia.[25] The Napoleonic Wars were dividing the world into trading blocs. France and Britain were imposing restrictions on transatlantic trade to bolster their strategic interests. France and the United States, meanwhile, had waged an undeclared conflict over shipping rights from 1798 to 1800 that saw the two countries' ships exchange fire across the Atlantic seaboard. A decade later, similar trade disputes would push the United States and Britain to war in 1812. In the Baltic Sea, Britain sought to use its naval power to control shipping from Danish, German, Swedish, and Russian ports. The trade wars would escalate until, by 1806, both Britain and France were seeking to enforce blanket trade bans with their rivals—bans that they applied not only to their own populations, but to their neighbors, too.[26]

In this context of trade wars, Russia's minister of commerce argued that his country needed a guaranteed outlet for its goods. The Pacific Ocean, he believed, could provide the answer. Rumyantsev saw the markets of China, Japan, and the Pacific Ocean as a vast opportunity. In a coordinated campaign with Rezanov and the directors of the Russian-American Company, a firm that managed the country's commercial interests in Alaska, Rumyantsev told Tsar Alexander that Russia's American colony could provide a springboard for a Pacific empire. As early as 1802, Alexander was receiving memos arguing that building up Alaska could boost Russia's trade and influence in China. Rumyantsev injected these ideas into discussions at the highest level of Russian politics. He encouraged Alexander to write to the Japanese emperor, proposing that their two countries open relations. He urged the tsar to send an envoy to China. These steps were comparable, one Russian aristocrat wrote, to the legacy "of Richelieu, of Mazarin," in their boldness. Such a vision was crucial, Rumyantsev convinced the tsar, for Russia to become a major power in the Pacific Ocean. And projecting Russian power in Asia, meanwhile, was critical in an era of trade blocs and global imperial conflict.[27]

"A DAGGER HELD TO THE THROAT OF THE RUSSIAN EAST"

Forging a Russian empire in the Pacific required not only willpower, but also a plan. Aleksandr Baranov, the merchant who was Russia's main official in America, was eking out a barren existence along the Alaskan coast, struggling against weather, hunger, Tlingit, and Bostonians. Rezanov devised a strategy that would resolve Baranov's logistical problems and expand Russia's empire in the process. Rezanov was "hot tempered," one of his colleagues recalled, "with a head more inclined to making castles in the air . . . than to making great deeds come true."[28] But Russia in the early years of Alexander I's reign was fertile territory for grand ideas about Asian expansion. And Rezanov sensed that, having already conquered its Siberian frontier, the Pacific was where Russian explorers could accomplish great deeds. If his empire-building plan worked, it would bring honor to him and glory to Russia. What more could a vain and ambitious young nobleman desire?

Rezanov's idea was straightforward: rather than supplying the Alaskan colonies with food from the Russian mainland, Alaska should trade with territories across the Pacific Ocean. Spain, for example, had colonies stretching along the Pacific Coast of North and South America, from present-day Chile to California. Japan was rumored to have a rich market, though Russians were not yet allowed in. Tropical islands were scattered across the South Pacific, as Captain Cook had discovered. If only Russians in Alaska had the ships, surely they could trade with these lands, too. Yet Baranov's men in Alaska had no ships to spare given their frequent shipwrecks in the cold waters of the North Pacific. Nor could Baranov's men build new vessels fast enough because outfitting ships required supplies such as rope and iron that Alaska lacked. The solution, Rezanov believed, was to send ships from St. Petersburg, through the Atlantic Ocean, around the southern tip of South America, up through the Pacific to Alaska. Such a voyage could explore the possibility of trade with Japan, Spanish America, and the Pacific islands, Rezanov argued, and provide the ships Baranov needed to supply Russian America.

There was only one problem: how to fund it? If sailing from Okhotsk to Alaska was complicated, the journey by sea from St. Petersburg to Novo-Arkhangelsk was, for Russia, unprecedented. Three centuries had passed since Magellan's crew first sailed around the world, but no Russian ship had yet done so. No Russian ship had even crossed the equator.[29] Russia's government found the prospect of exotic Asian trade appealing, but Rezanov knew that his voyage would be approved only if the tsar was convinced that the security of Russia's American territories depended on a round-the-world voyage. Otherwise the cost was simply too high.

In St. Petersburg, however, Rezanov's geopolitical arguments found a receptive audience. Fear of foreign influence in Alaska was growing. In 1800, Russia had sent a royal rescript to London demanding that the British cease "doing harm to establishments of Russian subjects . . . on the shores of North America." The British denied any wrongdoing, saying that any British explorers in the area were acting without the knowledge of the government. Yet Rezanov argued that potential English settlement on North America's west coast would be like "a dagger held to the throat of the Russian East." "The successes of the Russians with all their discoveries in the Northeastern Sea," Rezanov noted, "have always roused the envy of all the European powers doing business in America." That same year, the Russian-American Company moved its headquarters from Irkutsk to St. Petersburg. It was a no longer a regional firm led by Siberian merchants. Now the Company's leaders saw themselves as the cornerstone in a new, global Russian strategy.[30]

As St. Petersburg's frustration with other countries' activities in Alaska grew, so too did the case for Rezanov's round-the-world voyage. Commercial aims and empire-building impulses were intertwined. Minister of Commerce Rumyantsev wrote to Tsar Alexander in 1803: "No matter how much stronger the Company's establishments may become and no matter how hard it may try to maintain the prices of peltry in Kiakhta, the English and Boston men, who deliver their stuff from Nootka Sound and the Charlotte Islands directly to Canton, will always have the advantage in the [fur] business."[31]

The solution, the minister told the tsar, was for "the Russians themselves" to break "their way through to Canton." If Russia managed such a feat, the Russian-American Company would profit, and "the Russian-American colonies, seeing the opportunity for marketing in various places furs, fats, fish, and other natural products, would attract people of all kinds, tried in the sciences and arts, and would set about establishing mills and factories for the manufacture of metal objects, leather goods, and so forth. . . . Cities would finally arise out of the villages, through which the trade with the two Indies would, in time be established on a firm foundation." Other Russian diplomats dreamt of commerce with the Dutch colony of Batavia and with the Philippines. Rezanov's vision of expanding Russian influence across the Pacific was catching on. With promises of vast riches in Asian trade, the Russian-American Company received in 1803 a loan of 250,000 rubles to outfit two ships for its first round-the-world voyage.[32]

A "REPUBLIC OF DRUNKARDS"

In summer 1803, Rezanov set sail from the Russian port of Kronstadt on the *Nadezhda*, which, alongside its sister ship the *Neva*, would travel around Denmark and Britain, to Spain's Canary Islands off the African Coast, crossing the equator in late 1803. They rounded South America's southern tip, sailed past Easter Island, stopping in the Marquesas Islands in the South Pacific. Finally, they arrived in Hawaii, where the Russians were overcome by the islands' beauty—and their bountiful produce. "These islands will not long remain in their present barbarous state," one of the Russian officers predicted.

"They are so situated, that with a little systematic industry they might soon enrich themselves"—and even become the center of a struggle for control over the Pacific.[33]

The Russians did not stay long in Hawaii. Upon departing, the ships split, with the *Neva* sailing directly to Russian America while Rezanov's *Nadezhda* sailed to Kamchatka, arriving in July 1804. There Rezanov's crew regrouped, resupplied, and set off to Japan, with which Rezanov hoped to open trade. Yet he managed only to insult and to anger the Japanese, whose law strictly limited commerce with Europeans. After half a year of bullying the Japanese, Rezanov admitted defeat. Thwarted in Japan, Rezanov set sail to Alaska, arriving in August 1805, only to find the Alaska colonies were a mess.[34]

For one thing, Baranov was in a long-running feud with the Russian Orthodox Church. Missionaries wrote scathing missives to church leaders about the ills of Baranov's rule. Priests in Alaska declared to the Holy Governing Synod that "it is impossible for us to describe in detail the excesses, the pillaging and murder perpetrated against the natives here by Baranov . . . [who] says that we should not try to prohibit . . . shamanism (which he considers a form of worship)." Baranov was concerned with exporting furs, not with saving souls. Rezanov strongly backed Baranov. "Our monks have never followed the methods of the Jesuits in Paraguay; they have never tried to understand the beliefs of the savages," and, more importantly to Rezanov, "They have never understood how to become part of the larger policies of the government or of the Company." He saw little point in the church's activities. What good did they do? "They baptize the American natives and then when the natives imitate the monks for half an hour and can make the sign of the cross properly, the missionaries are proud of their success," Rezanov wrote. Yet "because the missionaries have too much time on their hands they have interfered in civil aspects of administration," he complained.[35]

Rezanov reported that these missionaries' complaints obstructed Baranov, whose efforts were crucial if Russia's American colonies were to be placed on a solid foundation. Rezanov had the utmost confidence in Baranov's ability. "The name of this distinguished elder is known in the United States of America, but unfortunately it has not yet reached the same status among his own countrymen; while he receives praise from other nations he drinks from the cup of bitterness of his own people. And Oh God! He accomplishes everything with such successful management!" Rezanov wrote. The other

Russians in Novo-Arkhangelsk were less impressive, Rezanov concluded, complaining that Alaska was a "republic of drunkards."[36]

Besides Baranov, the only people on the Alaskan coast who impressed Rezanov were the Americans. "Fifteen to twenty ships are coming from Boston annually," Rezanov warned the tsar in a letter sent from Alaska. "We are now like a man who is unarmed" in face of increasing American pressure. Rezanov's visit to Alaska further convinced him that the only way to push out the Bostonians was to find a better means of supplying Alaska. "The settlements in America cannot grow when the first necessity, flour, has to be shipped from Okhotsk, itself always in need of supplies and help," Rezanov told the tsar. On Kamchatka, the Russian colonists "are forced to eat half-rotted fish" and "birch bark," which "causes the outbreak of scurvy and other diseases." With Japan closed to trade, Russia must look farther afield and "purchase local products in the Philippine Islands and in Chile," Rezanov urged. This required more ships and more guns, both of which Russia's rivals had an advantage in. "How treacherous the Americans are," Rezanov complained, "and how well supplied with artillery."[37]

As Rezanov nursed his designs for expanding Russia's empire to all the corners of the Pacific, he faced a more immediate problem: as Novo-Arkhangelsk prepared for winter there was not enough food. Men received only one pound of bread per week, but this quickly proved more than the colony's meager supplies could sustain. Hunger produced illness, and illness made it harder to find food. "There is no bread since, as I hear, there is no one on Kodiak to prepare the fodder," Rezanov wrote, "and people are dying of hunger on Novo-Arkhangelsk because the Kolosh [native inhabitants], who are armed with splendid rifles and falconets, are waging perpetual warfare, and you have to catch your fish there under gunfire."[38]

In Novo-Arkhangelsk, the only sustenance was dried fish, sea lions, and an occasional seal. Those who came down with scurvy—and with such a diet there were many—received millet with molasses as well as beer made from pinecones. By the end of February, Rezanov recorded, eight of 192 Russians in the outpost had died while "sixty others were ill with the scurvy." The 1805–1806 winter was cold, but it was hardly worse than usual; most winters had left the Russians fighting hunger and disease. They faced a choice between greater reliance on the Americans—thereby sacrificing their position in the fur trade to rivals—or scurvy and starvation. Only a bold move could save

Russian Alaska and thereby salvage Russia's aim of staking out a greater role in the Pacific. Rezanov's hope that Japan could trade with Alaska had been thwarted. There was only one option left. Rezanov gathered a crew of thirty-eight sailors—though "only eighteen were in any degree fit for service," the others being "diseased and enfeebled"—and slipped out of Sitka Sound, tacked to port, and set sail—for California.[39]

"A BEAUTIFUL COUNTRY"

Europeans had been in California for only forty years when Rezanov decided that the California coast could provide the food that Russian Alaska needed. When the Spanish rulers of Mexico first heard news of Russia's arrival in Alaska during the 1760s, they sent an expedition northward to stake claim to the Californian coast. Spanish soldier Gaspar de Portolà established a settlement at Monterey, California, "to defend us from attacks by the Russians, who were about to invade us." An invasion was far from realistic in the 1760s—the Russians were still groping their way up the Aleutian Island chain—but the Spanish were right to suspect that the Russians were eyeing Californian coastline. In February 1790, Shelikhov, Rezanov's father in law, had told one Russian official that "all along the American mainland from the island of Kitak [Kodiak] to California . . . there have been distributed and left imperial markers, namely coats-of-arms and plates with the inscription 'Land Belonging to Russia.'"[40]

Rezanov sailed southward, hoping to establish a Russian presence in California. Despite the death and hunger that he left behind in Alaska, Rezanov believed that Russia faced the most favorable international environment in the Pacific Ocean since its explorers had first reached North American shores. This might not have been obvious amid the destruction of the Napoleonic Wars. The conflict in Europe distracted all European powers from paying attention to the Pacific. During late 1805, French and Spanish allied naval forces were decimated by British admiral Horatio Nelson's fleet at Trafalgar, so they couldn't deploy to the Pacific Ocean. The British, meanwhile, fearing Napoleonic dominance of the continent, kept their navy near Europe to continue threatening the French. Napoleon invaded Spain in 1809, preventing the Spanish from focusing on their American colonies, setting the stage for independence for Spanish America a decade later. In 1812, the British found themselves entangled in war with the United States, during which the Royal Navy harassed American shipping across the world, limiting the number of American merchants who could reach Alaskan waters and challenge Russian rule.

Even more important than Rezanov's perception of a power vacuum in the Pacific, however, was his boundless ambition. As he cruised southward past the mouth of Oregon's Columbia River, he did not know that a small group of Americans led by Meriweather Lewis and William Clark were wintering on the shore just five miles from where Rezanov briefly dropped anchor in March.[41] Yet even had Rezanov met Lewis and Clark on the mouth of the Columbia River, the Americans' overland journey would scarcely have impressed him. Had Russians not mastered the overland journey to the Pacific through thousands of miles of Siberian wilderness two centuries earlier? Had Russia not already established a series of outposts—small and hungry though they were—on the Pacific coast? Servants of the tsar had already established Russia's claim to the Alaskan and British Columbian coast. What did it matter if two or three dozen Americans had trekked to the Pacific? Rezanov was already establishing Russia's influence in California.

In late March 1806, with a "favorable wind" blowing, Rezanov's ship slipped through the Golden Gate into San Francisco Bay. "The Spanish shouted for us several times to anchor," Rezanov recorded, "but we merely replied 'Si Señor! Si Señor!'" before sailing into the bay and dropping anchor just out of range of Spanish cannons. He need not have feared Spanish attack. Per Madrid's regulations, the Spanish missions of California were prohibited from trading with foreigners, but the Spaniards proved welcoming hosts. Rezanov was met by Don Louis de Argüello, the son of the Spanish commandant, and treated to a "cordial reception," while his crew was provided "veal, vegetables, bread, and milk," which helped with the scurvy.[42]

Rezanov's crew was impressed by California's chocolate, but the wine was judged "ordinary." (The Spanish would begin settling California's wine country only a decade later, as they built new missions to stake out territory in response to Russia's arrival.) The Spanish also hoped to show the Russians a fight between a bear and a bull, but though "we awaited the time impatiently," one Russian recorded, "the bear had died in the night." The Russians had to be content with a normal bullfight, in which Spanish soldiers "killed one bull after another." The Spanish, mused one of the more reflective Russian sailors, "accustomed as they are to the sport from their youth . . . are no more affected by the sight of this worthless slaughter of animals . . . than the natives of [Pacific islands] are by the eating of human flesh." Most of the Russians were less introspective. Several of Rezanov's crew liked California so much that they tried to desert. They were quickly caught and interned on a desolate island in San Francisco Bay, which would come to be known as Alcatraz.[43]

Despite these diversions, Rezanov remained focused on finding a permanent means of supplying Alaska. Yet how to convince the Spanish in California to trade with Russia—trade that was prohibited by Madrid? As Rezanov strategized amid the banquets and bullfights, he met the commandant's fifteen-year-old daughter, Conchita. Rezanov's first wife had died in childbirth four years earlier. Conchita filled a void in Rezanov's heart and resolved the dilemma hanging over his empire-building plans. "Associating daily with and paying my compliments to the beautiful Spanish senorita, I perceived her active, venturesome disposition and character, her unlimited ambition, which at her age of fifteen, made her, alone among her family, dissatisfied with the land of her birth," Rezanov recounted. "She always referred to it, when we were joking as 'a beautiful country, a warm climate, an abundance of grain and cattle—and nothing else.'"[44] Rezanov offered a grander vision: to become the wife of the man who would knit together the Spanish and Russian colonies and thereby dominate the Pacific.

"ALL GRAND PLANS SEEM RIDICULOUS ON PAPER"

Rezanov wrote to his superiors in St. Petersburg that his courtship of Conchita was a "purely personal adventure," but his crew suspected otherwise. One of Rezanov's companions wrote, "The bright sparkling eyes of Doña Conception had made upon him a deep impression, and pierced his inmost soul." Yet this same colleague also reported that Rezanov saw the marriage as facilitating "business intercourse between the Russian American Company and the province of Nueva California"—a rather less romantic rationale.[45]

Rezanov's proposals for marriage and for trade both required the assent of leaders in Europe. As for the commerce, Rezanov hoped "that the possession of the Russians in America, as well as Kamchatka and Okhotsk, should be assured of a regular supply of breadstuffs from Nueva California." "I tell you frankly that we need grain," Rezanov told the Spanish governor, "which we can obtain from Canton, but, as California is closer to us and has surpluses that it cannot sell anywhere . . . we can take preliminary steps and submit them for approval and ratification by our [royal] courts." Don Argüello, however, told Rezanov that there was little hope that Madrid would approve such a deal. Rezanov's marriage proposal, meanwhile, required the approval of the pope because Conchita was Catholic and Rezanov was not. The Spanish agreed to supply Rezanov with cargo "of wheat, flour, barley, peas, beans, lard, salt, and small quantity of dried meat," but made no commitments for future trade without the support of Madrid.[46] Rezanov promised to hasten to Europe to obtain Madrid's assent for trade and the pope's approval for marriage.

In May 1806, Rezanov set sail from California, arriving back in Novo-Arkhangelsk a month later. In his absence, scurvy had killed seventeen residents of the Russian colony and left sixty others immobile.[47] Hearing stories of California's fertile agriculture, Baranov agreed with Rezanov that produce from California—by trade or otherwise—was crucial to the Russian colonies' survival. Before his return voyage to Europe, Rezanov dashed off a series of reports to high-ranking Russian officials, to the directors of the Russian-American Company, and to the tsar himself. Rezanov's report on California predicted "a million rubles" of annual trade with the Spanish colonies. "Our American territories would not be in want; Kamchatka and Okhotsk could be supplied with grain . . . Irkutsk would be relieved of the dearness of grain," Rezanov promised.[48]

If Russia were to "obtain permission to trade with California," Rezanov argued, "the company could establish granaries, and in the proposed southern colony, having treated the numerous savages kindly, it would at the same time commence grain growing and stock rearing, and, having organized trade with Canton, it would settle Chinese here." Some may "laugh at the expense of my far-reaching ventures but I adamantly insist that my proposals are the very crux of the matter and are very feasible. All grand plans seem ridiculous on paper." In Rezanov's defense, it was only a few decades later that Chinese workers began flooding into California to build the railroads that would connect California to North America's east coast. Russia needed a long-term vision, Rezanov urged. "If the government had thought earlier of this part of the world . . . if it had constantly pursued the perspicacious aims of Peter the Great . . . California would never have become a possession of the Spaniards. . . . [If] we overlook it, then what will our descendants say?"[49]

Not all Rezanov's crew were convinced by his vision of transpacific trade. One noted the "great distances" between California and Russian Alaska. Moreover, the "goods required in Nueva California are: cloths, manufactured articles, sugar, chocolate, wine and brandy, tobacco, iron and iron tools"—the very type of goods in which the Russian settlements "are no less in want—perhaps even more in want—than the Spanish in Nueva California." But Rezanov would not be deterred. He wrote to Tsar Alexander I that he "proposed to [the Spanish in California] a plan for lasting trade, which all of them accepted with much pleasure," though the Spanish officials had not, in fact, agreed to any such deal.[50]

Rezanov soon set off on the long journey from Alaska to Okhotsk, then overland across Siberia to St. Petersburg, to deliver news of California's riches to the tsar's court. He had an ambitious set of requests: from the Russian government, more money and ships to help build his transpacific empire; from the Spanish, the right to trade with California, and thereby to feed Russia's American colonies; and from the pope, the hand of Conchita Argüello in marriage, a union that would cement his ties with the Spanish missions along the California coast. Whatever feelings he had for Conchita, Rezanov loved his imperial visions more. "I weep," he wrote a colleague in early 1807, "that there is no room in my heart for her," overflowing as it was with grand dreams of transpacific empire. Yet Rezanov found neither love nor glory. En route to St. Petersburg, Rezanov "rode . . . on horseback over a very arduous route; on the way he was beset by frost and snow, [and] exhausted himself severely." In March 1807, amid the Siberian winter and only halfway home, Rezanov fell off his horse into an icy river, got a fever, and died.[51]

CALIFORNIA, "LAND OF RUSSIAN POSSESSION"

Rezanov was dead, but Russia's California dreams persisted. In Alaska, Baranov still struggled to feed his fur trappers and relied on American ships for supply. Rezanov's journey had convinced Baranov that he must either trade with the Spanish or establish a Russian settlement on the California coast. Backed by Russian-American Company leaders in St. Petersburg, Baranov tried both strategies. In 1808, he sent his most trusted aide to California to examine "sites for settlements" and solutions "to the problems of supply." Making landfall north of San Francisco, the Russians buried copper markers with the inscription "Land of Russian possession" and established a small outpost near Bodega Bay as well as a slightly larger settlement twenty miles to the north, which would become known as Fort Ross.[52]

The California settlements met one of Baranov's goals—to "steal a march on the North Americans," who were themselves exploring hunting grounds in the area—but they failed to supply Alaska.[53] California had rich farmland, but the coastline north of San Francisco, where the Russians settled, was less fertile. The weather was cold and foggy, the land heavily forested, and the soil heavy with clay. Moreover, even when the settlers at Fort Ross could grow a surplus of crops, transporting produce to Alaska proved difficult. There was no good landing at Fort Ross, and even Bodega Bay—a twenty-mile journey to the south—was exposed to stiff winds and the grinding Pacific surf, providing mediocre shelter to visiting ships. It was a poor imitation of either the harbor or the farmland of San Francisco Bay.

Convincing Spain to trade with the Russians was no easier. When the Russians first built Fort Ross, Spain was beginning its descent into a disastrous, half-decade-long war with Napoleon. The conflict on the Iberian Peninsula set off a series of revolts in Spanish America that would eventually see Mexico and California win independence from Madrid. Chaos in Spain ensured that Russia faced little pressure to evacuate its California settlements, despite Madrid's claim to the territory. Though the Californians established the mission of Sonoma—due east of Fort Ross—to prevent Russian expansion inland, they soon realized that the Russian settlers posed little threat. "I do not have a great mistrust of the Russians," one Californian official wrote to a superior in 1813, "but I do of the Americans—these I do not like, not at all."[54]

The Spanish government in Madrid nevertheless declined to approve trade with the Russians, so such trade as occurred remained small and formally illegal. The Russian-American Company repeatedly lobbied St. Petersburg as well as the tsar himself to apply diplomatic pressure on Spain, arguing that a deal with Madrid would bring "mutual benefit" and would mean that "the Bostonians would not be able to incite the wild savages." Foreign Minister

Rumyantsev told Russia's ambassador in Madrid of "the eagerness of the California inhabitants to open trade with Russia . . . since they have no way of marketing" their crop surplus.[55] Yet Spain did not budge.

The Russian-American Company continued to report that with "the introduction of agriculture, livestock breeding and various other economic enterprises and manufacturing operations" in California, "it will be possible to have more people there to build ships, and to have enough of all goods not only for the colony's own needs, but a surplus to be sent to Kamchatka and Okhotsk, which will thus have to rely less on the delivery of necessities from Russia and Siberia."[56] Yet farming on Northern California's coast continued to disappoint. For Alaska, the prospect of future trade was not enough—the Russians needed food now. Baranov turned his attention farther south—not south along the California coast, but to a chain of islands due south of the Russian settlement on Kodiak, in the center of the Pacific Ocean.

"A POLISHED AND CIVILIZED COUNTRY"

The first Russian ships to arrive in Hawaii had been the *Nadezhda* and the *Neva,* carrying Rezanov on his round-the-world-voyage from St. Petersburg to Alaska. In June 1804, they dropped anchor off the coast, astonished by the islands' beauty—and their plentiful food. "Here may be procured an abundance of swine, bread-fruit, bananas, cocoa-nuts, taro, yams, batatas [sweet potatoes], salt, wood, water, and other things particularly desirable for ship stores," wrote one Russian visitor. Moreover, the islands sat at the center of Pacific trade routes, "very commodious for all ships going to the north-west coast of America, to the Aleutian Islands, or to Kamchatka," as well as ships carrying furs from Northwest America to China. And they had "very secure bays." Hawaii was likely, this Russian visitor declared, to become a "polished and civilized country."[57]

The Russians were not the only Europeans to notice Hawaii's strategic location. Britain's Captain Cook had been the first European to discover the archipelago. On his arrival in 1778, he named them the Sandwich Islands and introduced firearms, venereal diseases, and smallpox to the population. At first, the British played a major role in the islands' politics, with an Englishman named John Young serving as an adviser to King Kamehameha, as the king tried to unite all the islands under his personal control in the early 1800s. Yet the Americans soon overtook the English as the most influential foreigners. Most of the ships docking at the port of Lahaina on Maui were American whalers or fur traders. American merchants dominated commerce in the capital of Honolulu. And American missionaries transformed Hawaiian culture by assaulting traditional religious practices and demanding that Hawaiians abstain from alcohol and from liaisons with visiting sailors.[58]

Tsar Alexander himself had been aware of the islands' strategic relevance for some time. From his first year on the throne, Alexander had discussed with friends and advisers Hawaii's importance for control of the Pacific Ocean. One of the tsar's mentors, a Swiss intellectual, emphasized to Alexander the risk that the British might annex the islands, a move that "deserves the attention of Russia, to which the fur trade provides the means for a very advantageous trade with China." St. Petersburg had heard similar assertions of Hawaii's importance from its agents in the field. Before his death, for example, Rezanov had written to St. Petersburg promising that one of Hawaii's kings wanted to open trade relations with Russia.[59]

Trade with Hawaii could resolve Russia's supply dilemma in its Pacific colonies. Foreign Minister Rumyantsev reported to the tsar that "these islands, which have a superb climate, are well situated to supply all of Asiatic Russia abundantly with their produce—coconut breadfruit, a sweet root from which good rum is distilled, sugar cane, millet, wild tobacco, pineapple, from which excellent wine is made, sandalwood and other woods similar to lignum vine, wild cattle and swine." The tsar's ministers, meanwhile, discussed among themselves the strategic relevance of the Hawaiian Islands in case of naval conflict in the Pacific.[60]

With multiple islands in the Hawaiian Archipelago—governed at the time by two warring local rulers—surely there was space for Russia, too? In 1806, King Kamehameha, who ruled the Big Island as well as the port of Honolulu, sent a message to Baranov in Novo-Arkhangelsk, saying that "he had learned from the accounts of people who had visited the Northwest Coast that the Russian settlements . . . sometimes experience great shortages of food" and proposed an annual shipment of "salt, pork, sweet potatoes and other provisions" in exchange for "sea otter pelts at a fair price." In 1807, when the Russian ship *Nikolai* sailed to Hawaii, King Kamehameha gave it gifts, including his own cape, to send to Baranov. The following year, Baranov sent the *Neva* to Oahu to "obtain adequate supplies of vital provisions." The Russians obtained a load of salt and sandalwood, which was highly valued in China and therefore by traders across the Pacific, but failed to win Kamehameha's approval for more regular trade between Russian America and Hawaii, perhaps because Americans feared competition and pressured Kamehameha to reject the proposal.[61]

It was Napoleon's invasion of Russia in 1812 that spurred a more active Russian policy toward Hawaii. As Napoleon marched toward Moscow, the French and Russian armies faced off near the town of Borodino, not far from Moscow. *War and Peace,* Leo Tolstoy's famous account of the Battle of Borodino, describes the test of a "great air balloon" intended for "use against the enemy." As the real Battle of Borodino raged, a German physician in Russian service named Georg Anton Schaffer was helping to build a balloon airship intended to "lift 40 men with 12,000 pounds of explosives, enough to destroy whole regiments." As the Russian army prepared its final stand against Napoleon, the airship was readied for flight, inflated with gas, began slowly to lift off the ground—and then crashed back to earth. The project was abandoned and the tsar's troops chased Napoleon out of Russia without the help of airships.

Schaffer, meanwhile, sought new adventures, signing up to work for the Russian-American Company. In 1813 he was sent on the *Suvorov* to Alaska. He proved no better with naval ships than with airships, and upon arriving in Novo-Arkhangelsk he was expelled from naval service for being "an intolerable person on board ship."[62] Baranov, in one of his most significant lapses of judgment, decided to make use of Schaffer, sending him on a mission to the south. Schaffer, Baranov concluded, was just the person Russia needed to open trade with Hawaii.

"A RUSSIAN WEST INDIA"

Schaffer set sail for Oahu in October 1815 with orders to befriend Hawaii's King Kamehameha and his wives, and to convince the king to trade with the Russians. Baranov sent Schaffer with a letter to Kamehameha, proposing that because "we are the closest neighbors . . . it is most appropriate that we, rather than anyone else, should establish with you friendly and mutually advantageous commercial relations." After what seemed like a promising opening to their relationship, Schaffer's dealings with King Kamehameha soured, and some royal advisers urged that he be killed.[63]

In May 1816, Schaffer decamped to the island of Kauai, where he immediately convinced that island's king that Russia could help in Kauai's struggle against rival King Kamehameha, who controlled the other islands in the Hawaiian Archipelago. Soon after Schaffer's arrival on Kauai, the island's king formally became a Russian subject, professing "his loyalty to the Russian scepter," and was awarded honorary rank in the Russian navy. One of Kauai's princes was awarded a silver medal. In return, Kauai's rulers promised to allow Russian settlements on the island, to permit trade in sandalwood and other supplies, and to place under Schaffer's command a force of 500 soldiers to lead in battle against King Kamehameha.[64]

Schaffer began preparing to conquer the other islands in the Hawaiian Archipelago. He bought several ships, at least one of which was purchased on Baranov's credit, and established three forts on Kauai, one at Waimea and two on Hanalei Bay. "My desire," he wrote the Russian-American Company's main office in St Petersburg, "is to have sent here from St. Petersburg two good ships with reliable crews and well armed." He claimed to have "reliable information" that the Russians' California settlement was "in danger of being destroyed by the Spaniards." With additional resources, Schaffer promised, he could defend Russian California, solidify control over Russian Kauai, feed Russian Alaska, and make Russia the dominant power in the Pacific. With the support of the king of Kauai, now a Russian subject, Schaffer believed he could expel the Americans from Honolulu. This would give him control of the best harbor between Shanghai and San Francisco, a crucial stopover for transpacific trade. All it required, Schaffer promised, was help from St. Petersburg. "Would His Imperial Majesty consent to send a frigate into the Pacific?" Schaffer asked.[65]

"ILLEGAL AS WELL AS HOPELESS"

Even as Schaffer pushed forward, however, Russia's leaders were pulling back. His Imperial Majesty would not send frigates to Hawaii. Schaffer's establishment of three Russian forts on Kauai marked the peak of Russia's transpacific ambitions.[66] Schaffer followed a grand tradition of the tsars' servants in the Pacific hatching exorbitant plans for empire, from Grigory Shelikhov's colony on Kodiak to Nikolai Rezanov's courtship of Conchita Argüello and the entire Spanish Empire.

For a time, those plans coincided with St. Petersburg's imperial designs. Yet the window in which Russia was willing to devote substantial resources or attention to the Pacific was closing. Russia after the Napoleonic Wars was consumed by its European responsibilities. True, the defeat of France and the decision by England to pull back from the continent left Russia the dominant power in Europe. Yet European hegemony brought responsibilities, including preserving agreement among the continent's great powers and preventing destructive revolutions of the type that had only recently been snuffed out in France. The costs of empire, meanwhile, were higher than Tsar Alexander had hoped, and the benefits less obvious than he had imagined. Facing more important issues like reshaping Europe after the Napoleonic Wars, the tsar began to roll back his empire's Pacific Ocean ambitions.

Schaffer was the first to be pulled back. Russian-American Company directors in St. Petersburg tried to resist the reverse course on which Tsar Alexander insisted. Upon receiving news that the king of Kauai had agreed to become a Russian subject, company directors wrote that same day to Baranov of "a most interesting and pleasant report from Dr. Schaffer on [Kauai]. . . . His Majesty might find it pleasing to dispatch some nature of directives along with the frigate *Kamchatka*." The company told another of its agents that Kauai was a "new and important possession," and informed Tsar Alexander that the Kauaian king had "transferred his citizenship and that of all islands under his domain and the inhabitants thereon to His Imperial Majesty." And they forwarded Schaffer's report to Foreign Minister Karl Nesselrode, along with Schaffer's request "to have dispatched from St Petersburg to here two good ships with full crews and appropriate armaments."[67]

Yet Schaffer's plans had already collapsed. In the time it took for letters to reach St. Petersburg from Hawaii, Schaffer had been chased off Kauai by angry Americans and shipped to China. From there, Schaffer traveled to St. Petersburg, aiming to convince the tsar in person that the Hawaiian Islands were the key to Russia's Pacific Ocean empire. "The Chinese will have to allow the Russian flag to wave in Canton," Schaffer argued. "The English and Americans will have their trade cut off. . . . The Sandwich Islands must be made a Russian West India and a second Gibraltar. Russia must have these islands at any cost!" Arriving back in Europe in summer 1818, he sent Tsar Alexander a flurry of memos, insisting that "the occupation of the Sandwich Islands would provide Russia with the opportunity to generate for itself alone trade in furs on the Northwest Coast of America . . . only then would the Russian Flag appear in Canton." He followed with a memo noting that "not on the Kurile islands, not on Kamchatka, not in Okhotsk, not on the Aleutian Islands, and not on our coasts of Northwestern America do they have any food, but on the Hawaiian Islands food is abundant."[68]

Russia's leaders were unconvinced. From the first reports that the king of Kauai was becoming a Russian subject, Alexander's diplomats had urged "attentive study" rather than quick action. The advantages of annexing Kauai are "illusory," the Russian minister in London reported, and "it would not be long before we could expect a hostile confrontation" with the "adventurous" Americans on the islands. The Russian-American Company was ordered to refrain from action on Kauai, with one minister grumbling to a colleague that "these islands . . . not only cannot bring any substantial benefit to Russia, but on the contrary, in many ways may cause extremely serious problems."[69]

In 1819, St. Petersburg admonished the Russian-American Company that the Hawaiian incident was "unpleasant" and that the company should exercise "the greatest caution." Even the Company now began to sour on Schaffer, seeing how much money he had squandered. And Baranov, who had sent Schaffer to Hawaii, was appalled by the doctor's combination of overreach and incompetence—and also by his wanton spending on Baranov's credit. In March 1817, the Russian-American Company directors in St. Petersburg wrote Baranov that "Dr. Schaffer is . . . no longer to be entrusted with any expedition at all."[70]

Hawaii, meanwhile, was forgotten. Even Schaffer eventually abandoned his efforts to convince the tsar to seize Kauai, quitting Russia entirely in frustration. He sailed to Brazil, entering the service of that country's emperor, publishing a book, and leading several thousand Germans to settle in the southern Brazilian state of Rio Grande del Sul. These Brazilian ventures were only slightly more successful than his attempt to seize Kauai for the tsar, and Schaffer died in obscurity in 1836.[71]

In California, too, St. Petersburg began to restrain the imperial ambitions of the Russian-American Company, having grown increasingly skeptical of California's utility. Despite the ambitions of the Company, the colony had yet to demonstrate any value. In 1816, according to the report of a Russian deserter, Fort Ross had multiple buildings, including a windmill, blacksmith, *banya* (steam bath), and 14 cannons, plus a population of 21 Russians, 100 natives, 100 sheep, 80 cattle, and 30 horses.

The Spanish, meanwhile, were growing angry at Russia's presence. Spain's minister in St. Petersburg declared that Russia's California settlements were "illegal as well as hopeless." Spain built a series of new missions north of San Francisco Bay, notably in Sonoma, encircling Ross and seeking to limit Russian expansion. A royal order from Madrid in 1817 demanded that Spain's local officials destroy Fort Ross, though the viceroy of New Spain halfheartedly agreed to do so only "if possible" and "without excessive risking of conflicts in matters of commerce."[72]

What was the point of tense relations with Spain, Russian diplomats wondered, to defend a colony of twenty-one Russians and several dozen farm animals? Pierre de Poletica, a Russian diplomat in Washington, wrote to St. Petersburg that the Russian-American Company's claim to Fort Ross was "far from being evident. . . . It is enough to look at the map to see that the colony in question was wedged into the Spanish possessions in California and the neighboring territory." The Company's claim to Alaska would look flimsy by the standard by which it claimed ownership of Ross. It only had a handful of settlements strung-out along the Alaskan coast. If the Russians could build a fort at "unsettled" territory less than a hundred miles north of San Francisco, what would stop the Americans from doing the same a hundred miles from Novo-Arkhangelsk?[73]

In 1819, the United States and Spain agreed that the northern border of California should be along the 42nd parallel, far to the north of Fort Ross, meaning that the United States, too, now officially recognized Fort Ross as a violation of Spanish territory. In 1820, under pressure from St. Petersburg, the Russian-American Company agreed to wind down its colony in California, telling Foreign Minister Nesselrode that it "would gladly abolish that settlement." Though it would take the Company two decades to sell the property, Fort Ross had failed.[74]

THE *UKAZ* OF 1821

As Russia extricated itself from Schaffer's Hawaiian adventures and limited Baranov's expansion in California, St. Petersburg decided it needed more direct control over Alaska. Tsar Alexander's willingness to countenance expensive and controversial expeditions across the Pacific had declined. The region no longer seemed central to Russia's aims, nor had it provided any obvious benefits. Confidence in Baranov, meanwhile, had begun to wane as his California and Hawaii initiatives soured. In 1816, St. Petersburg sent a naval officer to Alaska to tighten control over the territory. Upon arrival he reported finding dozens of problems with Baranov's management of the colony: feeding Baranov's pigs placed "a burden on the company," for example, and there was not enough rum at Fort Ross. The officer ordered Baranov to return to Russia.

Baranov departed Alaska "not without tears," it was reported. Even Tlingit headmen came to pay their respects. Though he had served the tsar loyally for nearly three decades, Baranov considered retiring in Hawaii or New England, but eventually decided to return to Russia. Setting sail in autumn 1818, his ship passed Hawaii and the Philippines before stopping in the Dutch East Indies. Four days after setting sail again, Baranov got a fever and died. He was buried in the warm waters off Sumatra, thousands of miles from the Alaskan frontier, where he sought riches and glory, and found neither.[75]

The naval officer who replaced Baranov in Alaska was little more effective than his predecessor. Better management alone couldn't resolve the problem of the Bostonians, whose presence in Alaskan waters only increased. As the Russian-American Company complained, "Every year ten to fifteen merchant ships come . . . from the North American United States. On these ships come [American] citizens who trade not only with the Company, but also with American savages." The Americans were not only fomenting Tlingit opposition to Russian rule, they were also undercutting Russian business. They "sell the sea otters to the Chinese for 50 rubles apiece; beaver pelts fetch 5 rubles each. . . . The Chinese give us a . . . lower price for our furs in Kiakhta, which is the only place we can sell them." Meanwhile the Americans "obtain furs from the savages, including as many as 10,000 to 15,000 sea otters per year"—pelts that would otherwise have been purchased by Russian traders.[76]

As early as 1808, St. Petersburg had pressed the Americans in Alaska to trade only with the Russian-American Company, not to native groups. That year Russia sent a formal protest to Washington against "clandestine and illicit trade" in firearms on the northwest coast. In 1809, Russia's foreign minister promised Tsar Alexander that "regarding the sale of firearms to island natives," he would "bring up this matter with the American minister here, [John Quincy] Adams."[77]

The Americans were unwilling to compromise. John Quincy Adams was particularly stubborn. An ardent American expansionist, he cheered the Bostonian merchants for undermining Russian control. True, there were only about a dozen American ships on the Northwest Coast each year, and one Russian naval officer reported that with "two or three naval commercial vessels of 16 guns . . . permanently stationed in American waters" Russia could "protect our possessions" and "prevent Bostonians from entering into trade with the American savages." Yet though Russia was able to send occasional warships, permanent stationing in Alaskan waters proved impossible.[78]

Adams also realized that, even if Russia found a way to defend its Alaskan colonies, it still had no efficient means of either supplying the settlements or getting furs to Chinese markets. "Russian vessels are not admitted at Canton," Adams noted to a colleague, so trade with China "can be done so conveniently and, probably, so cheaply by no others as by the Americans."[79] After a decade of painful experience—and failed ventures in California and Hawaii—the Russians knew that Adams was right.

When Russian diplomats nevertheless began taking a harder line against American traders, Washington refused concessions. The Russian-American Company warned that Russia risked losing its colonies to the Americans unless the tsar prohibited "any further interference with Russian business on the part of private North American hucksters."[80] But when Andrei Dashkov, Russia's minister in Washington, criticized the "injurious effects" of America's "illicit trade," American diplomats stonewalled.

Russian Alaska was saved, temporarily, by the War of 1812, as the British navy hounded American merchant ships, keeping them from Alaskan waters. But as soon as the war ended in 1815, they returned, with some Americans urging President James Madison to deploy naval forces on the Northwest Coast. The Russian-American Company redoubled its lobbying efforts in St. Petersburg, hoping for greater government support. In 1817, it proposed new regulations on foreign vessels in Alaskan waters. Even as Russia considered restrictions on American shipping, the US attitude toward Russia soured. In Congress and in the media, voices urging a confrontation with Russia grew louder, with one congressman noting that Russia had occupied Kauai and warning that Russia would soon "command the whole northern part of the Pacific Ocean."[81]

This was a vast overestimation of Russia's capabilities. Rather than expanding, Russia's Pacific presence was beginning a long decline. St. Petersburg was unwilling even to devote more resources to Alaska, its first colony across the Pacific. Russia's round-the-world journeys had been ruinously expensive, with one such voyage costing 700,000 rubles and returning with cargo valued at only 200,000 rubles. This was no sustainable method of supply. Stationing naval vessels in Alaskan waters, meanwhile, proved little more realistic. St. Petersburg opted instead for what it hoped would be a low-cost means of asserting its influence. In 1821, Tsar Alexander issued an *ukaz* (order) declaring Alaska "exclusively" Russian territory, claiming absolute control over its territorial waters, extending 100 miles offshore, and hoping that the Americans would comply.[82]

Yet Russia still had no means of supplying the Alaskan colonies without the Americans. No supply ship was sent from Russia to Alaska in 1822 or 1823, and the directors of the Russian-American Company admitted that voyages from St. Petersburg created "significant losses." Meanwhile, the Company suspended the payment of dividends in 1822 under financial pressure. At the same time, it requested permission to engage in barter trade with foreigners, which ran contrary to the aim of the *ukaz*, which was intended to reduce reliance on the Bostonians.[83]

More worrisome still was the Americans' refusal to recognize either St. Petersburg's vast claim to territorial waters or its restrictions on trade with native Alaskans. One reason for American obstinance was money: the profits from Pacific trade were substantial. In contrast to Russia's loss-making Alaskan trade, whalers from the Massachusetts city of New Bedford alone made $500,000 annually in North Pacific waters. "Congress is preoccupied with those settlements," as Russian minister in Washington Pierre de Poletica explained to St. Petersburg in early 1821, because of pressure from American traders. As soon as Washington was formally notified of the tsar's *ukaz*, America's "preoccupation" turned to anger. One congressman declared in early 1822 that the Russian claim must be "resisted." American traders took to the media, accusing the Russians of trying "to monopolize commerce and usurp territory."[84]

John Quincy Adams, now secretary of state, would not tolerate the *ukaz*. He wrote to the US minister in St. Petersburg in July 1823 that "the traffic of the citizens of the United States with the natives of the Northwest Coast was neither *clandestine* nor unlawful nor irregular." Moreover, Adams declared, the United States would not tolerate Russia's claim to territorial waters. The United States, Adams concluded, "cannot for a moment acquiesce to those regulations [the *ukaz*]." The US minister in St. Petersburg, Henry Middleton, clarified, lest the Russians misunderstand, that enforcement of the *ukaz* would mean war.[85]

Russia promptly backed down. Tsar Alexander had intended the *ukaz* as a last-ditch attempt to shore up his Alaskan colony. Yet no one in St. Petersburg believed that Russian America was worth the risk of war. In April 1823, Russia's new minister to the United States arrived in Washington with orders to resolve the dispute. Russian ships in the North Pacific were told to not enforce the *ukaz*. Adams adopted a maximalist position, arguing that Russia had "no territorial right" on North America.[86]

In his State of the Union Address on December 2, 1823, President James Monroe declared that "the American continents . . . are henceforth not to be considered as subjects for future colonization by any European powers"—a declaration that would come to be known as the Monroe Doctrine. Even without the doctrine, the United States had already proven that it cared more about trade, hunting, and fishing rights in North Pacific waters than Russia cared about its Alaskan colonies. Negotiations between the two powers began in St. Petersburg in early 1824, and Russia quickly conceded nearly every American demand. Merchants could trade in "any part of the great ocean" without restrictions "in navigation, or in fishing, or in the power of resorting to the coasts." Russia, meanwhile, agreed it would not settle any territory below 54′40 latitude, Alaska's current southern border. The subsequent year John Quincy Adams, the architect of America's expansion in the Pacific Northwest, was elected president. The Russian-American Company, despairing of its inability to placate either the Tlingit or the Americans, considered burning down Novo-Arkhangelsk and retreating to Kodiak.[87] The struggle for Alaska was over.

RUSSIA'S LONG RETREAT

Though Russian explorers had mapped the North Pacific coastline for decades, and though trappers such as Baranov spearheaded the country's settlements in Alaska, St. Petersburg's push into the Pacific began in earnest only with Rezanov's voyage to the Pacific in 1803. This push lasted barely a decade, peaking with Schaffer's efforts on Kauai in 1813. By the time St. Petersburg signed the treaty with the United States in 1824, repealing the *ukaz* and recognizing America's preponderance in North Pacific trade, Russia's rulers had concluded that their Pacific Ocean colonies were an unprofitable distraction.[88]

Both Fort Ross and the Alaska settlements hung on for several more decades, but they were roundly ignored. Russians struggled to justify why they should care. St. Petersburg no longer saw any point in expanding Russia's footprint in North America. By the late 1830s, the directors of the Russian-American Company noted that "sea otters have become almost completely extinct on the coast of California . . . [so] the settlement of Ross does not bring any material benefit." Nor had the colony ever succeeded in feeding Alaska. To the contrary, another Russian report concluded, "The expansion of the settlement's production could not under any circumstances come close to corresponding with the aims of its founding." In 1841, the Company sold the fort for $30,000.[89]

Had the Russians not sold Fort Ross, it would have been overrun by Americans. In 1848, gold was discovered in California, spurring a rush of settlers into the territory. Soon Americans were streaming toward the Pacific Coast, not only in California, but in the Oregon territory, too. In contrast to Russia's impoverished Alaskan settlements, "The opulence of the gold-bearing stratum [in California] is wonderful, unbelievable," one Russian observer marveled. It was difficult to see how the 1,100 Russians who populated Alaska could hang on given the tens of thousands of Americans flooding the Pacific Coast.[90]

St. Petersburg, moreover, increasingly perceived Russia's future not in remote Alaska, but in southward expansion along Russia's own Pacific coastline. "The ultimate rule of the United States over the whole of America is so natural that we must ourselves sooner or later recede," wrote Siberian governor-general Nikolai Muravev to Tsar Nicholas I in 1853. "We must

recede peacefully in return for which we might receive other advantages."
By the 1850s, after three decades of ignoring Alaska, Russia finally decided to
sell the colony, though the transaction itself would take another decade to
be completed. But Russia's attention had already turned elsewhere. In contrast to Alaska, separated from Russia by treacherous seas, it was "very natural
for Russia, if not to possess all of Eastern Asia, then to have sway over the
entire Asiatic seaboard of the Eastern Ocean," Muravev argued to the tsar.[91]
It was to this territory—the Kuril Islands, Sakhalin, the Amur River Valley,
and eventually toward Japan and China—that Russia now turned.

2

"RUSSIAN CONTROL WILL BE GUARANTEED FOREVER"

Nikolai Muravev and the
Conquest of the Pacific Coast

"HE WHO CONTROLS the Amur River, controls Siberia." So declared Nikolai Muravev, governor-general of East Siberia, in 1848. Gathering waters from Mongolia, northern China, and the Russian lands east of Lake Baikal, the Amur River stretches for over 1,700 miles before reaching the Sea of Okhotsk in a wide delta opposite the coastal island of Sakhalin. The river cuts a broad valley as it flows down to the Pacific Ocean, passing through highlands that, before the Russians arrived, had been inhabited by Jurchens, Mongols, and Manchus. It was the latter who named the river Sahaliyan, meaning "black river." The Chinese, translating from the Manchu, called the river Heilongjiang, the Black Dragon River. The Russians, perhaps drawing from an old Mongol name, called it the Amur.[1]

Manchus and Mongols named the river because they had long controlled its shores. When Manchu armies founded China's Qing Empire (1644–1912), Manchuria was united with China. Yet the Manchus focused their attention on extracting tribute and taxation from the rich farmlands of central China, ignoring their homeland in the far northeast. The territory remained sparsely populated, and there were few ethnic Chinese living in the area until the nineteenth century.

In geographic terms, however, the Amur fits more naturally into China than Russia. Russia's Siberian settlements are separated from the Amur Valley by mountains, with no waterways connecting the two regions. Before the construction of railroads, the Amur was far easier to access from Shanghai or Tokyo than from nearly any Russian city. To Russian supporters of seizing the Amur, this made the river valley attractive. It was difficult to run an Asian empire from the icy ports and hungry settlements of Okhotsk or Kamchatka. The Amur—farther to the south, providing access to what Russians believed was fertile farmland—seemed to offer a more durable base for expansion on the Pacific Ocean.

The first Russians had arrived in the Amur Valley in the 1600s, seeking furs, like all Russian explorers, but also seeking food. As Russians began to penetrate east of Lake Baikal, they followed the rivers, most of which flowed northward. Traveling along these rivers, they reached the Arctic Ocean and the Sea of Okhotsk, establishing settlements along the way. There was fur in these regions, and native peoples skilled in gathering food from the taiga forests, but no rich agricultural land. The Russian settlements in Siberia always depended on food deliveries from far-off farms in central Russia.[2]

Russians had heard rumors of a temperate country southeast of Lake Baikal and hoped to find fertile land for farming. The mountains on the southeast edge of Baikal were called the Yablonoi, a name that may have been borrowed from a local tongue, but which sounded like the Russian word for apple—a sign, some Russians hoped, of the food supplies in the valleys across the mountains. In 1643, setting off from Yakutsk, one Russian explorer traveled southward, eventually reaching a tributary of the Amur. He pillaged his way to the mouth of the river, his hungry band of men eating not only the inhabitants' food but also, some reports suggest, some of the inhabitants, too. Several years later, a second group of explorers entered the region, only to find a large Qing Empire army awaiting them. They were defeated by the Qing forces, and in 1689 the chastened Russians signed the Treaty of Nerchinsk, ceding the entire Amur Valley to the Qing Empire.[3]

For the next century and a half, Russia mostly ignored the Amur territory. In the latter years of the eighteenth century, Siberia's governor-general proposed to Catherine the Great that she annex the river valley as part of a broader strategy of carving up the Qing Empire. The plan was to work with Mongols and other dissatisfied groups in the Qing borderlands to "shake [the

Qing] to its foundations" and to establish a new port at the mouth of the Amur to trade with Asia by sea.[4] But Catherine did not implement the plan, in part because Russia had no Far Eastern army with which to invade China, and in part because she had plenty of foreign policy challenges on her western and southern frontiers. She focused instead on conquests in Poland, Ukraine, and the Black Sea coast, where she expanded Russian territory. In the Far East, by contrast, she let Russia's fur trappers set the agenda, and they explored Russia's far northeast, up the Lena River, toward the Arctic Ocean—far away from China.

Russia stuck with this strategy through the mid-1800s. There were furs aplenty in the North Pacific, though Russians had to delve ever deeper into Alaskan waters to harvest them. The trade with China was adequate, though Russians resented being forced by the Qing to trade through the overland border crossing at Kiakhta rather than using more efficient sea routes through Canton, as other European powers were permitted to do. The Amur Valley and Russia's border with China remained an afterthought for most Russian leaders. China was vast and powerful, and Russia was busy elsewhere.

"RUSSIA'S MISSISSIPPI"

China, however, was changing, and many Russians began to perceive new opportunities. When the first Russians reached the Amur Valley in the 1600s, the Qing Empire was far stronger than Russia.[5] The Qing reached the peak of its power in the late 1700s after successful military campaigns deep into Central Asia, in the Tibetan highlands, and along the borders with Burma and Vietnam. Yet signs of overextension and domestic decay quickly appeared. The empire was soon beset by internal revolts, both on newly conquered frontiers and in the Chinese heartland. The European merchants who traded along the South China coast, meanwhile, found that China's military was technologically backward. In 1839, trade disputes at the port of Canton set off a war between Britain and the Qing Empire, ending in a humiliating Chinese defeat. The Qing were forced to hand Hong Kong to the British and to open four additional ports to foreign traders.

For Russia, China's weakness posed risks and opportunities. Traditional trade patterns were upended as growing European commerce in south China ports reduced the price that Chinese were willing to pay for Russian manu-factured goods. Russian traders had long received tea from China in exchange for furs and manufactured goods. Now, thanks to the efficiency of maritime trade between Britain and China, it was cheaper to smuggle Chinese tea from England to Russia than to ship it overland from China to Russian cities.[6]

In 1843, a year after Britain forced China to open more ports to trade, the Russian government established a committee to examine commerce with China. St. Petersburg quickly realized it knew little about these far-off lands, and hardly anything beyond what could be gleaned from European newspa-pers. Russia had once led Europe in knowledge of Chinese affairs, thanks to its overland caravan trade. Now that trade was being undermined by Euro-pean competition, and Russia's privileged position in the Chinese market was waning. If Britain and other European powers were probing China's borders, perhaps Russia should too, if only to guarantee that it did not fall behind European rivals.[7] A Russian maritime voyage was proposed to explore the coastline along the Russian-Chinese border, in the hopes of finding a port more convenient than Okhotsk, the icy and poorly protected bay that still served as the main harbor for North Pacific trade. Perhaps the mouth of the Amur River, about which Russians knew little, might be navigable, some of the tsar's advisers hoped. Perhaps, too, it might be undefended by the Chi-nese. Not only did the Russians not know if the Chinese occupied the region—they were not sure whether Beijing considered the Amur delta its own.

Rear Admiral Evfimy Putiatin was tasked with organizing a maritime mission, but the voyage was quickly quashed. Foreign Minister Karl Nessel-rode was opposed, fearing that it would spark conflict with China or England. Finance Minister Yegor Kankrin, meanwhile, saw no point in "wasting" 250,000 rubles on a journey that "given undeveloped, or, better to say, non-existent trade in the Eastern Ocean," would provide no benefits beyond geo-graphical knowledge. After considering these objections, Tsar Nicholas I canceled the voyage, though he remained personally curious about the ge-ography. He approved a cheaper variant, an overland expedition to the Amur Valley, led by zoologist Alexander Middendorf. When Middendorf returned from the Far East, the tsar requested a private meeting with the explorer to learn more. Middendorf's travels convinced the tsar that the Amur was the "only path of communication from Siberia to the East, necessary to us for consolidating our hold on Okhotsk, Kamchatka, and the North American

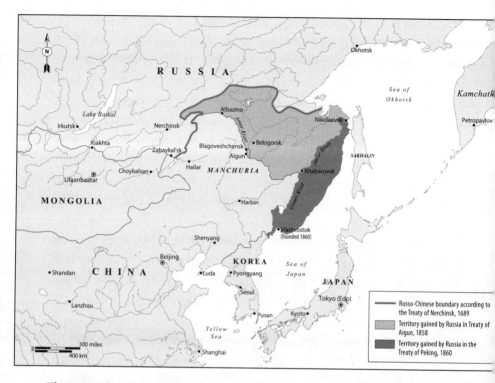

The Russia-China frontier, 1850s–1860s

Colonies," as Middendorf wrote in a report to the Russian Army's General Staff.[8]

In the early 1840s, Nicholas's interest in the Amur River was driven only by his own curiosity. Yet he was not the only Russian beginning to think differently about the future of the Amur River. Russian writers had referred to the valley as a "new Canaan" as early as the 1700s, but technology made the Amur seem newly accessible. By the 1840s, hundreds of steamboats were plying America's Mississippi. Why could the same technology not be brought to what one traveler called "Russia's Mississippi"? One Russian envisioned steamboats on the Amur bringing to Siberia "all the goods of the South and the East," from California, Canton, "even India."[9]

An American visitor to Siberia thought the parallels with his country's development were obvious: "The commerce" of Siberia, he wrote, "seeking a channel of communication with other countries and nations, must, of necessity, seek the sources of new rivers for an outlet." The Amur, the only great river flowing from Siberia to the Pacific, might even "become one of the greatest commercial arteries in the world." This American was not alone in thinking that the two countries' efforts to push toward the Pacific were linked. Middendorf, the zoologist who had explored the Amur, sensed something similar. "The great, although quiet migration of peoples of our time has now closed into a circle around the earth," he wrote. "Americans and Russians look at each other from hospitable shores across the ocean like neighbors."[10] The Americans had established rich settlements on their Pacific coast. Could Russia not do likewise?

MAINTAINING FRIENDLY RELATIONS WITH CHINA

Tsar Nicholas's curiosity about the Amur was counterbalanced by his innate conservatism and his fear of European revolutions. In the decades after St. Petersburg rolled back its Alaskan adventures, Russia had demonstrated little interest in the Pacific coast. European affairs seemed far more important. Nicholas was deeply afraid of revolution, and Europe seethed with tension, creating waves of revolt and revolution. When his brother, Alexander I, had died in 1825, a group of soldiers had risen up in opposition to the new tsar's ascension to the throne. The rebellion was easily put down, but it convinced Nicholas that he must always be vigilant, given the revolutionary ideologies sweeping Europe.

Nicholas surrounded himself with conservative advisers and tasked them with preventing revolution, whether at home or abroad. Expanding Russia's territory was not a priority. The goal, as Nicholas's foreign minister, Karl Nesselrode, explained in 1833, was to preserve "in the East, the existing treaty system and . . . in the West, to build a defensive system against the revolutionary agitation"—the type of agitation that Russia faced repeatedly, in the rebellion against the tsar in 1825, in the Polish revolt against Russian rule in 1830–1831, and then again in the pan-European revolutions of 1848.[11] An array of other revolts across Europe during the 1820s, 1830s, and 1840s demanded St. Petersburg's diplomatic attention, from Spain, to Belgium, to the states of Italy, the latter of which were marching toward unification. Neither the tsar nor his foreign minister had serious plans for territorial aggrandizement. They were too busy stomping out revolts in Europe, too burdened with foreign policy problems on their western frontiers to devote any attention to Asia.

It is easy to see why an aristocratic conservative like Foreign Minister Nesselrode thought that "the subversion of all social orders" represented the main threat to his Russia—and to his tsar. Of all the tsar's officials, Nesselrode was the most concerned about European stability and the least interested in Asia. Nesselrode's father was a German count who entered Russia's diplomatic service, and the young Nesselrode was born on a frigate off the coast of Lisbon, where his father served as Russia's ambassador. Nesselrode spoke little Russian, conducting all his official work as Russia's foreign minister in French. He served as a diplomat in Prussia and Germany before working with Tsar Alexander I at the Congress of Vienna, and eventually being named the tsar's foreign minister. When Alexander died in 1825, his successor, Nicholas, retained Nesselrode as foreign minister until the end of his reign.[12]

Nesselrode served the tsars loyally for four decades, but as early as the 1840s he began to look anachronistic. European politics were moving in a nationalist direction, but Nesselrode embodied the old French-speaking transnational aristocracy. A broader range of social classes were voicing opinions about foreign policy, yet Nesselrode could only speak to those Russians who were fluent in foreign languages. The question of European stability—both stable relations between the great powers and stable ruling elites within them—was to Nesselrode, like to Nicholas, an existential question. Revolutionary movements such as those that spread across Europe in 1848 threatened the multinational aristocracy that Nesselrode stood for.

Nesselrode's correspondence from the period covers all range of European conflagrations—from Italy to Denmark, Turkey to Moldova, Denmark's disputed province of Schleswig, and the middle-class "demagogues of Frankfurt." China, Japan, and the Pacific Ocean were barely mentioned. He did not see Asia as a priority so long as the border was stable and the tea trade was profitable. Trying to change arrangements with China would distract Russia from more important questions, draining resources that were better deployed on Russia's western border. Nesselrode was not alone: many of Tsar Nicholas's key advisers thought that Asia was best left untouched. "Our activities in Siberia," Russia's finance minister urged, "should be directed singly at supporting and maintaining friendly relations with China," thereby avoiding any complications in Asia.[13]

"THE EAST BELONGS TO US"

In 1847, Nikolai Muravev was appointed governor-general of Eastern Siberia. He immediately set out to annex the Amur Valley. Descended from an old noble family, schooled at the ultra-elite Page Corps military academy, Muravev was talented and ambitious, making the rank of governor-general at the age of thirty-eight, far younger than his peers. Before Siberia, he served as a military officer on the Russian Empire's other frontiers: on the Black Sea coast during the Russo-Turkish War of 1828–1829, against the Polish revolt of 1830–1831, and in the Caucasus during the late 1830s and early 1840s.[14] After resigning from the military, he was named governor of Tula, a province south of Moscow. As a soldier and bureaucrat, Muravev excelled at climbing Russia's bureaucratic ladder, reaching one of the most powerful positions in the Russian government.

Muravev's ideas and his policies reflected the contradictions of Russia's educated aristocracy. The Muravev family had a long history of participation in reform-oriented secret societies, even as family members benefited from the country's autocratic government and its economy powered by the labor of oppressed serfs. As governor of Tula, Muravev was said to be sympathetic to reformist ideas, including the abolition of serfdom and support for commerce. Later, in Siberia, Muravev established friendships with liberals and even radicals who had been exiled to Russia's far frontier. One such exile was Muravev's second cousin, the famed anarchist Mikhail Bakunin, who wrote in 1860 that the governor-general "desires the following reforms: in the first place, the abolition of the ministries (he is a notorious enemy of the bureaucrats, both in his attitude and his acts); and believes that at the first opportunity there should be established, not a constitution, and not a jabbering parliament of the nobility, but a temporary iron dictator under whatever name you choose."[15]

Whatever Muravev believed, it was certainly not in the multinational aristocracy of Foreign Minister Nesselrode. Nor did he believe in Nesselrode's absolute faith in stability as a lodestar of Russian foreign policy. Nesselrode feared change, lest it upset the balance in Europe. Muravev feared inactivity, lest rivals gain at Russia's expense. This debate between stasis and change was not only a matter of Russian foreign policy. It was also the central debate in domestic politics across Europe. In 1848, revolutionary forces in France, the German lands, and elsewhere had pushed for social and political changes, which Tsar Nicholas and Foreign Minister Nesselrode interpreted as a threat not only to their aristocratic allies, but to religion itself. Nicholas's proclamation against the revolutionaries was almost apocalyptic, declaring: "God is with us! Consider this, pagans, and submit, for God is with us!"[16]

Yet though the European revolutions sparked fear among Nicholas and Nesselrode, the revolutions of 1848 brought no change in Russia itself. Unlike much of Europe, Russia lacked a sizable urban middle class, and demands for political change were aired only secretly, among a politically marginal group of utopian intellectuals. Nevertheless, the tsar and his secret police perceived a threat amid the revolutionary tumult of 1848, arresting a circle of writers, government clerks, aristocrats, and would-be philosophers. The Petrashevsky Circle—named after the man in whose house they regularly gathered—had few coherent political beliefs beyond a desire for change. One acquaintance described Petrashevsky himself as "an extreme liberal, a radical, an atheist, a republican, and a socialist"—a confusing mix of political beliefs.[17] A young Fyodor Dostoyevsky was a member, but he went on to develop a political philosophy centered on Christianity, the opposite of Petrashevsky's atheism. Some participants in Petrashevsky's salons thought Russia should emulate Europe or the United States in modernizing its society. Others, drawing on the same nationalism that drove the 1848 revolutions in Europe, believed that Russia should develop its own traditions separately from Europe. They grumbled about the multinational aristocrats who ran the tsarist government—people like Nesselrode—fearing that these administrators did not have Russia's unique interests in mind.

One thing that united the members of the Petrashevsky Circle was discontent with the status quo under Nicholas I—a status quo that seemed impossible to change even as it dragged Russia into ever deeper backwardness. A second belief shared by many of Petrashevsky's friends was a desire for territorial expansion, a belief that new land could revitalize Russian society. With no opportunities to participate in domestic politics, ambitious Russians looked outward, and saw Siberia and the Amur Valley as an outlet. Liberals imagined creating Russian society anew, free of the ills of serfdom, in Siberian territory that they hoped would be Russia's equivalent of America's frontier. Young conservatives smitten by Russian nationalism argued that Far Eastern regions provided territory for Russia to develop separately from Europe, free of the old continent's corruption. Many would-be expansionists, such as Governor-General Muravev, were motivated by a mix of both liberal ideals and patriotic nationalism. They hoped that new territory in the Far East would help them transform Russia.

Aleksandr Balasoglo, another member of the Petrashevsky Circle, was convinced that the Amur Valley was the outlet for expansion that Russia needed. As early as the 1840s, Balasoglo was writing about Russia's Asian vocation in almost religious terms. "The East belongs to us unalterably, naturally, historically, voluntarily," he declared. "It was bought with the blood of Russia already in the pre-historic struggles of the Slavs with the Finnish and Turkic tribes, it was suffered for at the hand of Asia in the form of the Mongol yoke, it has been welded to Russia by her Cossacks, and it has been earned from Europe by resistance to the Turks."[18] What better place to find new territory than the virgin lands of the Amur Valley?

Governor-General Muravev had several social connections to the Petrashevsky Circle, so when he was appointed to govern Siberia—before Petrashevsky was rounded up by the secret police—Muravev turned to circle member Aleksandr Balasoglo for advice about how to govern "the East." Russia's future was in Asia, Balasoglo told Muravev: "Eastern Siberia, bordering on the Arctic on the north, the Pacific Ocean on the east, the Chinese Empire on the south . . . represents a natural link connecting all of these regions. . . . Across it and to some extent because of it, Russia enters into its multifarious relationships with China, Japan, innumerable Pacific islands, the whole American coast, and all of the Asiatic and European possessions which are playing any sort of part at all in the general life of the globe."[19]

Balasoglo confirmed Muravev's own belief that Russia's expansion was both necessary and inevitable. Balasoglo told the governor-general "everything I knew about Siberia, China, Japan, and the Eastern Ocean, and America," he recalled. Muravev enjoyed Balasoglo's first report so much, "he even wanted to read it to the emperor himself." The key to expansion, Balasoglo argued, was the Amur River, "the natural border" of Russia and China. "When the country is populated it will prosper quickly . . . creating an unescapable flow of hardworking, skillful, and sober people from these two empires into all parts of Eastern Siberia." The Amur would be to the Russian Empire what the rich Malayan port of Malacca was to the British, Balasoglo predicted, or like the Nile was to Egypt. "A holy location," the scholar concluded, "will not remain empty!"[20]

MURAVEV'S AMUR AGENDA

Muravev had little fear that the Amur would remain empty: his concern was the opposite. Other countries were beginning to encroach upon what Muravev viewed as Russia's rightful territory on the Pacific Coast. The French, for example, were expanding their presence in China, and showed little sign of losing their appetite for new trade routes. American whalers were hunting in the waters off Sakhalin and the Kurile Islands. When Russian sailors landed in the Kuriles in the 1850s, native Ainu yelled "Amerika! Amerika!" thinking that the Russians were Bostonians. Muravev noted the expansion of American and British whaling, reporting that "250 ships arrive for this industry annually and hunt 100 tons of whales."[21] While the Americans did not have the capability to seize territory on the Asian mainland, Muravev's greatest concern, the British, certainly did.

Although it was the United States that seized the Alaskan trade routes, ejected Russia from Hawaii, and limited Russian expansion in California, Muravev saw the British as a greater threat to Russian interests on the Asian shores of the Pacific Ocean. The British Empire had, after all, just seized Hong Kong from the Chinese in a war that proved the British fleet could sail across the globe to defeat the world's most populous empire. Britain already ruled India and dominated the Indian Ocean. Russians had been frightened by Captain Cook's exploration of the Alaskan coastline in the 1770s. Now, by the 1840s, British naval power in the Pacific Ocean had expanded substantially. Britain's ambitions had grown too.

Muravev closely tracked British successes in China, worrying constantly about the "five English ports" that Britain opened to foreign trade after the First Opium War. He suspected that British influence in China would continue to grow. Muravev's fear was less that Britain would seize large chunks of territory along Russia's Pacific Coast than that it would wean Siberia away from dependence on St. Petersburg. Russian officials openly discussed the risk that Siberia's isolation from St. Petersburg and Moscow "awakens the desire for the establishment of an independent country." All Russian leaders of the time remembered the United States' independence struggle. They had all lived through the wars in which Latin American countries achieved independence from Spain and watched the British and the United States intervene on behalf of the Latin American rebels. Muravev therefore warily eyed any British presence in Siberia. He had one English visitor deported. And he warned the tsar to "not allow in your empire the spread of English influence."[22]

Arriving in Siberia to take up his governor-generalship, Muravev launched a three-part strategy to strengthen Russian control: attract Russian settlers, develop Siberia's economy, and—most controversially—seize the Amur River, providing Siberia with a direct transport artery to the Pacific. Muravev was an early member of the Russian Geographical Society, a group he hoped would spread knowledge of Siberia and publicize the commercial opportunities he perceived in the region. To encourage Russians to move to Siberia, Muravev wanted to provide free land to settlers. Subsidies of 50 rubles were provided to each family that arrived, and colonists were freed from the obligation of military service, though those who took up the offer were often "starved and in rags."[23]

To boost the economy, Muravev needed to help local traders still reeling from the shock that Britain's expanding trade with China had put on prices in Kiakhta. Muravev reported frequently, and nervously, to Russia's finance minister about the gold flowing out of Siberia via Kiakhta, and about low levels of trade more generally. Meanwhile "private gold production in Eastern Siberia for a variety of reasons is declining," Muravev wrote to the finance minister in a separate letter, costing the province an additional source of revenue. "Sooner or later," Muravev grumbled the following year, "we will need to find other sources of state revenue and other directions for trade." He implemented a "buy Siberian" policy of preferencing Siberian over other Russian producers, with the aim of boosting local agriculture and other industries.[24]

An alternative was to find and exploit new resources. "The entire left bank of the Amur," Muravev wrote the minister of the interior in 1848, "is full of gold, and these places don't belong to anyone." This was far from true. For one thing, as Muravev noted, "occasionally Tungus people wander there, and at the mouth [of the river] there are Gilyak people." Beyond the inhabitants of the territory, the land was claimed by another empire—Qing China. Russians knew that the Qing considered the territory its own, though it wasn't clear whether Beijing had any real control over the area. Yet the prospect of gold only intensified Muravev's conviction that Russia must act immediately to grab the territory. "The English would only need to find out about [the gold], and they would by all means grab Sakhalin and the mouth of the Amur," Muravev worried, concerned about the future of the territories that his adviser, Balasoglo, predicted would be as crucial to Russia's future as the Nile was to Egypt. The Amur delta and the North Pacific coast were ripe for European imperial expansion, Muravev sensed. The only question was which empire would seize it. "If at the mouth of the Amur, instead of a British fortress, [there] stood a Russian fortress," Muravev wrote, "Russian control would be guaranteed forever."[25]

THE NEVELSKOY MISSION

When Muravev's tenure as governor-general of East Siberia began, despite the tsar's personal curiosity in the Amur, St. Petersburg had little interest in the region. A report had arrived in St. Petersburg in 1846 with news that the Amur River estuary was too shallow for large ships to navigate. If true, this meant it was closed not only to commerce, but also to foreign invaders. Foreign Minister Nesselrode, who feared that expansionist officials such as Muravev might push Russia into a conflict with China, cited news that the Amur was unnavigable in his effort to close off debate about further exploring the Amur. Closed to ships, Nesselrode told the tsar in December 1846, the Amur provided an outlet neither for invaders nor for Russian traders. "The river Amur," Nesselrode concluded, "has no significance for Russia." In 1848, the Russian government, noting the river's "inaccessibility to seagoing vessels," decided to "give forever to China the entire Amur basin."[26]

Whatever the desires of Nesselrode and the Europe-oriented grandees of St. Petersburg, many Russians were unwilling to give up on the dream of an Amur empire. Muravev had personal as well as ideological reasons to promote seizing the Amur. Absent territorial expansion, he realized, the governor-generalship of Siberia was a job of bureaucratic toil rather than military glory. A second advocate of expansion was Navy Minister Admiral Alexander Menshikov, who knew that without a decent port on its Pacific coast, Russia could never become a global naval power. Joining these two in calling for expansion was Gennady Nevelskoy, an officer in the Russian navy who was preparing for a mission to sail a supply ship, the *Baikal,* to resupply Kamchatka.

Nevelskoy had grander aims than simply delivering provisions, crucial though they may be, to the Kamchatkan port of Petropavlovsk. The continued need to supply Kamchatka and Alaska by sending ships from St. Petersburg limited the Russian Empire's expansion in the Pacific Ocean. Yet previous attempts to put the region on a sounder economic footing had failed. Nevelskoy noted with regret the unsuccessful Californian colony at Fort Ross and the persistent dilemma of feeding Alaska. He had followed closely the efforts to find supplies in tropical islands in the Pacific, but these proved unrealistic. As a result, Nevelskoy grumbled, Russian leaders treated Far Eastern provinces such as the Okhotsk region as a "necessary evil" rather than as a springboard for expanding Russia's power in the Pacific.[27]

Conspiring with Muravev and Navy Minister Menshikov, Nevelskoy lobbied St. Petersburg for approval to explore and even to occupy the Amur delta while on his journey, with the aim of proving that it was navigable by large ships. Yet occupying the Amur was something that many in St. Petersburg feared, lest it spark conflict with the Qing. Nevelskoy was given a contradictory set of secret instructions. After delivering his cargo in Kamchatka, he was to explore the Amur delta as well as the Sakhalin coast. His "primary goal" was to be "identifying a location suitable for settlement," but to do so in a way that did not anger China. This would prove impossible because—as most Russian leaders realized—the Qing believed the coast was theirs. St. Petersburg was keen to avoid any conflict with China and saw Sakhalin as the most likely location for a Russian outpost, on the grounds that the Amur delta was both probably unnavigable and occupied by the Chinese.[28]

Nevelskoy seized the opportunity to establish a new outpost for Russia in the Far East. In spring 1849, having deposited his cargo in Kamchatka, he set off in the *Baikal* through a cold fog, heading toward the eastern shore of Sakhalin Island. As the weather cleared, Nevelskoy sailed past the island's northern tip, into the straits separating the island from the Eurasian coast. A month after his departure from Kamchatka, the *Baikal* slipped into the Amur's mouth, finding—contrary to previous Russian reports—that the estuary was navigable. Pushing farther southward, Nevelskoy continued along the shores of Sakhalin until he reached the southern tip, proving that Sakhalin was an island, not a peninsula, as many had thought. Near the Amur's mouth, he established Nikolaevsk, an outpost named after Tsar Nicholas. Nevelskoy raised a Russian military flag and fired guns in salute.[29]

The Russians were not alone. Alongside Gilyak peoples, whom the Russians expected to find, Nevelskoy also came upon people he called "Manchus"—subjects of the Qing Empire. Although he reported to St. Petersburg that these Manchus were "merchants," they were probably Qing officials—contradicting his claim that the Chinese had no official presence on the Amur. Nevelskoy declared to the "Manchus" that all of the Amur region, stretching southward toward the Korean border, belonged to Russia. This was a vast territorial claim, which clearly contradicted both the Russia-China Treaty of Nerchinsk and prior Russian practice. It risked an open conflict with the Qing Empire—exactly what most of the tsar's ministers feared. Nevelskoy ordered one of his lieutenants to always keep the Russian flag raised and awaited further orders from St. Petersburg.[30]

In the capital, however, the appetite for expansion had soured. For one thing, news arrived from Kiakhta that the Qing Empire had heard of Nevelskoy's exploration of the Amur and was displeased. Most of the tsar's top advisers, including the ministers of foreign affairs, war, and finance, all feared conflict with China. Beijing could far more easily deploy forces to the Amur Valley than could St. Petersburg. Would the Qing Empire retaliate? And even if the Chinese held back, what benefit was there for Russia in the Amur? In trade and financial terms, the ministers predicted that the Amur territory would bring no great profit to Russia. In terms of foreign policy, they perceived only risk. Russia had no need for another far-off port, they believed. What benefit was there besides the personal glory of vain officers along the frontier? Nevelskoy saw himself as more as an empire builder than a navigator. And Muravev, a young and ambitious governor of a vast territory, perceived in the Amur a means of catapulting himself to greatness. As the war minister snapped at Muravev during one council meeting, "You're trying to erect for yourself a statue!"[31]

News that the Amur was navigable, however, encouraged Muravev and Nevelskoy to redouble their efforts. They launched a campaign of persuasion and misinformation directed at the tsar. Nevelskoy insisted that the native Gilyak peoples did not pay tax to the Qing—evidence, if true, that the Chinese had no sovereignty over the area. He also reported that the Gilyaks requested defense against the Manchus. Muravev took Nevelskoy's claims even further, writing in 1850 that not only were the Gilyaks independent of the Qing, but that Manchus themselves "admit that Gilyaks living on both banks of the Amur do not belong to the Chinese Empire," and that the Amur delta "belongs to the Gilyaks."[32]

Chinese anger over what Beijing perceived as Russian intrusions on its territory would soon prove this claim untrue. Muravev knew, however, that he had a winning argument, whatever the facts. He reassured Navy Minister Menshikov that Russians had a historical right to the Amur, noting that "in the course of the 17th century, Russian Cossacks and traders seized the coast of the Okhotsk Sea and the river Amur." In fact, the Russians' "seizure" of territory along the Amur had lasted only several years before they were roundly defeated by the Qing. But by 1850, this was ancient history—and the balance of power in the Far East had shifted. Muravev had well-rehearsed talking points on the "reasons it is necessary to take the mouth of the Amur River." First, "in Siberia there have long been rumors . . . of Englishmen at the mouth of the Amur, and God forbid if they establish themselves there before us." Second, "only by having in our hands the left bank of the Amur . . . can we open lines of communication with Kamchatka capable of guaranteeing Russian control of the peninsula." Third, "the shrinking of the Kiakhta trade is evidence that English traders in China cannot be positive for us"—and thus new trade routes were needed. The conclusion, Muravev thought, was obvious: it was necessary "to provide for our borders with China"—in other words, by moving the Chinese-Russian border southward.[33]

Rational arguments about the costs and benefits of expansion on the Pacific Coast would only go so far, so Muravev manipulated the tsar's desire for glory, too. In late 1850, as debate raged over the Amur, Muravev sent the tsar "a map of the river Amur and its delta, prepared by Nevelskoy," challenging the tsar to surrender a territory already mapped and settled, a land that required only imperial approval to be formally recognized as part of Russia. "All this is ours!" exclaimed the tsar. True, he noted, the territory would have to be defended with naval forces from St. Petersburg—no easy task. Reason counseled restraint, but emotions urged otherwise. "You are a little mad on the subject of the Amur," the tsar needled Muravev. But was it mad to think that, as other European powers converged on China, that Russia should have its fair share? And anyway, had not Russian forces already established an outpost on the Amur's mouth, named Nikolaevsk in honor of the tsar himself? Nicholas could not turn this down. "Where the Russian flag has been raised," the Russian emperor concluded, "it should not be taken down."[34] The Amur would be Russian.

"SIBERIA WILL CEASE TO BE RUSSIAN"

The Chinese would also have a say. St. Petersburg decided, per the tsar's orders, to keep its new Amur settlement, but also to refrain from immediately seizing additional territory, a position the Russians hoped would placate Beijing. The Foreign Ministry, meanwhile, continued to seek amicable relations with the Qing. In early 1851, Russia proposed to China that the two countries jointly defend the Amur against foreign attack. But the Qing had little interest in joint defense of what it considered its own territory. Before hearing back from the Chinese, Nevelskoy set out to solidify Russia's Amur holdings. The Russians began farming along the delta, though food supplies were scarcely above starvation level. The river itself was covered with ice all winter, only becoming navigable, Nevelskoy reported, as late as June.[35] It was not the most auspicious start.

Moreover, the international environment was darkening. In 1850, just as Nevelskoy was establishing his Amur settlement, China was plunged into a fourteen-year-long civil war, in which messianic rebels called the Taiping seized a large chunk of central China, conquering major cities such as Nanjing and twice besieging Shanghai. By obstructing trade, the rebellion encouraged European intervention. And by weakening the central government, the Taiping revolt reduced the costs to Europeans of meddling in Chinese affairs. Muravev received detailed reports about the Taiping, and worried to Russian Foreign Ministry officials that the Europeans might use the uprising as an excuse to intervene. "Our populous neighbor, China, weak as she is now from ignorance, might easily become dangerous under the influence or guidance of the English and French, and Siberia will cease to be Russian," Muravev warned in early 1853. The only solution, he believed, was to send more Russian troops to the region.[36]

Russia was underestimating the British threat in China, Muravev feared. It must not forget how quickly other powers could expand at Russia's expense. "Twenty-five years ago," Muravev reminded the tsar, "the Russian-American Company requested from the government the occupation of California, which at that time was still hardly controlled by anyone, expressing . . . its apprehension that soon this region would become an acquisition of the United States of America. In St. Petersburg this apprehension was not shared, and it was asserted that this could happen only in one hundred years."[37] In fact, the United States had quickly taken control of California. Might something similar not happen in China, given that country's domestic troubles and given growing English and French interest in the region? And China, the Russians soon realized, was not the only country in Asia whose weakness in the face of foreign pressure threatened to reshape the balance of power in the region.

THE OPENING OF JAPAN

"The American possession of California, and the rapidly expanding trade and industry there, are driving the Americans to desire places for trade on the coast of Japan," explained the report of the tsar's special committee. "The Government of the North American States, pursuing this goal, have decided to send forth a new maritime expedition . . . and thereby induce them to agree to American demands."[38] Well before Commodore Matthew Perry's flotilla of steamships slipped out of their Virginia harbor and set course for Tokyo, news had arrived in St. Petersburg that the United States was planning to send a fleet to force open Japan to US trade. Perry's mission was one of two separate fleets that the United States was sending to the Pacific, one to open ties with Japan, the other to reconnoiter the North Pacific coast— territory that Nevelskoy and Muravev were trying to seize. In May 1853, St. Petersburg sent Nevelskoy a detailed list of the American ships headed to Asia. Nevelskoy ordered his subordinates to treat the Americans well, and to deliver a series of lies: the Amur was dangerous to navigate, Russia had always controlled the Pacific Coast, and the entire area was a wasteland.[39] No need, in other words, for Perry's ships to stay for long.

Perry was not, of course, the first captain to try to open trade with Japan. Portuguese traders had arrived around 1542, before they were displaced by the Dutch. In 1638, the Japanese banned all other European traders from visiting Japan and limited the Dutch to Nagasaki Harbor. At that time, the Japanese scarcely knew of the Russians—and Japanese castaway Dembei had yet to arrive in Moscow. But since the late 1700s, the Russians had been the most persistent group of Europeans seeking to open new trade with Japan. Russian merchants such as Pavel Lebedev-Lastochkin, Adam Laxman, and Nikolai Rezanov each visited Japan, seeking to pry open trade. Each was rebuffed.[40]

Russia and Japan were both expanding in the region: Japan pushing northward and asserting control of Hokkaido and Sakhalin; Russia looking southeast from its North Pacific perch. Where Japanese and Russian explorers and traders overlapped, in the Sea of Okhotsk and on Sakhalin and the Kuril Islands, they found some interchange unavoidable. Relations were not easy. Vasily Golovnin, a Russian naval officer who was mapping the Kuril Islands, was captured and interned by the Japanese from 1811 to 1813 for violating Japanese territory. He emerged from captivity impressed by the Japanese. "If there will rule over this populous, intelligent, dexterous, imitative, and patient nation, which is capable of everything, a sovereign like our great [Tsar] Peter," Golovnin wrote, "he will enable Japan, with the resources and treasures which she has in her bosom, in a short number of years to lord over the whole Pacific Ocean."[41]

The Japanese, meanwhile, were affected no less than the Russians by foreign ships in North Pacific waters. In 1850, the Japanese counted eighty-six foreign whalers, mostly British and American, off the coasts of Hokkaido.[42] Tokyo was divided about how to respond, and Perry's arrival in Tokyo Harbor sparked a political crisis. For Russia, Perry's voyage was also traumatic. Soon after Nevelskoy received notice from St. Petersburg of Perry's mission, he was sent orders to occupy Sakhalin Island, lest it fall into the hands of the Americans. Nevelskoy established a settlement on Sakhalin and told the Japanese and the native Ainu he met that he intended to protect them from the Americans.[43] The Japanese were unconvinced, and by the end of 1853 Nevelskoy and the Japanese on Sakhalin were in a tense standoff.

For Russia, occupying Sakhalin was not enough to counter Perry's plans. Muravev feared that Japan "is already lost to us," given the English and American naval and commercial advantage in the Pacific. Officials in St. Petersburg were less certain. The appeal of opening ties with Japan—or even of subordinating Japan to Russian interests—was obvious. As one American noted, Russia's possessions in Alaska, Kamchatka, and the Kuril Islands "placed her [Russia] on every side of the Japanese empire but the south . . . if she possessed Japan, she would have an abundance of harbors, unrivalled in the world for excellency, and with her resources would command the Pacific." The Americans, of course, had a similar view of themselves, with one writing that if America united the California coastline with Japan it would be properly called "the Middle Kingdom."[44]

Whoever "opened" Japan to foreign trade, many analysts believed, would gain a dominant position in Asia. Meeting in spring 1852, the tsar's ministers concluded that the "expedition, taken by the North-American states against Japan, could have as a consequence changes to the political system of the entire Japanese government, which was thus far inaccessible to other nations." If the United States gained unique access to Japan, it would have an advantage in commerce, coaling stations, and naval facilities. More likely, the committee concluded, Perry's mission would "open for Russia the opportunity to open commercial relations with them."[45] But this would require clever Russian statecraft—and would mean getting a mission to Japan as quickly as possible.

"If the Americans are successful," the Russian government concluded, we cannot stay inactive." And the Americans, it was concluded, would likely succeed in opening relations with Japan, "peacefully by negotiation or with the use of violence." Admiral Putiatin was ordered to sail to Japan and to "convince the Japanese government to permit our vessels and our merchants to drop anchor." Territorial questions mattered, too: "When the negotiations about the borders begin, the issue of Sakhalin Island will arise. Compared to other islands, this island is of special importance to us, because it is directly in front of the mouth of the River Amur. . . . In the near future we might settle on some of the most profitable parts of this island." While the Americans may lay claim to the southern tip of Sakhalin, "we *definitely* cannot accept their right to possess the rest of [its] regions." Putiatin was given a letter from Foreign Minister Nesselrode to Japan's leaders, emphasizing the need to "determine clearly the borders between both empires" and the "sincere wish of His Majesty that the Russians will be permitted to come to the ports of the Japanese Islands."[46]

On October 19, 1852, Putiatin's flagship, the frigate *Pallada,* set sail from St. Petersburg, racing toward Japan. Had it not lost a mast in a typhoon near Hong Kong, the *Pallada* might have beaten Perry to Japan. Yet Commodore Perry arrived first, his ships dropping anchor off Tokyo Harbor in July 1853.[47] After issuing a series of threats, Perry left Tokyo, telling the Japanese that he would return the following year. The Japanese must either allow American ships, Perry said, or prepare for war.

Several weeks later, on August 21, 1853, Putiatin arrived off Japan, his ship's band playing "God Save the Tsar" as the *Pallada* entered Nagasaki Harbor. "Our patriotic feelings were aroused," one Russian officer remembered, "suffused with a pleasant awareness of the dignity of the Russian flag, under whose protection four ships had fearlessly appeared to open an empire of thirty million souls." For several centuries Japan had been "the locked casket whose key was lost, a country whose acquaintance was sought doggedly, with gold, with guns, with sly diplomacy."[48] Russians would use all three methods to force the Japanese to trade.

Putiatin demanded immediate talks with the Japanese, knowing that the Americans were determined to force their way in. He would wait one month for negotiations to begin, he told the Japanese, after which he would sail to the capital—breaking Japanese law—and demand direct talks with the Japanese government. In September 1853, negotiations began, and by early 1854, Putiatin had begun to win concessions from the Japanese. First, Japan agreed to set boundaries between Japan and Russia, which would require resolving the Sakhalin question and delineating ownership of the Kuril Islands. Second, Japan promised that "should our country finally permit trade, it will be first to your country."[49]

THE CRIMEAN WAR IN THE PACIFIC

Putiatin spent the winter in Manila before sailing north to Russia's Far Eastern territories. He arrived on Russia's Pacific Coast in summer 1854 to find a region at war.[50] The Crimean War had begun in 1853 as a conflict over the rights of Christian minorities in the Middle East yet quickly became a test of the future of the Ottoman Empire. Russia, which wanted to carve up the Ottoman state, confronted Britain and France, which sought to defend the Ottomans. The war's bloodiest battles were fought in the Black Sea, where British, French, and Ottoman forces landed on the Crimean Peninsula, home to the tsar's great naval base at Sebastopol. After a bloody year-long siege, Russian forces were defeated, laying bare the inadequacies of tsarist rule, including the Russian Empire's lack of railroads, which made moving troops and supplies difficult.

Because the Crimean War involved three of the world's greatest military powers, it was fought across the globe. The Pacific Ocean was a minor theater in the war, but the conflict transformed Russia's attitude toward the region. Siberian governor-general Muravev had been warning for years about the risk to Russia of British expansion in the region, advocating that Russia take additional territory and enhance defenses at the Kamchatkan port of Petropavlovsk. Now the British really were attacking, as the Royal Navy and its French allies tracked Russian ships across the Pacific, from South American ports, through Hawaii, as far as the Amur delta. To defend the new Amur outpost of Nikolaevsk—still only several years old—Muravev received permission from St. Petersburg to set out from Irkutsk and sail down the Amur River.[51] Petersburg had previously prohibited such a move, fearing China's response. War with Britain, however, meant that Chinese sensitivities were ignored.

Muravev also received permission to negotiate directly with Beijing over territorial questions. No longer would he be restrained by cautious officials in the capital. He sent the Chinese a note informing them of his plans to move troops down the Amur, ostensibly to defend against Britain and France. As he sailed down the Amur, local villagers fled their homes before him, though he tried to win friends by distributing gifts of silver. Chinese officials, inquiring why he was sailing through their territory, were told that Muravev was simply "making a short cut" that "would not cause any disturbance." When the Chinese asked how many men were making such a "short cut," Muravev replied, "Only a thousand men this time, and more to come." Having sailed through Chinese territory, in summer 1854, Muravev reached the shores of the Pacific. He found not the British fleet that he feared, but Putiatin, who had just arrived from Manila, bolstering Russia's naval power in the region.[52]

Unlike in Crimea, Russia's military in the Pacific fought well. British and French forces besieged Kamchatka in autumn 1854 but were rebuffed, giving Russia a rare Crimean War victory. Yet Russia remained outmatched when it came to military power in Asia. Russian commanders struggled to get messages to naval forces spread across the Pacific, from South America to Hawaii to China. Muravev decided to focus on what mattered most—the Amur. Despite Russia's successful defense of Kamchatka, Muravev ordered the peninsula's garrison to withdraw to Nikolaevsk, on the mouth of the Amur River, to defend the new territory from a potential British-French assault.[53]

The outbreak of war in the Pacific made Putiatin's mission of establishing relations with Japan even more important. The Japanese were not a military power, nor could they be relied upon to side with Russia against its rivals. But after Putiatin had left Japan in early 1854, the country had signed treaties not only with Commodore Perry, but also with a British admiral. Putiatin quickly returned to Japan, signing a treaty in February 1855 opening several Japanese ports for trade.[54]

As the war continued, Russia performed well in the Pacific, fending off British and French attacks, losing no territory, and managing to establish relations with Japan amid the fighting. Though the war itself was a stalemate in Asia, it transformed Russia's Pacific Ocean footing. Muravev had gained St. Petersburg's approval to withdraw forces from Kamchatka to the Amur delta, setting a precedent whereby the Amur settlement of Nikolaevsk became the most important of the country's Pacific outposts. In the process of defending Nikolaevsk, meanwhile, Muravev had sailed troops down the Amur, through territory China considered its own. Rather than resolving tension between the European powers, the Crimean War opened a new era of competition in Asia—a struggle that Russians like Muravev believed their country was now well placed to win.

"THE PEKING CABINET HAS BEEN LEFT VACILLATING"

Defeat in the Crimean War, therefore, encouraged Russia to double down in Asia. After agreeing to a peace treaty with Britain and France in 1856, Russia backed off its demands on the Ottoman Empire and accepted humiliating restrictions on its power in the Black Sea. Meanwhile, the death of Nicholas

I in 1855 and the accession of Alexander II transformed Russian politics. At home, Alexander II would become known as a great reformer, above all for his moves to free Russia's serfs, but also for embracing the construction of railroads and for supporting industrialization. Russia had fallen behind the European powers, Alexander realized, and it was time to catch up.[55]

Catching up meant not only domestic reform, though this was important. It also meant keeping up with Russia's imperial rivals. The Crimean War put a halt on the spread of Russian influence in the Black Sea and the Balkans for at least a decade, so Russia had no choice but "to shift our focus from the Near to the Far East," as one Russian statesman concluded. This decision was made easier by three factors. First, Foreign Minister Nesselrode was forced out after Nicholas's death. Nesselrode was replaced by Alexander Gorchakov, who was equally interested in avoiding war in China, but who lacked the bureaucratic clout to restrain Muravev. Second, during the defense of the Far East during the Crimean War, Muravev had already broken several taboos, including by sailing down the Amur through territory China considered its own. After the first such journey, St. Petersburg struggled to avoid a second or a third. As a sign of the growing Russian influence of the Far East, the naval flotilla in Kamchatka was renamed the "Siberian-Pacific Fleet," underscoring the link between Siberia and the Pacific. This link was only credible if Russia could transport personnel and supplies down the Amur. Even though the Anglo-French assault on Kamchatka in 1854 had failed, it proved that Russia's prewar military forces—with only dozens of men in the Amur region—were inadequate.[56]

A third factor facilitating Russian expansion in East Asia was that, just as the Crimean War was ending, a new war in Asia began. In October 1856, the British began bombarding the Chinese harbor of Canton, present-day Guangzhou, after the Chinese seized a ship flying a British flag. Soon both the British and French were waging the Second Opium War against the Qing Empire, deploying superior military technology to smash Chinese resistance. Meanwhile, the Taiping Rebellion inside China continued to spread, with Foreign Minister Gorchakov reporting to the tsar in 1856 that only four of China's provinces were untouched by unrest. China faced a "day of reckoning," reported a Russian informant in Beijing. With Beijing weakened and British demands growing, Muravev's prediction that China would be carved up seemed to be coming true. If Britain seized Beijing, wrote one leading

Russian diplomat, it would "paralyze all our beginnings on the shores of the Pacific and Amur."[57] Was it not time for Russia to act?

In February 1857, Rear Admiral Putiatin, fresh from diplomatic successes in Japan, was sent back to Asia, this time to guarantee that Russia won the same privileges from China that France and Britain looked set to receive upon conclusion of their war with the Qing Empire. Putiatin envisioned a two-part strategy to extract concessions from the Qing. He proposed moving Russian forces toward China, and even bombarding a Chinese port, to pressure Beijing to surrender territory in the Amur Valley. At the same time, Putiatin sought to convince the Chinese that Russia's demand for sparsely populated territory in the Amur valley was far less onerous than British and French efforts to push into China's heartland. On Putiatin's advice, St. Petersburg offered to send military advisers to Beijing and to transfer fifty large guns and 10,000 small arms to bolster their struggle against other Europeans. Yet the Chinese rebuffed Putiatin's territorial demands.[58]

Muravev was unwilling to wait for Putiatin's negotiations to play out, lest British and French military victories in China limit his ability to extract concessions from Beijing. In 1855, Muravev had told the Chinese he claimed the northern bank of the Amur, territory that the Qing insisted was their own. Muravev argued that Beijing "absolutely does not want to put itself on hostile footing with us." One of Russia's representatives in Beijing agreed, writing Muravev not to expect "any definite system of action on the Amur question . . . both because of the internal troubles and the lack of talent . . . the Peking Cabinet has been left vacillating . . . [and has] decided here on delaying tactics."[59]

Yet Muravev would not accept delay. One reason was growing optimism about economic development in the Amur region. The "excellent ports" in the "empty maritime region, fit for farming and all types of industry" were key to Russia's future development, one diplomat reported. An American businessman visiting Siberia exchanged letters with Muravev and at least one of his lieutenants, outlining plans to build railroads in the Amur. After all, the United States was considering building a transcontinental railroad of its own, and Muravev had visions of US-Russian cooperation to develop Siberia's economy. The American, meanwhile, expressed the optimism felt by many Russians when looking at the area: "Steamboats will take the place of the canoe and barge . . . and add, as it were, a sixth continent to the domain of civilization."[60]

The first step was to clear the region of Chinese forces. Without telling Beijing, Russia created a regional government for the Amur in 1856, formalizing control over the territory. That same year, St. Petersburg authorized Muravev to negotiate directly with the Qing over a new border in Siberia. The governor-general now demanded that China hand over land on both sides of the Amur River, and grant expanded rights for Russian traders, too. On May 28, 1858, after much feasting on lamb, piglet, and Chinese whiskey—and after Muravev threatened them by shooting off Russian guns throughout the night—the Qing representatives relented. The Treaty of Aigun recognized Russia's right to the Amur but left vague the question of the Ussuri River Valley, to the Amur's south. The tsar described the results of Muravev's negotiations as "immense," and decreed that the governor-general should henceforth be known as "Amursky," in honor of the river he had conquered for Russia. The Amur was the key to Russia's position in Asia. "I foresee," the tsar declared, "that it is here that future destinies will be decided."[61]

"CHINA IS LIKE A LAMB BEFORE THE SHEARERS"

"The English barbarians are the most unrighteous," a Chinese official complained, "but the Russian barbarians are the most cunning." Yet after the Treaty of Aigun was signed in 1858, it was the Chinese who proved cunning, or at least duplicitous, when Beijing refused to recognize its diplomats' signatures on the treaty. The same year that Muravev negotiated—or, from the Chinese perspective, imposed—the Treaty of Aigun, China's representatives also signed a deal with the British and French to end the Second Opium War. Yet it quickly became clear that Beijing had no intention of abiding by either treaty.[62]

The Russians were unwilling to let the Qing escape the concessions made in Aigun. Nor would the British and French tolerate Beijing's repudiation of their own treaty with the Qing. The British and French commanders marched on Beijing to enforce compliance. Russia, seeing Beijing under pressure, decided not only to enforce the provisions of the Aigun Treaty, but also to demand more territory, too. Tsar Alexander sent Russian officer Nikolai Ignatiev to Beijing to negotiate. Ignatiev was ordered to demand a new and more extensive treaty with the Qing. He was also given thousands of guns with which to supply the Chinese against the British and French. The aim, one foreign diplomat in China recognized, was that Russian "assistance [to China would probably end in passing China under a Russian protectorate, and the extension of Russian limits to the Hoangho [River], or the mouth of the Yangtze . . . China is like a lamb before the shearers."[63]

China at first resisted Ignatiev's military supplies and told the Russian envoy that it had only "loaned" the Amur to Russia. Ignatiev, meanwhile, grumbled about China's "negative attitude . . . to our territorial demands." He attributed Chinese intransigence both to Russian weakness—"our influence . . . in Beijing doesn't exist"—and to China's unhappiness with Russia's seizure of Chinese territories, writing that "Chinese, who have lived with us in friendship for over a century, have now come to look on us as enemies." In the end, though, Ignatiev prioritized Russian demands over Chinese feelings. He threatened to work with Britain against China, told Beijing that Russian "military settlers" were already occupying the disputed territory, and insisted that Russia would implement the Aigun Treaty whether Beijing agreed or not.[64]

While Ignatiev waited for an answer from Beijing, Muravev moved to seize the land he wanted. A Russian military officer was sent to explore the Ussuri River and reported finding no Chinese officials there. Muravev ordered his soldiers to "declare the existence of the Aigun Treaty across Manchuria" so that "residents there know that they lived on Russian land under our protection." His troops demolished a Chinese fort on the Amur, and after the Qing forces rebuilt it, Russians destroyed it again. Muravev knew the Qing dynasty was teetering on the edge of collapse. Even the normally cautious Foreign Ministry agreed that if talks with the Chinese stalled, Muravev should seize the Amur and Ussuri Rivers.[65] He eagerly complied.

Only after Muravev occupied the Amur and Ussuri Rivers, and as British and French forces pushed toward Beijing, did the Qing begin making concessions. The Europeans entered Beijing in October 1860, torching the Qing Emperor's opulent summer palace in retaliation after British and French hostages were tortured to death there. Soon after, the Qing capitulated both to the European powers and to the Russians, signing the Treaty of Beijing, by which China formally surrendered the Amur and Ussuri territories to Russia and offered extensive trading rights. Ignatiev gloated to the Foreign Ministry that he had received vast territorial concessions "without spilling any Russian blood." Muravev, for whom the treaty was the culmination of a decade-long effort to win the Amur River for Russia, celebrated with a glass of champagne.[66]

THE DECLINE OF THE AMUR DREAM

Russia had not only won its "Mississippi," it had incorporated into its empire a vast territory that had long been promised as a "New Canaan." In Irkutsk, Siberia's commercial center, the Treaty of Beijing was celebrated with toasts and speeches heralding "a new and original future." Russia's new lands, one speaker declared, would unite the country with "California and Panama from one side; newly opened China and Japan from the other; the Australian continent now being settled in the south; a multitude of various countries touching on the ocean from all sides. . . . The shift of the world historical field to the Pacific is entirely in accord with the laws of history." "Somewhere on this coast, near or upon the Amoor," one foreign observer predicted, "must be built the St. Petersburg of the Pacific."[67]

It was not only Russians who thought that the Amur would transform Russia into an even greater power. Friedrich Engels—whose own ideas about communism would later reshape Russian politics—declared that "Russia is fast coming to be the first Asiatic Power" because "the annexation of Mantchooria increase[s] her dominions by an extent of country as large as all Europe . . . and bring[s] her down from snowy Siberia to the temperate zone. In a short time," he predicted, "the Amoor will be peopled by Russian colonists." The strategic ramifications were profound, Engels believed, because the territory Russia had conquered was the key to power on Asia's Pacific coast. "Mantchooria menaces China," he explained, "and China and India, with their 450,000,000 of inhabitants are now the decisive countries of Asia."[68]

Engels's predictions would have been more accurate, however, had the great believer in historical materialism analyzed Russia's material position in the Amur Valley. The irony of the Treaty of Beijing is that it represented both the culmination of Muravev's dream of seizing the Pacific coast for Russia and the end of Russians' dreaming that the Far East was the land of Russia's future. Muravev's successes heralded not the beginning of a new era for Russian power in Pacific, but a three-decade-long period in which St. Petersburg roundly ignored the region.

True, Muravev was proven correct in his belief that "he who controls the Amur, controls Siberia." And St. Petersburg continued to fear foreign infiltration into Sakhalin Island, for example, lest the Americans or, more likely, the British, establish a perch for monitoring and intercepting traffic in and out of the Amur. Such an occurrence would be a "serious political evil and source of embarrassment, if not danger, in time of war," one Russian diplomat warned. And Sakhalin's coal supplies attracted the navy's attention as shipping shifted away from sail toward coal power. Yet thanks to Muravev's efforts to assert Russian sovereignty on the entire Pacific coast north of the Korean border, Europeans and Americans did not meddle. The only remaining territorial question—ownership of the long island of Sakhalin—was resolved peacefully in a treaty with Japan signed in 1867. That same year, Russia finally agreed to sell Alaska to the United States for $7.2 million, liquidating its claims in North America.[69]

By that point, the Russian intellectuals and politicians who had placed such great faith in the Amur's ability to revitalize Russian society had lost interest. The Petrashevsky Circle had long since dissolved. Its members were spared by the tsar from execution, but they split politically among themselves. The more liberal half embraced the reformist policies of Tsar Alexander II, supporting his efforts to abolish serfdom and modernize Russia. The nationalist wing, meanwhile, was infuriated by Russia's defeat in the Crimean War and directed its attention to revising the postwar settlement in Europe and the Black Sea Basin. The Amur had lost its appeal for both groups.

As Russia's elite turned away from the Amur, the country's merchants and peasants showed no willingness to pick up the slack in integrating the new territory into Russia. By that point, hopes that the Amur Valley would benefit from the type of commercial expansion or population boom that was visible on the opposite side of the Pacific—in California, say, or in Oregon's Willamette Valley—had been dashed. There may have been a superficial similarity between America's and Russia's push to the Pacific, but the Amur territory was not the Canaan that was promised. A fanciful effort to build a telegraph line from the United States, north through Canada, across the

Bering Straits that connect Russia and Alaska, and then on to Siberia, was canceled in 1867—the same year Alaska was sold—after a much shorter transatlantic connection was completed.[70]

Nor was the Amur the breadbasket that generations of Russians had hoped. Settlers there complained that the land was difficult to plow, and they had to buy flour and millet from Manchuria. True, at some point Russia might get a trans-Siberian railroad that would connect the Amur with Russia's European heartland. But that day would not come soon. The United States approved its first transcontinental railroad in 1862. Canada followed five years later. But it would take Russia a quarter century to begin its own railway connecting St. Petersburg with the Amur, and far longer to finish it. By 1880, two decades after solidifying control over the region, Russia had built just 125 miles of railroad track there, compared to over 23,000 miles in the rest of Russia.[71]

Worrying that not enough Russians were settling in the area, Muravev ordered military units to move there. When this proved insufficient, he assembled male convicts and poor women from Siberia, ordered them to choose partners quickly, and, according to one source, had a priest conduct a mass marriage on the banks of the Amur before making them, too, settle in the territory. Yet it was not surprising that Russian peasants saw little appeal in a far-off land with no infrastructure. Muravev's mass marriages and forcible resettlement had little effect. Few Russians moved to the territory for decades, and as late as the 1880s soldiers and military officials outnumbered civilian settlers.[72]

When explorer and geographer Nikolai Przhevalsky traveled down the Ussuri River in 1867–1869 he found few Russians. Those who were present lived in "filth, hunger, and poverty." Yet Russians were needed, Przhevalsky noted, because of the large population of foreigners in the region. There were several thousand Chinese living along the Ussuri River, he reported, and they dominated the seafood trade in the new port of Vladivostok—the St. Petersburg on the Pacific. The Chinese population sympathized with bandit groups called the Honghuzi, who would harass Russians in Manchuria for the subsequent half century, suggesting that not all Chinese were pleased with Russia's arrival.

Even as Russians stayed away, large numbers of Koreans in search of new land spilled over their country's border with Russia into the Ussuri Valley, though Przhevalsky warned his Russian readers that it was best to keep Koreans away from the border lest they think about uniting Russia's Ussuri territory with their homeland. The other peoples living in the region, Przhevalsky concluded, were even less impressive, displaying "no feelings, no wishes, no happiness, no hope." There is only "a small difference," he concluded, "between these people and their dogs." Whether animal or human, the population needed to be ruled, and Przhevalsky advised continuing to settle Russian Cossacks in the area, whose "main responsibility will be the supervision of the local Chinese population," potentially "decreasing the flow of new Manchus from Manchuria to our area," or even encouraging some to leave.[73]

Nevelskoy, the naval officer whose machinations had helped win the Amur's mouth for Russia, quipped that the region was "long fated to live like an army camp." He was right. With few settlers and little trade, there was no other option for retaining Russian control. Sakhalin Island, off the Amur coast, was in fact turned into a prison camp in 1869, continuing a tsarist and later Soviet policy of shipping undesirable people to the underpopulated Far East. When famed playwright Anton Chekhov traveled to Sakhalin toward the end of the century—a journey that nearly killed him—he found nothing but incompetence, cruelty, and suffering. Voluntary settlers on Sakhalin "failed," Chekhov reported, but the number of prisoners only multiplied, emaciated and often suffering from syphilis infections.[74] What Chekhov saw on Sakhalin Island was an accurate depiction of the Russian Far East: forced colonization by soldiers and prisoners, coupled with a small number of voluntary settlers, many of whom regretted their decision to move east.

Some Russians believed that better government might have made the new territories a success. Mikhail Bakunin, the anarchist cousin of Governor-General Muravev, argued that American governance could have made the Amur a "blessed land," but its Russian rulers were as "helpless as a child." But the Russian Far East was far harder to settle and develop than the American West. It was twice as far from St. Petersburg to Vladivostok as it was from New York to San Francisco. And Russia remained backward when it came to the types of transport—first steamships, then railroads—that could have facilitated connections.

Moreover, the Russian elite was focused more on glorious conquests than on transportation infrastructure. Muravev occasionally dreamed of railroads crisscrossing the Russian Far East, but he took no practical steps in that direction. The military officers who drove Russia's expansion in the region were primarily interested in expanding the map of Russia rather than the business of making use of new territories.

Having pushed forward Russia's borders and excluded other powers, the officers and officials who had dreamed for decades of the Amur had gotten most of what they wanted. True, the idea that the Amur territory could revitalize Russian society had fallen out of fashion. But Muravev's goal of seizing the territory from China had been achieved. The border with China was moved hundreds of miles southward. Britain was kept off the North Pacific coast, guaranteeing Russian supremacy. Tsar Alexander II had fulfilled his father's desire that "where the Russian flag has been raised, it should not be taken down." Nevelskoy, navigator of the Amur, received a promotion and began writing a long, self-aggrandizing memoir.

Territorial expansion accomplished, the pendulum of Russian attention swung back toward other affairs, leaving the Far East a backwater. Only a year after signing the Treaty of Beijing, Muravev stepped down from the governor-generalship of East Siberia. After conquering the river of his dreams, even he lost interest in the region. Muravev continued to follow news reports about the Russian Far East, but never returned to the lands of the Amur. When asked by one acquaintance why he resigned from the governor-generalship of Siberia, he asked, incredulous, "Did you want me to stay there and die?" Conquering the Amur Valley was glorious; living in an "army camp" on the desolate shores of the Pacific was not.[75] Muravev quit Siberia for a pleasant retirement, not on the banks of the Amur or Ussuri, but along the Seine, in Paris.

3

"WE CAN STILL REPEAT THE EXPLOITS OF CORTEZ"

Expansion and Retreat in China's Central Asian Borderlands

"FILTH, HUNGER, AND POVERTY"—this is what Nikolai Przhevalsky found on his trek through the Ussuri Valley in 1867–1869. Przhevalsky lived in an era that celebrated explorers more than any since the days of Columbus, da Gama, and Cortez. In Africa, British travelers such as Richard Burton won fame by mapping the continent's lakes, while David Livingstone searched for the sources of the Nile. Przhevalsky had read about explorers like Livingstone as a schoolboy.[1] What was a Russian adventurer to explore? Some Russians had earned respect, though not much glory, by trekking across Alaska. But by the time Przhevalsky began his travels, Russian America had been sold to the United States. Russia naval officers discovered islands in the Arctic, but Przhevalsky had no maritime skill—and anyway Arctic islands were desolate, ice-covered rocks. Przhevalsky wanted to take part in great events, but the frozen Arctic was a wasteland. Britain's explorers helped expand their country's empire, and Przhevalsky wanted to do the same. But where? The Arctic was frozen; Russian America sold; and the Amur and Ussuri were already being forgotten.

Previous generations of European explorers had mapped Asia's coast, but the continent's inner heartland remained, in Przhevalsky's mind, a mystery.

The plains of Mongolia and Kazakhstan; the deserts of Kara Kum and Tak-lamakan; the peaks of the Pamirs, the Tian Shan, the Himalayas—what did Russians know about these? Russian trading caravans had plodded across the Mongol plains and the Kazakh steppe for centuries, and Russian diplomats occasionally traversed the mountains and deserts to deal with neighbors on the other side.[2] But Przhevalsky sensed that there was territory to "discover" along China's Central Asian borderlands because Russians' knowledge of the region was limited, and because St. Petersburg had never treated learning more as a priority.

Along China's western borderlands were a diverse set of territories and peoples. The northwest was home to a mix of Kazakhs, Mongols, and Chinese. To the south was the fertile Yili Valley, a great trade hub that was cut off from the rest of China by snowy mountains, but which shared a broad, easily traversable river valley with the Russian-controlled Kazakh steppe lands. The Yili Valley was the Qing Empire's key outpost in Central Asia but it was also closely linked to Russia. As early as the 1840s, Russia had built roads to Yili to facilitate trade, while Russian frontier forces had established new towns along the portion of the Yili Valley that Russia controlled.[3]

Farther south still was a land called Kashgaria, named after its central trading city of Kashgar. Kashgaria was an immense desert bounded by mountains on three sides: the Tian Shan to the north, the Pamirs to the west, and to the south the Kunlun Shan, which stretch into the Himalayas. Snowmelt-fed streams trickled down to small towns and agricultural settlements at the base of these mountains, inhabited mostly by Muslims speaking Turkic languages. While most trade with Russia transited through the northern steppe lands, the towns of the south carried on a brisk commerce through high mountain passes with the Fergana Valley—an area that Russia was now entering. The 1860 Treaty of Beijing, which China had signed after Governor-General Muravev threatened war, gave St. Petersburg the right to open a consulate in Kashgar, Russia's first substantive foothold in the region.[4]

By the beginning of the 1860s, some Russians were beginning to think again about the Central Asian borderlands of China's Qing Empire: from Mongolia to the Altai, from the Kazakh Steppe to the Tian Shan mountains, from the peaks of the Pamirs to even the Himalayas and Tibet. As the Urals and Siberia became more densely populated, some Russians began looking southward for farmland, settling in Central Asia and grabbing land from nomadic Kazakhs who lived there. Russian military detachments clashed with the khans who ruled the river valleys surrounding the trade hubs of Bukhara, Khiva, and Kokand, to China's west.[5]

These Central Asian territories were no great prize in themselves, even though some Russians argued that Russia's conquest of them "is required by geographic and historical needs."[6] Przhevalsky, too, insisted that the inhabitants of Central Asia must be brought into what he called "the realm of civilized peoples"—if necessary, by force. Over the course of the 1850s, 1860s, and 1870s, the Russian Empire conquered most of present-day Central Asia, seizing lands from the khans in a series of small wars. Russian leaders rarely saw these territories as crucial in themselves, though some officials in St. Petersburg viewed them as part of a broader imperial sparring match with Britain for control of the Caspian basin, Iran, Afghanistan, even India itself.[7]

Russia's expansion into China's Central Asian borderlands was related to this southward march of the Russian Empire. But the military and geopolitical context was profoundly different. Unlike Central Asia's khans, China was a vast empire, sharing a border with Russia that stretched from the center of Eurasia all the way to the Pacific Coast south of Vladivostok. All of China's frontiers had to be considered with the Qing leadership in Beijing in mind.

Central Asia mattered to Russia because St. Petersburg was beginning to see these lands as part of a broader imperial struggle against Qing China and the British Empire for control over all of Asia. The Khan of Kokand traded with China and British India, having sent at least forty-eight trade delegations to the Qing Empire over the previous decades.[8] Central Asia's rulers had sent envoys to the British East India Company, too.[9] Lands that had long seemed to Russians as among the world's most isolated now appeared to hold the key to domination in Asia.

One reason for this is that Qing China appeared to be in inexorable decline. Muravev's seizure of the Amur and Ussuri Valleys in the previous decade was just one of many crises that the Qing Empire faced during the 1850s and 1860s as wars and revolts ripped across nearly all its frontiers. The Taiping Rebellion threatened major Chinese cities such as Shanghai until it was snuffed out in 1864. In the far southern region of Yunnan, meanwhile, along the Burmese border, a variety of Muslim ethnic minority groups revolted against Qing rule.[10] For Russia, rebellions and crises along China's eastern and

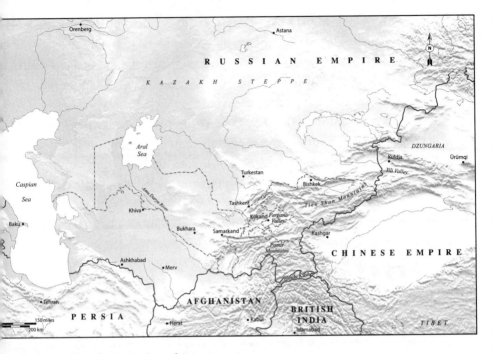

The Russia-China frontier in Central Asia, 1850s–1890s

southern borders seemed at first like no bad thing. Russia had no interests in far-flung Yunnan Province. If China were kept busy there, Beijing would have no energy to press for revisions to the Amur settlement, which the Chinese accepted only because they lacked the power to overturn it.

China's crises created opportunities for Russia, but they also posed risks. One risk was that, if Beijing's rule over its Central Asian periphery began to crumble, the aftershocks would spill over into Russian territory. A second risk, more dangerous still, was that Qing China's decline would benefit the British, giving them a chance to expand across the continent. Viewed from St. Petersburg, the British Empire looked as though it was encircling China and preparing to dominate all of Asia. For the British not only ruled India, on the opposite side of the Himalayas from China; they had also tried invading Afghanistan and were eyeing Tibet. Farther to the east, the British had already conquered the southern half of Burma, which bordered China's Yunnan region. British merchants, meanwhile, had received substantial trading privileges in Siam and were expanding their position elsewhere in Southeast Asia. Along China's coast, meanwhile, it was the British who had already defeated the Qing Empire in both Opium Wars, winning control over Hong Kong and special trading rights in many of China's great ports. Britain's presence was felt over thousands of miles of China's frontier. If the Qing lost control, and China splintered apart, Britain looked likely to pick up the most valuable pieces.

This would pose a profound challenge to Russia, of course. But some officials in St. Petersburg believed that Britain's growing presence along China's borders also presented opportunities. Perhaps, some officials argued, Russia could use the region to pressure its long-standing rival. Russia had no means of threatening Britain's empire by sea, but could it not march on India, the crown jewel of the British Empire? The idea had been long discussed by some Russian strategists, though many of them found the prospect of sending an army over the Himalayas absurd.

By the 1860s, however, the gap between the southern border of Russian Central Asia and the British Empire's frontier on the Hindu Kush had shrunk to only 1,000 kilometers. Leading Russian strategists such as Nikolai Ignatiev, the hawkish diplomat who had negotiated the 1860 Treaty of Beijing with China and who would spend the remainder of his career contesting British power in Central Asia and the Black Sea Basin, argued that "British statesmen should not indulge in pleasant illusions of their colonies being secured . . . [or of the] inaccessibility of routes through Central Asia." Even some disinterested observers thought that Russia could plausibly assault India. A Russian "attack upon India from the north," wrote *New York Daily Tribune* columnist Friedrich Engels, "has already abandoned the state of vague speculations and assumed somewhat definite contours."[11] As Przhevalsky first turned his attention to China's borderlands, all of Asia seemed up for grabs.

"A KIND OF EL DORADO"

By the mid-1860s, the crises on the Qing Empire's northern, eastern, and southern borderlands were finally reaching its western frontier. The yoke of Qing officials in the Central Asian borderlands wore ever harder on the local population, with the officials living "extravagant lives" while their subjects complained that they were treated like "dogs and sheep," paying higher taxes while losing access to government jobs. In 1864, the populace of the city of

Kucha rose up, attacking Qing officials and their allies with axes and hoes, burning their buildings, and chasing them out of town. The revolt whipped across China's western borderlands, and within six months local militias had wrenched control of the entire region, an area three times the size of France. Soon the rebellion reached the Yili Valley, the trading entrepot on the Russian border.[12] By the end of the year, nearly all of China's western border with Russia was governed by local warlords—or not governed at all.

Russia at first stayed studiously neutral, even as it suffered from the rebellion's side effects. In 1865 and 1867, Chinese forces were alleged to have violated Russian borders during clashes with rebel forces, but Russia did not retaliate, choosing only to reinforce the border and demand compensation for damages. St. Petersburg repeatedly declined to support the anti-Chinese rebels.[13] Though some Russians discussed intervening in China's Yili Valley to restore order—and to establish a Russian foothold—most officials in St. Petersburg and most of the military's officers on the Central Asian frontier initially preferred to avoid doing so. After all, St. Petersburg was busy suppressing a rebellion in Russian-ruled Poland during the mid-1860s. It would likely soon be at war again with one or more of the Central Asian khans. Russia had no need to get involved in China's civil wars—and most officials in St. Petersburg saw relations with China as far more important than any local warlord.

But even if Russia did not at first take advantage of the rebellion along China's western borderlands, others would. The greatest beneficiary of China's chaos was a warlord named Yakub Beg, a native of the Khanate of Kokand, in Central Asia's Fergana Valley, just to the south of the Russian Empire and to the west of Qing China's border. Yakub Beg had come of age battling Russian armies as they pushed into Central Asia. As a military commander ("beg" meant "commander" or "chief" in the local language), he amassed a small fortune collecting customs duties from the caravan trade, though his influence in Kokand later declined after his forces were routed by a smaller contingent of Russian troops.[14]

When the revolt broke out in China's Kashgar region, Yakub Beg saw an opportunity for redemption. His native Kokand had deep ties with Kashgar, sharing languages and customs, connected by centuries-old trade routes. In early 1865, half a year after the rebellion in Kashgaria broke out, Yakub Beg and several dozen followers set off from Kokand over the mountain pass toward Kashgar. In only two years, after a skillful military campaign and political skullduggery, the warlord established control over the southern half of China's western borderlands. He saw no reason to stop.

Russians soon wondered whether Yakub Beg's rise might redraw the map of China and reshape the distribution of power in Asia. The warlord had already signaled a desire to ally with Britain. R. B. Shaw, a British citizen, arrived in Kashgar from British India, reporting that the territory was strategically important and commercially "a kind of El Dorado." British interest in Yakub Beg subsequently rose. Would Britain ally with the warlord, helping him establish an independent state, detaching Kashgaria from China in the process? If so, the British boa constrictor would further encircle China. Suddenly it seemed that Yakub Beg might be a power broker even beyond China's tumultuous western borderlands, for China's fate would shape all of Asia.

"THE RICHEST PORTION OF THE ASIATIC PROVINCES"

The collapse in Chinese authority had "enormous political significance" and "adverse consequences" for Russia, one official warned. Russia's trade with the region plummeted, and Russia had to close its consulates in Western China after Russian trading warehouses in Yili and elsewhere were destroyed in the rebellion. Meanwhile, tens of thousands of refugees fled conflict in China by crossing the border into Russia. As Kyrgyz groups in China became embroiled in conflict, their allies among the Kyrgyz in Russia crossed into Chinese territory in the Yili Valley to join the war.[15] Even if Russia wanted to stay out of China's civil war, the war was spilling across the border into Russia.

Russian officials were at first reluctant to intervene against the warlord who controlled the Yili Valley, lest such a move anger China. So long as the rebellion lasted, Russian officials expected "secret relations" between the rebel government in the Yili Valley and Kyrgyz groups in Russia to continue. If the Chinese retook the area, however, such a reconquest would drive more refugees into Russian territory. And the Chinese had not been perfect neighbors. They, too, had supported "intrigues" among the Kyrgyz, while refusing to extradite "bandits" and "criminals" to Russia. Yet these concerns were subordinated to the belief that, as one Russian official noted, "it would be impolitic to retreat now from our traditional foreign policy" of friendship with China.[16]

As the war continued, however, this view was soon eclipsed by a contrary thesis: that passivity threatened Russia's prestige, and that an expansionist policy would be more fitting of a great power like Russia. The situation in the Yili Valley continued to worsen. It was no longer only that the war had devasted the borderlands, leaving "dried-up canals, abandoned fields, withered forests, and every few miles dismantled and ruined cities." The crisis threatened "the prosperity of our [frontier] regions, which depend on the establishment of order" across the border, wrote one leading Russian diplomat, noting declining trade and disruptive refugee flows. Even Foreign Minister Alexander Gorchakov, who was always cautious in Asian affairs, grumbled that the situation had become "intolerable."[17]

What to do? "Asians only respect force," War Minister Dmitry Miliutin argued, echoing a refrain often repeated by Russia's leaders, insisting that St. Petersburg must assert its interests by force. The Foreign Ministry feared that intervention would embroil Russia in new conflicts, chiefly with Britain, causing St. Petersburg problems on the European front. The Finance Ministry correctly assessed that territorial expansion would exacerbate Russia's budget deficit and disrupt trade. Russia's generals, however, were inclined toward military means, some because they sought glory in conquests, others because they thought a decisive solution was preferable to intermittent frontier skirmishes.[18]

The rise of Yakub Beg, who now controlled the lands just over the mountains from the Yili Valley, illustrated that traditional borders were being redrawn. The fate of empires was at stake. By spring 1871, even the Foreign Ministry, which was generally skeptical of Central Asian adventures, had concluded that "both the general interests of the state, and the special conditions of administration of our border zones with China make necessary participation" in China's conflict. Later that year, St. Petersburg authorized commanders in Central Asia to seize the Yili Valley. After a brief battle, Russian troops marched into the valley—territory that remained, at least in theory, Chinese.[19]

Russian forces quickly integrated the territory into their growing empire, administering the territory much like how it governed other parts of

Central Asia. It continued to settle the border area with Russians and conducted a detailed census of the peoples in its new territory in the Yili Valley to govern them more effectively. Russia also supervised the construction of churches and promoted trade in the valley.[20]

It did not look like the Russians ever planned to leave the Yili Valley. Why would they? There was little evidence that China could ever reconquer its western borderlands from the rebels. Tsar Alexander II explained to the Qing Court that Russia "pursues only the goal of rendering China assistance towards the restoration of her influence in the . . . Western provinces of the empire." But when Beijing told Russia that it would send an official to govern the Yili Valley, Russia's ambassador refused, saying his country would turn over the city only to a Chinese army capable of retaining control. The Foreign Ministry wanted Beijing to have "an adequate number of troops there" to guarantee that "communications with the Chinese interior can be completely secured." In 1872, Russia's envoy in Beijing went further, telling the Chinese that Russia would not leave until Beijing reconquered the city of Kashgar, an even more difficult military venture. Foreign Minister Gorchakov also thought Russia should seek Chinese guarantees for "the free development of our trade," while other officials sought compensation from China for the costs of occupying its territory. In the meantime, while China struggled to reassert control over its western borderlands, Russia ruled over a new region, which one traveler reported was "in every respect the richest portion of the Asiatic provinces recently occupied by Russia."[21]

"THE MOST CELEBRATED TRAVELER IN ASIA SINCE MARCO POLO"

In 1870, just as officials in St. Petersburg were deciding whether to occupy the Yili Valley, the explorer Przhevalsky turned his attention to Central Asia. In four journeys over the subsequent fifteen years, he crossed the Gobi Desert, traversed the Tian Shan, trekked through East Turkestan, and mapped the approaches to Tibet. He promised anyone who would listen that Asia offered Russia territory that would be easy to conquer, straightforward to rule, and a magnificent addition to Russia's empire. Many in Russia did listen, at least at first, and Przhevalsky's journeys were supported by powerful Russian officials, notably in the military. Przhevalsky served as an adviser on the army's war plans.[22] His reports and books were read widely by the Russian elite, and he briefed officials at every level, all the way up to the tsar.[23]

Przhevalsky's treks across China earned him not only worldwide fame but also respect from other Russians as an expert on all matters Asian. He was "the most celebrated traveler in Asia since Marco Polo," one Russian declared. The playwright Anton Chekhov declared that Russia needed Przhevalsky "as it needs the sun."[24] Przhevalsky's exploration of Central Asia was underwritten by the Imperial Russian Geographic Society and by the army, whose leaders were sympathetic to Przhevalsky's energetic expansionism. "So long as . . . Miliutin was at the Ministry of War," one of Przhevalsky's biographers has written, "Przhevalsky got whatever he asked for."[25]

What Przhevalsky wanted above all was new territory for Russia, which he saw as crucial to guaranteeing his country's position in Asia and on the world stage. He was far from alone among Russian officials in seeing the redrawing of Asia's map as both an opportunity and a threat. Those officials knew that China faced rebellions and crises along nearly all its frontiers. "Chinese power has always been weak in Western China," one Russian noted. "The Chinese have already several times conquered Turkestan . . . and as many times lost it."[26] At a time when Beijing's central authority was collapsing and European empires were on the march, what reason was there to expect that the Qing would reestablish authority? Certainly, expansionists like Przhevalsky saw no reason to respect China's border if Qing armies could not defend it. His critics "have soap bubbles they call ideals," Przhevalsky once philosophized, but "I have might as the only recognized criterion of right."[27]

In 1872, after Russian troops had marched into Yili, a Russian officer was sent to Kashgar as an envoy to Yakub Beg's government. The officer was received in majestic fashion, with Yakub Beg wearing a stately green robe and a white turban and providing his Russian guests a magnificent feast of local delicacies.[28] The Russians were not the only foreigners to arrive in Kashgaria, the host explained. The English had been there first. As early as 1871, Yakub Beg had sent an envoy to India with a letter to the British queen, requesting that he be allowed to buy muskets from the British. Soon the two parties signed a commercial treaty. The warlord had already sent an envoy to the Ottoman sultan too. The Ottomans and Yakub Beg not only shared religious ties, they were also both rivals of Russia. The sultan provided the warlord a military aid mission led by four Ottoman officers and "six large Krupp cannons," "one thousand old and two thousand new rifles," and materials for "the manufacture of gun powder." When the Ottoman delegation arrived in Kashgaria it was "greeted with joy and honored by a 100-gun salute."[29] Russians looked on nervously at Yakub Beg's imperial diplomacy.[30]

To Przhevalsky and other advocates of expansion, Yakub Beg's partnership with Britain and the Ottomans provided a perfect pretext for Russia to march forward, crush his emirate, and grab his territory—or, rather, territory that Yakub Beg controlled but that still belonged formally to China. Przhevalsky's rationale was simple: Russia was rising, China was declining, and St. Petersburg should acquire Chinese land now before it fell into the hands of a rival power. "There are many scores to settle with our haughty neighbor [China], and we are obliged to demonstrate to it that Russia's spirit and Russian courage know no match, whether at home or in the Far East," Przhevalsky argued. In spring 1874, Przhevalsky gave a lecture in St. Petersburg about his latest journey to Mongolia and Tibet, which War Minister Miliutin attended. The minister noted in his diary that "women are especially eager for these meetings, with a true thirst for knowledge. Przhevalsky more than anyone can attract listeners—and above all, the women. His energetic nature is visible in all his figure, in each word." It was as if Przhevalsky personally embodied the romance of imperial expansion. After the lecture, Miliutin invited Przhevalsky over to his house for tea.[31]

Sources do not record what Przhevalsky and Miliutin discussed as they drank their tea, but it is easy to guess. Przhevalsky told anyone willing to listen that Russia must expand at China's expense. The land that China had lost to Yakub Beg seemed a natural place to start. The warlord was "cunning," Przhevalsky wrote, and had "courage" and "guile." But he would struggle to retain power. Yakub Beg "hardly has a serious understanding of running a government," Przhevalsky wrote. His rule was a "bloody terror." He had imported allies from the Fergana Valley to run Kashgaria, where they served as "governors of the cities, commanders of the army, collators of taxes, and make up the guards of the emperor [Yakub Beg] himself." But the local population, Przhevalsky argued, finds these imported officials "worse than the Chinese" because they "steal from the population not only property but also wives and daughters."[32]

A Russian officer who met Yakub Beg in 1876 agreed with Przhevalsky that he was weak. "The knowledge of Kashgaria that we possessed," this officer reported, "exaggerated the real power" of the Kashgarian warlord.[33] If that was the case, should Russia not take advantage? Przhevalsky asserted that even residents of Kashgar hoped that Russia would invade. "Here," Przhevalsky promised, "we can still repeat the exploits of Cortez."[34] It was no surprise that Przhevalsky saw parallels with the great Spanish explorers of America. Could he convince other Russians to share his vision?

On May 9, 1877, while on one of his great treks through China seeking a path to Tibet, Przhevalsky met personally with Yakub Beg, who received him "graciously," though Przhevalsky later grumbled that all the camels the warlord gave him promptly died. Yakub Beg fared little better than his hapless camels. On May 29, shortly after meeting Przhevalsky, blood began pouring from Yakub Beg's nose, and he expired soon after. Some of his associates believed the he was poisoned, while the Chinese suspected suicide.[35] Perhaps he simply died. Whatever the cause, his successors could not hold on to power. By the end of the year, Chinese armies crushed the rebels in Kashgaria.

Yakub Beg's emirate was no more. But Przhevalsky's dream of conquest survived. Just after the warlord's death, Przhevalsky wrote to army leadership, declaring, "The present time is the most beneficial in which to set up relations with Eastern Turkestan." Russia controlled China's Yili Valley. The Qing Empire's army was marching westward across China, but Przhevalsky doubted that it could reestablish authority either in Kashgaria or in Russian-controlled Yili. Locals hated Qing officials as "infidels," Przhevalsky explained. Surrounded by weak neighbors, Russia should use the opportunity presented by its occupation of Yili to move its border yet farther south and west, Przhevalsky urged.[36] This meant yet further conquests of territory that China considered its own.

"WASTELANDS WE DON'T NEED"

Even as Przhevalsky and Yakub beg were meeting in spring 1877, Russia and the Ottoman Empire were slipping into war. As Russian troops in the Balkans and the Caucasus pushed into Ottoman territory, Central Asia at first seemed like a distraction. The Russo-Turkish War began in April 1877, and by November the Russian army in the Caucasus had seized the great Ottoman fortress of Kars. Soon Russian forces in the Balkans had swept Ottoman forces from Bulgaria, clearing the way for a quick march onto the Ottoman capital of Constantinople. By January, the Ottomans offered a truce, but Russia hesitated, wondering whether it should march on Constantinople and seize the Turkish Straits. London, fearing such a move, sent its fleet to the straits, threatening war.[37] Suddenly, Russia and Britain stood on the brink of war.

Russia's previous conflict with the British—the Crimean War of 1853–1856—had been a global struggle, stretching from the Baltic to the White Sea to Kamchatka. Now, after two decades of Russian expansion in Central Asia, any new war with Britain would have an additional theater of conflict, Russian strategists believed. Russian military officials quickly began calculating the risks to their Central Asian position. Some worried, for example, that British troops could land in Persia, threatening Russia from the south via Shiraz and Isfahan. One officer noted the risk of British meddling in Russian-held regions. "There is no doubt," he wrote "that England will fund and try to stir up against us Bukhara, Khiva, the Turkmen and maybe the southern Kyrgyz."[38]

Yakub Beg's death had spelled the end of his emirate, but it did not resolve the question of who would dominate Asia. Some Russian officials urged St. Petersburg to go on the offensive against Britain in the region. But most Russian leaders saw the risk of a European war as a reason for caution. The enthusiastic colonialism urged by adventurers like Przhevalsky began to seem less appealing. The July 1878 Congress of Berlin, which was charged with managing the end of the Russo-Turkish War, was a diplomatic defeat for Russia, with all its European rivals lined up against its expansionist designs. "Against [Russia] is not only England, but all Europe," Miliutin grumbled, realizing his country had no real choice but to stand down. The tsar had a similar view: the Congress of Berlin was a "European coalition against Russia under the leadership of Prince Bismarck."[39]

As Russia's diplomatic situation in Europe darkened, the Yili question returned to the agenda. In spring 1878, Chinese general Zuo Zongtang threatened Russia with war unless it left the Yili Valley. General Zuo had raised a powerful army. By putting down Yakub Beg's armies in Kashgaria and subduing the various rebel forces along China's Central Asian borderlands, Zuo met all of Russia's initial stipulations for returning Yili to the Chinese. China's government not only had armies ready to reoccupy Yili, it had more forces in the area than did Russia.

In the time between when Russia first occupied Yili and when China was prepared to reoccupy the area, however, Russia's demands had grown. When General Zuo took the city of Urumqi in 1876, a Russian diplomat told Beijing that before handing back Yili, Russia wanted new trade concessions, too.[40] Other Russians discussed whether their country might adjust the border in their favor before returning the territory to the Chinese. Some wondered whether Russia should return Yili at all. Was this not the territory over which explorers like Przhevalsky imagined Russia could forge an empire like Cortez? Even as advocates of restraint won the internal debate over pulling back from Afghanistan, supporters of a forward policy had turned their attention to Yili instead.

The Chinese saw that Russia was wavering on its promise to leave Yili, and threatened Russia with war. "It would be very unpleasant to have a clash with them" warned Konstanin Kaufman, governor-general of Russian Turkestan. "There would be no glory, no honor . . . it would be expensive, and given the geography, it could take place in three or four places and last long, without end. . . . If we invade them, we would have to fight and annex to the empire wastelands we don't need." Far better to give the territory back to the Chinese, Kaufman reasoned, and avoid both the wrath of General Zuo and "a most unpleasant war, a thankless war, expensive, unproductive, which given the obstinacy of the Chinese it would be impossible to predict the end of."[41]

On March 1879, the tsar's top officials and generals assembled to discuss the fate of the Yili Valley. In a three-hour long meeting, they debated the costs and benefits of returning the territory. In exchange for leaving Yili, Russia decided to request trade benefits, border adjustments, and provisions to ensure the safety of the local population, fearing Chinese retribution would again cause refugee flows and cross-border instability. Negotiations with the Chinese began later that year in Livadia, the tsar's summer palace in Crimea. The Chinese envoy shocked the Russians with his "great haste" in negotiations, offering Russia nearly every concession it requested.[42]

The final draft of the treaty, signed September 15, 1879, was therefore surprisingly favorable to St. Petersburg's expansionists. Russia received a chunk of territory along the present-day China-Kazakhstan border, including a larger share of the Yili Valley and control of the strategic Muzart Pass, the gateway into Kashgaria. China let Russia open new consulates in key Chinese cities such as Urumqi, Hami, and Turpan. On top of these new privileges, Russia demanded and received concessions on unrelated issues, including access to new trade routes in central China and to the Sungari River in Manchuria— suggesting that, to many officials in St. Petersburg, Yili was seen as a beach-head for further expansion into China. Finally, Beijing agreed to pay 5 million rubles to compensate St. Petersburg for the cost of occupying Yili. The treaty talks started with a Russian agreement to withdraw from Chinese territory but ended with a series of humiliating Chinese concessions. Beijing's Central Asian territories appeared to pass even deeper under Russian influence. "When it is perceived that Russia will still hold the province [of Yili] practically under her authority," one British newspaper noted, "it is much to be doubted if either the generals in Central Asia or the Ministers in Pekin will deem that there is much cause to feel grateful to the Czar."[43]

"WE CAN FIGHT IF WE WANT TO FIGHT"

The Chinese were furious about the concessions their envoy had made to the Russians. The British feared that Russia's "withdrawal" from Yili—a withdrawal that seemed only to enshrine Russia's imperial ambitions in the region— presaged a new wave of expansion. Over the previous fifteen years, Russia's expansionists had driven forward the borders of their empire. Some in St. Petersburg claimed that Russia's motives were only defensive, but the frontiers of the Russian Empire moved forward regardless. It seemed impossible to escape the conclusion that, as Queen Victoria wrote to her prime minister, "Russia is our real enemy and rival."[44] Chinese General Zuo Zongtang agreed.

Many Russians, meanwhile, continued to celebrate their country's expansion. Following a military victory against the Turkmen in Central Asia, Fyodor Dostoyevsky, the great novelist, declared that "in Europe we were hangers-on and slaves, while in Asia we shall be the masters. In Europe we were Tatars, while in Asia we are the Europeans." "Just let people begin to understand," Dostoyevsky continued, "that our outlet is in the Asia of the future; that our riches are there; that our ocean is there."[45] Many of Russia's intellectuals continued to gulp the punch that explorers like Przhevalsky had prepared, exulting in their country's superiority and seeing further territorial expansion as the natural result.

Yet Russia's fate in "the Asia of the future" depended on its relations with the other Asian powers. It was one thing to seize lands from poorly armed Central Asians. It was quite another to risk war with a great power. War was exactly what China threatened when news of the Treaty of Livadia—by which Russia extracted humiliating concessions from China in exchange for evacuating Yili—reached Beijing. All of China was stunned. At the court in Beijing and across the country, officials mobilized against the agreement. General Zuo argued that granting Russia an extensive presence in Yili and consulates throughout Western China would enable St. Petersburg to absorb the region. "We can fight if we want to fight," Zuo urged. "What do we fear?"[46]

Other Chinese leaders agreed. Beijing asked hundreds of officials to comment on the proposed treaty, and the feedback was clear: Russia's border changes, its trade privileges, its navigation rights on the Sungari River—all were unacceptable. Russia and China had demarcated their border after a treaty in 1868, so what justification was there for changing the border again, barely a decade later? "They want to copy the clever old methods of Spain's occupation of Luzon, Portugal's occupation of [Goa], India, and Holland's destruction of Java," two Chinese officials wrote. Beijing would not put up with this. In 1860, facing Britain, France, and Russia, Beijing had no choice but to capitulate. Now, Chinese officials wrote, it was the Russians who had conflicts on all fronts, having just concluded a war with Turkey and facing the ongoing threat of conflict with Britain. "The Russians' demands are even more extravagant than in 1860, but China's situation is more stable," one Chinese official declared. Beijing renounced the Treaty of Livadia and prepared to behead the "extremely stupid and absurd" diplomat who had signed the pact.[47]

On March 1, 1880, General Zuo was ordered to march west toward the Russian border. To prove he was ready for battle, he brought his coffin with him. With China repudiating the Treaty of Livadia and mobilizing its military, newspapers in Shanghai reported that war was imminent. If so, conflict would not be isolated in Yili. In 1878 and 1879, when General Zuo's forces first threatened to invade the Yili Valley unless the Russians withdrew, Russia began preparing for a global struggle, presuming that the British would not stay neutral if China and Russia went to war.[48]

Britain bolstered China's army by letting former British officers serve in the Chinese military. Famed British general Charles Gordon, who had whipped Chinese forces into shape when they fought the Taiping rebels in 1860, returned to China in 1880, ready to prepare its troops for war with Russia. Russian reconnaissance officers, meanwhile, were sent as far afield as Melbourne and Sydney in Australia, while the tsar's agents explored whether Irish residents of San Francisco, who hated the British, could attack the Royal Navy's station in Vancouver. Perhaps San Francisco could be a supply base for the Russian Far Eastern Fleet, some Russians thought. The Russian frigate *Morge,* meanwhile, visited the harbors of Southern China, including Macao and Guangzhou, to analyze their defenses.[49]

As the war scare intensified over the course of 1880, Russia's expansionists cheered the prospect of a clash with China. Nikolai Przhevalsky had long called for Russia to seize China's western regions, and the crisis over Yili provided the perfect pretext. In October 1880, Przhevalsky dashed off a memo from Mongolia titled "On the Possible War with China." The "obstinacy" and "pride" of the Chinese, he wrote, meant that the Yili crisis could only be resolved by the "force of arms." Of course, Przhevalsky noted, the Chinese under General Zuo apparently believed it would be "easy" to defeat the Russians, but they were forgetting the "lesson" dealt them by the British and French in the Opium Wars.

Przhevalsky believed that the Chinese—and, for that matter, Russia's General Staff—vastly overestimated Zuo's forces. It may be that the "best Chinese army" is now in Western China, approaching Russia's border—but it was not a force to be feared. Chinese forces, he wrote, were incompetent. "Few of the officers themselves know how to shoot," he explained. The Chinese army was full of bribery and theft. Moreover, though China had more troops, other factors favored Russia. The Mongols might well join Russia's side in a war, Przhevalsky hoped. Shipping men and material across China to Turkestani and Mongolian battlegrounds via camel caravans would take months, though Russia's supply chains were no shorter. Przhevalsky envisioned an invasion of China on three fronts: over the Tian Shan mountains, across the Mongolian plains, and along the Ussuri River in Manchuria.[50] Ultimately, he believed, the Manchurian theater would be key, because the Chinese would likely only surrender if the Russians brought force to bear on Beijing, whether by sending an army from Manchuria or by landing troops from the sea.

Przhevalsky was not the only Russian official to urge war with China. General Mikhail Skobelev, the hero of campaigns against the Turkmen, declared that violence was the only way to win respect in Asia. "Carry out a great slaughter, render them incapable of resistance, terrify and overawe them . . . this is my method for conquering Asia."[51] Przhevalsky agreed. And anyway, Przhevalsky argued, war had become "unescapable." If Russia avoided conflict with China now via "excessive concessions," Russia's prestige and credibility would decline, encouraging war later.[52] It was better to fight today, while Russia had the advantage.

"NO STRATEGIC VALUE"

Advocates of expansion into China's western borderlands, however, were beginning to lose the argument within St. Petersburg, especially as the Russian military's general staff began considering what war would entail. These officers were far less sure that Russia had such an advantage. General Nikolai Obruchev compared Russia to a comet, with a European core and "a horrifying Asiatic tail, stretching . . . to Vladivostok," which would be almost impossible to defend. Mikhail Veniukov, a lecturer at the Russian Staff Academy, noted that China could strike Russia in Central Asia, in Mongolia, or in Manchuria, the latter of which was easy to cut off from the rest of Russia. "From here one can expect great danger," he warned. The region's only lines of communication—its great rivers—were also the country's border with China, and thus were easily cut. During the Crimean War, Veniukov noted, Russia had needed to move heavy weaponry across North Asia, along the country's "enormous frontier." Military outposts on the Pacific coast were so isolated from Russia's heartland that they lacked supplies not only of arms, but even, at times, of food.[53]

In 1880, the Russian General Staff prepared a war plan in case of conflict with China. The plan would have taken two years to execute and would have required not only occupying Russian Turkestan but also deploying a naval expedition to seize Beijing. In terms of numbers, on land or at sea, China had a clear advantage. Russia had twenty-six ships in Chinese waters by April 1880, which in addition to having to confront China's navy might also face hostility from other European powers. Yet Britain—which was supporting China—had had twenty-three ships of its own near China. On land, the correlation of forces looked scarcely more favorable. The commander of the Russia's East Siberian military district reported in 1880 that China would mobilize 10,000 troops in the region if war broke out. Yet Russia itself sent only 5,000 men to bolster its defenses in the Far East.[54]

China now appeared a more serious rival than pundits like Przhevalsky had promised. Pressured by Russia from the north and west, and by the British and French along its coast, China had begun to take seriously its security. In place of the envoy who negotiated the humiliating deal with Russia in 1879, Beijing appointed Marquis Tseng, a skilled diplomat who had served as ambassador to Britain, spoke French and English, and knew how to play the European diplomatic game.[55]

On the military front, meanwhile, Russian intelligence agents tracked vast Chinese arms purchases, including "6,000 Snider carbines, 4,000 Vittena rifles, 3,000 Peabody-Martinis, 2,000 old Remington rifles, and . . . 15,000 Mausers." Some of these weapons were "old, cheap, and in a bad state of repair." But China was on track to acquire a total 260,000 rifles by 1881, plus artillery and torpedoes, Russian analysts reported. The scale of Chinese rearmament made Russian officials nervous. Moreover, although Przhevalsky believed that Chinese soldiers were "unenduring, unenergetic, and immoral," other Russian military experts noted that China had reformed its military with the help of European instructors. War with China would cost between 30 and 300 million rubles, the General Staff reported, concluding that war would be "calamitous" and that "all possible measures" were needed to avoid it.[56]

Whatever the claims of hotheads such as Przhevalsky, Russia's leaders decided to offer China new concessions to avoid war. China's demands for treaty revisions, including that Russia surrender valuable commercial concessions, were substantial. But the cost of war far outweighed any benefits from trade. Przhevalsky had promised great gains from imperial expansion, but on inspection the opportunities were more meager than he had promised. And Russia's own war minister was grumbling that the military situation was "disappointing." The Russians agreed to renegotiate the treaty.[57] In exchange, the life of the Chinese diplomat sentenced to beheading was spared.

Russia's strategy in the new talks was simple: offer concessions on every issue. Russia's chief negotiator described his aims as first, "avoiding war"; second, getting reimbursed for the expense of occupying Yili; and third, "re-establishing, to the extent possible, proper relations with China."[58] Russia agreed to redraw the boundary of the Yili Valley in China's favor, and to give up some of the trade privileges it had won. "We're giving concessions to them on every point," War Minister Miliutin noted in his diary, but he backed the policy nonetheless, as the only way "to escape what would be a war with China." Russia's chief negotiator declared that the territory in question "has no strategic value" and that any conflict would be "ruinous" given Russia's "gigantic frontier" and the need, if war broke out, to send troops from Odessa in the Black Sea to Vladivostok on the Pacific.[59]

Russia's new foreign minister, Nikolai Giers, agreed. The negotiations were "tedious" and the whole affair "detestable," he wrote to one of his officials, because Chinese matters were ultimately unimportant compared to pressing concerns in Europe. Russia's aim, Giers declared, was to "carry on the negotiations as fast as possible" so that it could withdraw its fleet and put "the long Chinese frontier on a peaceful footing." Indeed, it was in the West, not in China, where Russia had greater interests. The expansionist party had promised that a push into Central Asia would bring Russia substantial benefits at limited cost. Yet the burden had risen, and the benefits were elusive.

It was time, therefore, to turn Russia's focus away from the region and back toward Europe instead. "All our attention should be directed toward the Turkish coasts," Giers argued, "where one can foresee serious complications." Przhevalsky was in St. Petersburg in January 1881, meeting with Miliutin and receiving a medal from the tsar. Yet his advice on China was ignored. Despite the explorer's own exuberance about empire, and his desire to emulate Livingstone or Cortez, Russia's leaders were always of two minds about the country's Central Asian adventures. Now, the consensus view in St. Petersburg was that it was time to pull back on commitments in the region, reducing resources and trimming risk. Grabbing territory was one thing. Governing it was something quite different. Doing both without getting entangled in war with one of Russia's great power rivals was even more challenging. Przhevalsky promised Russia's rulers that Central Asia was ripe for Russian expansion, but many perceived more of a quagmire or swamp.

Even Russia's military leaders eventually rethought their support for Przhevalsky's uncompromising expansionism. Though Przhevalsky loudly insisted that the armies of Russia's neighbors were paper tigers, Russian military planners disagreed. Przhevalsky urged Russia toward war with China, hoping to strip the Qing Empire of its Central Asian frontier. St. Petersburg chose instead to call a halt to the army's march, trimming its commitments in the region as quickly as it had expanded them.

The month after Przhevalsky received a medal from the tsar, Russia's government abandoned his dreams of conquest in China. In February 1881, Russia and China came to a new agreement, with Russia assenting to a new border, more favorable to China, and with St. Petersburg also surrendering some trade privileges. Beijing celebrated the success of its pressure campaign, which by threatening war had forced Russia to back down. China, declared the British ambassador in St. Petersburg, "has compelled Russia to do what she has never done before: disgorge territory that she had once absorbed."[60]

"OUR HISTORY IS PLAYED OUT IN EUROPE"

The decision to stand down from war with China and to pull out of Yili inspired a broader reassessment of Russia's stance in Asia. The expansionist party, especially in the military, remained keen for new territory, promising glory and security. But the advantages of expansion had been far lower than promised. St. Petersburg doubted the benefits of marching into new, far-flung territories on China's borderlands in Central Asia; it was plenty busy at home. In 1881, Tsar Alexander II was assassinated when a bomb exploded in his carriage. His son, Alexander III, brought new advisers to the fore, including Ignatiev, Prince Meshchersky, General Skobelev, and journalist Mikhail Katkov, who advised that Russia refocus its foreign policy on more pressing matters in Europe.

Even General Skobelev, who had led Russia's military advance into Central Asia, believed that it was time to shift Russia's focus toward Europe. Like many other of Tsar Alexander III's advisers, Skobelev was now fixated on Germany, blaming "foreigners" (Jews and ethnic Germans) within Russia for the country's internal problems. "The foreigner is everywhere. . . . We are the dupes of his policy, the victims of his intrigues, the slaves of his power," he warned. This had foreign policy ramifications: "A struggle between the

Slav and the Teuton is inevitable. It will be long, sanguinary, and terrible, but the Slav will triumph." In this context, Katkov warned, Central Asia was a distraction: "Whatever makes Russia greater [in Asia] weakens her in Europe. Russia's role as a great power is not based there but on her rule over the Western marchlands and in her position on the Black Sea. Our history is played out in Europe and not in Asia."[61]

This had always been true, though adventurers like Przhevalsky promised vast Asian benefits. There were no great riches to be won on the peaks of the Tian Shan or in the Yili Valley, nor was there great glory, either, except in the imagination of geographers and explorers. Przhevalsky himself still managed to entrance crowds with his lectures and writings on the Mongolian deserts or the routes toward Tibet. But among Russia's rulers, the cost of the Central Asian campaigns had punctured the myths that Przhevalsky had enthusiastically inflated.

When Britain threatened war with Russia over the Central Asian oasis of Pendjeh in 1885, St. Petersburg quickly backed down and signaled that it would accept the status quo. "Everyone without exception thought that the war threatening us was senseless and [would be] terrible for Russia in its results," one of the new tsar's advisers confided in his diary. The tsar himself believed that the dispute need not "necessarily lead to a war with England." Russia had far bigger concerns than Central Asian frontiers, as the tsar's confidant Meshchersky admitted, noting that reports of Britain's preparation for war extended as far as "rumors of the English occupation of the Hamilton Island in the Japanese Sea."[62] If Russia feared a war with China over Yili during the crisis of 1880–1881, it had even more reason to fear a clash with Britain several years later, given that such a conflict would stretch from Europe, through the Middle East, all the way to the Far East. Some Russian officials would carry on Przhevalsky's dream of opening trade with Tibet or of detaching Kashgaria from Qing control. But St. Petersburg had already demonstrated that these were lands it was unwilling to fight for.

"JUST BUILD TWO RAILWAYS"

In 1885, Przhevalsky completed his final journey, across the Gobi Desert to the Yangzi River and back across the Tian Shan before reentering Russian territory. Upon his return, Przhevalsky praised his team "in the name of science, which we served, and in the name of our homeland, to which we brought glory." That same year also marked a turning point for Russia's imperial ambitions along China's Central Asian borderlands. St. Petersburg would continue to spar with London over the boundary markers in the peaks of the Pamirs, but without any of the vigor of its earlier expansion.[63]

In the course of his journeys, Przhevalsky had collected 7,500 specimens of "mammals, birds, reptiles, amphibians, fish and insects," as well as 1,600 plants, 216 of which were previously uncategorized. His services to science and tsar were unquestionable. Yet soon he was dead, slain by the typhus he had caught on the slopes of the Tian Shan. Anton Chekhov praised Przhevalsky's "noble ambition," "love of work," and "fanatical belief in Christian civilization," declaring that he personified "a higher moral force." "Reading his biography," Chekhov concluded, "none will ask, 'Why?', 'What for?' . . . but everyone will say: 'He's right.'"[64]

By the end of Przhevalsky's life, however, Russia's leaders had found his advice wanting. He urged Russian armies onward. But the tsar and his ministers would not take the risk. When expansion was easy, like grabbing Chinese territory in the Yili Valley after Qing authority had collapsed, St. Petersburg was happy to oblige its commanders. By the late 1870s, however, the costs of imperial expansion had mounted, while the benefits had proven illusory. Przhevalsky promised that territorial expansion would assert Russia's status, elevate the country's prestige, and bring glory to the tsar. This made for inspiring essays and entertaining lectures, reinforced by what War Minister Miliutin described as Przhevalsky's "energetic nature." But the romance of expansion alone was not enough of a benefit when the cost was war with two great imperial powers in Asia, the Qing and the British.

Some Russians adopted Przhevalsky's haughty attitude toward the Chinese, disdaining Beijing's military power and its ability to control far-off frontiers. But China was rearming after its humiliation by Europeans in the Opium Wars, while Russia faced new challenges at home and abroad. After the assassination of Tsar Alexander II in 1881, one Qing official suggested dispatching a Chinese mission to "advise the Russians in the arts of government."[65] Coming from an empire that had just suffered decades of internal rebellion, the Qing offer was a bit rich. But it was undeniable that Russia's rivals were getting stronger.

By the 1880s, therefore, Przhevalsky's memos to officials urging further conquest were politely ignored. He was a hero to Russian imperialists, but the era of imperial expansion along China's western frontiers was being wound down. Expansionism retained some popularity in the military and among officials in frontier provinces, but they were overruled by ministers in the meeting rooms of St. Petersburg's palaces.

When Przhevalsky had advised using Yili as a springboard for an invasion of China, another officer suggested that the province be traded to the Chinese for things that Russia's empire needed more—say, the funds needed to build a railway across Siberia. Even Russia's more romantic expansionists realized that Russia needed to develop its capabilities if it was to spar with other great powers. "Just build two railways" to Asia, Dostoyevsky promised, "and you shall see the results at once."[66] This was a more sensible policy than many of Dostoyevsky's more mystical pronouncements on Asian affairs. And it was this more measured approach that won out over Przhevalsky's romanticism. For now, the tsar's advisers concluded, Russia must establish a defensible border and focus resources elsewhere. When Britain threatened war over far off Asian lands, Russia offered concessions and agreed to demarcate the border. And when General Zuo Zongtang prepared his armies to march on Russia unless the tsar withdrew from Yili, St. Petersburg decided—uniquely among its Central Asian conflicts—not only to cut a deal with Qing China, but to retreat.

4

"TIGHTENING THE BONDS BETWEEN US"

Sergei Witte and the Trans-Siberian Railway

IN 1890, the heir to the throne was preparing for a Grand Tour. Tsar Alexander III's son Nicholas, twenty-two years old, would cap off his education with a voyage. The princes and aristocrats of Europe often traveled around the continent, visiting fashionable capital cities and touring Roman ruins. But the emperor and autocrat of all the Russias envisioned something grander for his son. The heirs to European kingdoms could visit Europe's capitals, but the empire that Nicholas would soon inherit spanned two continents, stretching to the shores of the Pacific. Should not the heir to the throne acquaint himself with these lands, too?

To accompany Nicholas on his voyage as guide, the tsar selected Prince Esper Ukhtomsky, a poet, aristocrat, explorer, collector of Asian art, and self-styled orientalist. The itinerary: the lands of "the East." Nicholas set sail for the Suez Canal and soon reached the African coast, where "pillars of sand rise and twirl, flying over the neighboring Arabian desert." He traveled through Egypt—"ancient heathen temples, palaces innumerable, hieroglyphics"— passed the Red Sea port of Aden, and then arrived in Bombay, "the India we have longed for."

The East seemed ever more exotic as the journey progressed. The "ancient, moss-grown rock-temples" of Ellora; "crowds of hindoos, performing their religious ablutions" in the Ganges; "half-naked aborigines" and "death-breathing volcanoes" on the island of Java; "native music, native dances, native sports" in "Siam—a land of Eastern fable"; China, the "Celestial Empire," a "vast and impenetrable body." After months of exploration, Nicholas arrived at his final stop, Japan.

For Ukhtomsky, the trip was intended not only to educate the tsar's son about the worlds beyond the borders of his empire. Nor was it solely to promote an image of Russia as an "Eastern" power, though Ukhtomsky certainly wanted foreigners to understand Russia's special status and wanted Russians to take up what he perceived as their unique Asian role. Above all, for Ukhtomsky, the voyage was to be a mystical experience. The Orient was a land of myth and wonder—a place, he wrote, where "the deadly prose of life has not yet begun to reign—where man and nature, good and evil, asceticism and worldliness, have not yet congealed." For Ukhtomsky this was less a Grand Tour than a pilgrimage.

Nicholas, by contrast, was more taken by earthly concerns: the "dancing-girls," the Indian wrestling match, the boar hunting in Jodhpur, and the tiger chase in Gwalior. The formal program of meetings and royal audiences bored him—"palaces and generals are the same all the world over," he grumbled to a relative—but as heir to the throne he had no choice but to participate. More interesting to Nicholas was assessing the military strength of the powers present in Asia. He reported back to his father on the low quality of British naval forces in the region.[1] "I was really surprised at the kind of rubbish [the British] send to the Orient," he wrote. "One would think that here"—at the heart of the British Empire—"they would keep a squadron more worthy of their maritime greatness. . . . This makes me all the happier, dear Papa, since we must be stronger than the British in the Pacific Ocean."[2]

This was a point on which Nicholas and Ukhtomsky agreed: Russia had the right and the responsibility to rule in Asia. True, scarcely a decade had passed since Nicholas's father had pulled back from expansion in Turkestan to avoid war with Britain or China. Alexander was hailed as the "peacemaker" by his subjects, thankful for sparing them the suffering of yet another great war. But even as Russia's interest in Central Asia dissipated, writers such as Ukhtomsky began insisting that East Asia "presents remarkable possibilities for the creative energies of the Russian people." Ukhtomsky was a great admirer of Sergei Witte, who served as finance minister and prime minister

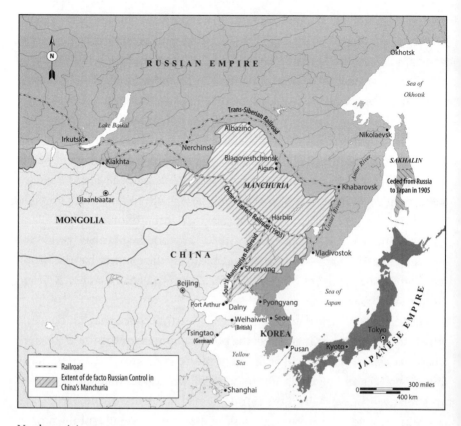

Northeast Asia, 1904–1905

for Alexander III and, later, Nicholas II.[3] Witte, however, was far less mystical than Ukhtomsky, seeing Asia in practical terms as a market for Russian goods and as a land where Russians could settle—if only Russia had a railroad to connect Russia with Asian lands and markets.[4]

RUSSIA AND THE ORIENT

"'Russia and the Orient' as a concept are one," Ukhtomsky declared, "only temporarily not existing as an entity." But the "Orient" that Ukhtomsky idolized was changing. By the time Nicholas set off on his Asian voyage in 1890, Russia was watching a new dynamic in the Far East. China was transformed in the decades after Governor-General Nikolai Muravev conquered the Amur

Valley in the late 1850s. The Opium Wars of 1839–1842 and 1856–1860 forced China's elite to admit that their country had fallen behind. A new generation of Chinese military leaders and bureaucrats took up the challenge. Li Hongzhang reorganized China's army and bureaucracy with Western technology, establishing academies for military officers, fortifying China's ports, purchasing ironclad ships, and investing in new arms factories. Li and other Chinese leaders built coal mines, telegraphs, cotton mills, railways, and steamships. They studied the West, sending students to learn from European powers, and building relationships with key European leaders.[5] China seemed, for a moment, to be gathering strength.

However, China was outpaced in modernization efforts by its smaller neighbor, Japan. After the visits of American commodore Matthew Perry and Russian admiral Evfimy Putiatin to Japan in 1854, the country had been cast into a political tumult that overturned the old order. Japan forged a new political system undergirded by a class of aristocrats committed to modernization and industrialization. Japan's Emperor Meiji declared that "knowledge shall be sought throughout the world so as to strengthen the foundation of imperial rule."

China and Japan were not the only empires recasting their governments and reforming their economies. Britain, France, Germany, and the United States were forging industrialized economies based on coal and steel. Railroads were stitching together far-flung territories. America's first transcontinental railroad was completed in 1867, connecting the Atlantic and the Pacific. Canada finished its own transcontinental railroad less than two decades later. A "Cape to Cairo" railroad across Africa became a dream for British imperialists as early as the 1870s.[6]

Russia was thinking about railroads too. The country had experienced a burst of modernization after defeat in the Crimean War in 1856. In his early years in power, Tsar Alexander II abolished serfdom and reformed the army. Yet as the tsar aged, his reformist zeal withered. His assassination in 1881 convinced his son, Alexander III, that reform presented more risk than reward. Yet even conservatives recognized that the world was shifting. Russia could, of course, refuse to use the new technologies. But then how could it keep up with rivals that were rapidly embracing them?

In Japan, Emperor Meiji stood forcefully behind his country's modernization. In Russia, like in China, the political elite was divided. China's emperors were weak and indecisive, while the bureaucracy was riven by ideological disputes and turf wars. Chinese conservatives saw similarities to Russia. "Only Russia resembles China in her supreme regard for monarchical power and in the awesome severity of her institutions," one Chinese official noted. Yet severity did not guarantee efficacy. "The government of Russia," one Russian diplomat explained, "although nominally an 'autocracy' . . . was far from being invested with the omnipotence which one associates with the idea of 'autocracy' or 'Tsarism.'" The government was in fact "a powerless federation of independent departments whose relations to each other were not always friendly, or even neutral, and sometimes partaking of the character of almost open hostility." And government had to reckon with a new force: "public opinion."[7] The country became ever more complicated to govern.

As the world's empire-building projects shifted into higher gear, Russia's leaders concluded that they had no choice but to compete. Prince Ukhtomsky insisted to anyone who would listen that Russia had a mission in the Far East. Russia would face little opposition as it pushed into Asia, he argued, because its role in Asia was natural, even inevitable. "Russia in reality conquers nothing in the East, since all the alien races . . . are related to us by blood, in tradition, in thought," Ukhtomsky insisted. "We are only tightening the bonds between us and that which in reality was always ours."[8]

Yet was Russia really an Asian country? The Russian Far East, which Muravev had conquered, remained scarcely populated. Chinese Manchuria, the territory on the south bank of the Amur River, had perhaps 6–10 million residents in the 1890s. Russia's Maritime Province, on the north bank of the Amur, had only 100,000 people. Elsewhere in Asia, Russians were a minor presence. British, French, and American traders had established trade networks across China, but there were only several hundred Russians living in China in the 1890s. And Russia's military power in the region remained weak. During Russia's forced withdrawal from Yili, one military official, lamenting his country's inability to move troops to the Far East, proposed giving Yili to China in exchange for a payment that could fund construction of a railway across Siberia. That proposal was rejected but illustrated how logistical difficulties constrained Russian power projection in Asia.[9]

Russia faced threats from European empires' expansion in China, but most Russians saw the opportunities in Asia as even more important. Chinese and Japanese markets were massive, providing a potential outlet for Russian manufacturers. As both countries built railroads, they would buy more European products. At the same time, China's weakness—and the prospect that it might be carved up by rival powers—suggested that new privileges and territory, too, might be on offer.

The mystical pronouncements of writers like Ukhtomsky gave expression to this expansionist urge. Russia was unlike the European powers, many Russians believed. The British, French, and Germans were imperialists. Russians were liberators. "Would it not be rather a crime," one Russian scholar asked, "were we to renounce the sacred duties designed to us and refuse to aid the 'oppressed'" peoples of Asia?[10] All these factors impelled Russia to take a broader role in Asia.

As Nicholas, heir to the throne, concluded his Asian tour, his last stop was Japan, the neighbor that had attracted Russian attention since the days of Dembei and Peter the Great. While Nicholas was visiting Japan's Lake Biwa, a Japanese policeman "leaped from the ranks, and, drawing his sword, dealt . . . a swinging two-handed blow" to Nicholas's head. The attacker raised his sword, preparing to strike again, but Nicholas sprang to the side. "At that same moment," Ukhtomsky recounted, "Prince George jumped . . . and struck the man from behind with a bamboo cane." One of Nicholas's servants "threw himself at the feet of the policeman, and, grasping them with his hands, brought him to the ground." A second servant picked up the assassin's sword and "with two blows, one on his neck and the other on his back, reduced him [the assassin] to a state of almost complete insensibility, and made it impossible for him to rise."

Why would a Japanese policeman try to murder Nicholas? His motives remain unclear. "Hatred of the Russians . . . is unknown in Japan," Ukhtomsky reported. The Japanese government was horrified, fearing that Russia might declare war to avenge the attack. Japan's emperor raced to the crime scene to show respect for Nicholas. Ukhtomsky insisted that Nicholas bore no grudge against the Japanese. The prince reported that "the first words spoken by His Highness" after the attack were "It is nothing, if only the Japanese will not think that this incident can in any way change my feelings toward them and my thankfulness to them for their cordiality." Other Russians suspected that Nicholas drew different conclusions. Sergei Witte, who would serve for over a decade as one of Nicholas's ministers, thought that the Asian voyage and assassination attempt "put its stamp on Nicholas II's reign." Russia would play a major role in Asia, as Ukhtomsky had envisioned, and as Nicholas's Grand Tour sought to prove. Whether that role would be peaceful, though, remained an open question.[11]

"COME HERE TO DIE"

Nicholas returned to Russia in May 1891, reaching Vladivostok, Russia's closest port to Japan. Upon arrival he unveiled a monument to Gennady Nevelskoy, the "bold and patriotic seaman to whom Russia owes possession of this land," for charting the Amur River and seizing the coastline for Russia. Nicholas was the first high-ranking royal to visit Russia's Far East. To mark the occasion, Tsar Alexander pardoned dozens of criminals living in Siberian exile. Nicholas spent his time in the Far Eastern outpost presiding over ceremonies such as laying the foundation of a dry dock in the city's harbor.[12] After a week in the Far East, only one task remained before Nicholas began his homeward journey up the Amur Valley, over the mountains, past Lake Baikal, through Siberia, back to St. Petersburg.

A year before Nicholas prepared to set off from Vladivostok to St. Petersburg, writer Anton Chekhov had traveled the same route in the opposite direction. It was not a voyage to look forward to. Except for several portions by river ferry, transport was by horse-drawn carriage, over bumpy tracks, with few comforts along the way. "Every joint and tendon in my body ached," Chekhov had complained, bemoaning "the lack of sleep, the constant fussing with the baggage, the bouncing up and down and the hunger. . . . The first few days were bearable, but then a cold wind started to blow, the heavens opened and the rivers overflowed." Chekhov reported "battles with the floods," "having to plough through mud and water in felt boots," his face "covered in fish scales because of all the wind and rain." And stopping along the way brought little relaxation because the typical Siberian town was "a dull and rather drunken sort of place; no beautiful women at all, and Asiatic lawlessness." Russians in Siberia, Chekhov concluded, "come here to die."[13]

Because transport across Siberia was little improved since the days of Aleksandr Baranov's Alaskan adventure, Vladivostok remained a backwater.

The city's name means "Lord of the East," but it was a settlement of "log huts and houses, some few with stone foundations . . . very rude in their construction . . . of an extremely temporary character. The roads leading in from one end to the other . . . are mere cart tracks, utterly neglected, and in wet weather deep in mud," one visitor wrote. "The general character of the place betokens indecision, mismanagement, and waste."[14]

The city's strategic potential was ignored, while its economic relevance was unconvincing. In the 1880s, one visitor reported, "Everywhere there are shortages and difficulties. The expenses are incredible. The reigning spirit of hard labor and exile crowns the oppression." With a population in 1875 of only 5,000, a number that included 350 convicts exiled there, Vladivostok remained a tiny Russian outpost on the Pacific Coast. And it was only tenuously Russian. Such commerce as existed was largely in the hands of non-Russians, with Chinese traders dominating trade in Vladivostok's main export, seaweed. Writers like Ukhtomsky could proclaim that Russia's Far East was "the key to the heart of Asia, the vanguard of Russian civilization." On the ground, things looked rather different.[15]

In the 1860s and 1870s, therefore, Russian leaders were primarily interested in limiting the Far East's burden on the rest of Russia. The territories across the border—Chinese Manchuria and Korea, the latter nominally independent though under the Qing Empire's tutelage—seemed even less interesting. Russia had hardly any trade with Korea until the mid-1880s. When Britain began encroaching on Korea in the 1880s, Russian officials generally urged a "hands-off policy." Russia's admirals, meanwhile, decided at the time that the country did not need a port on Korea's coast even if one became available.[16]

Chinese Manchuria during the 1870s seemed scarcely more appealing. In 1878, Russian general Alexei Kuropatkin wrote that seizing Manchurian territory would be "very unprofitable," and would destroy "the ancient peaceful relationship between China and ourselves." Worse, annexation "would result in many Manchurians settling in our territory," Kuropatkin continued, which would upset the already tenuous ethnic balance in the Russian Far East. "Our weak colonies would be swamped by the flowing tide of yellow . . . [and] Eastern Siberia would become quite un-Russian," Kuropatkin warned. "It must be remembered that it is the Russians alone who form, and will form in the future, the reliable element of the population."[17]

"LET A RAILROAD BE BUILT"

Russia's weak position in its own Far Eastern territories provided a mediocre springboard for empire. The country's leaders continued to worry about the "Yellow Peril," a fear that only grew over the course of the 1870s and 1880s. At first, this perceived risk was cited as a justification for ignoring Asia and for keeping a buffer zone between densely populated Asia and sparsely populated Siberia. Since Russia's conquest of the Amur and Ussuri Valleys, officials had warned that immigration of "too many Koreans could put us in a difficult position." In 1881, the government implemented a new program to support Russian settlers in the region, with the aim of boosting the "reliable" portion of the population. Even still, by the late 1880s, a fifth of the population of the region's largest towns were Chinese. In Khabarovsk, for example, one survey found 16,550 Russians, 4,555 Chinese, and 666 Koreans. Some native peoples such as the Chukchi spoke English, warned a senior adviser to the tsar in 1879, because they traded with British and American whalers. Official surveys found that native groups who lived near the border with China "considered themselves subjects of the Chinese emperor rather than the tsar." St. Petersburg responded by offering Russians additional incentives to settle in the region, as well as by restricting foreign investment.[18] But the more that foreigners were constrained, the less hope the territory had of prospering. And if Russia's Far East remained economically backward, why would Russians want to settle there?

Considering the logistical difficulties of supplying the Russian Far East, its economic backwardness was understandable. Yet the Far East was changing rapidly. Japan was modernizing and industrializing, catapulting itself into the first rank of world powers. China was riven by domestic political division and challenged by European imperialists, but it too was being transformed. Foreign trade attracted thousands of Chinese to metropolises such as Shanghai and Guangzhou (Canton), which ballooned in size. Foreign investment brought technologies such as the telegraph and the railroad to China in the 1870s.

As Asia modernized, the view that the "Yellow Peril" could be best managed by keeping a sparsely populated buffer zone between Russia and Asia became less credible. St. Petersburg could prohibit migration, but Russians knew that railroads would soon arrive in Chinese Manchuria, and that even more Chinese would be flowing northward. Could Russia maintain its hold on the Amur Valley? Russia needed a coherent policy toward China. "Instead of colonies, which all other powers search for at the antipodes, we have one alongside us and do not know how to make use of it," diplomat Vladimir Lamzdorf grumbled. There was opportunity to be had in Russia's Asian territories, many Russian leaders believed, if only the empire could figure out how to make use of them. There was only one solution, the tsar decided, decreeing in 1891: "Let a railroad be built."[19]

"THE ONE STATESMAN . . . SINCE THE DAYS OF PETER"

Tsar Alexander III had expressed interest in a Trans-Siberian railway in as early as 1886, though the Council of Ministers only allocated funds in 1891—the year that Nicholas, heir to the throne, arrived in Vladivostok after his Asian tour. By then, Russians had been discussing a Siberian railroad for decades. In 1857, Nikolai Muravev-Amursky, conqueror of the Amur Valley, had ordered a study of railroad routes from the Amur River to the Pacific. The Russian government received a series of fantastic proposals for railroads stretching from Europe to Asia, but the cost was enormous. It was not until the 1880s, after several railways had been built across the North American continent, that a Trans-Siberian route began to seem more realistic.[20]

Though the Finance Ministry worried about the cost, Sergei Witte urged his colleagues to focus instead on the vast opportunities a railroad would create. "All the data of the Ministry of Finance suggests that the Trans-Siberian Railway will not soon become a profitable enterprise, and building it will require enormous expenditure, placing a serious burden on the State treasury for a prolonged period," Witte wrote to Tsar Alexander. "But to assess the significance of the Trans-Siberian Railway from a narrowly financial perspective would be completely wrong."[21] Railroads were the dominant technology of the era, Witte believed. They were transforming the world, building empires, reshaping trade flows, driving industrialization. If Russia didn't build them, it would fall hopelessly behind. The view that Russia couldn't afford railroads missed the point. Railroads were the technology needed to propel Russia's economy forward, Witte insisted. Russia couldn't afford *not* to build them.

Witte's ascent to the highest levels of Russian politics had been made possible by railroads. He was born in Tbilisi, in Russia's Caucasus region, in 1849. His mother was descended from an elite family, but his father's predecessors were German speakers from the Baltic region who served the tsar as bureaucrats. Witte's family was plunged into relative poverty, at least compared to other aristocrats, after his father died unexpectedly, and Witte remained sensitive about status for the remainder of his life. Yet notwithstanding his elite lineage, Witte was by personality and career experience more a self-made man. He began clawing his way up not in a government ministry or the army—careers fit for a man of aristocratic birth—but in the railroad industry. After studying physics at university, he began work as an administrator for the Odessa Railroad, rising quickly through the organization. He moved to St. Petersburg several years later, and subsequently he was given a position in Kiev.[22]

Witte's personality and worldview were shaped by the railroad business. No other industry offered such opportunity for rapid advancement. Construction required specialized engineering knowledge, while optimizing rail transport used quantitative and managerial skills in which Witte excelled. His success in managing the country's railways left him contemptuous of Russia's other social classes. Only managers like him, capable of applying scientific methods to modern machines, could understand new technologies and harness them for the good of the empire. The masses were "herds of intelligent beasts" needing guidance from managers like him. Deciding, at one point in his career, to treat "everybody, of whatever social position as an equal," and deigning even to shake hands with lowly laborers, Witte found the behavior of feigned equality "a heavy strain on me, as all acting is to the unaccustomed."[23]

Yet however much he condescended to the Russian masses, Witte detested Russia's aristocracy even more. "The nobility," he wrote in his memoirs, "looks at the Russian Empire as a cow to be milked." The nobles are "politically a mass of degenerate humanity, which recognizes nothing but the gratification of its selfish interest and lusts, and which seeks to obtain all manner of privileges and gratuities at the expense of the taxpayers generally, that is, chiefly the peasantry."[24] Russia's noble class reciprocated Witte's enmity, and they opposed his policies, many of which required them to pay higher taxes.

Worse than his policies, many nobles believed, was Witte's personality. They saw him as coarse and uncultured, an arriviste who acquired influence not via a respectable profession but in the greasy railroad business. One Russian diplomat recounted that Witte "produced, on the whole, a great impression of force and originality," but added that "one thing which always affected me disagreeably in Count Witte was his voice, the notes of which sounded out of tune." Witte spoke not in the refined Russian language of the court in St. Petersburg, but with an accent from the Black Sea coast, where he had grown up. His decision to marry a Jewish divorcee did not help his social standing. His wife was not accepted into to St. Petersburg's high society even when he was serving in the highest positions under the tsar.[25]

Those willing to look past his manners and his marriage were struck by Witte's ability to crush anyone who stood in his way. "Witte's attitude toward people was based on deeply rooted contempt for all humanity," one rival remembered, criticizing his alleged use of bribery and financial incentives to achieve his goals. Another diplomat recounted that Witte managed to create a "state within a state," marshaling "an innumerable crowd of functionaries of all denominations and all ranks, a network of schools of lower and even higher grades, a vast territory—a veritable kingdom, in fact."[26]

Witte used this power over Russia's bureaucracy to transform the country. After leaving the railway industry he served as railway director in the Finance Ministry before being named transport minister and, shortly thereafter, finance minister. He was finance minister for eleven years, during which time Russia formalized an alliance with France, built a railroad across Siberia, invaded China, established a colonial empire in the Far East, and set itself on a path toward war with Japan. "Witte," one observer declared "was the one statesman who had arisen in Russia since the days of Peter."[27]

"EXTENDING TRADE TO ALL PARTS OF THE WORLD"

Witte believed that as the world industrialized, Russia had to change. The old way of doing business—in which aristocrats managed vast estates, exported grain, and used the proceeds to buy luxuries and fund vacations on the Mediterranean coast—was no longer viable. By the 1880s, it was not only

Britain and France that were building industries. Germany, the United States, and even Japan were investing in railroads and steel. Russia had fallen far behind. Germany, Witte believed, showed how Russia might catch up. He idolized the German economist Friedrich List, who in a famous pamphlet titled *The National System of Political Economy* attacked Adam Smith's policy of laissez-faire. Germany could only industrialize, List argued, by investing in infrastructure that knit the country together and by supporting industry with protected markets.

Witte sought to implement List's ideas in Russia. In 1889, he published a pamphlet titled "On Nationalism: National Economy and Friedrich List," that celebrated the idea of state support for industry. What Russian industry needed, Witte believed, was new markets. He sought to forge a unified national economy based on a single customs and tariff system, new infrastructure, and support for industry. This, Witte insisted, was the path to "economic power." Any country that implemented such a program would succeed in "extending its trade to all parts of the world" and even "establishing colonies." Did not Russia's "proximity to Asia," Witte asked, provide an advantage in commercial competition with England and other powers?[28]

To expand trade with Asia, however, Russia needed a railroad across Siberia. Only then, Witte argued in a memo to the tsar, could Russian products reach the 460 million people living in China, Japan, and Korea. Trade with the region already amounted to "no less than 500 million gold rubles," a sum that was likely to grow. By reducing transport times, a Trans-Siberian Railway would expand Russia's role in the tea and silk trade, improving its balance of payments. An Asian railway was the only way Russia could expand commercial interests in the region, Witte argued, accessing the new markets that were crucial to Russia's industrialization.[29]

In 1891, Tsar Alexander placed supervision of this new railroad under his heir apparent, Nicholas, who was just then arriving in Vladivostok after his Asian journey. On the morning of May 31, 1891, about two and a half kilometers outside of Vladivostok, a prayer was said. In the name of "the Father, the Son, and the Holy Spirit" as well as "His Imperial Majesty, the Sovereign Emperor, Autocrat of all the Russias, Alexander III," Nicholas used silver tools to lay the first stone and, "turning the first turf on the Great Siberian Railway," began construction on the project that would connect "the Far East by an uninterrupted line of rail with the heart of Russia."[30]

To make the railroad a reality, the tsar named Witte minister of transport before quickly promoting him to finance minister in summer 1892, giving Witte control not only the country's railway building, but also its tax system, its tariffs, and its government spending. Soon, he waded into foreign affairs, too, on the grounds that financial matters required interaction with other countries. Witte's core belief was that national power stemmed from commercial and industrial expansion, so he focused Russia's foreign policy on economic goals. In Asia, his aim was "peaceful penetration" rather than territorial aggrandizement or military expansion.[31] The Trans-Siberian Railway would enhance Russia's influence by expanding the economy and supporting trade.

Even when Witte argued that the railroad would bolster Russia's military preparedness, as he did in a memo to the tsar in 1892, he suggested that the navy's primary purpose in the Pacific was to protect commerce—an economic goal, not a geopolitical one. The Trans-Siberian Railway, he promised Alexander, would let Russia maintain a Far Eastern fleet "which in case of political complications in Europe or in the Asiatic East would acquire an especially important significance in dominating all commercial movements in the waters of the Pacific." Around the same time, one influential American senator justified his country's imperial expansion by arguing that "commerce follows the flag"—in other words, that building an empire would help American businesses. For Witte, the logic was the opposite: the flag, and the fleet, would follow and serve the interests of Russian commerce.[32] Trade with Asia, meanwhile, would support the industrialization of Russia.

THE PARTITION OF CHINA?

The Trans-Siberian Railway route from Moscow, across Siberia, to the shores of Lake Baikal, was relatively straightforward. The portion from Baikal to the Pacific was not. The greatest dilemma was how to reach Vladivostok, the railroad's terminus on the Pacific Coast. One option was to build the railroad along the Amur River, heading eastward from Baikal to Khabarovsk, then turning sharply to the right, tracing the Ussuri River southward toward Vladivostok. This route had the benefit of traversing only Russian territory. But it was far longer than the alternative: a straight line from the city of Blagoveshchensk to Vladivostok, cutting directly through Chinese Manchuria. With experts projecting that the railroad would take twelve years to build, the desire to shorten the route was strong.

As the tsar's advisers debated where to build the railroad in 1894, an uprising broke out in Korea, a territory that was officially a Chinese protectorate but which was a target of Japanese expansion. Korean rebels cried, "Down with the Japanese!," and soon China and Japan were at war, fighting for supremacy in Northeast Asia. One British official reported that "999 out of every 1000 Chinese are sure big China can thrash little Japan." Russians, like most Europeans, agreed, thinking that the war was "a foolhardy enterprise on the part of the Japanese military." Yet the Japanese sank China's fleet, landed troops in Korea and Manchuria, and seized the fortified Chinese harbors of Port Arthur and Weihaiwei, which defended the approach by sea to Beijing. The Qing Empire quickly sued for peace. Japan demanded tough terms: China was to hand over Taiwan, pay a large indemnity, surrender parts of the Liaodong Peninsula, and recognize Korea's independence, opening the door to greater Japanese influence there.[33]

Japan's easy defeat of China, however, again raised the question of whether the Qing Empire would be carved up—and if so, what Russia should do about it. Since Governor-General Muravev's conquest of the Amur Valley, St. Petersburg had mostly ignored the Far East, treating it as a geopolitical backwater. Now, however, the map of Asia was being redrawn, and Russia—led by Witte—saw opportunities. The Sino-Japanese War was not only a contest between two Asian powers, nor simply a new opening for British or French imperialism. It was "the consequence of the construction of the Siberian Railway," Witte believed. A partition of China was coming, and all the great powers "see in the Siberian railway a significant improvement of our chances in the event of such a partition." The commander of Japanese forces agreed, declaring, "The day the Trans-Siberian Railroad is completed will be the day that crisis comes to Korea, and when crisis comes to Korea, all the Orient will face upheaval."[34]

Japan's rising power now looked likely to threaten Russia's aims in the region. Japanese forces in Korea were not far from Vladivostok, terminus of the not-yet-complete Trans-Siberian Railway. Might Russia solidify its position by occupying "part of Manchuria," the navy minister wondered in January 1895? Perhaps it was better to take an island off Korea's coast, the Foreign Ministry proposed. Witte, however, focused on "gaining the time necessary for the completion of the Siberian railway, when we shall be in a position to step forward in the full panoply of our material means and take our proper place in Pacific affairs." Taking additional territory now, at a time when Russia was unable to defend it, made little sense. Instead, Witte worked with Germany and France to demand that Japan give up some of the Chinese territories it planned to occupy. Tokyo, facing a united front of European powers, relented. Witte declined to seize the Chinese lands that Japan relinquished, however, sticking with his strategy of economic advancement, helping Beijing pay its indemnity to Japan, and opening talks with China about building a railroad through Manchuria. Witte's goal, he explained to the tsar in summer 1895, remained the "strengthening of Russian economic influence in China"—not taking additional territory.[35]

"A NEW WORLD POWER THIRTY HOURS BY SEA FROM VLADIVOSTOK"

The new tsar, however, had different ideas. Alexander III had died in autumn 1894, during the Sino-Japanese War, bringing to power his son, Nicholas II. No Russian leader then or since has had such an extensive education in Asian affairs. Only three years had passed since Nicholas's Asian tour, and the images of his voyage were fresh: the Indian temples, the volcanoes of Java, the music, dancing, and sports. Yet what seemed to have stuck most in Nicholas's mind was a sense of superiority. Nicholas was confident, as were so many Europeans of his era, in the supremacy of the "white race" over the "yellow," and believed he had an obligation to rule over Asia.[36]

Witte would later argue that Nicholas's need for supremacy over Asia was driven by the attempted assassination by the Japanese policeman. Yet Nicholas feared many things, not only rising Asia. He had a nervous personality, worrying after his father's death whether he was capable of ruling Russia. "I am not fit to be a Czar," he whined to a relative. "I know nothing of the business of ruling. I have no idea of even how to talk to the ministers." Yet rule he must, despite complaining to his mother of having regular "fits of nerves" during which he "felt green and trembled all over." Throughout his reign, Nicholas lacked confidence when interacting with his most powerful ministers, Witte chief among them. Witte's enemies took advantage of the tsar's insecurities, whispering to Nicholas that "Witte is a revolutionary under the skin." Nicholas's insecurity mixed with racism to produce a toxic brew. True, his racism was not confined to Asia. His antisemitism was if anything even more virulent, and his correspondence was littered with anti-Jewish slurs. "An Englishman," Nicholas often declared, "is a yid." Yet it was in the Far East that racial thinking plus insecurity combined to inspire a foreign policy of aggressive imperialism.[37]

Whatever the drivers of Nicholas's attitude toward Asia, one thing is clear: where Witte wanted to expand Russia's trade and open new markets, Nicholas wanted territory. The tsar was not unique in this belief that territory in Asia would bolster Russia's geopolitical position. What other way, asked *Novoe Vremya,* an influential newspaper, could Russia respond to the "alarm at the emergence of a new world power thirty hours by sea from Vladivostok"? Japan's rise "scares us," the paper argued, because Japan might lose its "prudence" and become overly assertive, risking war with Russia. "The yellows are fighting; the whites must keep a sharp look out," it warned.[38]

In the past, the "Yellow Peril" had convinced Russians to stay out of Asia. Now it was reinterpreted as a justification for expansion and coupled with promises that an Asian empire would reestablish Russian greatness. Russia needed an ice-free port in which the navy could operate year-round, many concluded. "It is not necessary even to mention the necessity of such a port," one Russian writer exclaimed, "it is obvious." Nicholas was personally interested in the issue. In spring 1895, he received a report from Foreign Minister Lobanov arguing that Russia needed "an ice-free port on the Pacific Ocean." "Exactly," the tsar scribbled in the margin. "Our main and most dangerous rival in Asia is undoubtedly England," Lobanov's report continued. "Of course," wrote the tsar.[39]

Yet where Nicholas pushed for ports and territory, Witte, backed by the tsar's military officials, urged caution and a focus on trade instead. Any war sparked by Russian expansion would unite Britain and Japan against St. Petersburg, War Minister Pyotr Vannovsky warned. Yet Russia could mobilize at most only 15,000 troops in the Far East, hardly enough to defeat Japan and Britain combined. Nor was Russia's fleet prepared. The head of the General Staff, General Nikolai Obruchev, agreed, warning that "it is highly important not in any way to get involved in a war that would mean fighting over 10,000 kilometers" away, in which "we would have to send from afar every firearm, every bullet." It would take five months to move forces from Irkutsk to the Far East, while Japan's forces are already in position, the general pointed out. Conflict with Japan had the making of a "great disaster, and what's more, we wouldn't be protected in the West or in the Caucasus." Witte agreed, saying that rather than war, Russia should let Japan take Formosa, the Pescadores Islands, the fortified Chinese harbor of Port Arthur, "even the southern part of Korea—just not Manchuria."[40]

"PEACEFUL RELATIONS . . . WITH THE CHINESE COLOSSUS"

Witte hoped to settle the Far Eastern question at Nicholas's coronation ceremony, held in 1896, the second year of his reign. It was a grand event: the "exceptional solemnity," "magnificent vestiments," and "lovely music" were all "deeply mystical," witnesses reported—as majestic as "Versailles relived." The ceremony was more magnificent than the coronation of Nicholas's father Alexander had been, with "more spectators, more foreign guests, and more extensive newspaper coverage." It felt like "a play at the royal boxes of Europe and the grandstands of the world," one American journalist reported, feeling out of place at an event involving 412 royals from nearly every European royal house. Nicholas rode into the ceremony on a white horse, the *New York Times* reported. "He sat erect and looked every inch the Caesar he is."[41]

Caesar he may have been, but while Nicholas played the role of tsar, demonstrating his dominion over Asian peoples that Russia had already subjugated, his most powerful minister, Witte, negotiated with the real Asian envoys. Chinese, Japanese, and Korean officials were all invited to Russia in 1896, and Witte used the occasion to reassert his influence over Russian foreign policy, again seeking a strategy in Asia focused on economic influence rather than territorial expansion.

Chinese official Li Hongzhang was the guest of honor at the coronation, a sign of how highly Witte valued relations with China. On Li's trip to Russia, after transiting the Suez Canal, he was met by an honor guard led by Prince Ukhtomsky, who escorted Li to St. Petersburg, reaching the capital on April 30, 1896. Upon arrival, negotiations between Li and Witte began. "Tea was served with great and elaborate pomp," Witte recalled. "Then began the ceremony of smoking," with two servants managing Li's pipe and tobacco. "It was apparent," Witte believed, that Li "wanted to impress me with all these solemn ceremonies. On my part, I made believe that I did not pay the slightest attention."[42]

Smoking and drinking complete, the two got down to business. Beijing faced an enduring threat from Japan, plus the risk that European powers would again try to carve up Chinese territory. Witte proposed that Russia complete the Trans-Siberian Railway via the shortest possible route, from Lake Baikal, directly through Chinese Manchuria to Russian Vladivostok. The benefit to Russia was obvious. Such a route "would considerably shorten the line," avoid "great difficulties" in construction in the Amur Valley, and pass through a region with "more productive soil and more favourable climate." "The problem," Witte believed, "was how to get China's permission for this plan."[43]

China's weakness made this easier. A railway through China, Witte told Li, would help in case of war. Witte proposed that in exchange for the right to build a railway through China, Russia would agree to a defensive alliance against Japan. Once completed, the Trans-Siberian Railway would help China in case of war, Witte argued, letting Beijing access supplies from Europe even in case of a naval blockade. The railroad track would be the wide gauge used in Russia, rather than the slightly narrower track more common in Europe, making the railway interoperable with Russian trains but inaccessible by any lines that Europeans built elsewhere in China. And Russia would be given an array of tariff concessions "to improve the competitiveness of our goods compared to foreign goods."[44]

Li agreed to the treaty, with two amendments. First, the China Eastern Railway, as it would be called, would be built not by the Russian government but an ostensibly private company, to maintain the image of Chinese sovereignty. Second, Li was to receive several million rubles in side payments from Russia, in appreciation of his efforts in negotiating the treaty. The agreement was signed in Moscow in spring 1896, immediately after the coronation of Nicholas II. The tsar sent gifts to the Chinese emperor, including forty-eight crates of "lapis lazuli vases, golden cloisonné goblets, a diamond diadem, a silver dressing table and one large diamond to adorn the hats" of each of the emperor's advisers on foreign affairs. Yet Nicholas was involved only in the pomp and circumstance. The strategic logic behind the treaty was Witte's, who without expanding Russia's territory achieved his two main goals: "first, a great railroad extending as far as Vladivostok on a straight line . . . and, second, firmly established peaceful relations with our neighbor, the Chinese Colossus."[45]

"VAST, NEIGHBORING EMPIRES"

Peaceful relations with China, however, were no guarantee of friendly ties with Japan, Asia's rising military power. Though Witte saw his strategy of economic penetration in China as peaceful, the Japanese were not so sure. Nor were the Japanese sure that Witte would continue to manage Russian policy in Asia, given the tsar's preference for a more aggressive posture. By demonstrating Chinese weakness, the Sino-Japanese War forced all the great powers to reconsider their strategies in the Far East. Japan began to see Russia as its main rival in North Asia. Germany, meanwhile, perceived China's humiliation as an opportunity to assert itself in Asia. Witte, therefore, not only had to reckon with China, but with the great powers circling the ailing Qing Empire like vultures.

At Nicholas's coronation ceremony, therefore, Witte also sought to defuse tensions with Japan. Tokyo's envoy, military commander Yamagata Aritomo, wanted a deal over Korea, the territory that Japan had just wrested from Chinese control. In theory, Korea was independent, but after Japan ejected China from the peninsula, Tokyo and St. Petersburg were the two main external players. Inside Korea, different factions jockeyed for control of the Korean monarchy. In 1888, the Japanese allegedly tried and failed to kill the Korean queen with a poisoned birthday cake. She survived seven more years before Japanese agents hacked her to death in 1895. Korea's king, meanwhile, had taken refuge in the Russian legation, fearing for his safety.[46] With each great power backing a different faction, Russia and Japan appeared on the brink of a proxy war.

Arriving in St. Petersburg for the coronation, Yamagata proposed delineating spheres of influence in Korea, a de facto partition. The two sides agreed to reform the government and build telegraph lines. Yet on the crucial question of spheres of influence, the two countries, "desirous of preventing any collision between their armed forces," agreed only to "determine the sphere of action reserved for each" at some point in the future. The Russo-Japanese agreement provided Korea's king the assurances needed to leave the Russian legation and move back to his palace, confident he would not be dismembered like the old queen. Yet Russia and Japan left open a complicated question: Where was the boundary between their empires? Both countries interpreted the deal as allowing them to expand relations with Korea. Russia's envoy set off for Seoul in 1897 with instructions to establish a Russo-Korean bank, build a Russian telegraph, and "aim to have the customs administration transferred . . . completely into Russian hands."[47]

Japan was not the only country shifting the balance of power in Asia. The German Kaiser dreamed of empire, insisting that he deserved a Chinese port like Britain's Hong Kong. Beijing's weakness provided an opening. Berlin identified such a harbor in Qingdao, on the southern coast of the Shangdong Peninsula, just across the Yellow Sea from Korea. Upon the murder of several Christian missionaries in the area, Germany announced it was occupying the port and surrounding territory. St. Petersburg scrambled to respond, threatening Germany that unless it abandoned Qingdao, Russian forces would occupy a port of their own in China. Yet with imperial ambitions at stake, Germany would not budge.[48]

In fall 1897, Nicholas assembled his advisers to discuss. Must the tsar now follow through on his threat to reciprocate by seizing a Chinese port for Russia? Port Arthur, on the southern coast of Manchuria, would provide an excellent, ice-free harbor with easy access to Beijing and Korea, some advisers suggested. Witte, seeing that the "peaceful relations" he had so carefully constructed with the Chinese were at risk, urged patience. Only a year earlier, Witte reminded the tsar, Russia had signed an agreement with China "to preserve the Asian continent from a new foreign invasion." China was letting Russia build the Trans-Siberian Railway across its territory. If St. Petersburg seized a Chinese port it would imperil this arrangement. Indeed, "if Japan were to follow," taking a Chinese port of its own, "we would have to defend China, per our agreement" signed the previous year.[49] Japan might also be emboldened in Korea—another area where Russia had interests.

Anyway, Witte argued, Russia would be worse off with Port Arthur. It would be difficult to defend, especially before there was a railway connecting it with the Trans-Siberian line. Building such a railroad would require "several years" and "enormous expenditure." The navy minister agreed, arguing that the Korean coast offered better harbors than Port Arthur. Rather than seizing territory, Witte continued, St. Petersburg should seek new outlets on the Pacific via peaceful means, "on the basis of economic interests." Russia only needs "time" and "friendly agreements" with neighbors. By contrast, seizing Port Arthur would be a "great risk."[50] Rather than following the German example, Witte proposed sending a naval squadron to Tsingtao, pressuring the Germans to withdraw and preventing a new round of imperial powers demanding territorial division of the country.

The tsar, however, was unconvinced. If his cousin the Kaiser was acquiring new territories in Asia, should not Russia do so, too? The Far East, in fact, was one of the most common conversation topics of the two monarchs. "Willy," as the Kaiser referred to himself in their correspondence, regularly wrote cousin "Nicky" about the importance of Russia's role in Asia. This was a convenient stance for a German ruler to take, of course, because the more resources Russia devoted to the Far East, the fewer it would deploy in Europe, where Russia's military alliance with France threatened Germany's growing power. Yet Nicholas, insecure in his role as Russia's ruler, was easily bullied. "I shall certainly do all in my power to keep Europe quiet and also guard the rear of Russia so that nobody shall hamper your action towards the Far East!" the Kaiser promised. "For that is clearly the great task of the future for Russia . . . to defend Europe from the inroads of the Great Yellow race."[51]

The Kaiser's badgering was far from the only reason Tsar Nicholas decided to seize Port Arthur, against Witte's wishes. Nicholas had a long-standing conviction that Russia should dominate Asia, dating at least to his tour of "the East" before ascending to the throne. When, on Nicholas's orders, a Russian squadron sailed into Port Arthur in spring 1898, seizing its fortifications, many Russians saw this as recognition of their country's status as a great power. The Kaiser dashed off a memo to Nicholas declaring that "Your diplomacy has just scored another great success in China." It looked that way to Nicholas, too. Russia pressured China into signing a deal "by mutual agreement" to lease the harbor and surrounding lands to Russia for twenty-five years, during which Russia would build a railway connecting the port to the Trans-Siberian Railway. One Russian leader told a colleague he considered the twenty-five-year time limit simply a matter of "formality," doubting that it would be legally binding. The agreement was, Russia's government newspaper declared, the "natural result of the friendship between the vast, neighboring empires."[52]

Other countries were less impressed by this sign of Russian "friendship." Russia's ambassador in London reported that the British were preparing for war in case Russia's move caused a broader partition of the Qing Empire. In Tokyo, meanwhile, Russia's occupation of Port Arthur reaffirmed Japan's fear about Russia's ultimate aims. Witte might talk about trade and commerce, but Russia was expanding its territorial empire.[53]

Perhaps, some Japanese hoped, Russia might be willing to relinquish its role in Korea now that it had secured an ice-free harbor at Port Arthur. In early 1898, Tokyo stated "its willingness to consider Manchuria . . . as being entirely outside the sphere of Japanese interests, provided the Russian government was prepared to make the same declaration in regard to Korea." Russia's envoy in Tokyo urged his government to accept the Japanese proposal, which was "the best means of safeguarding our interests in the Far East." If Russia did not give Japan a greater "share of influence" in Asia, he warned, "the Japanese government will . . . resort to force." St. Petersburg, however, did not take seriously talk that Japan would go to war over the issue. Russia cabled Tokyo that it "took note with great satisfaction" Japan's declaration recognizing Manchuria as part of Russia's sphere of interests, but "could not make a similar declaration in regard to Korea." This was "rather lame and pointless," the Russian envoy in Tokyo grumbled, because it resolved none of the key disputes between Russia and Japan.[54] The Japanese agreed.

"DEFINITIVE COLONIZATION"

Russia was less inclined to compromise with Japan, however, because progress on the Trans-Siberian Railway was bolstering its imperial ambitions. In 1897, Russia celebrated the launching of a new railroad spur, connecting the Trans-Siberian with a new railroad that went southward through Manchuria to Port Arthur. The Russian government spent 45,000 rubles on "elaborate pavilions, with rich draperies and a fountain" for a festival in the Far East marking the occasion. Yet of the 200 of esteemed guests who were invited, only eighty attended, including a smattering of Chinese officials and a French admiral who happened to be visiting.[55] It was not the most auspicious beginning for the railroad that was envisioned to be the backbone of Russia's Manchurian expansion.

In other ways, though, Russia's presence in Manchuria and Port Arthur was beginning to look like a proper colony. Witte's critics would later say that he saw himself as a great empire builder, taking "as a model" Cecil Rhodes, who wanted to unite Britain's African colonies with a railway from Cairo to Cape Town. Britain was far from the only country engaged in such empire building. Germany was acquiring territories from Africa to China to catch up with European rivals. Japan was strengthening its position in Korea. And the United States, after its victory over Spain in 1898, had taken the Philippines, Guam, and Hawaii.[56]

Yet even as Russia's rivals gathered new lands, Witte still believed Russia should focus on economic expansion rather than territorial conquest. The acquisition of Port Arthur, however, which Witte had been skeptical of, gave St. Petersburg new interests to defend, and created new constituencies for a foreign policy that leaned ever farther forward in Asia. This trend was visible in matters from road building to religion. On the question of missionary work and religious sects in Manchuria, for example, Witte had to remind one influential adviser to the tsar that Russian religious law cannot apply in the region because "Manchuria doesn't belong to Russia, but is a province of" China. Yet as Russia strengthened its de facto control over Manchuria, the tsar's ministers had no choice but to concern themselves with matters such as where to build roads, whether to set up ferry services, and how this infrastructure should be funded.[57]

Port Arthur soon became a quintessential colony. In 1903, it had 14,000 Russian military personnel, 3,000 Russian civilians, and 23,000 Chinese. There was a notable gender imbalance given the large number of soldiers. Harbin, a railway hub to Port Arthur's north, had fourteen women for every 100 men, and was notorious, one Russian visitor recounted, as "the brothel . . . of the world." It was, a British visitor declared, "as ugly and uninteresting as any new prairie town can hope to be." Governing the territory was no easy task. Port Arthur had "two epidemics of plague and three of cholera between 1898 and 1902, spurring the Russians to build a water distillery for civilians in 1903. St. Petersburg also had to deal with angry locals, for example, when the Russians expropriated landholders in the region, setting off a riot.[58]

Russia's Far Eastern territories experienced riots because, for the first time ever, they began to attract substantial numbers of people. Thanks to the Trans-Siberian Railway, Russians began streaming eastward, looking for free land or new opportunities. In the quarter century after 1891, 5 million people settled in Siberia, many arriving in the lands bordering China. As in earlier periods of colonization, though, the empire's Far Eastern territories were as attractive to foreigners as to Russians. Somewhere between 60,000 and 200,000 Chinese laborers worked on the railway in addition to specialists such as rock drillers, who were imported from countries such as Italy and the United States.[59] Russia's government thought it was colonizing the Far East. But on the ground, it was not always clear who was colonizing whom.

Businesses moved in, too. Russians established gold and coal mining firms in Manchuria around the turn of the century, for example. Some Russian officials hoped to set up factories in Manchuria because "with the labor of the yellow race so cheap. . . . Russia will be able to enter the arena of worldwide production." Witte sought to take advantage of Russia's new position in China to strengthen its commercial presence. He wrote Foreign Minister Lamzdorf that establishing "a commercial port" in Russia's new territory is "of prime importance." Once the Trans-Siberian Railway was ready, goods could be shipped directly from Port Arthur to Europe, letting Russia "compete with the maritime path through Suez" for European trade with China and Japan, he argued. The railway was expensive to build, costing two and a half times the price per mile in European Russia, one official estimated. Yet so long as Russia had the territory, it might as well try to create demand for trade, Witte concluded, spending huge sums on infrastructure. Witte's investments may not have been profitable, but they were transformative. A French consul who traveled through Russian-dominated Manchuria noted, "All the classes of the Russian populace represented, from craftsmen and laborers to merchants and bankers. Russian and Siberian peasants are steadily replacing the Chinese element and Russian is spoken everywhere, even by the natives. That is indeed definitive colonization."[60]

Colonization came with costs, however. Barely a year after Russia's seizure of Port Arthur, a violent anti-foreigner rebellion broke out in China, supported by part of the Chinese government. The rebels, known as the Boxers, attacked Europeans and besieged their legations in Beijing. St. Petersburg received frantic telegrams from Russians stranded in Beijing requesting help.

"The situation is critical," one Russian diplomat warned in spring 1900. "Only a powerful and decisive action of the [foreign] powers can stop" the rebels. Everyone agreed that Russia must intervene to defend its interests in China—a country with which, just several years earlier, Witte had signed a defensive alliance. But how? War Minister Kuropatkin wanted to "crush Beijing," believing that a harsh response would best deter future misbehavior. Witte recalled Kuropatkin "beaming with joy" at the outbreak of the rebellion, seeing "an excuse for seizing Manchuria" outright, and planning to "turn Manchuria into a second Bukhara"—a new outpost, in other words, of the Russian Empire.[61]

Witte may have exaggerated Kuropatkin's eagerness for an invasion, but the war minister certainly had far grander ambitions than either Witte or Lamzdorf. The foreign minister repeatedly argued that Russia needed to calibrate its response to keep open the prospect of friendly relations with China in the future. "Our goal," Lamzdorf wrote to Russia's commander in Port Arthur, "should be limited to freeing the imperial mission [in Beijing], providing security for Russian subjects living in Northern China, and the reestablishment of a lawful government in Beijing"—not the permanent occupation of Chinese Manchuria.[62] Yet with Russian forces already present in Manchuria to defend the railroad to Port Arthur, a large-scale intervention would be straightforward. And the thousands of Russian subjects now living in Chinese territory would view restraint as a betrayal.

In response to the Boxer Rebellion, therefore, Russia not only freed the diplomats trapped in Beijing. It also occupied Manchuria, repressing the rebels there and protecting the railroad. At first, Russia planned to withdraw from both ventures immediately after reestablishing order. "The happiest day of my life," Tsar Nicholas wrote his mother, "will be when we leave Beijing and get out of that mess for good." Yet once his troops were in place, Nicholas found it difficult to pull back. He believed the military operation would help preserve future peace, telling his foreign minister that "the Asiatics deserved the lesson which they had been taught." War Minister Kuropatkin, meanwhile, delayed withdrawing troops on the grounds that Russia's railways would otherwise be undefended. Other Russian officials wondered if Russia should take advantage of China's disarray to grab new territory, perhaps the Chinese port of Tianjin. Witte opposed any such expansion of Russian interests, urging immediate withdrawal and arguing that occupation of Manchuria was "useless" and involved "huge expenditures." "By waging war against China, we are making eternal enemies out of the Chinese," he warned.[63] Yet Russia had already seized Port Arthur, built a new railroad through Chinese territory, marched troops to Beijing, and invaded Manchuria. The "peaceful relations . . . with the Chinese colossus" that Witte had negotiated just five years earlier, at the time of Nicholas's coronation, were no more. Russia was now arrayed against nearly every power in Asia. Yet its appetite only continued to grow.

"NOW I RULE"

On January 22, 1903, St. Petersburg's high society assembled for a ball in the Winter Palace. Guests were asked to wear costumes in the style of the seventeenth century. Princesses dressed as wives of Russian noblemen from the period, "richly embroidered and covered with glittering jewels." Men wore costumes of long coats with "golden eagles embroidered on the breast," silk shirts, silk trousers, and leather boots. "For at least one night Nicky wanted to be back in the glorious past of our family," one of the tsar's relatives mused.[64]

Less than three years had passed since Russia's easy intervention to crush the Boxer Rebellion and occupy Manchuria. It was only five years since Russia had established a naval base in the Chinese city of Port Arthur, only seven since Finance Minister Witte and Chinese envoy Li Hongzhang signed the treaty giving Russia the right to build the Trans-Siberian Railway as an almost straight line from Lake Baikal to Vladivostok, cutting across the territory of Chinese Manchuria in the process. Lord of the East—the meaning of Vladivostok in Russian—felt more accurate than ever. Was it not Nicholas who set in motion the construction of the Trans-Siberian Railway in a ceremony outside of Vladivostok after his Asian voyage? In barely nine years, Russia had begun building the first railroad across Eurasia, acquired an ice-free port on the Yellow Sea, and established itself as a great power in the Far East. Lord of the East, indeed.

As the nobility of St. Petersburg waltzed through the Winter Palace in January 1903, however, the tsar's Asian empire was increasingly precarious. Russia's ambitions had grown only larger, thanks to Nicholas's dalliance with adventurers who urged him ever forward in Asia. Yet the farther Russia pushed into Asia, the more it frightened and angered Japan, Britain, and other powers. Nicholas was blind to the risk. His ministers, including Witte and War Minister Kuropatkin, urged caution. But they were increasingly displaced by the tsar's informal advisers, some of whom had financial interests in Russia's expansion in the Far East. And Nicholas was cheered on by his cousin, the German Kaiser, who warned that Russia must redouble its efforts in the Far East to defend Christianity against the Yellow Peril.

Nicholas was not so naive that he failed to understand the Kaiser's aim of distracting Russia's attention from Europe. Nor did he like or trust the Kaiser, writing to his mother after one official meeting that it made him want to vomit. But the Kaiser knew which buttons to press. He warned Nicholas that "the 'Crimean Combination' [that is, the Franco-British alliance that defeated Russia in the Crimean War] is forming and working against Russian interests in the East. 'The democratic countries governed by parliamentary majorities, against the Imperial Monarchies.' History always will repeat itself," the Kaiser predicted. Fearing both democracy and his rivals in the Far East, Nicholas listened. He was concerned, too, about the Japanese, another frequent subject of the Kaiser's letters. "Japan is becoming a rather restless customer" in its efforts to train the Chinese army, the Kaiser warned: "20 to 30 Million of trained Chinese . . . led by fine, undaunted Christian hating Jap. Officers . . . is the coming into reality of the 'Yellow Peril' which I depicted some years ago."[65]

Nicholas's ministers urged caution. Witte foresaw a "major calamity." Military intelligence reported that Japan "is rushing to finish its shipbuilding program," suggesting that Tokyo's naval power was growing. Most Russian military analysts agreed. A special committee of the Naval Ministry highlighted the risk of war with Japan between 1903 and 1906, given Japan's rapid naval expansion. In reports to Russian leaders, the General Staff repeatedly highlighted Japan's willingness to fight. War Minister Kuropatkin insisted that Russia had far fewer forces in the Far East than would be needed in a conflict. Russia could win a war with Japan, he believed, but it would take a year and half and require an army of 300,000 men—far more than were easily deployed to the Far East. The adoption of European technology substantially increased the Japan's army's fighting power, Kuropatkin warned. Anyway, he insisted, Russia's core aim remained to protect its western front from rising

German military power. The Far East was undefended, but it was a distraction. "Never in the whole history of Russia has our western frontier been in such danger in the event of a European war," Kuropatkin warned in 1900. He repeated the argument two years later: "We have to return again to the West from the East."[66]

Yet with Nicholas in charge, abandoning the East was never a plausible policy. He believed that great power status in Asia was crucial to Russia's international standing. The Japanese would have happily agreed to delineate spheres of influence, yet the tsar repeatedly rejected any compromise. The only other option, Kuropatkin concluded, was to reinforce Russia's military presence in the Far East to deter a Japanese attack. This would require yet more spending on the Far East at a time when its enormous cost was already controversial. Witte had promised that his railroads would expand Russian trade, but by the early 1900s they continued to drain the budget. His enemies calculated that Russia's Far Eastern efforts cost the government 171 million rubles annually, equivalent to a third of Russian military spending, or 13 percent of the government's overall budget. Such a deficit was not necessarily economic destabilizing, as Witte well knew, but it was politically damaging nonetheless.[67]

Witte, meanwhile, was losing influence over the Far East to a group of aristocrats led by Aleksandr Bezobrazov, who owned a stake in a timber business in Korea and who saw territorial expansion as key to Russia's future in the Far East. Bezobrazov was an officer in the elite Chevalier Guard regiment. He spent his free time inventing new types of artillery shells, dreaming of empire in Asia, and urging the tsar to allow his timber firm—in which Nicholas himself owned a stake—to expand its business in Korea. Bezobrazov's main interest, one contemporary explained, was not "materialistic" but rather fulfilling his "dreams of grandeur. The idea of playing adviser to the Tsar captivated his imagination and the idea of influencing cardinal issues of state policy befogged his weak brain, and led him to conjure up . . . the chimera of Russian supremacy, perhaps over the whole of Asia."[68]

Supremacy over Asia was a theme that resonated ever more strongly with Nicholas. By early 1903, Bezobrazov was pressing the tsar to expand the Far Eastern army by 35,000 men and to "introduce into Northern Korea a mounted detachment of 5,000 men equipped with mountain artillery"—an idea that was certain to infuriate the Japanese. On top of this, Bezobrazov wanted to create irregular forces, disguised as "working parties wearing Chinese dress," but "carrying arms concealed in their supply wagons." This plan was rejected by Kuropatkin, but Bezobrazov nevertheless drafted Chinese bandits into a fighting force, arming them with Russian weapons.[69]

Nicholas's ministers complained to the tsar that Bezobrazov's schemes were pushing Russia toward war with Japan. "I cannot hide from your Majesty," Foreign Minister Lamzdorf said in 1903, "that the activities of Bezobrazov in the Far East are causing general uneasiness . . . His policy is likely to lead Russia into a nefarious war. . . . A war on account of the [Korean] forests would appeal to no one." Yet the ministers' complaints had no effect. Witte grumbled that "Bezobrazov is with the sovereign no less than two times a week—*for hours at a time*—he, of course, talks all sorts of nonsense and shady plans. . . . Not long ago, the Sovereign took fright over the fact that I was supposed suddenly to have *sold* all of Siberia's minerals to the English."[70]

Bezobrazov's greatest accomplishment was to amplify the tsar's interest in Asia while destroying any semblance of organization in the making of Russian foreign policy. Gone was the coordination between Russian diplomatic, economic, and military measures, replaced by unstructured conversations between tsar and friends. Nicholas encouraged Bezobrazov to "speak from the heart" when advising him. Bezobrazov responded by telling the tsar that Witte was "an instrument of the Yids and the Poles." Witte continued to warn that war would be a "major calamity for us," predicting "many casualties," "heavy economic losses," and "the strong hostility of [Russian] public opinion." The tsar, fed up with Witte's second guessing of his policies, fired him in August 1903. In his diary that day, Nicholas wrote: "Now I rule."[71]

"WE CANNOT AVOID WAR"

The Japanese believed that Witte's firing represented the "victory of the expansionist party" in St. Petersburg and concluded that Russia would only change course if threatened with war. In early 1904, therefore, the Japanese envoy in St. Petersburg repeatedly approached Russian diplomats demanding recognition of Japan's primacy in Korea. The tsar, believing in Russia's military superiority and distracted by St. Petersburg's winter balls, did not take the Japanese seriously. The Japanese struggled to get a response from the Russians, who could not be bothered to hurry.[72]

It was not only former ministers such as Witte who predicted that the tsar's policies would drive Japan toward war. The tsar's commander in the Far East, Admiral Yevgeny Alekseyev, warned that "we cannot avoid war" with the Japanese. In an abstract sense, Nicholas himself realized the importance of peace, noting that "Russia stands to gain enormously by every year of peace," particularly given the country's severe internal divisions. Yet he could not bring himself to agree to limit his ambitions in Asia, nor could he take seriously a people he saw as "short-tailed monkeys." The Japanese were "impudent," he complained. He wanted to ward off war not "by concessions which would surely precipitate hostilities" but by a "firm policy." "Russia is a big country," Nicholas declared to a Japanese official at a New Year's reception in early 1904, presuming that the empire's continent-spanning girth was an asset.[73] It was not. When the Japanese launched a surprise attack in February 1904, sinking part of the Russian naval squadron at Port Arthur, Russia's size impeded an effective response. Russians at first rallied around the flag. Writer Andrei Bely declared that Russia's "future is at stake" because "the destiny of our national ideals, our arts and language, depend on her [Russia's] mastery in Asia and in the Pacific in the twentieth century." Others praised Russia's noble effort to defend Europe from the "yellow danger, the new hordes of Mongols." Yet national ideals were of limited use in an industrial-scale war. Both Russia and Japan deployed new technologies and tactics as they struggled for control of Manchuria, including barbed wire, searchlights, trench warfare, contact mines. They threw tens of thousands of men at enemy formations in battles that presaged the carnage of World War I.[74]

General Kuropatkin, in charge of the war effort, struggled to get supplies to the front. He wanted fourteen military trains daily running on Russia's Manchurian railroad, but in 1904 had only three. Japan could ship troops to Korea in only twenty-four hours. Russia had to move men and material across 9,000 miles of territory via single rail line—so that when two trains approached from opposite directions, one had to pull to the side to let the other pass. Russian troop trains, often 100 wagons long, were filled to the brim with peasants being shipped to the Far Eastern front. The Russian military knew the railroads were Russia's great weakness. In 1902, before the war, Kuropatkin had written that "the immobility of the railroads" requires an "extremely cautious" foreign policy. When war came—the result of the tsar's extremely incautious foreign policy—Kuropatkin's prediction was borne out: "The most important factor to assist the Japanese in their offensive strategy and to impede us was the condition of the Siberian and Eastern Chinese railways," he wrote.[75]

Japan took advantage of the disarray in Russian supply chains and the delays in its reinforcements to push the tsar's forces back from Korea and from the Chinese coast. First, the Japanese sank part of Russia's Pacific Fleet, bottling up the remaining ships in their harbors. Then, sea lines secured, Japan besieged Port Arthur, the naval facility that Tsar Nicholas had seized, which fell to the Japanese in early 1905. From there, the Japanese army pushed northward into Manchuria, with Kuropatkin's failing to halt the Japanese advance, slowing their progress only at great cost in lives.

As the war ground on, Tsar Nicholas began to lose his hold not only on Korea, but on Russia itself. Even Russian officers began turning against the tsar. In 1905, the second year of war, Russian society exploded. St. Petersburg erupted in strikes and protests. In Moscow, revolutionaries threw up barricades and took control of the streets. In the countryside, peasants began seizing land and farm tools, at times even slaughtering their landlords. Across the country, soldiers began to mutiny.[76] Nicholas was petrified of the masses and horrified that they would question his right to rule.

"EVERYTHING . . . TO SECURE PEACE"

What was to be done? Tsar Nicholas had no clue. He froze in the face of danger. The disaster of war and revolution had discredited his favored advisers. Months before the protests broke out, Nicholas's hardline interior minister, Vyacheslav von Plehve, had cast doubt on "the closeness of danger." Some of the tsar's advisers had reportedly even speculated that a "small, victorious war" would help stave off the revolutionary surge. Amid slaughter in Manchuria and revolt in St. Petersburg, these old advisers saw their credibility dissolve. So, too, did those like Bezobrazov who had urged expansion in Asia, promising glory, spoils, and easy victory. In winter 1905, Count Sergei Witte emerged from the political wilderness, urging Nicholas to sue for peace.

"The only rational way out is to open negotiations," Witte told the tsar. "To go on with the war is more than dangerous: further sacrifices the country in its present temper will not brook without appalling catastrophes," such as cholera, and possibly famine. The war could be continued only with more money and more men, both of which could be obtained only "by the application of force" against the tsar's own people. If so, "the warriors of the Far East will inaugurate their warlike career on the very place of their recruitment," Witte predicted.[77]

Nicholas finally relented, agreeing to send a delegation to negotiate peace with the Japanese at a conference in Portsmouth, New Hampshire, mediated by US president Theodore Roosevelt. Nicholas placed Witte in charge of the negotiations, knowing that Witte understood the issues at stake, and that, if the talks failed, he would be blamed for the results. The Japanese, despite their military success, were suffering the strain of war at home and also wanted peace. Roosevelt, the ostensible mediator, prodded the Japanese to settle, hoping to prevent Tokyo from becoming too powerful in the North Pacific. The two sides reached a deal in mid-1905. Russia would recognize Japan's predominant position in Korea; surrender Port Arthur and the surrounding territories to Japan; and hand over the southern half of Sakhalin Island.[78] Witte, who had never wanted Russia to seize this territory in the first place, gladly agreed.

Upon his return home, Witte was named prime minister in November 1905, now tasked with domestic stabilization. With the war over, Russia could redirect its military toward suppressing its own population. And with the government no longer drafting soldiers to fight in Manchuria, peasants and workers had less interest in toppling the government. Witte encouraged the tsar to announce guarantees for civil rights, an elected legislature, and a constitution. Mobilizing connections forged during his long work as finance minister, Witte also organized a vast foreign loan—"the loan that saved Russia," he called it.[79]

By 1906, the revolution was over. Witte's program—ending the war, liquidating Russia's Asian ambitions, and offering political reform at home—had pacified Russia. Nicholas wanted none of this, but so long as peasants were marching with pitchforks, he had little choice. Stabilization, however, presented an opportunity to row back change. By May 1906, just months after Witte prevented revolution and preserved his dynasty, Nicholas fired him, declaring to his mother: "I have never seen such a chameleon of a man. That, naturally, is the reason why no one believes in him any more. He is absolutely discredited with everybody, except perhaps the Jews."[80] Soon Nicholas began rolling back Witte's reforms, beginning with an assault on the elected legislature that the tsar had reluctantly granted at the peak of revolutionary discontent in 1905. He refused to recognize the Duma's reform-minded majority, resorting to gerrymandering and repression.

Yet there was one policy from Witte's brief premiership in 1905 that Nicholas did not touch. He did not return to the Far East. The war with Japan had extinguished what Witte described as Nicholas's "unreasoned desire to seize Far Eastern lands." Yet Witte's vision of "peaceful penetration" had been discredited, too. The bubble of naive optimism had been popped. There were no vast riches to be had in trade with Asia, nor were there territories ripe for conquest. Russian engagement in the region had produced nothing but bills and bloodshed.

Witte may have been correct that Nicholas "does not possess the talents of either Metternich of Talleyrand," as the former prime minister wrote bitterly from forced retirement. But despite the tsar's tendency to land "in a mud puddle or in a pool of blood," there was one pitfall that he persistently avoided after 1905: he kept out of Asian affairs.[81] Nicholas seemed to have learned no other lessons from the experience of 1904–1905. He continued to anger Russia's rising urban middle class with his reactionary politics. He infuriated ethnic minorities such as Poles and Finns by closing their schools and repressing their languages. Most disastrously, he plunged his country into yet another disastrous war in 1914, this time with Germany and Austria-Hungary, two powers that were even stronger than Japan. But Nicholas was careful not to step again into the trap of Far Eastern geopolitics.

Amid the debate in 1905 over whether to make peace with Japan, Witte had written Kuropatkin that "we need a quick but lasting peace in the Far East." Nicholas fired Witte but retained his new strategy of ignoring Asia. One reason was that the war had not only exposed Russia's weaknesses, it had made Russia weaker still. The Russian navy, for example, had been the third largest sea power, but fell to sixth place after the Japanese sank much of its fleet. Now it was surpassed by Germany, the United States, and Japan— three countries that were using their newfound industrial power to build industrial-scale fleets.[82]

Given Russia's belated recognition of its relative military weakness in the region, the deal over spheres of influence that Japan continued to seek in Northeast Asia now seemed appealing. After the 1905 peace treaty, the two countries signed a subsequent accord in 1907 dividing Manchuria and Mongolia into de facto northern and southern spheres. In 1910, Tokyo and St. Petersburg signed yet another secret treaty pledging to defend the status quo in the region. The tsar agreed, writing that "Russia should enter into the closest relationship with Japan."[83]

When Chinese rebels overthrew the Qing dynasty in 1911, sparking concerns that European powers might intervene to carve up China, Russia cooperated closely with Japan. One goal, a Russian diplomat wrote, was to ensure against Chinese efforts "to ruin our solidary with Japan on Manchuria." The foreign minister wrote the tsar reiterating that in Manchuria "our interests correspond with Japan." The decision to recognize Japan's position in Northeast Asia—something that, before the 1904–1905 war, Nicholas was unwilling to do—helped give Russia a free hand in Mongolia in the period after the Chinese Revolution, when that territory asserted its independence from Beijing.[84]

Yet even amid the collapse of Qing China's authority in its province of Mongolia, along Russia's border Russian leaders adopted a cautious approach. Some writers close to Russia's War Ministry argued that Mongols could be "faithful subjects" of Russia, "fit for military service, and loving us. . . . We shall have a rich region with fertile land . . . we shall obtain an extensive market for selling our goods . . . we shall open a source abundant with raw materials." Yet this type of grandiose claim about the prospects for expansion in the Far East no longer rang true. In the days before 1904, Bezobrazov mustered similar promises to shape Russian foreign policy in the Far East. After 1911 in Mongolia, however, the Foreign Ministry's cautious course dominated discussion.

Sergei Sazonov, who was named foreign minister in 1910, opposed a "one-sided engagement" on the part of Russia in Mongolia, especially a military operation, given the "international constellation in Europe." "The internal situation in Mongolia," he reminded a colleague, "does not in any way affect our vital interests." Even after striking an agreement with Japan to divide the region into spheres of influence, with Mongolia falling in the Russian sphere, tsarist diplomats nevertheless continued their negotiations with China, seeking Beijing's consent for a Mongolia that was autonomous rather than fully independent. In 1913, China and Russia reached an agreement along these lines.[85]

Sparsely populated, economically marginal Mongolia was ultimately an afterthought. In the Far Eastern territory that mattered, Manchuria, Russia's position was in decline, even after the spheres-of-influence deals with Tokyo. One British visitor reported that "Russian interests are steadily losing ground in north Manchuria" to Japan and the Western powers. The share of Russian goods in Manchuria's imports was declining, falling below 20 percent by 1911—hardly the economic powerhouse that Witte had envisioned. Manchuria's chief export products, agricultural goods, had by then "passed into the hands of British, Japanese, and Germans," Russia's commercial rivals. Japan's footprint was growing rapidly, given Tokyo's predominant position in Korea. "Japanese coal supplies Harbin with most of its fuel . . . [and] Japan will soon have two banks in Harbin. . . . The chief complaint of Russians is the fact that their own banks" do not give them the necessary support," one observer wrote. "The Japanese carry on extensive financial operations in Harbin with Russians on very advantageous (to the Japanese) conditions, due to the non-existence of similar Russian lending organizations." As a result, Japan's trade was booming, with Japanese exports to Manchuria having "trebled in the last three years, whereas from Vladivostok the import has hardly increased at all."[86]

Some Russians believed their only hope of stemming their decline in Manchuria was to formally annex the territory, but this proposal went nowhere. St. Petersburg was resigned to surrendering its status as a major power in the Far East. Ultimately, it had little choice. Even before the war with Japan, War Minister Kuropatkin had warned that "Russia and the Imperial throne is threatened from the West, and not from the East. . . . Wilhelm and all of Germany is glad at each new expenditure of Russia in the Far East for, weakening ourselves in the west, we also gradually lose the right of Russia to a voice in European affairs, befitting Russia as a great European, and not an Asiatic power."[87]

The defeat by Japan had only intensified this dilemma. Like nearly all of Russia's leaders, Kuropatkin insisted that Russia's European interests mattered far more than its Asian ones. Tsar Nicholas could not disagree: his aggressive policies in Asia before 1904 were based on the false assumption that

St. Petersburg had the resources to project power in both directions simultaneously. The Japanese victory had proven this disastrously wrong. Rather than an outlet for Russian ambitions, the Far East had proven dangerous but useless. The economic gains that Witte promised proved illusory. Russia began to industrialize thanks not to Asian markets but European investment. Russian industry was centered in St. Petersburg, Moscow, and the towns of Ukraine and the Urals—far from the markets of China or Japan.

Though the benefits of Asia for Russia were mostly illusory, war with Japan was far costlier than expected. After 1905, Russia's elite united on the need for peace in the Far East. The new partnership with Japan, Russian diplomats believed, was not only useful in preserving peace in the Far East. It also bolstered Russia's nascent partnership with Britain against Germany. St. Petersburg was therefore willing to offer Tokyo substantial concessions to secure peace, undoing most of Witte's legacy in the process. Russia had no shortage of internal problems, the new foreign minister, Alexander Izvolsky, reminded a colleague: "Everywhere in Berlin, in Vienna, in Paris and in London people are infinitely more interested at this time with our internal affairs than our foreign policy." Though the tsar's government had stabilized the revolutionary tumult of 1905, everyone knew Russian society could again explode. New Asian adventures would only hasten its demise. "Everything [we do] is and must be to secure peace," Izvolsky declared. "Nothing is less debatable."[88]

5

"A NEW MECCA FOR THE EAST"

The Bolshevik Revolution in China

THERE WERE NOT many similarities between Count Sergei Witte, the great statesman of late tsarist Russia, and Karl Marx, the Anglo-German pamphleteer and activist who devoted his life to analyzing and overthrowing industrial capitalism. Witte celebrated the big coal, steel, and railroad firms that he believed would make Russia an economic and geopolitical great power. Marx saw them as "fast-blossoming capitalist swindle," oppressing the workers on whose labor they depended. Witte sought to protect Russia's imperial autocracy, while Marx condemned tsarist Russia as "the chief of European reaction." Yet Marx and Witte agreed on one thing: industrial capitalism was reshaping the world economy. The American colossus was laying mile upon mile of railroad track as it charged toward the Pacific Ocean. New classes of traders and laborers in China and Japan were producing goods for global markets. Capitalism may have emerged on Europe's Atlantic coast, but its focal point was shifting. "The center of world development," Marx declared in 1851, was increasingly on "the shores of the Pacific Ocean."[1] Witte could not have agreed more.

Marx's musings would not have mattered were it not for the collapse of the system that Witte had tried to modernize and defend. After firing Witte, Tsar Nicholas foolishly let his country march toward war with Austria-Hungary and Germany, rivals far more fearsome than Japan.[2] World War I went as catastrophically for Russia as should have been expected. By

February 1917, amid strikes and protests, Nicholas was forced from the throne. A group of centrists tried to create a constitutional republic, yet war, inflation, hunger, and mutinies eroded the moderates' hold on power. In October 1917, they were toppled by a group of far-left radicals, disciples of none other than Karl Marx.

"THE HOUR OF VICTORY FOR THE WORKING CLASS"

Marx had not, of course, expected a communist revolution to happen in Russia. Vladimir Lenin, Joseph Stalin, Leon Trotsky, and the other activists who seized power in 1917 began executing a playbook that Marx had intended for advanced industrial powers such as Britain, France, or Germany. Despite the best efforts of Witte's industrialization drive, Russia still lagged far behind. Stalin exaggerated when he called Russia a "country of the Middle Ages," but it had far more peasants than industrial workers, the people who, according to Marx's theory, were supposed to drive revolutionary change.[3] The early Bolsheviks therefore presumed that, if revolution could break out in Russia, it would certainly spread through more fertile European territory, too.

"No mercy to these enemies of the people, the enemies of socialism, the enemies of the workers," declared Lenin upon taking power in 1917. "War to the bitter end on the rich and their hangers-on!" The Bolsheviks declared class war against the tsarist order, seizing the property of the old ruling class, chasing landlords off their estates, and ousting industrial titans from their offices. Companies were nationalized, farmland distributed to peasants, the jewels of the aristocracy snatched by red activists. Tsar Nicholas II and his children were murdered in a basement in Central Russia, shot, stabbed with bayonets, their bodies drenched with acid to ensure that the Romanov dynasty would never return.[4]

A revolutionary regime needed a revolutionary foreign policy. The Bolsheviks exited the hated war, securing peace with Germany in 1918 by surrendering a vast swath of territory in Eastern Europe. They published the secret treaties signed by the tsar's Foreign Ministry, as well as any other documents that would embarrass the old order. And they cheered and supported the revolutions that seemed to be sweeping Europe.

The same forces that brought down Nicholas II—the pain, the hunger, the senseless bloodshed of World War I—were shaking all Europe's governments to their foundations. Germany's emperor, Kaiser Wilhelm, was forced off his throne, though seeing the fate of cousin "Nicky" in Russia he fled before revolutionaries could grab him. The Austria-Hungarian monarchy was overthrown and split into pieces. The Ottoman Empire, which had sided with the war's losers, was also dismembered, torn apart in a series of wars between Turks, Greeks, Arabs, and Armenians that stretched into the early 1920s.

It was not only the losers who were hit by the aftershocks of war. The victors were scarcely better off, as soldiers returned from the trenches demanding vast social changes to compensate for the carnage. Britain was wracked by strikes in 1918 and 1919, so the government fearfully devised a broad array of new housing and social benefits—"homes fit for heroes," as Prime Minister David Lloyd George promised—hoping to buy off social discontent. France faced a similar mix of protests and instability. Amid the nationalist revolutions of 1848, Marx had famously declared that the specter of Communism was haunting Europe. He had misread the 1848 moment, but in 1918, seventy years later, his predictions appeared to be coming true. The class antagonisms that Marx thought would drive communist revolution were visible to all on the streets of Paris and London.[5] Russia, meanwhile, was already proving that communists could take and keep power.

When revolutionary socialist movements erupted in German cities in late 1918 and 1919, therefore, neither rightists nor communists were surprised. When a communist government was proclaimed in Hungary in 1919, few Europeans presumed it would be the continent's last revolutionary uprising. Bolshevik Russia cheered these revolutions forward. "Having received the joyful news of the victory of the communist revolution in Hungary and Bavaria," the Bolshevik government in April 1919 sent "ardent greetings to their brothers in the struggle for the emancipation of the working class" and predicted that "the hour of victory for the working class in the remaining countries will soon strike." The Bolsheviks' foreign ministry—or the "People's Commissariat" as it was known in the workers' state—focused as much on greeting workers' movements in Europe as it did dealing with other European governments, regimes that they believed would soon be swept off the map. The Bolsheviks condemned the "brazen lies," "shameless falsehoods," and "provocations" of Europe's "deceitful" bourgeois media. And they called for "the proletariat of England, France, and Italy . . . realizing their fraternal solidarity with the toiling masses of Russia and Hungary," to rise up and cast off their chains.[6]

The Bolsheviks were not, however, the only political force with a revolutionary vision at the end of World War I. Where Lenin promised social revolution, American president Woodrow Wilson, who was in Europe for the Versailles Peace Conference in 1919, offered national independence instead of class warfare—an appealing option for countries wanting to cast off the chains not of local capitalists but of foreign colonialists. China embraced the revolutionary moment, but was divided over the type of revolution it wanted. Chinese revolutionaries had toppled the Qing Empire in 1911, but the new republic that replaced the old dynasty struggled to take hold. The republic's first president, Sun Yat-sen, resigned after only two turbulent months in office, handing power to a general. Intermittent civil war followed, during which the country was carved up between Chinese warlords and foreign imperialists. When the Japanese used World War I as an excuse to grab German imperial holdings in China, the Chinese people rose in protest, demanding that the Japanese leave. The May 4th Movement, as this revolt became known, joined the list of revolutionary upheavals of 1919.[7]

The Chinese protests seemed, at first, something different from the socialist revolutions of Budapest and Bavaria. True, some of China's first communists were radicalized by the May 4th Movement. At the time, however, the world's only functioning communist government, in Moscow, saw the future of world socialism as a European affair. During the revolutionary moment of 1919, the trends in Europe—the only continent, besides North America, with a substantial industrial working class—appeared to favor the communist movement. "We can and must now conduct an offensive policy," declared Stalin in 1920. His agenda: "Organizing an uprising in Italy, and in such states that have not yet bolstered themselves such as Hungary, Czechoslovakia (Romania must be smashed). . . . In short, we need to weigh anchor and take to sea while imperialism has yet to get ship shape."[8] Asia, a continent of peasants, did not yet feature on the Bolshevik agenda.

"THE ACHILLES' HEEL OF THE BRITISH EMPIRE"

The "imperialism" that Stalin and his colleagues in the Bolshevik leadership feared meant primarily the British Empire. Britain was still the world's strongest power, with a large fleet and a vast empire, which expanded farther after World War I. The war had crushed Britain's rivals: Russia was shattered, the Ottoman Empire partitioned, Germany disarmed. The main risk, in the eyes of most British strategists, was not a rival power, but a rival ideology, Bolshevism, which threatened stability at home and abroad. From the earliest days after the Bolsheviks took power, therefore, many in Britain wanted not only to limit the spread of communist propaganda, but even to roll back communist power. "The policy I will always advocate," the future prime minister Winston Churchill declared at the time, "is the overthrow and destruction of that criminal regime."[9] Britain's government, however, took a more measured line, searching for a modus vivendi with Russia's new government while taking steps to protect Britain's commercial and imperial interests.

When the Bolsheviks looked at British foreign policy, they focused on the angry denunciations of socialism in London's newspapers rather than the more nuanced reality of official policy. The deployment of British troops alongside French, Italian, American, and Japanese partners to Russia's far north, the Caucasus, and the Russian Far East seemed, to Bolshevik leaders, like an effort to encircle them and strangle socialism. Facing what appeared to be a mortal threat, some Bolshevik leaders wondered whether an assault on colonialism could weaken European capitalism.[10] All the capitalist powers had colonial appendages: Britain and France, of course, had vast empires, while Japan occupied Korea and Taiwan, and the United States ruled Hawaii and the Philippines. Lenin had famously analyzed the links between capitalism and colonies in his book *Imperialism: The Highest Stage of Capitalism* (1917), which argued that imperial ventures were a source of "super-profits" without which capitalism could not survive. Now that the world's only socialist state was in a struggle to the death with the capitalist powers, could Lenin's insight not be used against the communists' rivals? M. N. Roy, an Indian communist who was influential in Moscow during the 1920s, argued that undermining imperialism would destabilize capitalism. "Super-profit obtained from the colonies is the mainstay of modern capitalism," Roy argued, so "the breakdown of colonial rule, together with the proletarian revolution in the home countries, will overthrow the capitalist system in Europe." Stalin agreed that the "proletarian West cannot put an end to the world bourgeoisie without the support of the peasant East." Britain's Asian frontiers, Trotsky declared, were the "Achilles' heel of the British Empire."[11]

As the revolution in Europe sputtered, therefore, the Bolsheviks repurposed their promises of liberation to target "Eastern" peoples, notably the Turks, Persians, and Indians among whom the Bolsheviks hoped to find allies in the struggle against Britain. In September 1920, the Bolsheviks organized a conference called the Congress of the Peoples of the East in Baku to spread this revolutionary anti-imperial message. A British journalist in attendance reported a "wonderful accumulation" of peoples, "Asiatic costumes," "astonishing weapons," and "undying hatred of capitalism."[12]

In fact, the congress focused more on anti-imperial messages than on anti-capitalist agitation. Bolshevik leader Grigory Zinoviev closed the conference with a call to arms: "Slavery! Frightful slavery, ruin, oppression, and exploitation—that is what Britain brings to the peoples of the East. Save yourselves, peoples the East! Arise and fight against this beast of prey! Go forward as one man in a *holy war* against the British conquerors! Stand up, Indian exhausted by hunger and unbearable slave labor! Stand up, Anatolian peasant crushed by taxes and usury! . . . Stand up, Armenian toiler driven out into the barren hills! Stand up, Arabs and Afghans, lost in sandy deserts and cut off by the British . . . stand up and fight against the common enemy, imperialist Britain! Wave high the banner of the holy war!"[13]

Zinoviev's declaration was promptly translated into the languages of "the East," but his call for a "holy war" against the British—or "jihad," as it was rendered in Turkish, Persian, and Arabic—was mostly ignored. The image of an atheist Jew calling the Muslims of the East to a jihad was a bit rich. Another Bolshevik agent declared that "Moscow and Petrograd have become a new Mecca for the East"—also probably not an optimal message for attracting Muslims to the communist banner. But the bigger problem was that the countries Zinoviev had hoped would lead the anti-imperialist effort were becoming less ripe for revolution. In Turkey, Mustafa Kemal established an iron grip over the newly founded Turkish Republic based not on class solidarity but on Turkish nationalism. In Persia, Reza Khan seized power in a coup in 1921, declaring himself shah four years later—hardly the right ally for a social revolution. And in India, the British reduced dissent by tightening repression and offering elite Indians new opportunities to participate in government. Here, too, the scope for communist revolution rapidly receded.[14]

"THE GREAT STATESMAN OF MODERN CHINA"

Even as the Middle East stabilized, China appeared to be moving in the Bolsheviks' direction. China's May 4th Movement, the wave of protests against imperialism in 1919, provided fertile ground for communist arguments about the need to cast off foreign empires. Was not Bolshevik Russia standing up to the same powers that were oppressing China? In 1919, two months after the May 4th protests began, the Bolsheviks promised "to return to the Chinese people everything that was taken from them by the Tsarist Government," a commitment that appeared to include the China Eastern Railway, the old symbol of tsarist imperialism in Chinese Manchuria.

At a time when other powers, notably the Japanese, were strengthening imperialist privileges in China, the offer looked magnanimous. President Wilson had talked about self-determination, but it was the Russian communists who, it appeared, were undermining the imperial order. Chiang Kai-shek, one of the leaders of China's nationalist movement, declared the Soviet promise to relinquish the railway "the noblest move in the annals of international relations." Sympathy with communist Russia raced through China's politically active classes. One Western academic visiting China in 1920 reported that all his Chinese students "were Bolsheviks, except one, who was the nephew of the [former] emperor." The young radical activist Mao Zedong would later recall that "the Chinese found Marxism as a result of its application by Russians. . . . Follow the Russian way—that was the conclusion."[15]

To many of China's revolutionaries, however, the Russian way meant not anti-capitalism, but anti-imperialism. Sun Yat-sen, who had briefly served as the first president of the Republic of China after its founding in 1912, was looking for allies in his effort to oust the warlords who ruled China and replace them with constitutional government. Sun had been introduced to Russia's revolutionaries decades earlier, having met several in London in 1897.

Later, in Chicago, Sun crossed paths with a Russian activist named Mikhail Borodin, who was then living in exile as an American schoolteacher.[16]

Borodin was born in the province of Vitebsk in the Russian Empire. He had worked as a riverboat man, floating logs down the Dvina River, before moving to Riga, one of the empire's most industrialized cities. There, he joined the Bund, a Jewish socialist movement, though he appears to have abandoned Yiddish, his native language, and most other Jewish cultural and religious practices. In 1903, he attached himself to a more radical group of socialists led by a then obscure revolutionary activist named Vladimir Lenin. Two years later, Russia was plunged into in the 1905 revolution, and after it failed the tsar sent many would-be revolutionaries into exile. Borodin went to America, bouncing from Boston to Chicago before unrolling in Indiana's Valparaiso University, at a cost of $30 per semester. After moving back to Chicago, Borodin continued to associate with Russian revolutionary groups in exile, though he also assimilated to the bourgeois side of American life, starting a family and acquiring a business.

When his old comrade Lenin took power in St. Petersburg in 1917, Borodin abandoned his new life and raced back to Moscow. As the Bolshevik leaders began cultivating Sun Yat-sen in 1918, they not only found Sun receptive to an alliance, they realized that one of their agents had already met him. Borodin was promptly sent onward to China to establish a relationship with Sun's forces. Georgy Chicherin, the Bolsheviks' foreign minister, wrote to Sun, calling him "honored teacher" and praising him for noting "that the Russian and Chinese revolutions had common aims, that they are leading to the liberation of the peoples and to the establishment of enduring peace, based on the recognition of the community of interests of the two great proletariats, the Russian and the Chinese."[17]

The Bolsheviks had little experience with China. Borodin reported that he knew only "what I could read from this or that book, from several articles, and from what several Oriental comrades told me." Yet Borodin and his comrades were sure of one thing: Sun would be an excellent ally in the struggle against imperialism. A report in 1920, for example, declared that Sun was "very popular among the Chinese people" and that "he has sources of funds, and many capitalists regularly give him material support." Moreover, they believed that though Sun was not a Bolshevik, he was a leftist, providing a basis for an alliance. Lenin therefore prioritized the relationship with Sun, telling Chicherin "we must be kind in every way, write him regularly and, trying to be secret, send our man [Borodin] to Canton," the southern Chinese city where Sun's movement was based. Another agent wrote Sun with obsequious praise: "I dreamed that I would be able to personally meet with you, and, in that way, see the great statesman of modern China, fighting for its national liberation." "Our victory is your victory," Soviet newspaper *Izvestia* declared, "and our doom is your doom!"[18]

The Bolsheviks' praise for Sun Yat-sen was self-serving, but their belief in his influence was sincere, and they decided in the early 1920s to provide him all possible support. In 1922, they organized a grand conference in Moscow for the "Toilers of the Far East" to publicize Sun's cause. One Russian speaker asserted (inaccurately) that Russia's 1905 revolution had profoundly influenced the 1911 revolutionary movement against China's now-collapsed Qing Empire. A Japanese communist contrasted the capitalists' effort to stabilize China via free trade—a "means of exploiting China and Korea, Siberia and the other Far Eastern Countries"—with the socialists' plans to topple the old order. A speaker concluded the conference praising two converging streams: "the movement of the oppressed peoples which seek independence" and "the far mightier current of the conscious proletarian movement." "Give up your faith in Versailles and Washington," he urged Asians, and "do not believe the bourgeois intriguers."[19]

The Soviet Union provided not only rhetorical support to the Chinese revolutionaries, but money and guns, too. Borodin arrived in China in 1923 to organize support for Sun Yat-sen. He stayed with Sun for several years, not only coordinating relations between Sun and Russia's communists, but helping to lead Sun's Nationalist Party (called the Kuomintang, or Guomindang in Chinese), forging a party with active members and a well-organized structure, the type of which China had never seen before. The Nationalist Party constitution, for example, was written by Borodin in English before being approved by Sun and translated into Chinese. Borodin, Sun Yat-sen declared, was the "Lafayette" of the Chinese Revolution.[20]

To train the next generation of Chinese revolutionaries, the Soviet Union set up schools for them in Moscow. More significant still was the Whampoa Military Academy established in Canton to train officers to fight in Sun's army. Moscow sent its own officers, too: by 1925, there were over 1,000 Soviet advisers in China, experts in aviation, communication, and naval affairs. To arm

Sun's soldiers, Soviet Russia shipped guns and ammunition, too. First, "8,000 rifles, with 500 rounds of ammunition for each"; then, "an additional 15,000 rifles, machine guns, and artillery pieces." Throughout the early 1920s the Soviets micromanaged Nationalist Party affairs, even overseeing the party's budget for furniture.[21]

THE FAILURE OF REVOLUTION IN EUROPE

The Bolsheviks had time to consider the Nationalist Party's furniture purchases because their efforts to spark revolution in Europe had failed. In 1918, Lenin had declared that Bolsheviks would be "doomed if the German revolution does not break out."[22] "We do not know, nobody knows, whether it will triumph in a few weeks," Lenin said, or "perhaps even in a few days." But in 1918, the prospect that further revolutions would take years, even decades, was inconceivable to any right-thinking Bolshevik.

Lenin and his comrades had done everything possible to encourage such uprisings, seeing European revolutions as ideologically necessary, geopolitically useful, and, as Marx had prophesized, inevitable. "From provincial Moscow, from half-Asiatic Russia, we will embark on the expansionist path of the European revolution," Trotsky had declared. "It will lead us to a world revolution. Remember the millions of the German petite bourgeoisie, awaiting the moment for revenge. In them we will find a reserve army and bring up our cavalry with this army to the Rhine to advance further in the form of a revolutionary proletarian war. . . . You can almost literally hear the footsteps of history."[23]

Yet the footsteps of history marched in a more circuitous route than Trotsky expected. The first round of socialist revolutions in 1918–1919 sputtered out. Capitalist politicians in France and Britain restored stability by expanding social programs and repressing revolutionaries. In 1921, Germany's communists launched a new uprising, but it quickly fizzled. A subsequent revolt in 1923, again led by Soviet-backed German communists, was promptly crushed. Across Europe, the most audible footsteps were those of bourgeois parties on the march. In France, power alternated between center-left and center-right coalitions, with both groups solidly opposed to Soviet-style revolution. In Britain, the conservatives governed for most of the 1920s, their electoral success underwritten by anti-Soviet rhetoric. Italy saw an even more drastic swing to the right, as Benito Mussolini's fascists seized power in 1922.[24]

"VLADIVOSTOK IS FAR AWAY"

The failure of Bolshevism in Europe encouraged Soviet hopes that socialism would take root elsewhere. China's revolutionaries seemed like natural candidates to spread revolutionary fervor. If they succeeded, Soviet officials hoped, they would also help address an important dilemma for Moscow: how to provide security in the country's Far East? The Bolsheviks had no friends in Asia. It faced the same competitors that the Soviets' tsarist predecessors had confronted: China, Britain, the United States, and—most dangerously—Japan.

The Bolsheviks feared Japan, and not only because they had come of age during the 1904–1905 Russo-Japanese War. Though they blamed Tsar Nicholas and Count Witte for embroiling Russia in the war, they also remembered that Japan sank two Russian fleets and ejected the Russian army from its fortress at Port Arthur. It was a "shameful" conclusion to a humiliating conflict, one Soviet diplomat recalled. Stalin remembered the war as a "dark stain" that "left painful memories." The Far East, meanwhile, was as far away as ever, connected with the rest of Russia by a single railway and primitive air links. It remained sparsely populated and had comparatively few ethnic Russians. And it shared a long land border with China and a series of disputes with Japan.[25]

If Japan's military was powerful in 1904, it had grown only stronger in the twenty years since—a period in which Russia was torn apart by civil war, which lasted into the early 1920s. During the civil war, Japan led Russia's rivals in occupying Russia's Far East, with Japanese troops occupying territory from Vladivostok deep into Siberia. The Europeans and Americans had been ambivalent about the Far Eastern intervention, but the Japanese dove in, deploying far more troops than the Americans or Europeans and staying for several years after the other foreigners departed. The Soviets were therefore extraordinarily sensitive to Japan's position on the Pacific Coast, and feared that at a moment of weakness, Japanese troops might land in the Far East again. "Vladivostok is far away," Lenin warned the Japanese in 1922, "but it is still our city."[26]

Japan had benefited greatly from World War I, building its economy and expanding its power in Asia. But during the mid-1920s Tokyo was comparatively uninterested in foreign adventures. Civilian political parties restrained the military's desire for an expansionist foreign policy. And in 1923, Japan was struck by a massive earthquake, forcing the country to rebuild at home. None of this, however, assuaged Soviet concerns. The country retained "a powerful industry, navy, and army," Chicherin reminded his colleagues. Tokyo ultimately wanted the Soviet state dismembered, the Bolsheviks believed. Japan was funding and arming rebels inside the Soviet Union, they concluded. "Along the whole coast" of the Pacific Ocean, Chicherin warned, "Soviet power is so weak that the Japanese are, in fact, in charge, freely coming, exploiting local natural resources, and buying up furs for next to nothing from the local population."[27]

The core issue, to Chicherin, was the Chinese territory of Manchuria. Nikolai Muravev-Amursky had seized the Amur Valley and the territory around Vladivostok to provide Russia an outlet to the Pacific. Count Witte had built the Trans-Siberian Railway to guarantee that Russia could always reach Vladivostok. Yet the more territory Russia had on the Pacific, the more energy it took to defend. Defense meant keeping the railway line open so that troops and supplies could be shipped eastward in case of crisis. Manchuria, which jutted northward between Lake Baikal and Vladivostok, was an enduring threat to Russia's lines of communication to the Pacific Coast. The three provinces that made up Manchuria remained ostensibly part of China—as they had been even at the peak of tsarist railroad imperialism—but in the 1920s they were controlled by a Chinese warlord named Zhang Zuolin, who was funded and armed by the Japanese. And the Japanese, Stalin repeatedly warned, remained a grave threat. "Don't trust Japanese diplomats even for a second," Stalin wrote one of his diplomats in 1924. "Trust facts."[28]

"THE DEMOCRATIC CHARACTER OF SOVIET POWER"

How should the Soviet Union defend its Far Eastern border? Was it better to pursue an offensive or defensive policy? To Moscow, Japan and China were part of the same dilemma. Soviet leaders threatened that "if foreign hands interfere" in Sino-Soviet relations, they would be "mercilessly cut off."[29] But everyone knew that Japan was deeply ensconced in Chinese politics. Japan's army and navy were a permanent threat to Russia. Tokyo's influence in China, meanwhile, gave it additional levers with which to pressure the Soviets. China, for its part, was divided between competing warlords, some funded by Japan, others trying to undermine Japanese influence, with many selling the services of their armies to the highest bidder. Tokyo's imperial ambitions in China, including the occupation of the Liaodong and Shandong Peninsulas, which controlled sea lanes to and from Beijing, infuriated Chinese nationalists. The May 4th Movement against Japanese imperialism had sputtered out, but China's port cities continued to seethe with anti-Japanese anger even as warlords such as Zhang collaborated with Tokyo.

China's warlords, meanwhile, fought among themselves for control over the country's government in Beijing. Several groups of warlords emerged in different parts of China. They, not the Beijing government, were the country's real rulers, collecting taxes, providing order, even organizing basic public services. The government in Beijing served at their pleasure. In the decade after 1916, China had six heads of state, as rotating warlord coalitions put their preferred figureheads atop the government.[30] So long as China remained divided, the Soviet Union believed, it would invite foreign interference, bringing other great powers closer to the Soviet Union's Asian borders. How could the Soviet Union defend its interests?

One option was to cut deals with the warlords. The Soviets tried this in the early 1920s over the China Eastern Railway. Though they had declared in 1919 their intention to return "to the Chinese people, without any compensation, the Chinese Eastern Railway," by 1921 they had rolled back this promise, insisting that "Russian rights on this railway remain in full force." Claiming control over tsarist railroads involved reputational costs for a country promising to be an anti-imperialist force. One Bolshevik agent warned that Soviet policy "in China should in all its declarations constantly demonstrate the full lack of imperialistic interests . . . to underline the democratic character of Soviet Power." Sun Yat-sen, for his part, cautioned that any use of Soviet military force around the Manchurian railroads would "have difficult consequences for long-term Russian-Chinese relations."[31] But the need to ensure that Moscow—not Japan—controlled the railway was too important to the Soviets, and slogans about the evils of tsarist imperialism in China were quietly shelved.

In fall 1923, Soviet envoy Lev Karakhan arrived in Beijing to negotiate over the Manchurian railroads, and to open formal diplomatic relations between Soviet Russia and China. Stalin urged him to finish the talks quickly. "We need an agreement as a legal guarantee against a repetition of conflicts" over the China Eastern Railway, he wrote Karakhan. Months later, in spring 1924, the Soviets signed a deal with Beijing opening diplomatic relations and providing for joint management of the railroad. The Soviet Union and the Chinese also agreed not to engage in propaganda "directed against the political and social system of either contracting party."[32]

Yet even after the deal with Beijing—and a subsidiary deal with Zhang Zuolin, the warlord who controlled Manchuria—Soviet interests remained difficult to defend. Manchurian military authorities arrested the Russian manager of the China Eastern Railway, for example, before releasing him after several days. Several months later, ships belonging to the railway were seized in the Sungari River. The Japanese had not actively opposed Soviet settlement of these issues with the Chinese government or the Manchurian authorities, but the Soviets nevertheless saw Tokyo's hand in Chinese obstructionism. The "aggressive Chinese-ization" of the China Eastern Railway, Chicherin argued, "is clearly inspired by the Japanese," whom he believed were also "preparing an aggressive policy against the Mongolian Republic," another territory along the China-Russia border where Japan had an interest.[33] It was not effective, Soviet leaders believed, to cut deals with the impotent Chinese government in Beijing. And Manchurian warlords like Zhang Zuolin, they soon found, were not to be trusted.

The warlords knew how to extract taxes and raise armies from China's agricultural regions, but they struggled in China's prosperous central and southern coast. Cities such as Shanghai, Nanjing, and Fujian had become major international ports, thanks in part to the treaties that gave foreign merchants preferential legal treatment. In the three-quarters of a century since the First Opium War, these port cities had been transformed by trade and commerce, drawing in hundreds of thousands of peasants from the countryside seeking work, and building a small but powerful group of Chinese tycoons who ran banks, trading houses, and factories. New schools and universities trained a burgeoning class of students, educated in foreign languages, who protested China's government and foreign imperialists alike. And by the 1910s, China had even begun to develop industry, especially in "cotton textiles, flour, matches, cigarettes, cement, canned food, bean oil, and even coal and iron."[34] Industrialization created factory workers—a proletariat, in Soviet parlance—who constituted only a tiny share of China's overall population, but who were concentrated in strategic choke points such as the ports of Shanghai and Canton through which the produce of China was shipped to the world.

It was in Canton (now Guangzhou) where Sun Yat-sen established his government-in-waiting, attracting support from students, workers, and capitalists across the South China coast. The Bolsheviks were already shipping guns and money via Borodin to support Sun's efforts. Could the Nationalist Party not expand its influence across China, perhaps even take Beijing? If an allied revolutionary party took power in China, would this not resolve the Soviet Union's security dilemma in Asia? Chicherin was optimistic. Soviet-style revolution had been repeatedly defeated in Europe, but Asia seemed different. Was it not a region where the Soviet Union could win allies, undermine rivals, and advance its agenda? China's tumultuous politics seemed to provide an obvious opportunity. "The historical significance of the surprisingly rapid development of Chinese democracy, spread by the Nationalist Party, is clear," Chicherin declared. Warlords and imperialists "cannot hold back the historical development of China."[35]

"THE CAMP OF IMPERIALISM AND THE CAMP OF SOCIALISM"

To the Soviets, the mid-1920s seemed to signal a change in the "historical significance" of China's Nationalist Party. A defensive strategy in China no longer seemed tenable. It was time to push back against imperialists of all stripes, to undermine their colonial interests in China, and to carry forward the red banner. Soviet aims in China shifted from defense to offense. How best to execute a forward policy in China? In spring 1925, Sun Yat-sen lay dying, and Stalin worried that without him, Soviet influence in China might disappear. "How are things with Sun Yat-sen?" Stalin nervously wrote Karakhan in March 1925. "How the hell did he decide to die now? Are there people in the Nationalist Party who can replace Sun Yat-sen if he dies? This is a big question, and we need to pay special attention to it."

The issue wasn't only whether a new Nationalist Party leader would work well with the Soviets. Stalin was prepared to send additional agents and extra funds. The bigger question was if the Nationalist Party after Sun would have the support from society needed to expand its army. "One division organized along Soviet lines is, of course, small," Stalin lectured Karakhan. "We need to set up several divisions. Without that things are impossible in China." For a credible army, the Nationalist Party needed "a real base for rallying elements capable of constructing an all-national Chinese government." The army, in turn, must be "a real army, connected with the people," not like the warlords' mercenaries. "That's why we need to pay special attention to improving and staffing the army," Stalin instructed.[36]

Sun died one week later, and Karakhan ordered Soviet flags to half-staff. Sun's last words, Karakhan claimed, were "If only Russia will help. If only Russia will help." Yet before Soviet Russia would increase its help, Karakhan needed an answer to Stalin's question. Did the Nationalist Party have "a real army, connected with the people?" Was it more than a collection of military leaders funded by China's capitalists? Stalin had long argued that "the world has been split into two camps," as he declared in 1919, "the camp of imperialism and the camp of socialism," a view that became official Soviet policy two years later. What differentiated these groups? Stalin explained: "In *their* camp are the United States, Britain, France, and Japan with their capital, with their armaments, with their experienced agents and equally experienced administrators. Here, in *our* camp, are Soviet Russia with the young Soviet republics, and the growing proletarian revolution in the European countries."[37]

This distinction was clear enough. It suggested that the Nationalist Party—which was on the Soviet "side" given its opposition to China's warlord-dominated government in Beijing—was in the socialist camp. Before his death, Sun Yat-sen had not been so sure. He wondered to a colleague why "the youth seek wisdom in Marx, when all the basic ideas of Marxism were to be found in the Chinese Classics." And in 1923, he had formally declared, "The Communist order or even the Soviet system cannot actually be introduced into China," because the conditions were not ripe.[38] Chinese nationalist leaders were certainly not in the "imperialist camp." But they did not sound like socialists, either.

Yet Marxists knew better than to listen to political declarations. They focused instead on the correlation of social forces within the Nationalist Party.

"Does China *really* have a movement, and how deep is it?" Stalin asked his underlings. Does "the Nationalist Party have roots [in society] and are they real living roots?" This was the key question. As early as 1905, Lenin had argued that, even during bourgeois revolutions, proletarians could participate and eventually take a leading role. The Nationalist Party was clearly bourgeois. It was financed by major Shanghai and Canton businesses. Yet so long as Soviet analysts saw evidence that left-wing elements were playing an ever-larger role within the Nationalist Party, they could argue that the revolution was progressing along the lines Lenin predicted. On this metric, the news from China was positive. One Soviet agent reported to Moscow that "modern industry is growing rapidly, especially with the help of foreign capital" even though it is "an extremely small part of the population" and the peasantry remained politically inert. Another Soviet official, meanwhile, saw even China's warlords as evidence of modernization, interpreting "the power of these military governors . . . [not] as merely militarist violence" but as "centers of bourgeois development."[39]

Reports from Borodin seemed to confirm this thesis. A month after Sun died, Borodin wrote Moscow that factional disputes within the Nationalist Party were shifting to the advantage of left-wing groups. "All the work that is being undertaken by the Nationalist [Party] in the peasantry is run by us," he wrote. "There, the split with the rightists will have no relevance. Work among the workers is undertaken exclusively by us." The forces of reaction, he argued, were "powerless" within the Nationalist Party. Canton, another Soviet informant reported in the year of Sun's death, is a "small Leningrad or a small Moscow, and not even that small."[40]

Since the early 1920s, the Soviets had backed the Nationalists on the rationale that the party would incubate the communist presence as China prepared for more genuinely revolutionary changes. Stalin declared that the party was "revolutionary" and a "workers' and peasants' party," even though it was run by a collection of capitalists and their hangers-on. "The Nationalist Party suffers from many errors," Chen Duxiu, the cofounder of the Chinese Communist Party had argued in the 1922, but "nevertheless it is the only revolutionary democratic group in China." Moscow therefore ordered Chinese communists to "become part of the Nationalist Party" to pave the way for socialism. Even Trotsky, the arch-radical in Soviet debates who believed in the necessity of immediate socialist revolution, had initially backed collaboration with the Nationalist Party. By Sun's death in 1925, this policy seemed to be working. What other country in Asia had such well-developed communist party cells?[41]

Reports from China, moreover, suggested that left-wing groups were gaining traction. In April 1925, a month after Sun's death, a strike broke out in Tsingtao, before quickly spreading to Shanghai, then across the country. In June, protesting workers in Canton were killed, sparking a year-long expansion of the strikes to Hong Kong, the British colony off the south China coast. The revolutionary movements of the East, Soviet leader Zinoviev declared in October 1925, "are advancing like a torrent." "A new, exceptionally important factor has appeared," he emphasized several months later: *"the movement in China."*[42]

"ASSISTING THE . . . EDUCATION OF THE ASIAN PEOPLES"

By the mid-1920s, the revolutionary movements of the East seemed attractive because the Soviet Union was frozen out of Europe, and because Soviet leaders perceived a global economic and political shift toward the Pacific. The years 1924–1925 brought a series of setbacks in Europe. The Kremlin had opened formal diplomatic relations with Great Britain in 1924 only to see British politics erupt in anti-Soviet fury later that year over the publication of correspondence alleged to document Soviet meddling in British politics. Then, London and Paris signed the "Locarno Treaties" with Berlin, establishing economic and security cooperation between Western Europe's status quo powers, on the agreement that the parties lock the Soviets out of Europe.[43] Europe was set for a period of capitalist stabilization. The Kremlin saw little hope for immediate revolution.

What to do? Chicherin told a party congress that the British goal was "to soften us, to make us . . . give up our policy in the east." The solution was to do the opposite: "Any speculation that through some changes [i.e., concessions] in our Eastern policy we may gain any advantages in the West is . . . empty chat, based on the ignorance of history and our true position in both the West and the East," he declared. "We must unambiguously postulate the unquestionable importance of our Eastern policy."[44]

This meant redoubling Soviet efforts in Asia. Stalin, who was then consolidating power at home after Lenin's death, delivered a series of speeches over the course of 1925 emphasizing the need to focus on Asia. On January 19, he declared that "the international situation is beginning to change radically," driven by "the liberation movement in general in the East. . . . This is bound to turn the ruling classes in the Great Powers against us . . . for they know that the seeds falling on this fruitful soil in the East will grow and mature."[45]

Moscow then signed a treaty with Japan to improve ties, giving the Soviet Union a freer hand to promote revolution in China. Chicherin celebrated the agreement as "a real revolution in Far Eastern politics . . . the end of the entire period of intervention, civil war, and unsettled conditions in the Far East." In March, Stalin declared that "national liberation movements . . . [are] damaging capitalism in the rear." In May, he reiterated that "in Europe the revolutionary tide has begun to ebb" but that "our country is no longer alone" thanks in part to "the oppressed peoples of the east." Chicherin observed similar trends: "the present situation in Europe has . . . uncertain characteristics, [but] the direct opposite can be observed in the Asiatic States."[46]

What did the Soviet Union desire in Asia? Stalin set out his aims in a major speech in mid-1925. Soviet policy, he argued, should pursue the following goals in Asia:

1. To win over the best elements of the working class to communism, and to create independent communist parties.
2. To form a national revolutionary coalition of the workers, peasants, and revolutionary intelligentsia against the coalition of the conciliatory national bourgeoisie and imperialism.
3. To secure the hegemony of the proletariat in this coalition.
4. To fight for the emancipation of the urban and rural petty bourgeoisie from the influence of the conciliatory national bourgeoisie.
5. To ensure that the liberation movement is linked with the proletarian movement of the advanced countries.

The final point—the link between national revolution and the success of communism—was, in Stalin's view, the key. A movement could be considered revolutionary, and thus useful, if it supported the position of the world's main proletarian state, the Soviet Union. In mid-1925, a Japanese journalist asked Stalin, "The Japanese people have a slogan, 'Asia for the Asiatics.' Do you find a common ground . . . [with] your revolutionary tactics?" Stalin replied: "In so far—and only in so far—as the slogan 'Asia for the Asiatics' means a call for a revolutionary war against Western Imperialism." The Soviet Union, Stalin wrote, was the only "bridge between the socialist West and the enslaved East."[47]

Stalin was not, of course, the first person to see Russia as a "bridge" between East and West. Many of the tsarist statesmen of his youth held similar views, whether Prince Esper Ukhtomsky's spiritual conception of Russia's connection between East and West, or Witte's hope that the Trans-Siberian Railway could facilitate transport and trade between Europe and the Pacific. The Bolsheviks redeployed this concept in communist garb. The first issue of *Novy Vostok*, a new journal the Bolsheviks created for the study of "Eastern" countries, declared that "Far back in Russian history, Russia not only possessed Asian territories, but had been to a considerable degree itself an Asian state. This fact on the one hand gives Russia the right to participate in charting the destiny of the Asian countries, and, on the other hand, imposes on her the moral duty of studying Asia, its peoples, and its history, as well as of assisting the political development and education of the Asian peoples."[48]

"OUR POLICY IN CHINA HAS BEEN ABSOLUTELY RIGHT"

Optimism about the revolutionary wave crashing over China was widespread in the Soviet Union. There were some setbacks, of course. Borodin had in the course of his work caught both dysentery and malaria and had barely survived a typhoon while at sea. He was haunted by pessimism and despair, writing Karakhan at one point that "the only communism possible in China today is the communism of poverty . . . of people eating rice with chopsticks out of an almost empty bowl." But most Soviet officials were willing to take whatever kind of Chinese communism they could get, even the impoverished sort. Most Bolsheviks also remained willing to continue betting on the alliance with the noncommunist Nationalists, provided that their leader, Chiang Kai-shek, continued to work with China's small communist party. After all, one Soviet report noted in early 1926, "The Nationalist Party, such as it exists now, has been created by us . . . [and] there has not yet been a case, when any measures proposed by us were not accepted."[49]

It was possible, of course, to see reasons for concern. In late 1925, a group of right-wingers in the Nationalist Party met in the Western Hills outside of Beijing and plotted to limit communist influence in the party. Some Soviet officials worried that the communists were failing to conduct adequate "political work, bringing about a weakening of their influence." Another Bolshevik noted that that though the Nationalist Party had perhaps 500,000 members, there were only 4,500 people in Chinese Communist Party cells.

Yet pessimism about Chinese communism was the minority view among Soviet observers. Most perceived the left on the rise. "The workers movement has substantially grown, starting with a wave of economic strikes," one Soviet agent in China noted in February 1926. "We see economic strikes in Shanghai, Hankou, Nanjing, Tianjin. . . . And for the first time in China we see workers not only struggling against foreign entrepreneurs, but also against Chinese capitalists." "It is impossible to say anything negative" about the Nationalists, Karakhan declared that same month.[50] Chicherin also urged investing yet more in the alliance with the Nationalists, advising Karakhan to redouble support on the grounds that "our policy in China has been absolutely right and produced grand results, exceeding even our expectations."[51]

In China, however, Nationalist leader Chiang Kai-shek was less convinced by his party's alliance with the Chinese Communist Party. Chiang cared little about communist ideology. He knew that he needed Soviet aid to unify China, but he worried that communist influence within the party subverted his personal control. Given Borodin's role in founding the Nationalist Party and the Soviet role in the Whampoa Military Academy, which trained the party's military leaders, Chiang had reason for concern. He was constantly on the lookout for rivals trying to subvert him, and feared adversaries with communist backing. In March 1926, Chiang heard rumors that the communists in Canton were plotting against him, mobilizing naval ships as part of a potential coup. Borodin happened to be on a trip, away from Canton, so Chiang struck quickly, ordering his troops to shut trade unions and to lock up Chinese communists.[52] When Borodin returned from his trip, Chiang acted as though nothing had changed. He immediately requested that Soviet advisers, including Borodin, continue their support. Having solidified his control over the Guomindang, Chiang wanted to keep Soviet aid flowing.

Moscow debated how to respond. Some Soviet leaders argued that the Chinese communists should withdraw from the Nationalist Party now that Chiang had purged leading communists. The debate was between two strains of optimism: Trotsky's belief that the USSR should abandon the Nationalists and support immediate communist revolution, and Stalin's assertion that the communists' alliance with Chiang was moving China closer to revolution. Trotsky insisted that "only woeful philistines and sycophants can believe that the national liberation of China can be achieved by moderating the class struggle" against the capitalists and the Nationalists. Stalin's allies retorted that tension within the Nationalist Party was caused by "the mistakes of the Canton communists," and that with the existing policy "the movement of the great people's mass of workers and peasants" would inevitably "develop and strengthen." Stalin pushed the Soviet Politburo to agree "to intensify the work of the Communist Party within the Nationalist party." In practice, this meant not changing Soviet policy at all. Indeed, as Chiang launched his "Northern Expedition," a vast military offensive against the Chinese warlords in July 1926, Soviet military advisers played a central role—despite Chiang having assaulted the Chinese communists in Canton just four months earlier.[53]

"A CHINESE MOSCOW"

As Chiang's armies marched northward with Soviet military support, Stalin's policy appeared justified. When Nationalist forces captured the crucial metropolis of Wuhan, in central China, in fall 1926, labor unions set up a left-leaning Nationalist Party government there. Wuhan seemed the perfect place for China's proletarians to stand up. The city had a long revolutionary tradition. In 1911, mutiny by military units in Wuhan had set off the revolt that toppled the Qing Empire. Since then, Wuhan had industrialized rapidly thanks to its position as a commercial entrepôt and railroad junction. It had acquired a steel mill so advanced that it exported even to the United States. The city was, one journalist declared, "the Chicago of China" thanks to its industrial base. With a sizable proletariat working in its factories, Wuhan was as likely as any Chinese city to drive a communist revolution. Stalin's bet on Chiang looked increasingly justified. Under its left-wing Nationalist Party government, Stalin declared in September 1926, Wuhan "will soon be a Chinese Moscow."[54]

As 1927 began, Stalin's predictions appeared to be coming true. The workers' movement in China was growing ever stronger, with Shanghai workers launching a major strike in February. Nationalist Party armies, meanwhile, were marching northward, advised by Soviet officers and armed with Soviet rifles. They took Shanghai in late March and Nanjing several days later, solidifying Nationalist Party control over almost all the South China coast, including the country's most industrialized areas and its commercial hubs. Europeans interpreted Nationalist Party success as evidence of Soviet meddling. The most influential foreign newspaper in China, the *North China Herald,* declared that "all Soviet Russia's activities have been spent on an attack on Great Britain in China. It has been and is a war between Soviet Russia and the British Empire." The British agreed, seeing the Russians as "permeating" Shanghai. Canton was said to be "honeycombed" with communist spies.[55]

Moscow celebrated these advances. In 1927 more than half of all the editorials in the Soviet publication *Communist International* mentioned the successes of the Nationalist-Communist alliance in China. As Nationalist Party troops marched toward Shanghai, Soviet officials argued that the "the Shanghai proletariat . . . could provide tremendous influence on the long-term revolutionizing of the entire National Government." Like Wuhan, the city with the left-leaning Nationalist Party government, Shanghai had a militant labor movement, and Soviet agents reported that "conditions are ripe for the proletariat to exercise hegemony through the government." In Shanghai, one Soviet report declared it "entirely possible and necessary to create a Soviet-style government."[56]

Soviet officials continued to admit, as one put it in March 1927, that Chiang Kai-shek "has counterrevolutionary tendencies," but insisted that "he also plays a progressive role, carrying out the struggle against imperialism." The march on Shanghai seemed like evidence that the Nationalist Party was winning in urban areas that ought to be conducive to proletarian power. "We have within the Nationalist Party," one official declared, the ability "to strengthen from below the left wing . . . [and] to strengthen our strategic, nodal position within the army and the government." As Stalin put it in April 1927, the alliance between right-wing factions of the Nationalist Party, the left-wing Nationalist forces in Wuhan, and the Chinese communists was developing in China's favor. "Why drive away the Right, when we have the majority and when the right listens to us?" The Nationalist Party must be "be utilized to the end, squeezed out like a lemon, and then flung away."[57]

THE CANTON COMMUNE

It was Chiang Kai-shek, however, who squeezed the lemon first. Fearing the growth of communist influence in Shanghai's growing labor movement, Chiang assembled a coalition of bankers, industrialists, and gangsters who agreed to crush the communists. In early hours of the morning of April 12, 1927, Chiang's forces struck against the city's leftists, firing wantonly into labor union headquarters and burying one of their opponents alive. Perhaps 300 leftist militants and activists were killed, 500 arrested, and several thousand forced to flee. Shanghai business and foreign capitalists alike applauded Chiang's work in handily dispatching the communist threat. China's leftists were sent reeling. Chiang's own son, who was living in Moscow and studying Russia's revolution, publicly declared his father an "enemy of the Chinese working masses."[58]

Simultaneously, European powers and Manchurian warlord Zhang Zuolin launched their own pressure campaign against the Soviet Union. Zhang raided the Soviet embassy in Beijing, grabbing and publishing documents detailing the work of Soviet agents in China, including the funds and arms they provided to their clients.[59] Then, in London, British police raided the office of a Soviet trading firm called Arcos, alleging that it was a front for intelligence efforts and publishing its documents, too. (The USSR explained that the firms' rifle purchases were for a hunting expedition.)[60]

Yet Chiang Kai-shek's massacre of the Shanghai communists did nothing to shake Stalin's faith in his alliance with the Nationalist Party. After the Shanghai Massacre, *Pravda* reported "bloody carnage among the Shanghai proletariat" but interpreted the slaughter as evidence that "the Chinese revolution is being born in hard labor," predicting that "the Chinese will stand closer than ever to the side of the *revolutionary* Nationalists, the Nationalist Party without Chiang Kai-shek." The "left Nationalists" were, in Soviet parlance, the part of the party that was governing the city of Wuhan with support from the labor unions. Borodin, writing from Wuhan in early May, urged Moscow to stick with its policy, noting the Wuhan government's support for left-wing ideas such as a "radical solution to the agrarian question."[61]

During Moscow's May Day celebration in 1927, therefore, Soviet Communists carried Chiang Kai-shek's portrait through Red Square next to those of Stalin, Lenin, and Marx, as if Chiang's recent massacre of Chinese communists had not happened. Several weeks later, Moscow concluded that "recent events have entirely confirmed the point of view of the Communist International concerning the Chinese Revolution and have brilliantly confirmed Lenin's predictions. . . . [It is wrong to conclude] that these defeats menace the fate of the revolution as a whole." Indeed, Moscow warned against underestimating "the powerful and unorganized movement of the toiling masses" in China, led by the Nationalist Party.[62]

True, even Stalin worried about the future of Wuhan's left-wing Nationalist government, which was the most visible success of the "toiling masses" in China. Stalin wrote to two aides in late June expressing concern "that Wuhan will lose its nerve" and submit to Chiang Kai-shek's control. "We must insist adamantly on Wuhan not submitting. . . . Losing Wuhan as a separate center means losing at least some center for the revolutionary movement, losing the possibility of free assembly and rallies for the workers, losing the possibility of the open existence of the Communist Party, losing the possibility of an open revolutionary press—in a word, losing the possibility of openly organizing the proletariat and the revolution."

Stalin sent notes to Wuhan urging the city's government to form a revolutionary army, break ties with Chiang, and seize leadership of the Nationalist Party. The Soviet leader's confidence in his position was unchanged. He wrote an aide in early July that "our policy [in China] was and remains the only correct policy. Never have I been so deeply and firmly convinced of the correctness of our policy . . . as I am now."[63]

The left-wing Nationalist forces in Wuhan chose not to heed Stalin's advice. In July, they moved against the communists in Wuhan, purging them from the government and forcing Borodin to flee Wuhan, crossing via the old camel trail across the Gobi Desert, back into Soviet territory. Stalin denied that this was a setback. In an editorial in *Pravda* he argued that China's situation was not like Russia in 1905—when the revolution was crushed by tsarist forces—but like Russia in mid-1917, just months before the Bolshevik takeover. The failure of the Wuhan left-wingers was simply a "stage of development" on the road to the ultimate victory.[64]

The alliance with the Nationalist Party was dead, but revolutionary dreams were not. None of the setbacks in Wuhan prevented either Stalin or his aides from perceiving new openings for revolution. After all, Canton—the base of the Nationalist Party, which had a relatively developed left-wing movement and working class—was seething with discontent. The mood was febrile, one Soviet agent noted in late November 1927, citing the "reactionary" Nationalist Party government, the "arrest of workers [and the] breaking of strikes. Among workers there is deep unhappiness, a fighting mood." The city was poorly defended, manned by only three regiments of soldiers plus police, scarcely capable of defending the city, to say nothing of the peasant uprising that Soviet reports promised was "swiftly developing" in the surrounding countryside.[65]

Sensing opportunity, Stalin jumped. "It is clear," he told a congress of the Soviet Communist Party in early December "that the Chinese revolution has not yet led to an outright victory . . . [but] great popular revolutions in general do not attain final victory in the first round." "Only the blind and the timid," he continued, "can doubt the Chinese workers' and peasants' advance." Stalin pushed to the side the evidence from a telegram received on December 3, warning that "the Communist Party here [in Canton] is extremely weak," fixating instead on additional information received on December 5 that "at the current moment Canton is completely clear of military forces." On December 10, he ordered Soviet agents to strike. "In view of the . . . mood among the masses and a more or less favorable situation on the spot," he wrote to his agents in Canton, "we do not object to your proposal and recommend that you act confidently and decisively."[66]

At 3:00 a.m. on December 11, 1927, Chinese communist and Soviet agents launched an insurrection in Canton, seeking to strike at the heart of the Nationalists' power base and to forge a revolution without Chiang Kai-shek. For a day, the communist forces held the city, forming a Soviet-style government and decreeing an eight-hour working day and other policies to benefit the city's laborers. Yet scarcely forty-eight hours after the revolt broke out, Nationalist troops backed by European powers marched into the city and crushed the communist rebellion.

The uprising was, one of Stalin's rivals declared, "foolhardy, ill-conceived . . . a typical adventure." Chiang Kai-shek, now in control of most of China, responded by ejecting Soviet diplomats from the country. Even Soviet leaders finally seemed to register the failure of their revolutionary efforts in China. Their trust in Chiang Kai-shek, their bet on the "left Nationalists," and their final gamble on a communist revolt had all failed. The Canton uprising had "world-historical meaning," one of Stalin's allies declared a month later, from which the Soviet Union must draw "lessons." But the "meaning" of the Canton uprising did not bode well for the fate of communist revolution. Stalin's revolutionary tactics in China had failed.[67]

"THE GENGHIS KHAN OF THE RUSSIAN REVOLUTION"

There were multiple "lessons" of "world-historical meaning" that one might draw from the Soviet Union's failure to spark revolution in China. One was that the Soviet Union's offering—Marxist class struggle—did not appeal to a country of peasants. Stalin does appear to have concluded that peasant societies were not as ripe for revolution as he had hoped. A second lesson, though, was that revolution and international friendships need not necessarily be linked. Perhaps socialists could collaborate with nonsocialists. Perhaps they could even embrace imperialist tactics in pursuit of socialist power.

This was a complex lesson for some true believers to swallow. Lenin had taught that the key antagonism in international politics was not between different anti-imperialist groups, like the Chinese Nationalists and the Soviet Union, but between imperialists and socialists. This had been the basis for Stalin's "two camp" theory. Yet as Chinese Nationalists repeatedly assaulted Chinese communists, Stalin shifted toward a different thesis, defining a revolutionary not as someone who wants socialism, but as someone who supports the world's greatest socialist: Stalin. "A *revolutionary*," Stalin declared in 1927, "is one who is ready to protect, to defend the USSR without reservation, without qualification, openly and honestly . . . without wavering, unconditionally."[68]

Stalin's ideological gymnastics did little to mask the deeper traditions of politics into which he now tapped. He was, in the words of a colleague, "the

Genghis Khan of the Russian revolution," and in the late 1920s it was to the Mongol borderlands that the Soviets turned as they reconsidered their country's foreign policy in Asia. "Let's not forget that Russia is an Asiatic country," one senior Soviet diplomat declared, a country inclined not toward Europe but to "the way of Genghis Khan and Stalin." Stalin himself had studied the history of the Mongols. In one book that he read, he underlined the phrase: "Genghis-khan destroyed many people, saying 'The death of the vanquished is necessary for the calm of the victors.'"[69]

The Mongol Empire provided a complicated example for the Soviet Union to follow, however. Genghis Khan had united all of Eurasia, of course, a territory that corresponded roughly with the modern USSR. But like the Soviet Union, the Mongols' domain under the Great Khans was stopped at the borders of Japan and Poland even as Mongol unity was undermined by bloody internal dissent. The parallels were not entirely promising, especially for a leader like Stalin who was in the middle of his own equally bloody campaign to crush domestic rivals.

Yet it was to Genghis Khan's ancestral homeland, the territory stretching from Lake Baikal to the Pacific Ocean, that Soviet foreign policy increasingly turned. In Mongolia, the Bolsheviks struggled to reconcile their anti-imperial rhetoric and their geopolitical designs. Mongolia was a country divided among itself and strung between Russia and China. Tsarist Russia had spent the 1910s trying to detach Mongolia from China, a process that was accelerated by the collapse of the Qing Empire. The dissolution of the tsarist empire complicated matters further, as a White Russian officer, Baron Roman von Ungern-Sternberg, worked with Mongol leaders to declare an independent Mongol state. The Bolsheviks defeated the baron's forces in late 1921 and then backed a "people's revolution" in Mongolia in 1924.[70]

The establishment of socialism in Mongolia did not resolve the question of sovereignty, however. China continued to claim the territory. Soviet diplomats twisted and turned to explain how their country simultaneously supported Chinese sovereignty and the Mongol People's Republic that the USSR had helped to establish. In 1924, Soviet foreign minister Chicherin explained to a Chinese interlocutor that "We recognize the Mongolian People's Republic as part of the Chinese Republic, but we recognize also its autonomy in so far-reaching a sense that we regard it not only as independent of China in its internal affairs, but also as capable of pursuing its foreign policy independently." The subsequent year, he coupled this expansive definition of "autonomy" with military threats, warning that in case China sought to reestablish control, the "Mongolian people would certainly resist and the Soviet Union would not just sit by and watch but would immediately support them."[71] The Soviet Union supported China's sovereignty over Mongolia, in other words, so long as China did not try to use it.

This type of old-school geopolitics, with a focus on consolidating Soviet borderlands, was replicated in Tannu Tuva, a remote, mountainous land to the west of Mongolia. Today a province of Russia, Tuva had been previously part of Qing China and was also claimed by Mongolia. The Soviets continued the tsarist-era practice of treating the territory like a Russian protectorate. Working with the population of ethnic Russian settlers as well as factions of the Tuvan majority, Moscow ensured that Tuva followed the Kremlin's foreign policy line, even though its status remained disputed. In 1926 Moscow pressured Mongolia to recognize Tuvan independence after the two territories' border was delineated.[72]

In the early 1920s, Moscow had felt the need to temper its territorial and revolutionary ambitions in Mongolia and Tuva, along its border with China, to better promote its agenda of anti-imperialism and socialism across Asia. By the end of the decade, however, as the Kremlin's efforts to spark a Soviet-style revolution in China had failed, and as the Chinese communists were on the run, Moscow saw little downside in replacing promises of socialist brotherhood with the tactics of old-school geopolitics.

Tuva was an early example of this. In the late 1920s, the Soviet Union asserted more direct control over Tuvan and Mongolian affairs, via the same tactics that Stalin was using to solidify his control at home. In the Soviet Union, in 1928, Stalin launched the first Five Year Plan to build heavy industry, and announced the collectivization of farmland, replacing the country's vast peasantry with state-controlled farmers. This burst of radicalism was intended not only to create the conditions of socialism within the USSR, but also to sweep away any remaining opponents of Stalin's personal control.

The same tactics were deployed in Tuva and Mongolia, too. Between 1928 and 1930, Moscow worked with local radicals in Tuva to overthrow the government, which had collaborated with the local Buddhist clergy, to bring to power a Soviet-style regime. Monasteries were closed and Buddhist lamas were persecuted as the Soviet-backed forces sought "the liquidation of the feudal chiefs as a class," echoing slogans used to fight class enemies in the Soviet Union.[73] Tuva became ever more dependent on Moscow, until it was formally incorporated into the USSR in 1944. Mongolia, meanwhile, launched its own set of collectivization policies and purges under the leadership of Khorloogiin Choibalsan, who ruled Mongolia until his death in 1952. The Mongolian People's Party faithfully governed its country as a Soviet puppet until the USSR dissolved. The Mongolian borderlands would be ruled by Moscow.

"FIRM" BUT "FLEXIBLE"

The sparsely populated Mongolian mountains and steppe lands were always less important, though, than Manchuria, which had been the focus of Russian, Chinese, and Japanese empire building for half a century. As in Mongolia, the collapse of Stalin's hopes for socialism in China drove the Soviet Union to embrace more openly imperialist tactics in Manchuria, too. Manchurian warlord Zhang Zuolin was assassinated in 1928, probably by Soviet agents. He was replaced by his son Xueliang, a playboy and notorious womanizer said to have seduced Mussolini's daughter. The assassins may have hoped that the younger Zhang's vices would make him more pliable to foreign pressure, but Xueliang proved loyal to Chinese leader Chiang Kai-shek and was an inveterate opponent of foreign meddling, whether Japanese or Soviet, in Manchuria.[74]

As Zhang Xueliang refused to bend to Soviet demands, Moscow's relationship with him, and with China more generally, deteriorated over the course of 1929. The Soviet Union's push for concessions sparked a backlash within China. In May, Chinese authorities ransacked the Soviet consulate in the Manchurian city of Harbin, publicizing Soviet diplomats' support for communist subversion and distributing photos of the stoves in the consulate that the Soviets allegedly used to burn secret documents. In June, the Chinese shuttered Moscow's trade office in Manchuria. Then, they grabbed control of the China Eastern Railway, firing Soviet-backed officials and replacing them with White Russians who lived in the area. The Kremlin saw Tokyo's hand behind every Chinese move, concluding that Japan was "encouraging further aggression by the Chinese and unnerving Chinese public opinion with rumors."

After issuing an ultimatum that China ignored, the Soviet Union attacked Chinese Manchuria by land and air in summer 1929. When Moscow's strategy in China had focused on supporting Chiang Kai-shek, the Kremlin had sent Soviet arms and advisers, but never substantial numbers of troops. Now, after the break with Chiang, Stalin decided it was time for new tactics, deploying several thousand troops as well as military planes and riverboat gunships to pummel the Chinese in Manchuria into recognizing Soviet predominance.[75]

The 1929 Sino-Soviet War lasted only a few months. On paper, it was a tremendous victory for Moscow. The Chinese suffered perhaps ten times as many casualties, while the Kremlin bludgeoned China into accepting Soviet control over the tsarist-era railroad concessions in Manchuria. "We've won," Karakhan exclaimed to a colleague. "The Chinese look like cowards, running away, asking to start negotiations." Stalin, meanwhile, dreamed that Soviet military successes had the effect of "undermining the authority of Chiang Kai-shek's government, a government of lackeys of imperialism." He urged his lieutenants to take advantage of their military superiority to push for a Mongolian-style people's government in Manchuria. "We have to go for *bigger things* now," he told his aide Vyacheslav Molotov in October 1929, meaning a *"revolutionary* movement" that could play the role he once hoped Chiang Kai-shek would occupy. Stalin ordered Molotov to organize an army "chiefly made up of Chinese, outfit them with everything necessary (artillery, machine guns, and so on), put Chinese at the head of the brigade, and send them into Manchuria with the following assignment: to stir up a rebellion among the Manchurian troops, to have reliable soldiers from these forces join them . . . to form into a division, to occupy Harbin . . . [and] establish a revolutionary government (massacre the landowners, bring in the peasants, create soviets in the cities and towns, and so on). This is necessary. This we can, and I think, should do. NO 'international law' contradicts this task."[76]

The Red Army's defeat of the Chinese gave the Soviets an open door in Manchuria. Yet the surge of enthusiasm that accompanied military victory faded quickly. Stalin and other Soviet leaders were soon reconsidering the idea of arming a brigade of Chinese and establishing a revolutionary government in Manchuria. The international mood was darkening, raising the risks of adventures in Manchuria. Scarcely two weeks after Stalin ordered Molotov to prepare a revolutionary movement in Manchuria, the tumbling of share prices on the New York Stock Exchange set off a chain of events that would transform Soviet foreign policy in Asia. Manchuria and Wall Street may have been on opposite sides of the world, but they were tied together by networks of credit and by commodity prices.

At first the Soviets seemed to think that the Wall Street crisis served their interests. Had not Marx taught that capitalism was doomed? But as economic shockwaves ricocheted across the world, the Soviet Union soon felt less secure. A year earlier, in 1928, Stalin had launched his collectivization of the Soviet Union's farms, expropriating millions of peasants, repressing farmers who were relatively well-off, and casting the rest onto vast collective and state farms. As countries responded to the depression by raising protectionist tariffs, commodity exporters like the Soviet Union were vulnerable. One of the aims of collectivizing Soviet farmland had been to control grain exports and thus to fund the construction of Soviet industry. Plummeting grain prices on the world market threw a wrench in this strategy. Stalin's response was to double down, declaring to Molotov in 1930, "Once again: *We must force through grain exports*"—which funded industrialization—"*with all our might*."[77] With such a vast transformation underway at home, the Kremlin's scope for foreign adventures grew more limited.

The effects of the Great Depression on international politics also constrained Soviet ambitions in Asia. The capitalist powers were thrown into economic and political crisis, but Stalin feared this would make them more aggressive. "The Poles are certain to be putting together (if they have not already done so) a bloc of Baltic states," Stalin wrote Molotov in September 1930, "in anticipation of a war against the USSR." Earlier that year, the Poles and the Germans, the two great rivals of the USSR in Central Europe, signed a commercial agreement that appeared to defuse their enmity, allowing both to focus their foreign policies against the Soviet Union. In German parliamentary elections, meanwhile, the Nazi Party won a fifth of the seats by promising to confront the "Judeo-Bolshevik" threat, their popularity enhanced by the economic crisis. The greatest losers from the Depression were Japan's hapless liberals, discredited by their country's descent into depression. As Japan's civilian leaders lost power, the country's military leaders set the agenda at home and abroad. Their main interest was Manchuria, where they advocated an aggressive policy designed not only to subjugate the Chinese, but also to lock out the Soviet Union.[78]

On the question of relations with Moscow, Japan's militarists had a point. Had the 1929 war not proved that Stalin's expansionist aims in Manchuria threatened Japan's interests? Tokyo had stood aside in 1929 while Soviet forces assaulted the Chinese, but it did not yet look like Stalin was moderating his aims. Japanese policymakers, like the Kremlin's other rivals from Paris to Warsaw, had looked on nervously as the Soviet Union scored an easy victory over the Chinese. Did the 1929 Sino-Soviet War not prove, asked Japanese militarists, that the "Manchurian problem" would be resolved by force?[79]

Though the Japanese interpreted the 1929 war as evidence of Soviet expansionism, Moscow was beginning to question whether the conflict had been worth it. Just months after the 1929 war, after the excitement of victory had subsided, a more sober interpretation emerged. True, the Red Army had beaten Chinese forces in Manchuria. But the war also proved that Stalin's aims of retaining railroad privileges in Manchuria in the face of Chinese nationalism and Japanese imperialism—and of sustaining a forward policy in China more generally—could only be secured by force.

Compared to the promises of friendship with China's revolutionaries, which had been the premise of Soviet support for the Nationalist Party since the early 1920s, the war with China in 1929 underscored how disastrously Moscow's China policy had failed. Rather than uniting with China against the imperialists, Soviet policy had alienated the Nationalist Party and China's warlords alike, both of which collaborated with capitalist powers. China's tiny communist movement, meanwhile, played hardly any part in the 1929 conflict. The war with China looked like a victory but compared to the great expectations of the early 1920s, it felt like a defeat. By mid-1931, facing renewed disputes with both Japan and China, Soviet leaders realized that their dreams of revolution had failed. They began to consider pulling back from maximalist positions in Manchuria. In August 1931, the Politburo discussed steps to avoid "exacerbating relations" with the Chinese. Stalin supported this policy, calling for an approach that was "firm" but also "flexible."[80]

WITHDRAWAL AND LIQUIDATION

The military victory over the Chinese in Manchuria therefore marked the peak of Soviet ambition in Asia and the beginning of a turn toward a more defensive posture. Stalin's strategic orientation since the 1920s had been to push forward in Asia, taking advantage of the opportunity he perceived in

China's revolutionaries, whom he hoped would spread socialism and undermine imperialism. By the clash with China in 1929, these hopes had been extinguished. The Soviet Union could expand by force, but it won allies only in places like Tuva and Mongolia—where it installed them by force. Elsewhere in China, ambitious aims had either failed or proven more costly than they were worth.

The year 1929, therefore, marked the last gasp of Stalin's forward policy in China. His efforts to spark a pro-Soviet revolution in China had failed, winning the enmity of Nationalist Party leader Chiang Kai-shek in the process. His shift toward more traditional imperialist tactics, pressuring China to acknowledge Soviet predominance in Manchuria, had been no more productive, inspiring further Chinese distrust. During the years in which the Bolsheviks had spent their time managing the Chinese revolutionaries' furniture budget and meddling in Nationalist Party factional politics, they had accomplished nothing of value, distracting themselves from more important matters even as the international picture darkened. Marx may have predicted the crisis of capitalism, but the Soviets had not expected the 1929 stock market crash or the international destabilization it caused. The greatest risk, meanwhile, was at home, as Stalin's drive to collectivize Soviet agriculture caused a famine in the early 1930s that killed millions.

Moscow's forward policy in Asia was therefore promptly abandoned as the USSR pulled back from China and offered embarrassing concessions to Japan. The Kremlin's definition of its critical security interests in Asia was scaled back. Soon even core interests such as the China Eastern Railway were redefined as expendable. The railroad itself—thought by Moscow to be worth a war in 1929—was sold several years later, liquidating the primary legacy of Count Witte and Tsar Nicholas's railroad imperialism. Reacquiring the railroad was the only substantial accomplishment of Soviet foreign policy in China in the 1920s, but Moscow now judged this to be of little value. The Soviet Union made this decision despite complaining about repeated violations of Soviet rights on the railway, including even "mass arrests of Soviet citizens." But the Kremlin had come to conclude that owning a railroad in Manchuria was a liability, not an asset. As one European diplomat pointed out in 1932, the effort to assert Soviet influence in Manchuria was "a wild and reckless military adventure that never brought any additional strength or profit to Russia but was, on the contrary, a running sore and a source of weakness."[81]

This was not the first time that revolution at home coupled with a sense of failure abroad had caused Russia to pull back from the Far East. In 1905, after tsarist Russia's defeat by Japanese armies on Manchurian battlefields, Count Witte—the great advocate of casting open Asian markets—not only made peace with Japan, but reduced Russia's role in China and recognized Tokyo's military predominance in Manchuria. Stalin, too, suffered defeats and disappointments in China that deflated his expectations that an Asian revolution was imminent. Following Witte's example, Stalin discarded offensive operations, and shifted focus toward conciliating the Japanese while deepening his own revolution at home.

When Japanese analysts suggested that the USSR had adopted a policy of "withdrawal" from the Far East or a "liquidation" of its position, Soviet newspapers vociferously objected.[82] Yet there was no denying that Stalin had surrendered a railroad that had been Russian for over three decades, or that he had scaled back ambitions in a region that just several years earlier he had seen as a central front in the global revolutionary struggle. For the fifteen years after 1929, Asia would be a secondary priority for Soviet foreign policy. Stalin's forces vigorously defended their Far Eastern border but abandoned offensive aims. Soviet leaders had once perceived the "footsteps of history" marching across the Mongolian steppe and the Manchurian plains. By the early 1930s, however, the Genghis Khan of the Russian Revolution had abandoned his expansive vision and beat a hasty retreat.

6

"WE MUST HAVE OUR HANDS FREE"

Stalin's Drive for Hegemony in East Asia

"BOLSHEVIKS ARE NOT fortune tellers," Stalin's aide Vyacheslav Molotov warned an assembly of collective farm workers in 1933. "We do not want to be caught unaware."[1] Moscow had been surprised two years earlier, on September 18, 1931, when reports emerged of an explosion near the city of Mukden (now Shenyang). A bomb, it was reported, had detonated along the South Manchurian Railway, which ran from the center of Manchuria to the coastal cities of Dalny and Port Arthur, formerly the prize possessions of Nicholas II's Asian empire, now governed by Japan. The alleged explosion was said to have blown a thirty-one-inch hole in the track.

Blaming the Chinese for the explosion, Japan launched a series of punitive military strikes across Manchuria. An official statement from the Japanese military commander declared, "The South Manchuria Railway is the property of the Japanese Empire. . . . We will not permit any other country to 'lay a finger on it.'" Japan alleged "constantly recurring incidents in violation of Japanese rights and interests" and declared it would take "drastic measures to maintain these vested rights and interests and to make secure the prestige of the Imperial Japanese Army."[2] Soon Japanese troops were streaming across Manchuria.

The Soviet Union's decision to pull back from Manchuria and abandon its ambitions in the area had not produced peace. Competition over the region had only intensified after the USSR's brief war with Chinese forces in 1929.

China, which officially ruled the region, struggled to increase its actual control. Zhang Xueliang, the local warlord, continued to assert his freedom of maneuver against China's central government and foreign powers alike. Japan, meanwhile, which already ruled Korea and the former Russian ports along Manchuria's southern coast, had broader designs. In Tokyo, civilian authorities lost control of foreign policy, and the military's leading generals struggled to control hawkish younger officers eager for territorial conquest. Across Korea, Manchuria, and the rest of China, a series of riots and boycotts between rival nationalities added to the tension.[3]

Everyone knew that the fate of Manchuria held the key to Asia. If China could consolidate control, it would halt Japanese imperialism. If Japan seized Manchuria, it would gain a springboard for dominating all of China. The South Manchurian Railway, which carried the produce of Manchuria to the ports along the Yellow Sea and thus to world markets, was vital to both Chinese and Japanese plans. Count Sergei Witte was long dead, but Manchurian railroads remained central to the region's empire-building schemes. For the South Manchurian Railway "is no strangling narrow-gauge trackage stretching across the steppe," one journalist explained. "It is a thoroughly modern, adequate, forward-looking railway. The equipment is American, the track is standard, the cars and locomotives are American-built and of the latest type." The goods carried by the railroad, moreover, were on the leading edge of Asia's industrialization. For a region that had been a backwater seventy-five years earlier, when Governor-General Nikolai Muravev-Amursky first sailed down the Amur River, Manchuria now represented the cutting edge of economic progress in Asia. In addition to the Fushan coal mines and the Anshan steelworks, the region boasted "soil generally of almost exhaustless fertility . . . immense potential resources in agriculture, timber and mineral wealth," and "modern flour mills, bean-oil mills, soap works, sugar refineries, sawmills, distilleries, breweries, glass factories, tanneries and ore mines." Manchuria rivaled all of Asia in industrial potential.[4]

It was no surprise, then, that the Japanese saw Manchuria as a stepping-stone to a broader Asian empire. After the alleged Chinese attack on the South Manchurian Railway, Japanese forces began occupying towns along the entire length of the railroad on September 18 and 19.[5] The Soviet Union hesitated. The Politburo met on September 20 but lacked good intelligence on what was happening in Manchuria. On September 22, two of Stalin's lieutenants sent a telegram to the Soviet leader at his vacation home in Sochi explaining that they had no clarity on Japanese intentions. Stalin assumed the worst, concluding that Japan was dead set on "expanding or enhancing spheres of influence in China."[6] The Soviet Union, which had proven itself militarily dominant over the Chinese in Manchuria just two years earlier, was about to be displaced by Japan.

What to do? Nothing, Stalin decided. As more information about the so-called Mukden Incident emerged, it became less clear that the explosion ever happened. The official Japanese government account of the incident stated that the bomb blew a thirty-one-inch hole in the railway, but that an express train nevertheless crossed the site of the bombing, where the train "was seen to waver unsteadily to one side and then recover its equilibrium with sufficient rapidity to avoid any derailments." There was no doubt that the express train crossed the site of the "explosion," for it arrived in Mukden on schedule at 10:30 p.m. That a train could cross a thirty-one-inch hole without derailing defied belief. Indeed, the only evidence of any hole in the tracks was Japanese official statements, for there was no photograph of the damaged railroad. An American official sent to investigate concluded that "the Japanese Army planned the whole thing." A British official reported doubting "whether it ever occurred" at all.[7]

Whether or not the Mukden Incident was cooked up by the Japanese mattered little to Stalin. Chinese leaders thought that the USSR might intervene militarily to counter the Japanese. A Soviet diplomat told a Japanese officer in Manchuria that the USSR was prepared to defend its interests by force; this was a bluff. Within five days of the "incident," Stalin had decided that the USSR would take no stand on the Manchurian question, which was an issue for the Chinese and Japanese to sort out. He told Molotov and Kaganovich that Soviet military intervention was "ruled out" and that even "a diplomatic intervention would serve no purpose." The Soviet Union wound down its propaganda against imperialist Japan and even proposed a nonaggression pact with Tokyo. Molotov all but endorsed Japan's seizure of Manchuria as a "cautious" step.[8]

Stalin recognized, of course, the threat that the Japanese invasion of Manchuria posed. Over the course of late 1931, Japan established control over the entire Manchurian region, deploying thousands of troops and recruiting locals into military units, further boosting the number of forces under Tokyo's command. Every mile that Japanese troops marched northward through Manchuria put them a mile closer to the Soviet border. Had the Japanese so desired, one diplomat believed, they could have crossed into Soviet territory and cut the Trans-Siberian Railway "within a few hours." Japan had demonstrated, moreover, that it would not be bound by international law, even by the 1928 Kellogg-Briand Pact, which obligated signatories not to use military force to settle disputes. International law experts puzzled over how Japan could have violated a treaty it had signed just three years earlier. Japan cited self-defense. Unlike the international lawyers, Stalin had little difficulty in comprehending how "self-defense" could be used to justify invasion. He was familiar with the setting up of puppet states, as Japan did in 1932, when it declared the independence of "Manchukuo," as it called the Manchurian territory under its control, explaining its move by pointing to US military interventions in the Caribbean.[9]

Because Stalin understood Japan's motives, he had a clearer sense than most Western observers of Tokyo's likely next steps. The Soviet Union, he told Commissar for Defense Kliment Voroshilov, "needs military preparation in the Far East." Voroshilov agreed that "the Japanese are really undertaking intense work to prepare for war."[10] Yet Soviet leaders saw their own preparation for war in the Far East in defensive rather than offensive terms. Manchuria was not worth a war, they believed, having fought one only two years earlier against the Chinese. Instead, Stalin opted for a policy of appeasement, avoiding a clash with Japan at all costs. Responding to reports in 1932 that Japanese planes were violating Soviet airspace, the Kremlin told military commanders that "Japanese fascist military men" were trying to provoke a conflict, and that they should "categorically forbid shooting." Shortly thereafter, Stalin wrote Politburo member Lazar Kaganovich that Moscow should avoid further entanglement with Manchuria by declining to say whether it would recognize Japan's Manchurian puppet state. He proposed telling Tokyo instead that the decision was "being delayed somewhat by the vacations" of party leaders.[11]

The League of Nations, forced by China to investigate the Mukden 'incident,'" took every possible step to avoid angering the Japanese. The international commissioners sent to the region to research the facts had to walk delicately around the truth, referring only to "the so-called incident" without adjudicating what had actually happened.[12] But even this whitewashing of reality in Manchuria—where everyone knew that the Mukden Incident was concocted by the Japanese Army—was too provocative for Moscow. The Soviet Union declined to cooperate with the League of Nations investigators lest the commission's report embarrass Japan. Molotov mocked the League as having "not the slightest effect" in Manchuria. The Soviet Union even refused to let the League of Nations commission travel through Soviet territory en route to Manchuria. "You know very well," Molotov declared to a committee of Soviet leaders, "that we have never placed our hopes in the League and its commissions."[13]

"REINFORCE THE DEFENSES"

In what did the Soviet Union place its hopes? It is often argued that Stalin trusted in spheres of influence to secure his borders, with his subjugation of Eastern Europe in 1939 and again in 1945 the prime examples.[14] Less frequently noted is how the Kremlin's ambitions expanded and contracted in the Far East, metastasizing when Stalin turned his attention toward the region, shrinking when Moscow concluded that the costs were high and the benefits questionable. The Soviet Union's definition of its security interests fluctuated not only alongside shifts in the distribution of power, but also by changes in the Kremlin's appetite for risk and its enthusiasm for expansion. Sometimes spheres of influence were seen to be worthwhile, sometimes not.

The 1930s were a period of declining ambition in Asia, reducing the Kremlin's sense that spheres of influence would suit Soviet needs. Soviet leaders perceived a wide array of threats in the early 1930s. Molotov continued to warn about "white bandits . . . the Denikins, Kolchaks, and Wrangels," the leftovers of the old tsarist order who still harbored hopes of casting out the Bolsheviks and retaking power. Aging tsarist generals living in exile were still hallucinating about counterrevolution, but these reactionary forces were far less capable than Soviet leaders imagined.[15]

More dangerous was what Molotov described as the "external danger . . . the hostile bourgeois states . . . who dream of the early downfall of the Soviet government." The Romanians, Latvians, Lithuanians, Estonians, and Poles were prickly new nations that hated and feared Soviet Russia. The French and the British, Europe's great bourgeois powers, remained imperial rivals of the Kremlin in Europe and in Asia. And it was only in 1933 that the United States finally recognized the Soviet Union as the legitimate government of Russia, though Washington remained deeply skeptical of communism.

When the Japanese seized Manchuria and set up a puppet state there, however, any risks to the Soviet position coming from the West were hypothetical. Europe in 1931 was still living the illusion that the Great War might actually have ended all war. The League of Nations included all the European powers, though the United States and the USSR remained on the outside. All the great powers except the USSR had signed the Kellogg-Briand Pact outlawing war.

When Japan seized Manchuria, therefore, the Soviet Union's international environment was as benign as at any point during the 1920s or 1930s. Its western border was as secure as at any time during those two decades. The USSR itself faced the self-inflicted internal turmoil of the shock industrialization and the collectivization of agriculture. But even with the domestic political tumult, the Soviet Union was certainly more powerful in 1931 than it had been in the 1920s, at the peak of its campaign of meddling in China's civil war. Stalin's decision not to confront the Japanese in Manchuria is hard to explain, therefore, by Soviet weakness or vulnerability. In 1931, the Soviet Union was as strong as at any point since the Bolsheviks' seizure of power and faced no other immediate foreign crises. But the Soviet leadership decided that Manchuria was not worth a fight. Nor was a sphere of influence in Manchuria or Northeast Asia likely to bolster Soviet security, Soviet leaders decided, in a reversal of their position from several years earlier.

By 1933, a year and a half after Japan solidified control over Manchuria, Europe's peace began to crumble. The Great Depression caused most countries to shift toward short-sighted, self-serving policies, letting security problems fester. The Nazis' seizure of power in Germany in 1933, meanwhile, created a host of new threats to Europe's peace. Adolf Hitler openly promised to rebuild German military-industrial might, to seize "living space" in Eastern Europe, and to fight the "Judeo-Bolsheviks" that he believed wielded power not only in Germany, but worldwide. Everyone in the USSR remembered how German armies had crashed through Imperial Russia's defenses during World War I, tearing down the tsarist system in the process. Soviet leaders knew they could not trust the Versailles Treaty's limits on German rearmament because they themselves were selling weapons to the Nazis, part of their strategy of stoking competition between capitalist powers.[16]

Suddenly the Soviet Union faced urgent threats on both its European and Asian frontiers. But its tactics in these theaters differed sharply. In Europe, the Kremlin launched an active diplomatic effort, while in Asia the USSR spent several years pleading with Japan to sign a toothless nonaggression pact, building up its military forces in the Far East but otherwise remaining mostly passive.

On the European front, the USSR started by cutting alliances with Germany's rivals. Moscow signed a Treaty of Mutual Assistance with France in 1935, after Hitler formally repudiated the Versailles Treaty's prohibition on Germany rearmament. The French had little choice but to work with the Soviets against Hitler, even though many French policymakers feared the Bolsheviks as much as the Nazis. Britain was harder to deal with because British leaders believed they had room for maneuver. Many in London sympathized with Hitler's critique of the Versailles Treaty as unfair. Many British leaders also wanted to avoid war at any cost. The Royal Navy was still second to none, rivalled only by the Americans, so some British officials thought that German expansion in Europe might not threaten the United Kingdom's far-flung empire. Soviet diplomats reported to Moscow that leading British politicians were advising Prime Minister Neville Chamberlain to "avoid war at the price of any humiliation."[17] Stalin doubted that Britain could be trusted to oppose German expansionism. He thought London was more likely to cut a deal with fellow capitalists in Berlin, creating a "united imperialist front against the USSR."[18]

As Hitler's power grew and as Europe marched closer to war, Stalin took further measures to prepare. He appeased Hitler by continuing secret military cooperation. He explored enhanced alliances with the democracies of France and Britain, though he doubted they had the spine to resist the Nazis. He waged a proxy campaign against Germany by supporting leftists in the Spanish Civil War. He dropped the USSR's rigid opposition to Europe's moderate social democrats—whom he had long derided as "social fascists"— allowing Europe's communists to support center-left "Popular Front" governments in France and Spain, hoping to lock the right out of power.

"Reinforce the defenses," Molotov had urged Soviet Communist Party cadres. On the European front, this meant an active defense.[19] Across the European front, the 1930s were a period of diplomacy, of creativity, of mobilizing communist parties, of arming their military wings, and of subverting potential anti-Soviet alliances. The Soviets believed their defensive perimeter in Europe ran from Madrid to London, Paris to Prague.[20]

"IT IS ONLY NATURAL THAT THEY WILL BE SHOT"

In Asia during the 1930s, however, "reinforcing the defenses" meant something rather different. Soviet foreign policy in the Far East focused less on shaping regional politics than on strengthening the Red Army and purging untrustworthy cadres. Soviet diplomacy remained inert, cautious, and defensive. Stirring the pot in Asia, Stalin had concluded after the disastrous 1920s, risked only trouble. The defensive orientation that Stalin adopted after Japan's seizure of Manchuria in 1931 persisted even as Japan built up its military and then launched a massive invasion of the rest of China in 1937. To be sure, Moscow retained a wide network of agents abroad, using them for espionage and subversion.[21] But the Kremlin's willingness to take risks had declined sharply from the days of managing Sun Yat-sen's furniture budget as he tried to conquer China. In the 1930s, the dominant Soviet strategy was to hunker down, seeking to defend the country's eastern border, thereby preventing foreign subversion or a Japanese invasion.

Gennady Nevelskoy, the naval officer who had claimed the Pacific coast for Russia in the 1850s, had predicted a century earlier that the region was "fated to live like an army camp." Stalin's crash military buildup guaranteed that the region would remain an army camp for the next half century, too. The Soviet Union poured resources into Far Eastern defense, yet the military's demands were insatiable. "Six bombers for the Far East is nothing," Commissar for Defense Voroshilov screamed. "We need to send no less than 50–60 . . . and as soon as possible." The Soviet Union built new fortifications, established new bases, and deployed a dozen additional submarines in the region. By 1939, the Far Eastern Army had twice as many tanks, eight times as many armored cars, and at least 100,000 additional men compared to when the Japanese first seized Manchuria.[22]

Yet the dilemmas of Far Eastern defense were the same as they had always been. Arming the region was scarcely easier in the 1930s than it had been at the outbreak of the Russo-Japanese War in 1904. Despite massive railway investment during Stalin's industrialization campaign, Soviet war preparations still depended on "slow-moving and vulnerable columns of horse transport." Only in 1937 was a second track added to the Amur Railway in the vulnerable section between Vladivostok and Khabarovsk. Meanwhile, almost all the population of Siberia and the Soviet Far East lived in a string of towns along the southern border, within easy striking distance of Japan's armies in Manchuria. The Trans-Siberian Railway was also just across the border, at high risk of being severed by Japanese forces in a conflict. Without the railway, meanwhile, Vladivostok was indefensible. Kamchatka was even more exposed, because it could only by supplied by sea, via shipping routes patrolled by the Japanese navy. This was the perilous military situation that during the 1920s had led Stalin to resurrect Tsar Nicholas II's dream of controlling Manchuria, on the belief that additional territory would provide additional security.[23]

In Europe during the 1930s, the Soviet Union equated territory with security, concluding that effective defense required diplomacy across the continent and military commitments as far away as Spain. In Asia, by contrast, the Kremlin adopted a rigidly defensive posture. Geography suggested the need for a buffer zone along the Manchurian borderlands, but the Soviet leadership decided otherwise. Instead of pursuing an active defense, the Soviet Union stood by as its Asian influence was liquidated during the 1930s. In Japan, the Communist Party was suppressed by police so effectively that Moscow nearly lost communication with its leadership. In most the rest of China, communists were harassed by the government and forced to retreat deep into the countryside.[24]

All this was a marked change from Soviet policy in Asia during the 1920s, a shift that is difficult to explain by what Soviet analysts would have called "objective factors." Military technology was little changed. Japanese aims remained expansive, and the militarists in Tokyo faced few checks on their authority, with many describing in public their dreams of seizing Russian territory in the Far East. China, meanwhile, was decentralized and divided, as it had been in the 1920s. But the Soviet Union, burned by its Chinese and Manchurian misadventures, decided during the 1930s that though the threat of invasion was greater, the best strategy was cautious, even passive, defense.

Moscow's main tactic in Asia during the 1930s was to purge its own population, seeking to eliminate the risk of subversion. Soviet leaders and citizens alike worried about the loyalty of the Far Eastern population in the event of war. One citizen sent a letter to Voroshilov warning of "the rapacious appetite of Japan" and pointing out that "the population of our Far Eastern region is quite small." During the 1930s, the Kremlin arrested or deported many of the ethnic Chinese and Koreans who lived the Far East, fearing that they were collaborating with Japan. Of 35,000 Chinese in the region, 11,000 were arrested and 8,000 deported. Every ethnic Chinese living either in Vladivostok or elsewhere within 60 miles of the border was forcibly moved. Among the region's Korean population, nearly all—over 175,000 people—were relocated, some to as far away as Ukraine. At least several thousand people were arrested after resisting deportation. The region's native population was replaced by "supporters of the Soviet system" brought in from other parts of the USSR.[25]

Brutal treatment of ethnic minorities was coupled with purges of the Far Eastern Army and party elite in 1937 and 1938. *Pravda,* the USSR's most important newspaper, declared that the Far East was infiltrated by spies, saboteurs, and hidden enemies. The Japanese were indeed supporting some anticommunist Russian exiles, but the Kremlin vastly exaggerated the threat. By liquidating nearly all the leaders of the Soviet Union's Far Eastern region, the Stalin-era purges hit the Far East harder than most parts of the USSR. Many residents of the Russian Far East were alleged to have plotted with Japan to separate their region from the USSR. To ensure loyalty, military forces in the Far East were split into three different armies, each reporting directly to Moscow. The Far Eastern province itself was divided in two. Perhaps 15,000 people were killed in the purges, with several hundred thousand repressed in some fashion, whether deported, jailed, or sent to a gulag—8 percent of the region's population.[26]

This brutality addressed threats that were mostly imaginary, but it made Soviet leaders in Moscow feel more secure. The creation of vast labor camps expanded the ethnically Russian population of the Far East, even though these new ethnic Russians were mostly prisoners. Kolyma, one of the largest gulags, had 170,000 prisoners by 1941, of whom 40 percent had been convicted of "counterrevolutionary activities."[27] As thousands of people were deported, purged, jailed, or killed, Soviet leaders displayed growing confidence against the threat of Japanese subversion or a Japanese attack.

When Ivan Maisky, the Soviet ambassador in London, was told by the Japanese ambassador there that the chances of the two countries concluding a nonaggression pact had grown, Maisky gloated in his diary: "Well, well! That's what it means to have a mighty air force in Vladivostok!" When Winston Churchill told Maisky that the Red Army "scared the living daylights out of the Japanese . . . because they understand perfectly well that in the space of a few hours your air force can turn Tokyo and Osaka into piles of ash," Maisky credited the Soviet Union's military buildup and industrialization efforts.[28]

The Soviet Union had the opportunity to test its military strength in a series of small clashes with Japanese forces along the Mongolian and Manchurian borders. Japanese sources reported 152 small scale incidents between 1932 and 1934 alone. Both sides blamed the other, or their Manchurian and Mongolian proxy forces, for the cross-border raids.[29] Though Japanese military officers feared that these skirmishes were probes in preparation for potential offensive operations, Soviet leaders focused solely on defending the border.

Indeed, Moscow's appetite in Asia shrank even as its military power grew. Rather than using its military presence in the Far East like in Europe, where the Kremlin supported left-wing movements and badgered neighbors to offer concessions, the sole aim in Asia remained border defense. In 1936 in Moscow, the Soviets hosted a reception for the Japanese military attaché, who had completed his tour of duty and was returning to Tokyo. At the event, the attaché told Commissar for Defense Voroshilov, "Many border incidents have occurred. . . . All Japanese soldiers on border duty should be ordered to carry a flask of sake in their pockets. Now, Marshall, please order all your troops also to carry a small bottle of vodka with them. When Japanese and Russian soldiers run into each other on the frontier, all they will have to do is . . . share a couple of drinks." Voroshilov objected: "No, colonel, borders don't mean this. . . . If anybody violates the borders, it is only natural that they will be shot." This was a crude statement of the principle that Foreign Minister Maxim Litvinov had articulated immediately after Japan's seizure of Manchuria: "We have no need of other land, but neither will we surrender a single inch."[30]

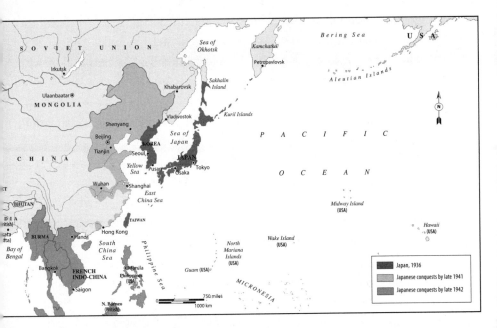

The Pacific Ocean in World War II, 1937–1942

THE STALIN-HITLER PACT

The Soviet Union may have had "no need of other land" in Asia, but the Kremlin had a different strategy on its European frontier. Unlike in Asia, where the Soviet Union's relative strength grew over the course of the 1930s, Stalin's military had no reason for confidence about a potential clash with Germany, which was rearming rapidly. Hitler was "betting on a long war," Soviet intelligence warned. Another military intelligence briefing cautioned that the countries of Central Europe—Poland, Hungary, and especially Czechoslovakia—would expand "the military potential of Germany" once they were incorporated in Hitler's Reich, functioning not as a barrier to German expansion, but as a "trampoline." Hitler's capabilities were strong and growing, and his intentions were clear. The Führer's angry ravings about Judeo-Bolshevism were shaping German foreign policy, Soviet intelligence concluded. One agent sent Moscow information on a meeting of top German leaders reporting that "the main goal of the Fuhrer is the struggle with the real enemies—the Soviets."[31]

By 1939, in the face of growing Nazi military power and Hitler's hatred of communists and of Russians, Stalin worried that a capitalist alliance against

Moscow was not only possible, but likely. Had the British and French not tolerated the Nazi annexation of Austria in 1938, despite promising never to do so? Had they not colluded with the Nazis to dismember Czechoslovakia, with British prime minister Chamberlain infamously declaring in September 1938 that "peace was preserved," even though Czechoslovakia was not? Soviet diplomats in Paris reported that even the French feared that the British would cut a separate peace with Hitler. When Stalin proposed a formal alliance with Britain and France in April 1939, the British avoided giving a clear answer.[32]

Facing these threats, Soviet leaders decided that the best strategy was to push forward Soviet borders, taking even more territory. As talks with the democracies dragged on inconclusively, and as Soviet intelligence reported that a Nazi invasion of Poland was imminent, Stalin cut a deal with Hitler.[33] The neutrality pact between Berlin and Moscow epitomized Stalin's strategy of "forward defense" in Europe—and drew a sharp contrast with his policy in Asia. The aim was to turn Eastern Europe into a buffer zone between Nazi Germany and the Soviet heartland. The Soviet Union's relative weakness, the Kremlin believed, necessitated territorial expansion.

The Stalin-Hitler pact, therefore, divided Eastern Europe and gave the Soviet Union a free hand in the Baltic States, eastern Poland, parts of Romania, and even Finland. This proved an enormous strategic error for the Kremlin, providing Germany an opportunity to defeat France—Russia's historic partner in restraining German power—while Nazi armies grew and gained battlefield experience. Stalin's annexation of Eastern Europe, meanwhile, earned him the enmity of small nations that might have been partners against the Nazis. On top of this, the Nazi-Soviet pact made the two empires direct neighbors. Rather than a buffer zone, the only thing dividing the Red Army from the Wehrmacht was a nearly 1,000-mile-long common border. Stalin equated his new territory, however, with security. On the European front, the Kremlin believed that expansion provided the most trustworthy defense.

"A DAGGER POINTED AT THE HEART OF JAPAN"

In Asia, by contrast, the Soviets stubbornly stuck with the opposite approach. Even as Stalin met with Nazi foreign minister Joachim von Ribbentrop to sign documents dividing Eastern Europe into Nazi and Soviet spheres, the

Red Army in Asia was inflicting a devastating defeat on the Japanese—"the only language these Asiatics understand," Stalin told von Ribbentrop. For the entire summer of 1939, thousands of Soviet and Japanese forces had clashed along a vast but now forgotten battlefield called Nomonhan. By September the Red Army had won a crushing victory. This, Stalin told Ribbentrop, would teach Japan a lesson. "After all," he added, "I am an Asiatic, too, so I ought to know."[34]

Soviet and Japanese forces had skirmished repeatedly along the Manchurian and Mongolian frontiers during the early and mid-1930s, but the scale of fighting intensified toward the end of the decade. First, in June 1937, the two sides clashed over the border along the Amur River, with the Japanese sinking one Soviet gunboat. Then, in summer 1938, the two sides fought near Lake Hasan, on the Soviet border with Japanese-controlled Korea, with the Red Army inflicting three times as many casualties on the Japanese than it suffered.[35]

In 1939, tens of thousands of Soviet and Japanese troops clashed at Nomonhan. Japan suffered at least 20,000 casualties during several months of fighting. The Red Army won a decisive victory, with the Soviet press celebrating the "liquidation" of Japanese forces, proudly listing the Japanese artillery and tanks captured by the Red Army. Japan soon agreed to a ceasefire. Soviet diplomats in Tokyo concluded Japan's losses had "produced an extremely strong impression on all circles of Japanese society . . . [in light of] 'unprecedented' manpower losses by the Japanese army." One Soviet intelligence agent, meanwhile, reported that the defeat caused a "panic" in Tokyo. The Red Army drew similar conclusions, with Soviet general Georgy Zhukov bragging about inflicting an "unheard-of defeat on the handpicked Japanese troops" and describing the battle as "a very useful school of combat experience." Thanks in part to the defeat of the Japanese, one leading historian of the Red Army has concluded that "Stalin believed . . . his army was powerful and ready."[36]

The battlefields on which Soviet and Japanese armies fought—along the shores of the Amur River and the Manchurian frontier—were the same territories where Soviet and Chinese forces had contested control of the Manchurian railroads in 1929, and not far from where Governor-General Muravev had fired off guns during his negotiation with Chinese officials, threatening them unless they surrendered the Amur Valley. Given Stalin's voracious appetite for land in Europe, one might have expected a Soviet military victory in Asia to have been accompanied by annexations. In negotiations after Nomonhan over the location of the Manchurian border, the Soviet Union mostly got its way, with Japan offering concessions to avoid further fighting.[37] Yet Stalin sought nothing more than a favorable border demarcation. Only a decade earlier, he had dreamt of dominating Asia, as had his tsarist predecessors. Now, having established military superiority over Japan, he sought no changes at all.

Stalin was satisfied with the status quo in Asia despite a series of what he believed were foreign policy masterstrokes. In the West, he had faith that the pact with Hitler would provide security on his European border. In Asia, meanwhile, after Nomonhan, Japan was stretched thin. Its armies had already invaded China, pushing south from their Manchurian stronghold, seizing Beijing, Shanghai, Nanjing, and Wuhan, as well as many of the ports on China's southern coast.

The Chinese government seemed unlikely to win the war—Chiang Kai-shek's military situation was "tense and difficult," Soviet agents reported—but so long as China kept fighting, most of Japan's armies would be tied up. And China's "powerful anti-Japanese movement" should not be underestimated, advised Soviet diplomats in China, noting that Chiang was rearming with foreign help. Soviet military intelligence reported that many Japanese officers advocated further expansion along China's Yangzi River and toward Guangdong Province.[38] This would embroil Japan yet further in China, tying down resources far from Soviet borders.

Along the Soviet border in Manchuria, meanwhile, Japanese puppet forces were "weak," Soviet agents reported, while the Japanese military itself was so worried about its position that it was sending new recruits there rather than to active battlefields in China. "Why are you so afraid?" one Japanese official in Moscow asked, noting the scale of Red Army forces in the Far East. "Your aviation . . . is a dagger pointed at the heart of Japan."[39]

The Soviet victory over Japanese forces at Nomonhan changed nothing about Soviet strategy, however. The balance of power shifted, but Soviet tactics and objectives did not. The overreaches of the 1920s had been seared in the minds of Soviet leaders. In contrast to Europe, where Stalin believed his position was weak and yet used his negotiations with the Nazis to grab more territory, Stalin declined to push forward against the Japanese despite the Red

Army's victory in battle. In Asia, "reinforcing the defenses" continued to mean hunkering down, not the construction of buffer zones. Moscow sought nothing more than a meaningless nonaggression treaty with Japan—a piece of paper that would remain valid only so long as the Red Army retained the upper hand.

"LET US DRINK TO THE ASIATICS!"

As the struggle at Nomonhan was winding down in September 1939, Nazi armies rolled into western Poland, prompting the British and French to declare war on Germany. Stalin stuck with his policy of active defense on the European front. Having secured his Asian frontier with the victory at Nomonhan in summer 1939, Stalin invaded Poland from the east, dividing the country in accordance with the secret Nazi-Soviet agreement. Shortly thereafter he threatened to invade the Baltic States unless they allowed tens of thousands of Soviet soldiers to occupy their territory. Two months later, in November, the Red Army invaded Finland. The next summer, Stalin bullied Romania into surrendering its eastern territory of Bessarabia, which the Soviet Union promptly annexed.

The situation in Europe was darkening, but Stalin continued to redraw borders in his favor, bolting new European territories onto the Soviet state, presuming that more land in Europe meant more security, too. He kept expanding westward even as Hitler won a series of victories over Poland, then Denmark, Norway, Belgium, the Netherlands, and—shockingly—France, which surrendered in June 1940. As the Battle of Britain raged over the English Channel, it seemed for a moment in mid-1940 that even the British Empire might sue for a compromise peace. Such an outcome would have been disastrous for the Soviet position. But it did not deter Stalin from continuing to grab territory in Eastern Europe. He finished occupying Romania's province of Bessarabia, for example, after the fall of France. His appetite in Europe grew alongside Hitler's power.

There was a strange contradiction between Stalin's strategies on his western and eastern fronts. It was in Asia that Stalin's armies had demonstrated their military superiority by inflicting a stinging defeat on the Japanese. Yet it was in Europe that Stalin "wanted to change the old equilibrium," as he told Western diplomats. In the first months of war, German armies had proven themselves far stronger than anyone expected. In comparison with the Nazi Blitzkrieg, the Red Army performed dismally in Eastern Europe. Its war with tiny Finland, launched in late November 1939, was a disaster. The Finns fought the Red Army to a standstill in subzero temperatures in the forests of Karelia, before finally agreeing to surrender some territory around Leningrad. The Winter War, as the clash with Finland became known, did not provide a reassuring message about Soviet military capacity in Europe. Yet Stalin retained his belief that the best strategy in Europe was to grab yet more land.[40]

In Asia, where the Red Army's track record was far stronger, Stalin made no demands after his military victory beyond asking the Japanese to sign an unenforceable nonaggression treaty, by which both sides promised to retain the status quo. When the Japanese proposed that the USSR abandon its support for Chiang's Nationalist government and the Chinese communist rebels, the Kremlin did not object.[41] Instead, it bent over backward to address Japan's concerns, treating Tokyo's willingness to sign a nonaggression pact as a great diplomatic success rather than a humiliating concession to a power that it had defeated in battle the previous year.

The combination of military victory with diplomatic concessions was not a usual feature of Stalin's diplomatic playbook. But he had been embarrassed too often in the Far East to ask for anything more. He had been burned by overinvesting in Sun Yat-sen, then burned again by trusting in Chiang and the influence of left-wing forces in China's Nationalist Party. Now, simply avoiding entanglement in Asian affairs was success enough. He went out of his way to show respect to the Japanese. After negotiating the pact in Moscow, Stalin personally escorted Japan's ambassador to the train station, a courtesy that Stalin never gave to other world leaders.[42] Though the Japanese army sat only dozens of miles from Vladivostok, the Kremlin never considered padding Soviet defenses by adding a small buffer zone in Manchuria or Korea. It was not that Soviet leaders failed to wring concessions out of the Japanese. They never really tried.

Less than two months later, contrary to all of Stalin's expectations, Nazi armies crashed across Soviet frontiers in June 1941, besieging Leningrad and reaching the outskirts of Moscow by autumn. Once war with Germany began, Stalin's peace deal with the Japanese seemed prescient. The Japanese, meanwhile, soon attacked Pearl Harbor; Hitler declared war on the United States five days later. By late 1941, the Soviet Union was allied with the United States in the struggle against Nazi Germany, while maintaining a studious neutrality in the conflict between the United States and Japan.[43]

So long as Nazi troops were deep in Soviet territory, the Kremlin focused all its energy on the European front. Whenever Soviet diplomats considered the postwar world, they struggled to conceive of substantial aims in Asia. In late 1941, one Soviet diplomat set out a postwar plan to Stalin, arguing that after the war the USSR would face a "united front of the capitalist powers," and should therefore prioritize its European borders: "Germany, Hungary, Romania, and Finland." This required "defanging Germany and its allies," both by changing borders and by imposing reparations. Only then could the USSR think of other regions, including the Pacific coast. In Asia, this diplomat's main proposal was to better protect Soviet sea lines of communication, via the straits around the Kurils and Sakhalin Island. So long as Soviet sea lanes were free, this official saw no other Soviet interests in Asia worth mentioning.[44]

During the war Soviet foreign policy in Asia sought only to maintain neutrality. This was no easy task, given that all the region's great powers were involved in the war. After the Nazi invasion, the Soviet Union had mined the waters of its Pacific coast, accidentally sinking multiple Japanese ships. The Japanese, meanwhile, complained that Vladivostok served as a port for US shipments of military supplies—intended, the Kremlin promised, for use against the Nazis. The Japanese also feared that the Soviet Union might sell airbases on Kamchatka, or even Kamchatka itself, to the United States.

Given that Kamchatka was as easy to access from Alaska as from Vladivostok, Tokyo's fears were not unfounded. The United States did ask for airbases in the Russian Far East, though the Kremlin repeatedly rebuffed these requests in the early stages of the war. Thousands of US-made airplanes nevertheless flew from Alaska to the Soviet Far East as part of Lend-Lease aid. Because these were intended for the USSR's war against the Nazis, they did not violate the Soviet-Japanese Neutrality Pact, though Tokyo looked on warily.

When US warplanes occasionally made emergency landings in Soviet territory, Japan lodged vitriolic complaints. Even American vice president Henry Wallace's visit to Siberia in 1944 sparked Japanese anger. Yet Moscow and

Tokyo kept relations stable even as they waged war on each other's allies. Japanese ambassador Yosuke Matsuoka told Stalin that he attributed the two countries' relationship to shared values: the Japanese practiced "moral communism" and the Soviets had "political-economic communism." Stalin saw things differently: "You are an Asiatic. So am I." "We're all Asiatics," Ambassador Matsuoka responded. "Let us drink to the Asiatics!"[45]

"RUSSIA MUST WIPE OUT THIS BLACK SPOT"

The world war transformed how all the great powers viewed international politics. The British started the war as the world's greatest empire, on which the sun never set: Canada, the Caribbean Islands, several Pacific archipelagos, New Zealand, Australia, Singapore, Malaya, Burma, India, South Africa, most of the East African coast, the Persian Gulf, the Suez Canal, Cyprus, Malta, and more. Churchill had promised a war of "blood, toil, tears, and sweat," and the British Empire ended the war bankrupt and exhausted. India left the empire just two years after the war's end, setting off two decades of decolonization, in which the maps of Africa and Asia would be redrawn.

For the Americans, the war proved they could deploy power with ease in Asia and Europe, defeating rivals on their home turf. The United States acquired a global network of military facilities, while the retreat of the British and the defeat of the Germans and Japanese opened new lands to American influence. Most US politicians envisioned a postwar retreat from Europe and a substantial drawdown from Asia. President Roosevelt hoped that the "Four Policemen"—the United States, Britain, the USSR, and China—could keep order in their respective regions, while the United States could rely again on the Atlantic and Pacific Oceans for defense. Yet as the end of the war approached, and as the great powers built new generations of strategic bombers that could fly ever farther, the oceans seemed like less trustworthy defensive barriers. American leaders began to consider retaining the military presence abroad that they had built for the war.[46]

For the Soviet Union, too, the war transformed thinking about global politics. "After the defeat of Hitler," recounted one of Stalin's deputies, the Soviet leader "believed he was in the same position as Alexander I after the defeat of Napoleon—that he could dictate the rules." Over the course of the war, the Red Army had surprised everyone, including Soviet leaders themselves, by annihilating Nazi armies on the plains of Eastern Europe. By mid-1945, the Soviet Union stood confidently astride all of Eurasia.

As Soviet power grew, the country's ambitions expanded. Stalin began to think not only of Soviet borders but also of world maps. After the war with Napoleon, Tsar Alexander I had reorganized Europe, reducing the size of France, expanding Prussia, forging a confederation of the small German states, recognizing Swiss neutrality, reshaping the Italian duchies and city states, even reshuffling ownership of former French colonies as far afield as the Caribbean and Ceylon. When Stalin looked at the portraits of Imperial Russian generals Mikhail Kutuzov and Alexsander Suvorov hanging in the Kremlin conference room, he thought not primarily of Alexander I's rule making at the Congress of Vienna, but rather of the territorial changes that Alexander's generals had won on the battlefield.[47]

Alexander I had also overseen the expansion of Russia's ambitions in Asia. His explorers and naval captains had pushed across the North Pacific, establishing an archipelago of settlements along the Pacific Rim from Kamchatka to Kauai, Sitka to San Francisco. Alexander's Asian ambitions were partly the result of a perceived power vacuum in the Pacific, but they were mostly driven by dreams of expansion—a feature of great expectations rather than objective calculations.

Stalin, too, saw a power vacuum in Asia when he surveyed the Pacific Rim at the end of World War II, but like Alexander, his perception was as much the result of his own optimism as of objective changes in the distribution of power. Before 1944, Stalin's policy in Asia had been one of strategic defense. The embarrassing defeats of the 1920s had reduced Stalin's interest, convincing Soviet leaders that the costs of advancing in Asia were high and the benefits few. Hence the policy of nervously defending the border with Manchuria, declining to use the Soviet military advantage.

Hence also the Soviet acceptance of the status quo in Mongolia, a Soviet protectorate that China claimed as its own. The Kremlin armed and funded the warlord who governed China's westernmost Xinjiang province, along the borders of Soviet Central Asia, but even here the primary aim was not to expand Soviet territory but to keep Japan out.

During the war, the Soviet Union long refused to join the Americans and the British in their struggle against Japan. Instead, after Pearl Harbor, the

Soviet Union observed strict neutrality vis-à-vis Tokyo, maintaining normal diplomatic relations until the final weeks of the war. It even let Japan drill for oil on Soviet territory on Sakhalin Island while Soviet allies torpedoed Japanese battleships and firebombed Tokyo.[48] The only expansion of Soviet territory in Asia was the 1944 annexation of Tannu Tuva, a sparsely populated land nestled between the Soviet Union and Mongolia, which until the 1930s lacked its own written language, and which the Soviets had long governed as a de facto colony.[49] Except for this, Stalin's policy in Asia between 1930 and 1944 was one of strategic defense.

By 1944, however, Soviet thinking about Asia began to shift. Simply holding the line against Japanese expansion no longer seemed an adequate goal for a country that was powerful enough to defeat the Nazis. It was natural, perhaps, that Soviet confidence in Asia grew alongside its military successes in Europe. But Soviet ambitions grew, too. Before the war, Stalin had wanted buffer zones in Europe but not in Asia. As Soviet power expanded, however, new territory in Asia began to seem more appealing. The mistakes of the 1920s began to recede from the memory of Soviet leaders.

The policy of strategic defense in Asia that had defined Soviet policy since the collapse of Stalin's revolutionary optimism in the 1920s was therefore abandoned. It was replaced with a new faith, hope that after Japan's defeat the Soviet Union could become the greatest power in Asia, spreading its influence and its political system. At the end of the war in Europe, the Japanese army still controlled the most valuable territory in Asia: Korea and Manchuria, the Chinese coast and Taiwan, Saigon and Singapore.[50] But Japan was on the verge of defeat, and all this territory now seemed up for grabs. Moreover, the Kremlin's worldview had shifted. It was no longer enough to maintain existing borders in Asia. Soviet leaders began to think in terms of expansion. As one Soviet diplomat told an American journalist, after the war Stalin thought of "security in terms of territory—the more you've got, the safer you are."[51]

The Kremlin's appetite for Asian influence and Asian territory grew rapidly beginning in 1944. In January, Ambassador Maisky wrote that "the Soviet Union is uninterested in unleashing a war against Japan, but is very interested in a military defeat of Japan" by the United States, hoping that such a result would allow for border changes on Sakhalin Island and the Kuril Archipelago. Just months later, Soviet ambitions had expanded far beyond these islands. In July, the Soviet ambassador in Tokyo wrote to Moscow that after

Japan's defeat the Kremlin must dominate not only the islands off the Pacific coast, but all of East Asia. Listing Soviet wartime aims in Asia, he mentioned "the status of Manchuria," "the Chinese Eastern Railway . . . seeing that it was ceded to Japan under pressure," "Korean independence," "the Liaotung Peninsula of China, with the former, actually Russian, town of Dairen [Dalny], and the Russian naval fortress of Port Arthur." Tsar Nicholas II's territorial dreams had suddenly reemerged. The Soviet ambassador wanted not only wanted to resurrect the old Manchurian empire, but to seek "the complete annulment of the Portsmouth Treaty," which marked the humiliating end to the 1904–1905 Russo-Japanese War. "Russia must wipe out this black spot," he declared, and resurrect its role as a great power in Asia.[52]

THE YALTA CONFERENCE

Stalin knew that power and influence could be acquired only by struggle. Pointing at the vast Soviet territory colored red on a world map, he declared to a comrade visiting from Yugoslavia in 1944 that the British and Americans—his ostensible allies—"will never accept the idea that so great a space should be red, never, never!"[53] By early 1945, Stalin's armies were in the final stages of vanquishing the Nazis on the battlefield. He knew that he must next outmaneuver the capitalists at the negotiating table. It was one thing to dream of world maps. Getting the other great powers to agree to restructure international borders in the Soviet Union's favor was substantially more complicated. To so, Stalin hosted his two wartime partners, Winston Churchill and Franklin D. Roosevelt, in an old tsarist place near the Crimean resort town of Yalta.

The British and Americans may have been the USSR's wartime allies, but Stalin did not believe they would be postwar friends—either with each other, or with the USSR. The "Big Three," as the leaders were known, tried to keep up appearances of alliance. Churchill, long an ardent opponent of socialism at home and abroad, made a toast "to the proletariat masses of the world."[54] Roosevelt went further, offering not only rhetorical compromises, but real territory, in a futile effort to appease Stalin's desire to redraw the map.

Each of the "Big Three" believed his country deserved a special role in setting the rules of the postwar order. There were vast differences, however, in what this vision of a special role entailed. "Marshal Stalin," notes from the Yalta Conference record, "made it quite plain on a number of occasions that he felt that the three Great Powers which had borne the brunt of the war and had liberated from German domination the small powers should have the unanimous right to preserve the peace of the world. . . . He said that it was ridiculous to believe that Albania would have an equal voice with the three Great Powers who had won the war"—a convenient position for someone seeking a dominant position in Eastern Europe and East Asia after the war. Neither Roosevelt nor Churchill desired complete equality between nations, though they each tried ineffectively to stand up for "the rights of people to govern themselves," at least in places like Poland and elsewhere in Central Europe, where there had been functioning nation-states before the Nazi and Soviet invasions in 1939.[55]

Western demands that countries in Central Europe deserved autonomy were ultimately sacrificed to military realities: the Soviet Union had troops in the area; the United Kingdom and the United States did not. In Asia, too, military thinking drove Roosevelt's policies. He was fixated on the challenge of defeating Japan. It was not yet clear that the atomic bomb that US scientists were developing would work, and, even if it did, there was no guarantee that the bomb would win the war. At the Yalta Conference, therefore, Roosevelt subordinated all other goals in Asia to guaranteeing that the USSR would finally join the war against Japan, as it had promised previously that it would do after the defeat of Germany.

At Yalta, Stalin reiterated his willingness to join the Pacific War, provided that certain "political conditions" were met. One such condition, agreed to in advance with American diplomats, was the transfer of the "the southern half of Sakhalin and the Kuril Islands" to the USSR, thereby securing Soviet shipping lanes to and from Pacific Ocean ports. Second was "that the Soviet Union be given the use of a warm water port at the end of the South Manchurian Railroad," with Stalin proposing Dairen, formerly called Dalny, when it had been the centerpiece of Tsar Nicholas II's Far Eastern empire. The third condition, Stalin told Roosevelt, was use "of the Manchurian railways," with Stalin noting that "the Czars had use of the line running from Manchouli to Harbin and from there to Dairen and Port Arthur." These three conditions, alongside a separate US-Soviet deal to manage Korea jointly after the war, amounted to a resuscitation of Russia's position in the Far East before the disastrous 1904 war with Japan.

When Roosevelt proposed that Soviet railway and port rights in Manchuria be managed together with China, which ostensibly controlled Manchuria, Stalin insisted: "If these conditions are not met," he told Roosevelt, "it would be difficult . . . to explain to the Soviet people why Russia was entering the war against Japan. They understood clearly the war against Germany, which had threatened the very existence of the Soviet Union, but they would not understand why Russia would enter a war against a country with which they had no great trouble. . . . However, if these political conditions were met, the people would understand the national interest involved and it would be very much easier to explain the decision to the Supreme Soviet."[56]

Roosevelt assented to Stalin's requests in Asia, just as he gave way to Stalin's demands over Poland and Central Europe. The Kremlin's vision of a restructured Asia faced only one remaining problem: the USSR wanted to take territory from the Japanese, but the two countries were not at war. Indeed, the Japanese were offering the USSR concessions in a desperate effort to preserve Soviet neutrality. Tokyo proposed handing over certain islands and promised to make Manchuria neutral territory.[57] It pledged to govern Asia jointly with the USSR after the war—and thus exclude the United States—hoping that this would appease the Kremlin.

Soviet leaders, however, were unimpressed. The Soviet ambassador in Tokyo warned Moscow not to expect "changes in Japan's position in Manchuria, Korea, Kwantung, or North China" except in case of Japan's "military defeat." The Soviet Union, therefore, began preparing for war. At the Yalta Conference with Roosevelt and Churchill, Stalin had promised to join the war and "break Japan's spine." Any extension of the Soviet-Japanese Neutrality Pact was therefore unacceptable. Nor could the Soviet Union wait until 1951, the year it expired. "The Pacific War will end much sooner," one Soviet diplomat warned, "and we must have our hands free by then."[58]

"EXPAND THE BORDERS OF OUR FATHERLAND"

On April 5, 1945, the Soviet Union freed its hands by notifying Tokyo that it would not extend the neutrality pact. A month later, Soviet leaders convened and decided for war. The only question was when the war would start. America's dropping of the atomic bomb on Hiroshima on August 6, 1945, set the schedule. Stalin's spies had reported many details of the American nuclear weapon program, but Stalin had not been forewarned of the date the bomb would be dropped. Fearing that Japan might surrender before the Soviet Union could enter the war, Stalin accelerated his invasion schedule. On August 9, the day the second bomb was dropped on Nagasaki, Tokyo was notified that "the Soviet Union will consider itself in a state of war with Japan." The Kremlin ordered thousands of Red Army soldiers to storm over the border. Sakhalin, the Kuril Islands, Manchuria, and Port Arthur: in scarcely three months after the Nazi surrender, Soviet armies had reestablished the borders of Tsar Nicholas I's Asian empire before the Russo-Japanese War.[59]

Japan capitulated quickly, though Soviet forces continued fighting on the Kuril Islands for several days after the surrender to ensure that Red Army occupied them before the Americans. Though the Soviet Union had justified its declaration of war on Japan by telling Tokyo's ambassador that "Japan is fighting with the United States and Britain, which are the allies of the Soviet Union," the wartime allies were rapidly becoming postwar rivals. Competition with the United States shaped some Soviet actions, for example when a stern warning from Washington dissuaded the Kremlin from trying to occupy Japan's northernmost main island of Hokkaido. Moscow also chose to divide Korea with the Americans along the 38th parallel—despite some Soviet military officials' belief that new naval bases were "necessary"—with Moscow judging instead that it was best to avoid an unnecessary conflict with Washington.[60]

More striking, though, was the expansion of Soviet ambitions in the face of horrifying evidence of America's military power in Hiroshima and Nagasaki. The atomic decimation of two of Japan's largest cities was the most visceral example of American military might. The US Navy's "island hopping" campaign across the Pacific, meanwhile, had proven that the Pacific Ocean was no insurmountable barrier, while the Normandy landings had demonstrated that vast armies could be landed by sea. In 1945, after Japan's surrender, the United States landed troops in China and Korea to enforce the departure of Japanese armies. Soviet military observers watched nervously, for example, as four US aircraft carriers sailed along the North China coast around the approaches to Port Arthur in September 1945.[61]

Evidence of America's military capabilities and willingness to project power in Asia did not deter Soviet ambitions. Some historians have argued that the United States ordered the atomic bombing of Hiroshima and Nagasaki to frighten Moscow.[62] The Kremlin did not act as though it felt threatened. Quite the contrary: as the atomic bombs exploded in summer 1945, Stalin announced that he was casting off his defensive position in Asia and re-embracing the expansive goals of his tsarist predecessors. It was Tsar Nicholas to whom Stalin turned. "As is well known," Stalin declared upon the end of the Pacific War in August, "in February 1904, when the negotiations between Japan and Russia were still going on, Japan, taking advantage of the weakness of the tsarist government, unexpectedly and treacherously, without a declaration of war—attacked our country." He continued: "The Russian defeat in the Russo-Japanese War left a painful memory in the consciousness of the Russian people. It left a black mark on our history. We the old generation have waited for forty years to remove this mark. This day has finally come."[63]

The day had come not only to reestablish Russia's position before the humiliating defeat by Japan in 1905 but also to reverse the retreat that Stalin himself began around 1930. In some cases, Stalin's aims were even broader than the tsars'. In the Korean lands about which Aleksandr Bezobrazov had dreamed, the Soviet Union helped establish Kim Il Sung as a communist autocrat. In Manchuria, meanwhile, Soviet forces reasserted control over the railroad system that Count Witte had built, and over a territory that Russia had not controlled for several decades. The railroad—which a decade earlier Stalin had sold, on the grounds that owning it provided few benefits for the USSR—was now again a priority. Stalin received regular updates on matters as detailed as railroad staffing decisions, involving his top lieutenants in the issue, too. To get the railroad running after the war, the Kremlin poured funds into its reconstruction. This was supplemented by the establishment of local governments and the dispersal of funds to support Soviet operations in Manchuria. "Our political influence in Manchuria has grown markedly," one Soviet official reported proudly in 1946. Soon Stalin was receiving admiring letters from Chinese students studying the "great Russian language, the language of Lenin and Stalin."[64]

The balance of power in Asia after 1945 had not obviously shifted in Moscow's favor. True, the United States had defanged Japan. But it had done so by proving that the US military could cross the Pacific Ocean with ease and obliterate Japanese cities in devastating bombing raids. Japan's armies were gone, but America's strategic bombers remained. Atomic weapons did, too.

American bombers that could reach Tokyo or Nagasaki could also strike Kamchatka or Vladivostok. The Soviet Union had been devastated by the war, while America was the strongest it had ever been. In 1945, at the end of the war, the United States landed marines in China, and the US Navy patrolled the seas between China and Japan.

Stalin's perception of an opening in Asia was therefore as much the result of expansionary enthusiasm as it was a sober calculation of the military balance. Tsar Nicholas's empire was restored. Molotov dreamt even of Alaska, before concluding that "the time was not yet ripe."[65] Yet even if Alaska remained beyond the Kremlin's reach, much had been gained. As the world's map was redrawn, the Kremlin perceived a new chance to expand Soviet power in Asia—and expand its territory, too. "My task as minister of foreign affairs was to expand the borders of our Fatherland," Molotov remembered proudly from his retirement. "It seems that Stalin and I coped with this task quite well."[66]

"CHINA HAS STOOD UP!"

Soviet ambitions expanded alongside the Kremlin's perception that, having won the war, it had a right to redraw the world map. But this was not the only impetus to growing ambitions. Ideas and politics mattered, too—notably the sense that in Asia Soviet ideas were winning. Over the course of the 1940s, revolutionary Marxism-Leninism seemed to be taking root in North Korea. More importantly, it was victorious in China's civil war. Perhaps, these events suggested, even the expansive territorial aims that the Soviet Union had set out in the postwar period underplayed the opening that was available to Soviet influence.

Immediately after the war, in 1945, the Soviet Union had looked at China primarily through a lens of realpolitik. Manchuria must be incorporated into the Soviet Union's sphere of influence, with its railroads and its ports coming under Soviet domination. But the rest of China, Moscow believed, would be governed by Chiang Kai-shek, ideally in charge of a weak and divided government, as the country had been ruled for decades. Even before the war with Japan ended, Stalin signed a treaty with Chiang's government recognizing its legitimacy and leaving Mao Zedong's communists hanging out to dry. In exchange for this treaty, Chiang's China tolerated Russian dominance of the Manchurian railways on the grounds that, as Stalin reminded the Chinese, "Russians built them." Port Arthur, the former Russian naval base, was also "built by Russia," Molotov added. Once Chiang accepted this deal—the Kremlin recognized his government, and he recognized Soviet dominance in Manchuria—Moscow's ambassador in China proudly reported seeing "no contradictions" in relations between the two powers.[67]

The Soviet Union worked with Chiang's Nationalist government because, like most analysts at the time, the Kremlin believed that Chiang would govern China long after World War II ended. After the collapse of the revolutionary project in China in the 1920s, Stalin still viewed the Chinese communists as untrustworthy. During the war, after all, Mao had repeatedly declined to obey Soviet requests. On five different occasions between 1941 and 1943, Stalin had ordered the Chinese communists to send forces into North China to tie down Japanese forces there; each time Mao refused. Mao himself told colleagues that "we should listen to the Soviets, but we should not listen to them completely." This approach triggered Soviet fears that the Chinese were what Stalin called "radish communists"—red on the outside, white on the inside. One US diplomat reported that Molotov believed that "the so-called Chinese communists are not in fact communists at all."[68]

On top of this, Soviet policymakers struggled to imagine that Mao could win China's long-running civil war. Stalin repeatedly told aides that "the CCP and working class are still too weak to become the leaders in the struggle against the aggressor." China's communists had only a million troops with little heavy weaponry, while Chiang had 4.5 million men armed with modern technology. Because of these asymmetries, the Kremlin bet that Chiang would continue to rule China. During the war, the Soviets had directed nearly all their military aid to Chiang, not to the communists. One historian found that the Soviet Union provided the communists with only "6 antiaircraft guns and 120 machine guns" during the war—vastly less than it had provided Nazi Germany in the years before World War II. "For the bourgeoisie, weapons," the Chinese communists had grumbled, but "for the proletariat, books."[69]

China's communists, meanwhile, were trying to improve ties with America. Communist leader Zhou Enlai told one US envoy that he believed that Chinese democracy "should follow the American pattern" and pledged his support for "industrialization, free enterprise, and the development of individuality." The Chinese communists turned to the United States because the Soviet Union was ambivalent about their revolutionary efforts. When the Soviet Union invaded Japanese-occupied Manchuria in 1945, Red Army units received orders that "in Manchurian cities freed from the Japanese, Chinese flags can be raised by administrations appointed by Chiang Kai-shek"—not by the Chinese communist forces that were ostensibly the Soviet Union's ideological allies. Stalin also let the Nationalists deploy representatives alongside the Red Army during the invasion. But after World War II ended, Stalin also began more actively supporting China's communists with weaponry, notably by shipping them armaments the Soviets had captured from defeated Nazi armies.[70]

Yet neither Stalin's ambivalence nor Chiang's armies could reverse the rise of China's communists. A decade of Japanese rule in Manchuria had weakened right-wing Chinese forces and empowered the left. The communists happily accepted into their ranks Chinese soldiers who had served in Japanese-led armies, bolstering communist forces. Chiang, meanwhile, struggled to craft a vision that would appeal to landlords and peasants alike. Mao's communists had a clearer message—"Liberate all of China!"—and by spring 1946 communist forces controlled Manchuria's urban areas. Over the next three years, they swept their rivals from the country's biggest cities—Beijing and Tianjin, Nanjing and Shanghai—until Chiang himself had no choice but to flee to Taiwan. "China has stood up!" Mao declared.[71]

Even in the final stages of China's civil war, however, Stalin's attitude toward Mao and the Chinese communists remained cautious. Stalin personally managed the China portfolio, keeping "all things related to China in his own hands," one aide remembered. "Even minute requests . . . were forwarded to Stalin alone." His approach toward Mao remained skeptical, influenced by the disastrous experience with the Chinese communists during the 1920s. In summer 1948, for example, when the Chinese communists had Chiang's forces on the run, Stalin refused to let Mao visit the Soviet Union—even though Mao had already acquired a new pair of shoes for the trip—on the grounds that the Soviet "grain harvest" meant that "top party officials are leaving for the provinces." In January 1949, as Chinese communist forces mopped up their last remaining Nationalist Party rivals, Mao again requested to visit Moscow, and was again rejected, with the Kremlin telling the Chinese to "avoid being hasty."[72]

Stalin continued to worry that the Chinese communists lacked ideological orthodoxy, wondering in late 1948 whether they might side with Josip Broz Tito, the Yugoslav communist leader who disputed Stalin's status as the leader of international socialism. Stalin simultaneously feared that the Chinese might be too leftist, urging them in March 1949 to adopt a policy of moderation and to "cooperate" with the "national bourgeoisie," avoiding the radicalism that doomed Stalin's early efforts in China. Mostly, he continued to worry that they could never win. In April 1949, Stalin hesitated about whether to extend loans to China's communists as they reached the final stages of their military struggle. "Are there any pilots?" he worried to a colleague when considering the state of the People's Liberation Army in July 1949. "Are there any seamen?" There were not many, in part because the Soviet Union had long avoided helping build the Chinese communists' military.[73]

Stalin's own views shifted, however, along with the correlation of forces in China. By 1949, Mao's stunning victories were undeniable. Chiang's bourgeois regime had survived Mikhail Borodin's conspiracies in the 1920s and war with Japan in the 1930s. Yet Mao's peasant armies were tearing it to the ground. Perhaps other bourgeois governments were weaker than expected. Perhaps, Stalin began to wonder, Soviet-style systems were primed for expansion.

By 1949, "people's democracies" had been established across Eastern Europe, from Poland to Romania. As the Cold War ramped up in Europe, Western powers dug in against communists, stamping out left-wing movements at home and mobilizing against them abroad. As early as 1946, senior Western leaders had declared the existence of an "iron curtain" across Europe and urged containment of Soviet influence. By 1948, the Marshall Plan had signaled the division of Europe into two separate economic blocs, while an intensifying standoff between the United States and the USSR over the status of divided Berlin demonstrated that Washington was willing to deploy its vast military power to preserve its position in Europe.[74]

In Asia, however, the door seemed open to the expansion of Soviet influence not only to the former borders of Tsar Nicholas II's empire, but beyond. Asia seemed ripe for the expansion of communist parties, too. Japan's rightists—the great enemies of communism across Asia—were being defanged in the late 1940s by the US occupation. Chiang's anti-communist forces had been chased out of China. And China was not the only Asian country with a communist party. In the northern halves of Korea and Vietnam, communist parties were also growing in influence, led by "solid and intelligent" communists, Stalin believed.[75] Even India, which gained its independence form the British Empire in 1947, was flirting with left-wing ideas, opening space for socialist advances.

When several Chinese leaders visited Moscow in summer 1949, Stalin hosted a dinner in their honor. A global transformation was underway, he told them. The simultaneous collapse of Imperial Japan and Chiang's China had created a surge of optimism, ambition, and even revolutionary fervor that was impossible to resist. The Soviet Union was shifting into forward gear, further abandoning its pre-1945 policy of strategic defense in Asia. Now was the time for offensive thinking. "The center of revolution shifted from the West to the East," Stalin told his guests, "and now it has further shifted to China and East Asia. I saw that you already play an important role . . . but at the same time I say that your responsibility has grown even more. You must do your duty." The aim? "Revolution in the countries of East Asia." The question wasn't only China's future, but Asia's and the world's. "Let's add to China's population of 475 million the populations of India, Burma, Indonesia, the Philippines. . . . The peoples of Asia are looking to you."[76]

"THE TEACHER OF REVOLUTIONS"

On October 1, 1949, Mao Zedong proclaimed the creation of the People's Republic of China in front of cheering crowds on Beijing's Tiananmen Square. Two months later he arrived in Moscow, after finally receiving Stalin's approval to visit. In theory, the two countries were revolutionary allies. In practice, Moscow was the big brother. "If on some questions differences should arise," one Chinese delegation promised Stalin, China's Communist Party, "having outlined its point of view, will submit and will resolutely carry out decisions of the Soviet Communist Party." Mao needed Soviet acquiescence as he solidified control over his borders and built an industrial base. He had no choice but to tolerate Soviet haughtiness in exchange for aid, at least so long as he was preparing his revolution at home. On February 17, 1950, in his farewell speech at Moscow's railway station, Mao cited the "complete understanding and profound friendship" between the two countries before declaring: "Long live the teacher of revolutions the world over, the bosom friend of the Chinese People, Comrade Stalin!"[77]

Mao was not the only Soviet client looking for favors from Stalin. Kim Il Sung, whom the Soviet Union had installed as leader of the the northern half of Korea, had grand designs of uniting the peninsula under his control. Kim wanted to invade the South, but he could not succeed without support from his Soviet patrons. He repeatedly badgered Stalin with requests for permission to invade—sending forty-eight telegrams on the subject, by one count—but made little progress. The lavish celebrations of Stalin's seventieth birthday that Kim organized across North Korea did not appear to help either. In September 1949, for example, Kim asked the Soviet ambassador for "permission to begin military operations against the south . . . if the international situation permits, they are ready to move further to the south." But the international situation did not permit, the Kremlin decided. It sent in response a long list of questions to better assess the North Koreans' fighting potential, the answers to which proved that Kim's armies were not ready for war. In fall 1949, even Kim admitted to the Soviet embassy that it might be "politically disadvantageous" if the North were to start the conflict. "North Korea does not have the necessary superiority of military forces," Soviet analysis concluded. "Very little has been done . . . to organize forces for a general uprising."[78]

Yet as the revolution in China progressed, Stalin's appetite did, too. The proclamation of the People's Republic of China in late 1949 made Soviet leaders wonder if Asia's other socialist and communist parties might also defeat their rivals in civil wars. Korea, a territory Stalin had mostly ignored when Asia's postwar borders were drawn in 1945, suddenly began to seem like an appealing avenue for expansion. Mao's ramshackle party of peasants had cast out a government backed by the great powers. Could not other communist parties replicate this success?

Mao had vast armies and was "no longer busy with internal fighting," Stalin mused, so Chinese forces could now be deployed in Korea. The Communist Revolution was "important psychologically," too, Stalin noted, demonstrating both the power of "Asian revolutionaries" and the unwillingness of American-led forces to "challenge the new Chinese authorities militarily." If the Americans had stood aside as the communists toppled Chiang's government in China, surely they would do the same in a territory as insignificant to US interests as Korea. Yet the more surprising shift was in Soviet perceptions of whether Korea was worth risking a conflict at all.[79]

On January 19, over a boozy lunch with the Soviet ambassador, Kim declared that, with the Chinese revolution complete, his divided country was "next in line" for unification by communist forces. He promised that "the [Korean] People's Army could be in Seoul in several days." Stalin told his colleagues that, with communist forces now in charge of China, the "international situation" had "changed." He had previously restrained Kim, but now gave Pyongyang a green light to invade. Stalin pressed Mao to support the war effort. The Chinese, having declared that they "must lean to one side" in the new Cold War, agreed.[80] Korea—a territory that Stalin had treated as a sideshow in 1945—now seemed worth a war.

In June 1950, North Korean troops streamed across the line of control into South Korea. In a month, they had nearly destroyed the nationalist regime in the south, isolating the South Korean army along a narrow strip of land along the coast. Although the Americans had previously signaled that they would not defend South Korea, they reacted angrily to the North's invasion. In September 1950, the United States landed tens of thousands of troops in South Korea, alongside allies such as Australia and Turkey, and quickly drove northward. By October the American-led forces were preparing to cross the 38th parallel that had divided the peninsula before the war. Stalin urged the North Koreans to redouble resistance, telling Pyongyang to "mobilize all its resources and stop the attack."[81]

Soon the Chinese plunged into the fighting. Mao had launched a "hate America campaign" at home, whipping up sentiment against the capitalist powers. As the US-led forces approached the Yalu River, which marked the border between China and Korea, Beijing ordered the People's Liberation Army into the fray. With complete surprise, they crashed into the allied forces, pushing them back across the 38th parallel and temporarily seizing the capital of Seoul in January 1951.[82] Soon after, the war stabilized roughly along the prewar border.

Stalin urged his Chinese and North Korean allies to keep fighting, though the war had reached a stalemate. China's "firm position" has already produced "positive results," Stalin wrote Mao in February 1952. US peace proposals are "fraudulent provocations," he wrote Kim several months later, and must be rejected. The Americans need not be feared, he told Mao's deputy Zhou Enlai in August, because they "are not capable of waging a large-scale war. . . . Every American solider is . . . occupied with buying and selling. . . . What kind of strength is that? America's primary weapons are stockings, cigarettes, and other merchandise."[83]

Conspicuously absent from the fighting against the Americans was the Soviet Army. Stalin's enthusiasm for expansion in Korea was not matched by his willingness to use force. He had miscalculated the American response and was surprised by Washington's willingness to send tens of thousands of troops to Korea. He had also misjudged his own risk tolerance, and even his own interest in Korea. Stalin authorized the Soviet air force to deploy secretly to the skies above Korea but refused military support beyond that. Asked by the Chinese whether he would send Soviet troops to Korea, Stalin demurred, writing Mao that "we long ago announced the prompt, complete withdrawal of our forces from Korea."[84]

Having just survived a war with Hitler, Stalin was not known for squeamishness. Yet he "quivered" with fear at the thought of open participation in the war in Korea, one of his colleagues remembered. "He knew that we were weaker." He also knew that Korea was, ultimately, a sideshow from the Soviet Union's far more critical interests, such as the occupation of Germany or the growing division of Europe into two separate camps. The peninsula was worth a war when it seemed likely that the United States would stand aside as North Korean armies swept out their southern rivals. But as soon as the United States intervened, Stalin's expansionary enthusiasm waned. Over the course of three years of fighting, Stalin urged his Chinese and North Korean allies onward. His own advisers, meanwhile, looked on nervously, hoping that a way out of the conflict could be found. The Chinese and the North Koreans, for their part, came to realize that Stalin's suggestions were not always formulated with their best interests in mind. "If I had always followed Stalin's advice," Mao recalled several years later, "I would have been dead."[85]

"WHO NEEDED THE WAR?"

The first of the two leaders to die, however, was Stalin, felled by a stroke on March 5, 1953. His successors immediately reversed course on foreign policy, offering concessions in search of peace in Korea. On March 9, at Stalin's funeral, Georgy Malenkov, who briefly succeeded the old dictator, declared "the possibility of the prolonged coexistence and peaceful competition between capitalism and socialism." Six days later he announced a "peace initiative" on the premise that "there is not one . . . question that cannot be decided by peaceful means on the basis of mutual understanding." The testing ground for this new theory, the Soviet leadership decided, would be Korea.

Fourteen days after Stalin's death, the Council of Ministers agreed that "it would be incorrect to continue the line on this [Korean] question that has been pursued until recently, without making changes to this line that are appropriate to the current political moment and which flow from the interests of our peoples, the people of the USSR, China, and Korea, interested in the consolidation of peace." The new goal: "to end the war in Korea as soon as possible." Stalin's position on the subject could not be followed "mechanistically," his successors declared. Indeed, it was promptly discarded.[86]

What explains this rapid change in policy? Like Stalin, his successors feared that the Korean conflict might engulf them in a broader conflict with America, perhaps even nuclear war. More importantly, they saw no purpose in the conflict, and no benefits remotely corresponding to the war's costs. Nikita Khrushchev, who would soon begin consolidating power, used an antiwar message as a battering ram against his political opponents in the Soviet elite. The war had been a pointless enterprise from the outset, Khrushchev argued. It caused America to strengthen its military position in Asia and reinvigorated Japanese anticommunism.[87] Pointing his finger at Molotov, Khrushchev declared that Stalin and Molotov's foreign policy had "mobilized people against us." "We started the Korean War," Khrushchev continued. "Now we cannot in any way disentangle ourselves. . . . Who needed the war?" he asked.

The Kremlin now urged its allies in Beijing and Pyongyang to offer concessions to the United States. Upon receiving news that the new Soviet leadership was ready to end the war, Kim was "very excited" and "very happy," the Soviet envoys who delivered the message reported.[88] The Soviets and their allies offered concessions on all the major issues of disagreement with the United States, and the two sides rapidly moved toward a peace deal. Just months after Stalin's death, the Korean War was ended, with the two sides' forces divided by a demilitarized zone that was little different from the border line on which the war began.

Why had the war in Korea gone so wrong? Beginning in 1944, Stalin's military victories over the Nazis had jolted him into rethinking the Soviet Union's position in Asia. Realizing his military strength, he abandoned the Soviet approach from the 1930s of treating the region solely as a dilemma of defense. Securing the border from Japanese assault—and securing the Russian Far East from Japanese subversion—had been at the top of Stalin's priority list. When he had opportunities to take new territory, especially in the strategically crucial Manchuria region, he declined to do so, both in 1929, after defeating the Chinese in battle, and in 1939, after defeating the Japanese. Security in Europe required spheres of influence, Stalin believed, but Soviet foreign policy in Asia only necessitated border defense.

Stalin's victories over the Nazis expanded both his sense of possibility and his appetite. Perhaps his earlier policy along the Manchurian border and in the Far East had been too cautious. Perhaps Japan's defeat opened the door to territorial expansion, beyond the small islands on the Pacific coast that the allies had agreed would be handed over to the USSR. Perhaps Mao's victory in China's civil war signaled that—in contrast to the disastrous adventures of the 1920s—Asia's peasant societies were now ready for communism. By 1945, Stalin had decided that Asia's map was ripe for redrawing.

For half a decade after 1945, Stalin had shifted into forward gear, backing China's communists, permitting an invasion of South Korea, prodding the Chinese to join the Korean War, throwing many tens of thousands of People's Liberation Army soldiers against the far more advanced American military. Stalin had hoped that the Korean War might catalyze a broader expansion of Soviet influence in Asia, demonstrating that America was unwilling to intervene on the Asian mainland and perhaps even undermining US influence in occupied Japan. Even after the war in Korea went badly wrong for the Soviet Union's allies, Stalin urged them onward, insisting that they were weakening the imperialists on the battlefield.

This was nonsense, as Stalin's successors realized. The war was a bloody stalemate that had provoked the United States to station forces on the Asian mainland, only several hundred miles from Vladivostok. The Red Army might have been victorious over Nazi armies, but Stalin was wrong to interpret this as evidence that armed expansion would now work in Asia. To the contrary: Stalin's expansionary dreams had backfired. At the Yalta Conference, he managed to win back several offshore islands from the Japanese, including the southern half of Sakhalin and the Kuril Archipelago. But he also earned the United States as a military rival in Asia. He lost Japan, too, as its right-wing forces were strengthened by the communist invasion of South Korea, and as Tokyo deepened its alliance with the United States. Even Stalin's successes in Asia proved temporary, as relations with communist parties in China and North Korea quickly deteriorated. After Stalin's death, therefore, his successors rowed back the old dictator's expansionary ambitions, speaking instead of "peaceful coexistence" and seeking to expand Soviet influence in global forums like the United Nations and in the Third World. The idea of waging war to expand Soviet interests in Asia was quietly set aside.

7

"THE GREAT HOPE OF HUMANKIND"

Soft-Power Socialism in Asia

"WHAT DID WE KNOW about India?" Nikita Khrushchev asked in his retirement, looking back on his years at the helm of the Soviet state. His views, he recalled, had been "superficial" and "simply primitive."[1] Nevertheless, he had placed decolonizing Asia at the center of his foreign policy, hoping to win new friends and increase the Soviet Union's global influence. The countries of South Asia received independence from Britain in 1947 and 1948, setting off a chain reaction of demands for decolonization. Most the countries of Southeast Asia were beginning their march toward independence, too, some with communist guerrilla movements and bloody civil wars. China, too, had cast off the imperialist yoke, defeating the Japanese during World War II and ejecting the European and Americans from their concession zones in the country's main port cities. Mao Zedong's communists had toppled the imperialists' ally, Chiang Kai-Shek's Nationalist Party, a government of landlords and the bourgeoisie—or so, at least, it seemed from Moscow. Everywhere Soviet leaders looked, a wave of decolonization and anti-imperialism appeared to be crashing over all of Asia.

Khrushchev concluded, therefore, that time was on his side. The arc of history was bending toward the victory of socialism. He jettisoned Stalin's dark pessimism and the old dictator's approach to Asia, which in its final decades had seen the region through a military lens. Stalin had defended Soviet borders against Japanese expansionism in the 1930s, but his own imperial ambitions in Korea inspired a dangerous American response. Upon Stalin's death, Asia was militarized and divided, and the Soviet Union had replaced one Pacific Ocean rival—Japan—with the United States, a more fearsome foe.

Khrushchev believed that Stalin misunderstood the forces that were driving world politics. He saw an opening for a different strategy. Military power was important, but Khrushchev did not believe it was the only thing that mattered. Nor, he thought, was war with the capitalists inevitable. Instead, Khrushchev declared a new era of "peaceful coexistence" in which the Soviet Union would "bury" its capitalist rivals not with thousands of troops but with economic success and ideological vigor. Soviet foreign policy abandoned Stalin's postwar interest in changing borders and redrawing maps. Khrushchev believed that the nations of the world were naturally turning toward the Soviet Union, recognizing his leadership. "Expanding the borders of our fatherland," Stalin's aim in Asia at the end of World War II, was replaced by a new strategy. Finding new friends, spreading the message of socialism, mobilizing support at the United Nations—this was how Khrushchev intended to make the Soviet Union a great power in Asia and on the world stage.

In November 1955, just after consolidating power following Stalin's death, Khrushchev took off from Moscow in a two-engine Ilyushin-14 on a journey to India, Burma, and Afghanistan. The trip left an "unbelievable impression," Khrushchev said, recalling years later the "rich colors" of their clothing, the "men's headwear (white or green)," and the "beards woven into many little braids. It all seemed fantastic to us, like a theatrical performance." Khrushchev spent several weeks in the region exploring the foothills of the Himalayas; inspecting a dam on Punjab's Sutlej River; traveling to the India-Nepal border; visiting Bombay, Calcutta, Kerala, and Madras; and receiving as a gift a 200-year-old sword. He visited historical sites like the Taj Mahal. He saw monkeys and rode an elephant. "It was so exotic," he remembered. "We thought that India without elephants and elephants without India were simply inconceivable." It was as if Khrushchev was replicating Tsar Nicholas II's journey to the lands of "the East," though the Soviet general secretary appears to have skipped the tiger hunt and the "dancing-girls" that kept Nicholas entertained.[2]

Like his tsarist predecessor, Khrushchev's main purpose for his visit was geopolitical. Nicholas's Grand Tour came as he was preparing to assert Russian influence in Asia, seeking to expand his power in China and stand up to the other great powers of the Asia-Pacific region, including Britain, Japan, and the United States. Khrushchev picked up this agenda and added a new element: ideological exhortations on behalf of socialism. Nicholas saved his attacks on rivals for his private letters to his father. Khrushchev waged a cold war in public, attacking US president Dwight Eisenhower and denouncing the Soviet Union's rivals in front of crowds of "hundreds of thousands or even millions," embarrassing his Indian hosts. Khrushchev thought the trip was a roaring success.[3]

Khrushchev visited India, he told his colleagues, because he believed it was "Kerensky-like"—that is, similar to Alexander Kerensky's provisional government that ruled Russia for several months in mid-1917 after Tsar Nicholas was toppled but before Lenin took power.[4] India was ruled by a bourgeois elite interested in social reform, not unlike Kerensky's government before it was ousted by the Bolsheviks, Khrushchev reasoned. He thought that India was evidence that much of Asia, including many of the newly independent countries that would soon become known as the Third World, was ripe for socialism. From Africa to Latin America, South Asia to the Middle East, Khrushchev's advisers reported that new social classes were taking power. Stalin had ignored politics in these regions, in part because many had long been ruled by European powers, in part because his experience in China in the 1920s had suggested that peasant societies could not build communist governments. As decolonization began in the late 1940s, however, Khrushchev was impressed by the apparent radicalism of many Third World rulers—and by the visible weakness of the West.

During Stalin's final decade, Soviet foreign policy often looked like Russian imperialism clothed in socialist garb. Khrushchev and his allies had different ideas. In the 1950s, Asia appeared to be the region most ripe for Khrushchev's strategy of soft-power socialism. The Soviet leader hoped he could improve ties with China by dispensing with Stalin's colonial mind-set and condemning the old dictator's territorial ambitions. Khrushchev sent Anastas Mikoyan, his right-hand man, to China in September 1956. In a speech during the trip, Mikoyan noted that in the 1920s Lenin had envisioned a partnership between Russia, China, and India, suggesting that something similar might now be possible between Asia's great anti-imperialist powers.

In the first decade after the Bolsheviks had seized power in 1917, their prediction of a socialist surge in "the East" was disappointed. Now, with India's independence in 1947 and the establishment of Mao Zedong's People's Republic of China in 1949, the tide seemed to have turned decisively. The revolution was now finally coming to fruition, shifting the balance of power in Asia. Khrushchev and his allies like Mikoyan dreamed of socialism's victory across the continent, hailing socialist allies like the Chinese Communist Party as "heroic" and describing anti-colonial leaders like Sun Yat-sen as "the great hope of humankind."[5]

SOFT-POWER SOCIALISM

Khrushchev was a true believer in socialism because he was Soviet socialism's greatest beneficiary. Lenin, Stalin, and their colleagues in the early Bolshevik leadership had come of age under the tsars, and many, like Lenin, were from middle-class backgrounds. The socialist state that they forged in the 1920s was built to improve the lives of poor metalworkers like Nikita Khrushchev. Born in 1894 to a poor family along the Russia-Ukraine border, Khrushchev was in his early twenties at the time of the Bolshevik Revolution. As someone who had worked in the metalworks of the industrializing Donbas region, Khrushchev was a member of the proletariat that Soviet socialism was supposed to serve.

For Khrushchev, Soviet socialism had delivered. The new socialist state needed young proletarians to staff the Communist Party, providing education and opportunities for many thousands of young people from families of workers and peasants. Having survived the purges and show trials of the 1930s, Khrushchev had by middle age acquired status and power that was almost inconceivable for someone born in his social position under the tsars. On his fiftieth birthday Khrushchev had become the most powerful official in Soviet Ukraine. By his sixtieth birthday, this former metalworker was consolidating power over all the Soviet Union. It is no wonder Khrushchev thought that socialism worked.

Khrushchev was an expert at accumulating power, but he never managed to acquire culture. British prime minister Harold Macmillan found him a "fat, vulgar man," while British Labor Party leader Hugh Gaitskell thought he was "a rather agreeable pig." America's Sovietologists agreed, with US diplomat Charles "Chip" Bohlen reporting that Khrushchev was "not especially bright." Soviet leaders always had an inferiority complex in negotiations with Western powers, especially the United States, but Khrushchev had twice the sensitivity of most Soviet leaders, believing that Westerners looked down upon him because he was Soviet and because he was a poorly educated boor.[6]

Khrushchev never pretended to be more sophisticated than he was. He did pretend, however, that the Stalinist purges were something that happened to him, rather than something that he participated in. From retirement, he tried spinning a story that he played little active role in the repressions, blaming them on the fact that "there was unquestionably something sick about Stalin"—as if the lieutenants who faithfully executed his orders were somehow blameless.[7] Nevertheless, Khrushchev was the Soviet leader who denounced Stalin in a speech to Soviet Communist Party cadres in 1956 that condemned the personality cult that the old dictator had constructed. Though Khrushchev had Lavrentiy Beria, one of his rivals for power, shot through the forehead, his other political opponents were allowed to live, and sent to humiliating posts far from Moscow. The use of violence in Soviet politics plummeted.

So, too, did the use of force in Soviet foreign policy, marking a major shift from Stalin's strategy. Khrushchev's years in power combined two seemingly contradictory trends: a new foreign policy doctrine of "peaceful coexistence" coupled with an array of standoffs with the United States that risked nuclear war. From the status of divided Berlin to the Suez Crisis, from Iraq to the Cuban Missile Crisis, Khrushchev repeatedly found himself in nuclear show-downs with the United States. He was impulsive in all aspects of life, and at times had been a foreign policy hawk, for example as the only Politburo member in 1945 who backed an invasion of Japan's northernmost main is-land of Hokkaido.[8] Some Western observers therefore interpreted Khrushchev's nuclear brinkmanship as evidence that he was dead set on pressuring the capitalist powers with whatever tools were available.

All of Khrushchev's nuclear threats were bluffs, we now know, because he was never willing to wage nuclear war. He probably exaggerates some-what in his memoirs in claiming that once he "learned all the facts about nu-clear power . . . I couldn't sleep for several days." When his rival Georgy Malenkov first argued that a nuclear war couldn't be won, but would instead mean "destruction of world civilization," Khrushchev criticized him for ignoring Soviet doctrine. Yet within a year or two of consolidating power, Khrushchev had changed his mind, along with many Soviet leaders. Kliment Voroshilov grumbled that the invention of the atomic bomb meant that "we'll all die in a few generations." Khrushchev insisted that the Soviets and the United States "presently possess such means of destruction to make war unthinkable, if not impossible."[9] Believing that the USSR nuclear arsenal had secured the country against surprise attack, Khrushchev felt comfortable undertaking unilateral troop reductions.

To win support from the Soviet elite for his policy of peaceful coexistence, Khrushchev had Marshal Georgy Zhukov, the former commander of Soviet forces during World War II, endorse the slogan, giving a speech declaring, "The foreign policy of the Soviet Union proceeds from the wise counsel of Great Lenin of the possibility of peaceful coexistence and economic competition of states, irrespective of their social or state structure." In the years after Stalin's death, a startling number of foreign disputes were resolved via Soviet concessions, including border disputes with Finland and Turkey, disagreements with the Western powers over the treaty that would govern neutral Austria, and ties with Yugoslavia, which though socialist had incurred Stalin's wrath by not submitting to his demands. For Khrushchev, peaceful coexistence meant competing with the West but not waging war with it. Success was to be measured in terms of progress toward socialism at home and the USSR's ability to convert more countries to socialism abroad.[10]

The territory most ripe for socialism, Khrushchev believed, was the decolonizing world. By the early 1950s it was clear that the British and French Empires were splintering and that the world would soon have dozens of new countries, many led by people who were angry at the West for decades of colonial rule. Soviet leaders saw an opportunity. Nearly three decades had passed since the Stalin-era period of overoptimism about China's revolution in the 1920s. And Khrushchev and his advisers believed that, with the old dictator dead, they could construct socialism in a more effective and humane manner. Khrushchev's advisers devised a theory called the "non-capitalist path," which they hoped would provide a road to "socialism without kolkhozes," referring to the collective farms that Stalin violently forced peasants to join in the late 1920s and early 1930s, killing millions.[11] Karen

Brutents, a foreign policy adviser to Khrushchev's government, recalled the period as an age of "euphoria" about decolonization.[12]

Soviet euphoria over decolonization came first in Asia, where as early as the 1940s key countries were winning independence from Western powers. In 1946, the Philippines was granted independence from the United States. The next year, India and Pakistan became independent, followed by Burma and Ceylon (now Sri Lanka). Indonesia's independence was recognized by the Netherlands the following year. French Indochina was also marching toward decolonization, albeit along a lengthy and bloody path. In the early 1950s, decolonization in Africa still seemed years away, despite rumblings of change. The Middle East consisted mostly of countries that were ostensibly independent but remained under British or French tutelage. Outside of the Caribbean, Latin American countries had been independent for over a century, though were mostly ruled by right-wing regimes. During the early 1950s, when Khrushchev first took power, it was Asia that seemed to be changing most rapidly.

For a moment, moreover, it seemed that Lenin's prediction of a Russia-China-India alliance might come to pass. In 1954, Indian and Chinese leaders formally agreed that their relations should be governed by principles of mutual respect for sovereignty and peaceful coexistence. The subsequent year, they met in Indonesia at the first Afro-Asian Conference, asserting that the decolonized world deserved a larger voice in international affairs. Khrushchev did everything he could to support this apparent entente. He backed India in its dispute with Pakistan over the territory of Kashmir, for example. And the Kremlin placed India at the center of its economic aid efforts, on the grounds that aid was the only way to "commence more serious competition with the U.S.," as Mikoyan put it. Even when Soviet specialists questioned the efficacy of aid to India, Khrushchev stuck with the policy, hoping that it might cement that Russia-China-India partnership that he believed he was forging.[13]

India was not the only place where decolonization had produced gains for socialism and influence for the USSR. France was losing its control over Indochina, its colony in Southeast Asia, with its military under attack from Ho Chi Minh's communist guerrilla forces. Backed by China and the USSR, the Vietnamese rebels forced the French to the negotiating table. In talks in Geneva in 1954, France agreed to divide Vietnam, de facto surrendering the northern half to the control of the guerrilla movement, allied with Moscow and Beijing. Here, too, it looked like socialism was on the march. President Eisenhower worried that the establishment of a socialist state in North Vietnam would set off rebellions across the region, with Western-backed regimes falling like "a row of dominoes." Khrushchev agreed that this was likely as the socialist wave crashed over Asia and as Soviet influence spread. "History is on our side," he declared to a group of Western diplomats in 1956. "We will bury you!"[14]

THE "GREAT FRIENDSHIP" UNRAVELS

In the early and mid-1950s, Moscow's policy on decolonization and the Third World won staunch support from the Kremlin's socialist allies in China. Mao told Soviet ambassador Pavel Yudin that Beijing placed great importance on ties with nonaligned India, declaring that "drawing the peoples of Asia to our side is an extraordinarily important matter." Mao "stressed the enormous importance" of Khrushchev's trip to South Asia for bolstering the "common cause" of socialism. China itself, Mao noted to Yudin in a different meeting, provided "aid to such countries as India and Burma," and Mao praised Soviet promises "to build a metallurgical facility in India," which he said had "made an enormous impression on Burma, Indonesia, and other Asian countries."[15]

The greatest recipient of Soviet aid in Asia, however, was China, which had asked the USSR to help it build an industrial economy. From 1953 to 1956, the USSR built 205 factories in China at a cost of $2 billion. Half of this aid is estimated to have been directed toward China's military buildup, including, Moscow promised, an atomic bomb. The effort was "the greatest transfer of technology in world history," concluded one historian who has studied the matter. The Chinese were grateful for the aid, at least at first. Mao's translator recalled that the Chinese leader "appreciated" the aid and that Khrushchev's new approach "greatly improved the situation Stalin left behind." Mao told Yudin that Indian prime minister Jawaharlal Nehru was "astonished by the scale of the Soviet aid and the conditions on which this aid was being given." The "Great Friendship" that Mao and Stalin had declared in early 1950 was finally being realized.[16]

Below the slogans about socialist brotherhood, however, the Soviet Union was diverging from its communist partners in Asia. As Mao dragged China deeper into his chaotic radicalism, Soviet leaders' doubts about his leadership grew. After Stalin's death, Soviet leaders dreamed of putting mass repressions behind them and of forging a socialism based on popular support rather than threats and violence. As the scale of repression declined in the Soviet Union, however, it expanded in China, where Mao shifted toward ever more radical revolutionary stances, expropriating land, forcing peasants into Communist Party-led farm "cooperatives," and harassing, purging, and in many cases killing Chinese who were guilty of having parents who had been traders, landlords, or business owners.

Speaking with Yudin in 1955, Mao noted that China's leaders "foresee the inevitability of various difficulties" in forging cooperatives and overcoming "the resistance of the class enemy. This year 600,000 people were arrested. About two million hostile elements will be repressed. . . . These figures do not include the counterrevolutionary elements exposed this year during a purge of urban institutions and public organizations." Landowners' estates were seized, business owners' firms were expropriated, and hundreds of thousands of people faced threats and violence, replicating the worst of Stalin's repressions. The Soviet ambassador reported: "This, Mao Zedong said laughing, we call a 'peaceful transition.'"[17]

There were few friends of the Chinese landlord class or the bourgeoisie among Soviet leaders. But there were many skeptics of Mao's methods, which seemed reminiscent of the Stalinism that the Soviet Union was just beginning to cast off. In the late 1950s, Mao launched the Great Leap Forward, a campaign intended to collectivize agriculture and build industry. The aim was to replicate Stalin's program of crash industrialization, but on an accelerated timetable. Mao argued that the creation of People's Communes helped with "strengthening the party leadership with the great masses of the people." In fact, Soviet analysts reported, the search for "greater, quicker, better" in the transition to socialism created suffering and chaos. The neighboring communist state in North Korea looked scarcely more attractive: its economy was a mess, while its political system was defined by "subservience and servility" despite that most party officials considered the radical line of the country's Communist Party and government "mistaken."[18]

Soviet leaders' support for such radicalism declined further after 1956, when Khrushchev condemned Stalin in a speech to Communist Party officials. Stalin was guilty of "the most cruel repression, violating all norms of revolutionary legality, against anyone who in any way disagreed with Stalin, against those who were only suspected of hostile intent, against those who had bad reputations. . . . [Stalin] used extreme methods and mass repressions at a time when the revolution was already victorious, when the Soviet state was strengthened. . . . [His rule was marked by] intolerance, his brutality, and his abuse of power," Khrushchev declared, stunning his audience with previously unthinkable critiques of their longtime leader. Now, Khrushchev said, the USSR would "eradicate the cult of the individual," which, he argued, had made possible Stalin's repressions.[19]

Khrushchev did not invite Chinese officials to his speech, nor did he notify them in advance that he planned to denounce the man previously praised as the "teacher of revolutions." When Mao learned of the speech, he grumbled that Khrushchev had "made a mess" and was "helping the tigers harm us" by letting news of the speech leak to the West. Chinese communists continued to praise Stalin as a "great Marxist Leninist," despite his "serious mistakes." When Mao spoke about the speech with Yudin in mid-1956, Mao complained not about Stalin's repressions but about his imperialist attitude toward China, listing a litany of Stalin's perceived errors in relation to China, including over "the joint exploitation of the Chinese Changchun Railway," the "naval base in Port Arthur," "four joint stock companies [that] were opened in China," and that "at Stalin's initiative . . . Manchuria and Xinjiang were practically turned into spheres of influence of the USSR." In Mao's eyes, Stalin's main error was his imperialist tendencies, not his personality cult. Anyway, Mao told Yudin, "Stalin had made mistakes not in everything, but on some certain issues."[20]

When Soviet leaders visited China, they briefed their Chinese colleagues on the Soviet Union's success in overcoming Stalin's personality cult. Mao was unimpressed and annoyed, in part because he was trying to build a personality cult of his own. In 1958, Mao told Khrushchev that "criticism of Stalin's mistakes is justified" but that "out of Stalin's 10 fingers, 3 were rotten ones," implying that Stalin had gotten 70 percent of things right. "I think more were rotten," Khrushchev retorted. "Wrong," Mao insisted.[21]

It might have been possible to overlook these disagreements if they had been only matters of ideology. But the debate over Stalin was also a question of prestige: Who would lead the socialist world? Mao had been willing to tolerate all manner of indignities in the days of Stalin, whom he had perceived as the legitimate leader of the international communist movement and who in the late 1940s and early 1950s was willing to support Mao's own aggressive foreign policy line. After Khrushchev denounced Stalin's tyranny and declared his support for peaceful coexistence, however, differences between the Soviet Union and China began to grate.

Khrushchev saw himself as a great advocate of decolonization, including in relations with China. He tried to differentiate himself from Stalin, mocking his predecessor's efforts to seize China's gold and diamond mines and describing the Soviet Union's unequal treaties with China as "a mistake. . . . an insult to the Chinese people. For centuries the French, English, and Americans had been exploiting China, and now the Soviet Union was moving in." Khrushchev took genuine steps to resolve issues with the Chinese, for example by liquidating jointly owned companies in 1954, which Beijing perceived as a legacy of imperialism. But the Soviet Union struggled to shake off its sense of superiority, while the Chinese remained extraordinarily sensitive to slights real or imagined.[22]

Khrushchev tried emphasizing his anti-imperialist credentials to Mao, noting that "even in Finland, a capitalist country, we liquidated our military base." "Our course is crystal-clear," he continued. "We render assistance to former colonies; there is not a single clause in our treaties that would . . . contain encroachments on the independence of the country which we assist." Yet when Khrushchev proposed that the two countries establish a joint submarine force in China, Mao heard echoes of colonial subservience. "There was a man by the name of Stalin, who took Port Arthur and turned Xinjiang and Manchuria into semi-colonies, and he also created four joint companies," Mao reminded Khrushchev. "These were all his good deeds." "Do you really consider us red imperialists?" asked Khrushchev, exasperated, thinking that his global vision of Soviet-backed decolonization ought to have established his anti-imperialist credentials.[23]

Mao did not agree. In July 1958, Mao attacked Soviet ambassador Yudin for what Beijing perceived as colonial attitudes in the USSR. "You never trust the Chinese! You only trust the Russians! [To you] the Russians are the first class [people] whereas the Chinese are among the inferior who are dumb and careless," Mao hissed. Moscow's proposal to jointly operate a submarine fleet in China, to be constructed with Soviet technology, sparked continuing anger. "If [you] want joint ownership and operation, how about have them all—let us turn into joint ownership and operation our army, navy, air force, industry, agriculture, culture, education. Can we do this? Or, [you] may have all of China's more than ten thousand kilometers of coastline and let us only maintain a guerrilla force. With a few atomic bombs, you think you are in a position to control us," Mao told Yudin, comparing the proposal to previous Russian control over Dalny and Port Arthur. "You have often stated that the Europeans looked down upon the Russians," Mao concluded. "I believe that some Russians look down upon the Chinese people."[24]

"WE WILL NOT FIGHT OVER TAIWAN"

Even these disputes may have been manageable had the two countries' foreign policies continued to align. But Mao's invective against the Soviet Union's red imperialism began to peak just as he most needed Soviet support. In August 1958, Mao ordered large-scale shelling of two offshore islands controlled by Taiwan, Quemoy (now Jinmen) and Matsu. In response, the United States threatened nuclear war unless Beijing backed down. Khrushchev's focus on peaceful coexistence and on competition for global influence was clashing with Beijing's regional goals.[25]

Khrushchev was no stranger to nuclear confrontations with the United States. But it was one thing for Khrushchev to be threatening nuclear war himself, knowing that he controlled the launch button. The situation on the Taiwan Straits was something new and disconcerting because Khrushchev did not control Mao. Quite the contrary: Soviet leaders worried that Mao was crazed and irrational on the question of nuclear war. Mao had a long track record of publicly downplaying the significance of nuclear weapons. In 1956, two years before the Second Taiwan Strait Crisis, for example, he had declared that "War will be all right. . . . We should not be afraid of war. If there is war, then there will be those who will be killed. . . . I believe that the atomic bomb is not more dangerous than a large sword. If half of humanity is killed during this war, it will not matter. It is not terrible if only one third of the world's population survives."[26]

Nuclear showdowns provide an incentive for leaders to sound crazy. If Mao's adversaries believed he was willing to use such weapons, they would approach him with care. So Mao may have just been bluffing in writing off two-thirds of humanity. Yet Mao repeatedly made statements that sounded numb to the human toll that nuclear war would bring. How could Soviet leaders be sure what he actually believed? Mao told Khrushchev that "if worse came to worst and half of mankind died, the other half would remain, while imperialism would be razed to the ground and the world would become socialist." "I looked at him closely," Khrushchev recounted. "I couldn't tell from his face whether he was joking or not."[27]

Perhaps Mao actually believed that the socialist world could use nuclear weapons for military advantage. When Khrushchev visited Beijing, Mao took the Soviet leader to a swimming pool where they talked politics. "Lying next to the swimming pool in our bathing trunks," Khrushchev recounted, "Mao Zedong said to me, 'Comrade Khrushchev, what do you think? If we compare the military might of the capitalist world with that of the Socialist world, you'll see that we obviously have the advantage over our enemies." Khrushchev responded: "Comrade Mao Zedong, nowadays that sort of thinking is out of date. You can no longer calculate the alignment of forces on the basis of who has the most men. Back in the days when a dispute was settled with fists or bayonets, it made a difference who had the most men. . . . Now with the atomic bomb, the number of troops makes practically no difference to the alignment of real power and the outcome of a war." Mao replied to an astonished Khrushchev that "the atomic bomb was itself a paper tiger." Mao "obviously regarded me as a coward," Khrushchev concluded.[28]

Mao believed that confrontation with the United States could help him consolidate power at home and keep the Chinese Communist Party on a radical course. "Besides its disadvantageous side," Mao noted in 1958, "a tense [international] situation can mobilize the population, can particularly mobilize the backward people, can mobilize the people in the middle, and can therefore promote the Great Leap Forward in economic construction." Moreover, Mao insisted, the Americans were to blame for the Second Taiwan Strait Crisis. The shelling of the offshore islands would "teach the Americans a lesson." "The Americans have bullied us for many years so now that we have a chance, why not give them a hard time?" Mao saw the US Air Force bases and several thousand troops deployed on Taiwan as hostages. "America's neck is hanging in China's iron noose," he declared. "We will kick America, and it cannot run away, because it is tied up by our noose."[29]

Publicly, the Soviet Union backed Beijing. "For outside consumption," Khrushchev told Mao, "we state that . . . in case of an aggravation of the situation because of Taiwan the USSR will defend the PRC [People's Republic of China]." Khrushchev told Eisenhower that "nuclear blackmail toward the PRC will intimidate neither us nor the People's Republic of China," adding that "if the PRC is attacked with [atomic] weapons, the aggressor will instantly be repulsed by similar means." "The American navy should be recalled from the Taiwan Straits, and American soldiers should leave Taiwan and go home," Khrushchev continued. "We are completely on the side of the Chinese Government, the Chinese people."[30]

Privately, Moscow's message was much more mixed. On the one hand, Soviet leaders told Beijing that "as for us, we can say that attacking China means attacking the Soviet Union." But Khrushchev warned Mao that he had created a dangerous situation, noting Eisenhower's declaration that the United States "will defend Taiwan. Therefore, a kind of pre-war situation emerges." Mao insisted to Soviet foreign minister Andrey Gromyko that China "was ready to take all the hard blows, including atomic bombs," leaving the Soviet leadership, which was barely able to navigate its own nuclear standoffs with the United States, fearful that Mao might deliberately drag them into war. Khrushchev grumbled that his swimming pool summits with Mao were "nauseating," and concluded that Mao and his colleagues were "unbelievably courteous and ingratiating . . . but it was all too sickeningly sweet"—especially with the threat of nuclear apocalypse hanging overhead. "We do not want war over Taiwan," Khrushchev warned Mao, despite public Soviet promises to defend China. "We think you ought to look for ways to relax the situation."[31]

The Soviet Union wanted peace, believing that in the struggle with the United States time was on its side. Mao wanted Taiwan and was unwilling to wait passively for socialism to spread. Disagreements over the Taiwan Strait spilled over into China's other border disputes. The next year, in 1959, after an uprising in Tibet, the territory's religious leader, the Dalai Lama, fled to

India. Beijing blamed India for supporting the Tibetan rebellion, but the Soviets defended Prime Minister Nehru, who had welcomed Khrushchev on his visit to India four years earlier. "We may say that Nehru is a bourgeois statesman," Khrushchev told Mao. "But we know about it. If Nehru leaves, who would be better? . . . We believe that the events in Tibet are the fault of the Communist Party of China, not Nehru's fault." "No," replied Mao, "this is Nehru's fault." "Why did you have to kill people on the border with India," Khrushchev retorted. "One can resolve disputed issues without spilling blood."[32]

The relationship spiraled downward. "Khrushchev is very infantile," Mao declared. "He does not understand Marxism and Leninism . . . he is easily cheated by the imperialists." Soviet leaders, meanwhile, blamed Beijing for its confrontational relations with the United States, as well as with many of the decolonization nations that Moscow was courting, including Burma, Indonesia, and India. In internal discussions, Soviet leaders feared that Chinese provocations were causing unnecessary divisions in the socialist camp.[33]

Mao's decision in 1962 to invade the Himalayan territories that it disputed with India further worried the Kremlin. "One cannot mechanistically repeat what Lenin said many decades ago on imperialism and go on asserting that imperialist wars are inevitable until socialism triumphs throughout the world," Khrushchev declared at a gathering of communist parties in 1960. He continued: "In present conditions when there are two world systems, it is imperative to build mutual relations between them in such a way as to preclude the possibility of war breaking out." But Mao was increasingly less committed to the thesis that there were "two world systems." He thought that Khrushchev had betrayed Stalin's legacy and abandoned the socialist path. After the Soviet Union made clear, as Khrushchev had told Mao, that "we will not fight over Taiwan," Beijing concluded that it must fend for itself. Moscow, meanwhile, decided that China was a volatile and unreliable partner. Less than a year after the Second Taiwan Strait Crisis, the USSR canceled its nuclear cooperation with China and began winding down aid to the People's Republic.[34] The alliance with China, which Khrushchev had hoped would spur socialist victories across Asia and the decolonizing world, was no more.

THE CLASH WITH CHINA

"The revisionist Khrushchev clique is nothing but a betrayal of socialism and communism," Mao declared in 1964, condemning the Soviet leader for having "defamed the dictatorship of the proletariat" and "paved the way for the restoration of capitalism."[35] The ideological disputes continued over the course of the early 1960s, contradicting the unity on which Khrushchev's hope of a socialist wave depended. In foreign policy, too, Moscow and Beijing were at odds on a growing number of issues. China's willingness to risk war with the United States over Taiwan conflicted with Khrushchev's vision of peaceful coexistence. When Soviet leaders told Mao, "we will not fight over Taiwan," they saw themselves has promoting peace; Mao saw them as betraying the anti-imperialist agenda. As Mao drove China's internal politics toward ever greater radicalism via the Great Leap Forward and the Cultural Revolution, compromise with the Soviet Union became ever less tenable. Instead, Khrushchev's criticism of Stalin and his desire for peaceful competition with the imperialists were interpreted in Beijing as evidence of Soviet "revisionism"—in other words, that the Kremlin was no longer a proper Marxist-Leninist government.[36]

By the 1960s, therefore, relations between the two communist superpowers had sunk into a deep freeze. After the Cuban Missile Crisis, during which Khrushchev had withdrawn nuclear missiles from Cuba in the face of American military pressure, Chinese newspapers criticized Moscow for having "caved in" to US demands. In response, Khrushchev pointed out that the Chinese—vocal critics of imperialism in other regions—had failed to eject the British from Hong Kong or the Portuguese from Macao, despite the fact that these imperialists were in China's own backyard. The Chinese hit back by noting the legacy of Russian imperialism in Northeast Asia, where the memory of Tsar Nicholas II's and Stalin's colonial policies toward Port Arthur and the Manchurian railroads was still fresh.[37]

As the two sides sparred for leadership over the international communist movement and traded barbs over their commitment to anti-imperialism, they began to see each other as dangerous not only to the unity of socialism but to their own security. In 1964, the Soviet defense minister drunkenly urged Mao's deputy Zhou Enlai to depose his boss. China detonated its first nuclear weapon that same year, shocking the Kremlin, though Beijing still lagged the Soviet Union in terms of technology and firepower. The People's Liberation Army made up for this in sheer numbers, however, giving Soviet officials nightmares of hundreds of thousands of troops streaming northward over the two countries' 4,150-mile-long border.[38] Mao's repeated declarations that he feared neither nuclear war nor millions of casualties—now aimed at the USSR as well as at the Americans—suggested that the Soviet technological advantage might not be as decisive as the Kremlin hoped.

In late 1964, Khrushchev was on holiday in Crimea when he received an urgent demand from his colleagues that he return to Moscow. Upon arrival in the Kremlin, Khrushchev was told that he would have to step down from power. Seven years earlier Khrushchev had defeated a similar coup attempt, narrowly winning a vote of confidence among the Central Committee and sending his opponents into internal exile. By 1964, however, he had alienated nearly every powerful group in the Soviet Union, in part because of his volatile domestic policies, in part because of his repeated foreign policy crises with the United States, culminating with the Cuban Missile Crisis in 1962, bringing the world to the brink of nuclear war and contradicting Khrushchev's own promise to pursue a policy of peaceful coexistence. Realizing that he had been outmaneuvered, Khrushchev agreed to resign "for reasons of ill health."[39]

The removal of what Mao called the "revisionist Khrushchev clique" did not, at first, cause substantial change in Soviet foreign policy in Asia. The primary dilemma—relations with China—was unaffected by Khrushchev's ouster. The new Soviet leaders, including General Secretary Leonid Brezhnev and Council of Ministers chairman Alexey Kosygin, toned down criticism of Stalin and happily attacked Khrushchev's mistakes, both of which Mao appreciated. But they were unwilling to recognize Mao as the leader of international socialism, as he implicitly demanded. Nor were they any more willing than Khrushchev to let Beijing drag them into a world war. Mao, meanwhile, continued to rely on international tension to whip up fanaticism at home.

In February 1965, Alexey Kosygin arrived in Beijing in a last-ditch effort to salvage relations with Beijing. Like Khrushchev a half decade earlier, Kosygin offered compromises that Mao rebuffed. Kosygin proposed "that if we met at the highest level, then in two hours we would be able to resolve many matters which would not be able to be resolved during usual negotiations." Mao rejected the offer of negotiations to address the two countries' differences. "I do not agree with your methods," he told Kosygin. "If open polemics continue, nothing terrible will happen . . . heaven will not fall, trees will still grow as before, fish will swim in water, and women will still be giving birth to children. . . . I am against discontinuing the public polemics. All this will last yet another 10 thousand years—less is impossible." [40]

Why was an improved relationship "impossible"? First, Mao declared, "I do not agree with the line of these [Soviet Communist Party] congresses, with the fact that Stalin turned out to be already so bad, that there was some cult of personality. And now you are saying that Khrushchev created his own cult of personality." Mao then announced that he would like to extend an invitation to Khrushchev—the Soviet Union's deposed former leader—to visit Beijing, an insulting intervention into Soviet domestic politics. [41]

Next, Mao turned to foreign policy, where he condemned what he saw as Moscow's lackluster efforts in confronting capitalist powers. Mao wanted a more aggressive policy against the imperialists. Kosygin told Mao that he sensed a contradiction: "On the one hand you are saying that it would be good to live without a world war for about 10–15 years; on the other hand, you are calling for a war. . . . I am convinced that, in reality, you are against world war." "We are against world war," Mao retorted, "but we are in favor of a revolutionary war whose goal is to overthrow imperialism." "If the imperialists impose a world war on us," one of Mao's colleagues added, "then one has to fight." [42]

So long as Mao ruled China, Sino-Soviet rapprochement would be impossible. The history of disputes dating back to Stalin weighed heavily on his thinking. His radicalism prevented any compromise. As the 1960s progressed, Soviet leaders perceived him as increasingly volatile as he dragged his country deeper into the Cultural Revolution. Moscow grew worried about the security of its long border with China, especially after an effort to demarcate the border failed to reach agreement in 1964, with neither country willing to surrender its claim to disputed islands in the Ussuri River.

That same year, Mao had seemed to call the entire Soviet Far East into question, declaring that "there are too many places occupied by the Soviet Union. . . . China has not yet asked the Soviet Union for an account about Vladivostok, Khabarovsk, Kamchatka, and other towns and regions east of Lake Baikal, which became Russian territory about 100 years ago." There was little substance behind Mao's claim to Kamchatka, which the Chinese had never controlled. But he was not wrong to say that only a century had passed since Governor-General Nikolai Muravev-Amursky marched his troops through the Amur Region in violation of the Qing Empire's claim to sovereignty, establishing Russia's control over the territory at gunpoint. Soviet newspaper *Pravda* responded to Mao's comments by threatening "dangerous consequences."[43]

In March 1969, the Chinese attacked Soviet border patrol units on an island in the Ussuri River, catching Soviet forces by surprise. Fighting continued for several weeks, leaving at least several dozen dead on each side. Later that year, a second clash erupted along the two countries' Central Asian borderland, in present-day Kazakhstan. The Soviets struggled to make sense of the Chinese assault, which was unprovoked and served no military purpose. Many Soviet analysts concluded that amid the craze of China's Cultural Revolution Mao had lost all grip on reality. As the Cultural Revolution churned through Chinese society, the Soviets prepared for war. The Soviet air force was put on high alert and bombers were redeployed from Eastern Europe to the Far East. Military exercises simulated war with China. And a KGB agent in Washington asked a State Department official how the United States would respond in case of a Soviet airstrike on China's nuclear facilities.[44]

Gone was the dream of a Russia-China-India alliance against imperialism, ended by a decade of disputes and weeks of skirmishing along the Sino-Soviet border. Gone, too, was the idea, popular early on in Khrushchev's tenure, that socialism might sweep across Asia. The only major country that socialism had swept through—China—was now a rival of the USSR. Soft-power socialism in Asia had produced little socialism and even less soft power. The attention that Khrushchev placed on relations with countries such as India and China had produced little of value. The Indians and Chinese had quickly found themselves in a bitter border dispute, tearing apart the Afro-Asian unity they had proclaimed in 1955. And China itself had attacked the Soviet Union, questioning its hold on territories that had been Russian since the days of Muravev and Count Sergei Witte. "Where the Russian flag has been raised," Tsar Nicholas II is said to have declared, "it should not be taken down." Soviet leaders were no more willing to surrender either territory or status, especially to someone like Mao.[45]

"THE PARTNERSHIP BETWEEN AMERICAN IMPERIALISM
AND BEIJING'S HEGEMONISM"

The Kremlin backed down from a large-scale war with China, in part because it feared Mao's response and in part because the Chinese halted their border attacks after 1969. As the USSR and China settled into a decade-long deep freeze in relations, Soviet leaders devised a new strategy in Asia. The USSR's foreign policy challenge in the 1970s was substantially more difficult than during the optimistic early days of Khrushchev's time in the Kremlin. Now Moscow had to deal with its volatile southern neighbor while continuing to wage a Cold War with the United States. Soviet leader Leonid Brezhnev turned to gallows humor, joking that he was lucky: the Chinese planned to shoot him when they invaded, whereas they planned to boil alive his colleague, Comrade Mikoyan. A second coping mechanism was a campaign to rename Soviet Far Eastern cities and towns whose original names derived from Chinese or Mongol words. In the face of Mao's territorial claims, these towns were given proper Russian-sounding names instead.[46]

More substantive was the Soviet military buildup in the Far East, as soft power was replaced with harder variants. Gone was the idea that the spread of Soviet ideas could win friends or influence in a way that might meaningfully shift the balance of power. Brezhnev and other Soviet leaders remained committed Marxist-Leninists, but these concepts were reflected through the lens of the Kremlin's strategic interests. The most effective way to shift international politics to benefit the Soviet Union, they believed, was by ensuring that the correlation of military force was moving in their direction.

Between 1965 and 1973, Soviet military manpower in the Far East region tripled. The Soviet naval presence in Vladivostok grew by a similar magnitude. Mobile missiles, nuclear-capable rockets, and tactical ballistic missiles were all deployed to the region. By the mid-1980s, there were 103 submarines in the Soviet Pacific Fleet, 86 large surface combat ships, and 2 aircraft carriers. In 1974, meanwhile, Brezhnev announced plans to build the Baikal-Amur Mainline, a vast new railroad connecting Siberia to the Far East, which would facilitate military resupply in case of war.[47]

The biggest problem for the Soviet Union, however, was that its most powerful rivals were improving relations with each other at the expense of

Moscow. In 1969, at the time of the Sino-Soviet border clash, Beijing, Moscow, and Washington had all seen each other as military and political threats. In the early 1970s, however, the United States and China began slowly reestablishing ties, recognizing that the Soviet Union was each country's biggest challenge. US national security adviser Henry Kissinger visited Beijing in 1971 to begin the process of opening relations between the two countries. President Richard Nixon went to China the subsequent year for talks with Mao Zedong. Washington and Beijing opened formal diplomatic relations in 1979, following a decision by Japan to reopen ties with the People's Republic of China several years earlier.[48]

Now the Soviet Union's greatest capitalist and socialist rivals were openly cooperating against Moscow. Fearing the combined power of Washington and Beijing, the Kremlin began tentative discussions over détente with the United States. But it long resisted anything similar with China, on the grounds that the previous several decades had proven that Mao was not someone they could work with. Indeed, Soviet leaders feared that China remained a military threat throughout the 1970s. Having already tried soft-power methods under Khrushchev, Soviet leaders believed that the USSR had no option but to lean ever more heavily on its military to defend itself against Chinese threats. "We should expect that the PRC's foreign policy will develop in the direction of implementing its great power, nationalistic, and hegemonic plans," one Soviet internal analysis declared in 1973, recommending measures to "decisively counter Beijing's hostile activities directed against the Soviet Union and other socialist countries, to unmask the efforts of Maoists who are counting on weakening the unity of fraternal nations." The strategy was "to unmask the real propositions of the Chinese leadership," to "take all possible steps to counter Maoist activities," and to "counter Beijing's hegemonic ambitions" across Asia and worldwide.[49]

"A SYSTEM OF COLLECTIVE SECURITY IN ASIA"

Khrushchev had seen the countries of Asia as a beachhead of socialism and as potential allies in the Cold War against the United States. Brezhnev, trying to improve ties with Washington to free up resources for containing China, also hoped to find allies in Asia. In 1969, months after the first Sino-Soviet border clash along the Ussuri River, Brezhnev delivered a speech calling for "a system of collective security in Asia."[50] Brezhnev's proposal marked a new strategy toward the region. Like Khrushchev, Brezhnev would seek friends in Asia. Unlike Khrushchev, Brezhnev's proposal was for an alliance not with China, but against it.

Brezhnev's vision was an Asian collective security system linking countries such as India, Vietnam, North Korea, Afghanistan—and potentially even capitalist countries like Japan—in a joint effort to contain Chinese influence. The Soviet Union spent the entire 1970s devoting its diplomatic energy in Asia to assembling an anti-China coalition. It found little success. One obvious participant in an anti-Chinese agenda ought to have been India, which won its independence from Britain in 1947 and struck a foreign policy course away from the Western powers. India's relations with China were a perpetual problem. "I do not think there is any country in the world which is more anxious for peace than the Soviet Union," declared India's first leader, Jawaharlal Nehru, "but I doubt if there is any country in the world . . . which cares less for peace than China."[51] After India and China's brief border war in 1962, which China won handily, India had no choice but to cozy up to Moscow. It became one of the Soviet Union's most important markets for arms, for example, and backed the USSR in international forums like the United Nations.

Despite New Delhi's reliance on Soviet support against China, however, it responded warily to the Kremlin's efforts to assemble an anti-Chinese alliance after 1969. India leaned toward the USSR, but it still claimed to adhere to a foreign policy of "non-alignment." Joining an anti-Chinese grouping would contradict this. India signed a Treaty of Friendship and Cooperation with the USSR in 1971, but despite the best efforts of Soviet diplomats, it declined to agree to anything stronger against the Chinese. Instead, by the late 1970s India had begun to reinvigorate relations with the West, for example by deciding in 1978 to buy Anglo-French Jaguar fighter planes rather than Soviet MiG-23s.[52]

Perhaps this was to be expected with a country like India, which despite its politicians' flirtation with socialist ideas remained an obviously capitalist country. But Asia's socialist states proved no less problematic as the Kremlin sought to assemble its anti-China coalition. The Democratic People's Republic of Korea, for example, was not particularly grateful for Soviet support during the Korean War. In the 1960s, the Kremlin had cut aid to North Korea, hoping to coerce it to take Moscow's side in the Sino-Soviet split, but this succeeded only in creating new problems in the relationship. Given Pyongyang's ongoing struggle with South Korea—and the American armies still stationed there—it had little choice but to stay on at least decent terms with Beijing. Soviet efforts to pressure Pyongyang therefore proved ineffectual.[53]

Socialist North Vietnam, however, proved a more pliable ally against China. In the 1960s, the Kremlin had worried about Hanoi's "radical views" and "pro-Chinese orientation." After Vietnam's communists united the country under their rule in 1975, their relations with Beijing deteriorated, and they strengthened ties with Moscow in response. In November 1978, the Soviet Union and Vietnam signed a treaty promising to coordinate in the face of security threats. The next spring, China invaded northern Vietnam, spurring the Soviet Union to send fourteen ships to the South China Sea, while several hundred Soviet workers were dispatched to Vietnamese ports to speedily unload supplies for Hanoi. The Kremlin also flexed its military muscles along the Soviet-China border, reminding Beijing that China faced security threats from both the north and the south. That same year, Vietnam gave Moscow access to former US military bases at Danang and Cam Ranh Bay, and the Soviet Union stationed several dozen ships there plus fighter, bomber, and reconnaissance aircraft. The Kremlin also ramped up economic and military aid to Vietnam.[54]

The year 1979, however, was also when the Soviet Union's position in Afghanistan began deteriorating. Afghanistan had never been part of the Soviet sphere, but amid tension with China and the United States, and as the Iranian Revolution developed in an Islamist anti-Soviet direction, Afghanistan appeared to be taking on more importance. It bordered Iran, China, Pakistan—an American and Chinese ally—and also the Soviet Union's Central Asian republics. Though there had been few problems on the Soviet-Afghan border since the earliest days of Soviet power in the region, the shared ethnic and religious ties between Afghanistan and Soviet Central Asia worried leaders in Moscow. The prospect that "the West and China" might collaborate to undermine Soviet influence in Afghanistan also worried Soviet officials.[55]

Afghanistan's politics were more tumultuous than usual in 1979, and the Kremlin saw the machinations of the CIA at work. KGB chief Yuri Andropov wrote Brezhnev in December of "a possible political shift to the West" among Afghanistan's leadership, which could lead to a "policy of neutrality" or even "anti-Soviet steps." Against the warnings of the Soviet Union's military leaders, the Politburo opted to send in Soviet troops, with Andropov reckoning that two brigades would be sufficient. The goal, he told Brezhnev, would be "defending the gains of [Afghanistan's] April Revolution, establishing Leninist principles in the party and state leadership of Afghanistan, and securing our positions in this country."[56] Soviet troops streamed in, and after they failed to secure peace, more were sent. Soon there were tens of thousands of Soviet troops spread across the entire country. Gone was Khrushchev's policy of spreading socialism in Afghanistan by building schools and bakeries. To the Soviet Union's neighbors in Asia, it seemed as though the "rugged Russian bear" that a century prior had menaced the British Empire in Afghanistan was again on the march.

The decision to seek a military solution to the Soviet Union's dilemma in Afghanistan marked the final defeat of Brezhnev's effort to contain China. It had been a decade since he had launched his proposal for "collective security" against Beijing. Now, the Soviet Union seemed to most countries like the primary military threat. Nearly all the Soviet Union's neighbors in Asia began hedging. Even India, long Moscow's closest friend in the region, moved further toward a neutral position. Countries such as Japan, a historic rival of China, responded to the Soviet military buildup by improving relations with Beijing and tightening ties with Washington. Most Southeast Asian countries, meanwhile, saw the Soviet Union primarily as a fearsome military threat. Because the Kremlin pursued its military buildup on autopilot, it ignored other means of influencing the region's smaller countries. In the mid-1980s, for example, Soviet trade with the six Southeast Asian countries in the ASEAN group amounted to roughly $500 million, compared to their $24 billion in trade with the United States and $29 billion with Japan.[57] Lacking diplomatic and economic leverage, looking like a dangerous military menace, the Kremlin found itself locked out of Asia.

MAOISM AFTER MAO?

By the end of the 1970s, the effort to contain China had failed. Other Asian countries were uninterested in banding together against Beijing. The USSR's belligerence had bolstered the budding entente between China and the United

States, and Beijing was no more willing to offer concessions. In 1980 Soviet policy in Asia was stuck, condemning Maoism, focusing on its military tools while alienating the region's other powers. Whatever the inadequacies of Khrushchev's soft-power socialism, Brezhnev's militarized alternative looked little more effective. The line from Moscow remained the same far after its policies had clearly failed to achieve their aims. Moscow reminded its ambassadors abroad of the danger of coordination between "Chinese representatives" and "imperialist circles, above all with the USA and their intelligence services." Several months later, Moscow warned that "the partnership between American imperialism and Beijing's hegemonism" is "spreading to the military sphere" and creating "a new negative phenomenon in world politics."

What to do? As long as the Soviet military was in Afghanistan, the Kremlin would face the animosity of most countries in the region. Even into the beginning of the 1980s, however, Moscow saw no reason to change tack. The Kremlin bet instead that Sino-American cooperation would collapse on its own accord. As one leading China expert in the Soviet Union told his colleagues: the Chinese are hoping to modernize "using Western technological help and credits and have no other capital to pay for this help but anti-Sovietism." All Moscow had to do was wait, because "the Chinese never befriend anyone for a long time."[58]

The Chinese had befriended the Americans, however, and even if their amity did not last forever, it made the Soviet Union deeply uncomfortable while it continued. Moreover, by the early 1980s the Soviet Union's effort to build an anti-China coalition had produced no results. Efforts to reinforce its military position in the Far East, meanwhile, frightened neighbors and intensified mistrust. At the same time, new US president Ronald Reagan was ratcheting up pressure on the Soviet Union to a level unseen since the early Cold War. Washington armed anti-Soviet rebels in Afghanistan and other proxy wars, built up its military, and denounced the Soviet Union as an "evil empire." "There has never been such an unbridled and aggressive administration in the USA as that of Reagan," Brezhnev complained to a colleague. The USSR's Eastern European client states, however, were unhappy with Soviet tension with "Chinese hegemonists," seeing little security threat themselves from China's military. Yet Brezhnev's only concession so far had been to promise Beijing that it would pursue a policy of noninterference in Chinese politics.[59]

China itself was changing, however. The Cultural Revolution had wound down in the early 1970s, and Mao died in 1976. Some in the Soviet Union, notably those experts who wanted to retain a hard line against Beijing, argued that little had changed. "Maoism without Mao," is how they described post-1976 Chinese politics, suggesting that anti-Soviet views and ideological volatility would continue. One Soviet analyst told East German colleagues in 1977 that China's new leaders were changing little: "basically it is just the continuation of Maoist policy."[60]

Soviet China experts such as Oleg Rakhmanin, a top Communist Party official, and Mikhail Kapitsa, who was appointed deputy foreign minister in 1982, insisted that the only changes were cosmetic. *Far Eastern Affairs*, the Soviet Union's main journal on the region, hewed to a similar line: "The present Chinese leadership . . . continues to pursue the hegemonistic policy bequeathed by Mao Zedong of accelerating the militarization of the country, whipping up anti-Sovietism, aggravating international tension, and leaguing with imperialism." The new leader, Deng Xiaoping, wanted to modernize his country, but this did not mean moderating the anti-Soviet line. As the USSR's Foreign Ministry reminded its officials, "There is absolutely no basis for concluding, as some do, that Beijing's alleged adoption of a 'modernization program' represents a new political course. . . . 'Modernization' is the best means of preparing for war." If such an analysis was true, there was little scope for Sino-Soviet rapprochement.[61]

Not all Soviet analysts agreed with this line, however. Some pointed out that the new Chinese leadership rejects "the Cultural Revolution . . . which cost the Chinese Communist Party so dearly." Soviet leaders began toning down slightly the propaganda war. By 1981, Brezhnev's speeches no longer argued that Deng was slavishly following Mao's line, admitting that "changes were occurring" and that "to some extent, China's leadership was overcoming the Maoist legacy." In 1982, the Soviet Union sent two China specialists to Beijing for talks, though the conversation achieved nothing.

Later that year, Brezhnev traveled to the Soviet city of Tashkent to deliver a speech on Soviet policy toward China. "We have never tried to interfere in the internal life of the People's Republic of China," Brezhnev declared. "We did not deny and do not deny now the existence of a Socialist system in China. . . . We have never supported and do not support now in any form the so-called 'concept of two Chinas' [i.e., Taiwanese independence]. . . . There was no and is no threat to the People's Republic of China from the Soviet Union." Brezhnev's logic, explained one of his speech-writers, was simple: "Mao is gone . . . so something must be changing, and not for the worse."[62]

"OUR TWO COUNTRIES ARE GEOPOLITICAL ENEMIES"

Beijing noted Brezhnev's change in tone, with the Chinese media describing his Tashkent speech as full of "attacks"—using a softer term than their usual "slander." Yet China wanted action, not words. Beijing had three main de-mands: that the Soviet Union withdraw from Afghanistan, cut its support for Vietnam's invasion of Cambodia, and reduce its military presence in the Far East, along China's northern border. By the early 1980s, the Soviet Union's war in Afghanistan had become a quagmire. Moscow had few concrete in-terests in Southeast Asia and was backing Vietnam's war in Cambodia pri-marily because Hanoi was a partner in Soviet efforts to contain China.[63]

On top of this, many Soviet analysts realized that their country's military buildup in the Far East had created a security dilemma. Moscow had "a faulty assessment of the threat from China, which forced us to concentrate very large forces in the Far East," one influential Soviet analyst noted. This "was interpreted by the Chinese as a threat forcing them to increase both their nu-clear and their conventional forces and their political and military coopera-tion with the West." Meanwhile, the China-US rapprochement that Moscow most feared was, by the early 1980s, facing new difficulties, as Washington and Beijing clashed over Taiwan and over a US refusal to transfer advanced technologies to China.[64] All these factors suggested that there was space for the Soviet Union to adjust its foreign policy and improve ties with Beijing.

The Soviet Union's top leaders in the early 1980s all issued statements sug-gesting a desire for better ties with China, but all were in ill health, unable to push forward change. Brezhnev believed that his Tashkent speech in 1982 had induced Beijing to take a softer line. But there was little to show for it, and Brezhnev died soon after delivering the speech. His successor, Yuri Andropov, had long advocated compromise with China, and surrounded himself with many well-informed foreign policy advisers. Yet Andropov, too, was in poor health, and died after only a year and a half in office. His successor, Konstantin

Chernenko, also issued statements advocating better ties with China, but died after barely a year in power.[65] Thus there was little pressure from the top for a change in tack.

The Soviet bureaucracy, meanwhile, was dominated by officials who wanted a tough line against the Maoists that they believed still governed China. The upper levels of the Foreign Ministry, the leading Asia-focused research institutes, and the Communist Party were controlled by anti-China hawks tied to the military-industrial complex. Defense Minister Dmitry Ustinov was an inveterate opponent of any change to military positioning in the Far East. Despite Chinese complaints, Ustinov argued in the early 1980s that the Soviet Union could not remove forces based in Mongolia that frightened China, because such a move would mean losing "a very good post" in the Far East. Indeed, despite Brezhnev's Tashkent speech, in the early 1980s the Soviet military buildup in the Far East continued on autopilot. New SS-20 intermediate range nuclear missiles were deployed in the region, worrying Beijing. More troops were sent to the Far East, too, with the USSR's military forces in the region expanding from forty-six divisions in 1981 to fifty-three in 1985.[66]

Anyone proposing dialogue with China was attacked by these officials who resisted change. The anti-China clique compiled dossiers on their internal enemies, in one instance trying to link a Soviet advocate of rapprochement with Beijing to a "Zionist conspiracy aimed at praising capitalist tendencies in the PRC." A Soviet diplomat's suggestion that the two countries' relations might be improving was immediately rejected by his superior. "Are you crazy? Our two countries are geopolitical enemies and this factor will never go away."[67] This same diplomat was ordered in the 1980s to write a critique of Chinese territorial claims on the Soviet Union, even though Beijing was no longer repeating Mao's claim that "there are too many places occupied by the Soviet Union." This diplomat recycled Soviet anti-Chinese propaganda from the 1960s to appease his superiors, changing only the date on the document.[68]

This internal opposition obstructed Brezhnev's tepid outreach to the Chinese. Most Soviet diplomacy in the first half of the 1980s seemed as if the country was simply repeating anti-Mao diatribes from two decades earlier while continuing to reinforce its military position. As Oleg Rakhmanin, the greatest opponent of China among Soviet foreign policy experts, told col-

leagues in February 1985, "The current direction in Chinese foreign and domestic policy [is] strongly negative. The People's Republic of China does not
want a true normalization of relations with the USSR. The Chinese . . . pose
territorial claims to the Soviet Union . . . [and] cooperate with the imperialist
powers on a global scale." "China," he added, "just like the U.S., favors revising borders and agreements which regulate the post-war political reality."[69]
There was no scope, therefore, for any concessions to Beijing beyond the
slightly toned-down rhetoric that Brezhnev had already offered. To Rakhmanin and other officials who had a stranglehold over Soviet foreign
policy in Asia, the military buildup remained of prime importance, even
though Soviet influence in Asia continued to decline.

A large military presence in Asia could defend the Soviet Union's borders,
but it did little to advance Soviet interests. By most metrics the USSR was
less influential in Asia in 1980, after years of military buildup, than it had been
at the time of Khrushchev's ouster in 1964. It was easy to criticize Khrushchev, of course. His domestic policies were volatile and often ineffective; his
diplomacy was no less impulsive. Despite promising "peaceful coexistence"
he had repeatedly brought the Soviet Union to the brink of war with the
United States. His soft-power tactics—embracing socialist ideas and handing
out aid to left-wing allies—ended up accomplishing relatively little for Soviet
interests.

But Brezhnev's more confrontational policy did little better. Facing attacks
from Mao's China, Brezhnev built up the Soviet Union's military position and
tried assembling an anti-China coalition in Asia. But he had little to offer countries in the region and struggled to separate the strengthening partnership
between Washington and Beijing. His decision to invade Afghanistan, taken
in a haphazard fashion in the twilight of his time at the helm of the Communist Party, marked the ultimate failure of his strategy in Asia. By the early
1980s, the region had ultimately forged a system of "collective security," as
Brezhnev wanted. But the collective security that had emerged saw Asia's
greatest powers lined up not with the Soviet Union, but against it.

8

PERESTROIKA AND THE PACIFIC

Mikhail Gorbachev's Opening to Asia

IN SUMMER 1986, in the cold waters of the North Pacific, the Soviet Union's Pacific Fleet launched one of its largest military exercises in years. Several dozen surface ships maneuvered in the Sea of Okhotsk, around the Kurile Islands, in the waters north of Japan, not far from the Soviet Union's submarine base at Kamchatka. Fighter planes buzzed overhead. Submarines lurked under the sea. Foreign military observers—Chinese, Japanese, and American—watched warily. Russia's navy had a long history of sailing these waters, as the legacy of mariners and explorers from Nikolai Rezanov to Gennady Nevelskoy attested. Russia's leaders had seen the islands of the North Pacific as strategically important territories since the beginning of the 1800s, and this focus intensified over the course of the Cold War. Under Leonid Brezhnev and his successors, the Soviet military's footprint in the Far East had grown substantially, fulfilling its responsibilities for defense not only against the Americans and their Japanese partners, but also against the Chinese.[1]

One of the key strategies of the Soviet Navy in the Pacific was "bastion defense"—gathering their ballistic missile submarines in the Sea of Okhotsk and ringing the region with the fearsome military might that was on display in the exercises of mid-1986. Soviet ballistic missile submarines were crucial to the country's nuclear second-strike capability against the United States, and therefore needed to be defended at nearly any cost. Yet they were noisier than US submarines and thus vulnerable to detection in open seas.[2] So they were husbanded in coastal "bastions" such as the Sea of Okhotsk. The Soviet Far East as a whole was treated as a bastion, too—strategically important, ringed with military facilities, defended with nuclear weapons. A region that Nevelskoy had predicted would be an "army camp" was, throughout most of the Soviet period, dominated by the Soviet Army and the military-industrial complex. Many of the region's residents had arrived in the Far East when they were shipped to Stalin-era gulags and then decided to stay in the area after being released. Some of the region's territories, such as the Kuril Islands and Kamchatka, were accessible only to Soviet citizens with a special permit. Vladivostok, the most important city of the Russian Far East, was completely off limits to foreigners.

By the mid-1980s the Soviet Pacific Fleet had around 800 ships, compared to the 230 American vessels stationed in the Pacific Ocean. Yet the US Navy was not the only rival about which the Soviet Union worried. Encouraged by Washington, Japan had rearmed, becoming a substantial military power. Tokyo established a de facto cap on defense spending of 1 percent of gross domestic profit (GDP), but as Japan's economy boomed over the course of the Cold War, Japan's military budget grew too. Yet it was not the capitalist powers, fearsome though they were, that most worried Soviet military planners in the Far East. In 1964, Beijing had tested its first nuclear weapon. In 1969 it had attacked Soviet defenses along the two countries' Manchurian and Central Asian borderlands—the same territories that had been contested by tsarist statesmen such as Nikolai Muravev and Count Sergei Witte.[3] China's military capabilities were less capable than the "imperialist" Americans and their Asian allies. But Beijing seemed more likely to start a war.

By the 1980s, therefore, the USSR's military had decisively reinforced its position in Asia. This kept Soviet borders secure, but it also degraded Soviet influence in Asia. The USSR's formidable military frightened nearly all the country's neighbors. Rather than submitting to Soviet demands, they joined up against it. Even former archrivals in Washington and Beijing had begun cooperating against the Soviet Union. Yet the Kremlin resolutely refused to change tack for over a decade.[4] Hardliners in the Soviet Communist Party had obstructed efforts to improve ties with China or to restrain military deployments in the Far East. Instead, they had launched new military adventures, supporting Vietnam's invasion of Cambodia, and invading Afghanistan themselves. And the more heavily they leaned on military power, the more Soviet leaders found themselves isolated from other regional powers and locked out of Asia.

"THE CENTURY OF THE PACIFIC"

Despite the old guard's commitment to the Brezhnev-era status quo, new ideas were brewing in the upper echelons of the Soviet Communist Party. Within the Soviet bureaucracy, officials were asking how the Soviet Union might refashion its foreign policy and reassert its influence in Asia. This new thinking was driven in part by generational changes. Younger cadres saw the aging Soviet leadership as "uncultivated, mediocre, and poorly educated," as one analyst put it. A second impetus for change was that the old policies weren't working: China and America had opened relations with each other, despite their ideological differences, while the Brezhnev-era proposal for "collective security" among Asian powers against China had flopped. A third factor was that Soviet propaganda about Japan's militaristic government and South Korea's repressive regime looked increasingly out of date. With the exception of the Soviet Union, Asia's economies were booming. Many of the Kremlin's Cold War punching bags—including capitalist Taiwan, South Korea, and the Philippines—were, in the 1980s, casting out dictators, building new democracies, and connecting their economies to the outside world. If the Soviet Union did not update its strategy in Asia, it looked likely to fall even farther behind.[5]

The most obvious critique of the Kremlin's strategy of militarized, anti-China containment was that it had failed. Rather than strengthening the Soviet Union, this policy had left the Kremlin with many enemies and few friends. The cost of two decades of military reinforcement in the Far East had been high, shifting resources toward the Soviet Union's gargantuan military-industrial complex at the expense of domestic consumption or technological innovation. Excessive military spending was an important cause of the Soviet Union's stagnating economy. Foreign Minister Eduard Shevardnadze later estimated that "confrontation with China cost us 200 billion rubles." Unhappiness over the cost of Soviet foreign policy was visible in relations with Asian client states such as Vietnam, which the Kremlin armed and bankrolled. Over the course of the 1980s, Hanoi's requests for support began to face growing skepticism from Soviet policymakers, who demanded a "full balancing of trade," which must occur not with Soviet subsidies, but "in convertible currency" at "world market prices."[6]

Several influential analysts and Communist Party officials argued that it was time to reduce the USSR's emphasis on small countries that happened to be ideological allies, and to improve relations with bigger, more influential countries instead. Small countries had learned that if they parroted Soviet slogans, they would receive cash and arms in exchange. When the Communist Party of Vietnam issued press releases praising Brezhnev, the Soviet leadership felt important on the world stage—but what other benefit did such ideological proclamations provide the USSR? The cost was substantial, not only in the rubles spent bankrolling ideological allies, but also in the regional conflicts that these "allies" dragged the Soviet Union into.

Refocusing Soviet foreign policy would require Moscow to recalibrate its policies in Asia, where it had a handful of small friends and several powerful rivals. One influential Soviet academic suggested that a "multi-polar strategy" would produce better foreign policy results. Which powers might the Soviet Union pursue better ties with? In the mid-1980s, Ronald Reagan's United States seemed like an implacable opponent, but influential foreign policy expert Georgy Arbatov advised Soviet leaders that "peace with the Chinese should be promoted" and that the USSR could reinvigorate relations with Japan. Alexander Yakovlev, who would play a key role advising the Soviet leadership in the late 1980s, called for "new steps in developing relations" with Japan and China.[7]

An additional factor driving shifts in Soviet thinking about its foreign policy in Asia was growing skepticism about socialist ideology itself.[8] Marxist-Leninist ideas had been reinterpreted multiple times between Lenin and Brezhnev, sometimes with a lens that focused on supporting socialist movements worldwide, at other times emphasizing the defense of socialism within the USSR. During some periods, notably in Stalin's final years, the success of "socialism" appeared to be roughly equivalent, in the eyes of Soviet leaders, to Russian territorial expansion. Whatever the definition of "the victory of socialism" in foreign policy terms, the concept of socialism itself began looking outmoded to many in Moscow, because the Soviet Union's deep stagnation discredited the thesis that state socialism was working. In the 1950s, the typical Soviet citizen was poor, but the Soviet economy was growing rapidly and living standards were improving. At that time, even American economics textbooks predicted that the USSR would overtake the United States economically.[9] Thirty years later, the optimism of the Khrushchev era had been replaced by a deep depression. The Soviet economy had stopped growing and was being overtaken by capitalist countries that had previously lagged far behind. Soviet politics and society, meanwhile, had sunk into a deep freeze, with Brezhnev's senility a metaphor for the tired Soviet system more generally.

"Socialism" therefore became less convincing as a foreign policy goal, at least as it had been traditionally interpreted. Yakovlev declared that it was time for "unorthodox approaches" and "doing away with old stereotypes." He adopted a new view: "The class enemy," he wrote, is "a partner in solving global problems on the basis of mutual interest." Rather than collapsing under the weight of its own contradictions, capitalism was likely to persist for an "indefinite duration," making "peaceful coexistence" not a "sort of respite . . . [but] the only possible way of existence." Moreover, Yakovlev argued, "security in the present-day world can be genuine only if it is universal and equal. . . . Nothing should be done that could be regarded by the other side as a growing threat to its security."[10]

The old guard in the Soviet leadership thought these ideas were heretical. But a growing number of Soviet officials found them realistic and refreshing. Applied to Asia, they suggested new and radical approaches to diplomacy in the region. Was there room for exploring relations with capitalist South Korea and Taiwan, with which the Soviet Union had no formal relations? Could ties with Japan, on deep freeze for decades, be reinvigorated? Might the security dilemma with China be resolved, allowing both sides to draw down forces patrolling the border? The intellectual climate began to shift away from the ideological and militarized approach to Asia.

Rethinking Soviet foreign policy in Asia seemed doubly necessary because the region appeared set to play a decisive role in the future of the world economy and political system. The 1980s were a period when, across the world, many analysts perceived the West as declining and Asia rising. Japan seemed to be setting the tone. Its technology had caught up to America's. It spent a greater share of GDP on research and development, for example, presaging rapid future growth, too. During the 1980s, Soviet analysts closely followed Japan's economic miracle, which was driven by high-tech manufacturing, cheaper production prices, and better management practices. Japan's state-led capitalist model appeared to be more efficient, which is why it was exporting high-tech manufacturing goods to the United States. Soviet scholars read influential books such as Chalmers Johnson's *MITI and the Japanese Miracle* and Ezra Vogel's *Japan as Number One*. A Soviet journal translated the concluding chapter of Paul Kennedy's *Rise and Fall of the Great Powers*, which asked whether the United States was falling behind relative to Japan. The answer, many Soviet analysts believed, was yes.[11]

Instead of the West, the future of the world economy appeared to be shifting toward Asia. In the clash between American and Japanese capitalism, Soviet scholars argued, Tokyo would come out on top. Associating Japan with militarism, as the Soviet Union had long done, no longer made sense. Japan had devoted its resources to economic growth, with spectacular results. During the early Cold War, Soviet scholars were discouraged from discussing Japan's economic miracle, or even from using the phrase with skeptical quotation marks. But it was impossible to deny. The USSR's own economic forecasts predicted that Japan would grow at 5 percent during the 1980s, far faster than either the West or the USSR.[12]

Japan's rapid growth was matched by its neighbors in Asia. "It was in no way expected that such a powerful spurt on the path of progress would be seen from an Asian country," one Russian historian noted.[13] Across East Asia, previously poor countries were industrializing rapidly, from South Korea to Singapore, Taiwan to Hong Kong. Soviet scholars did not use the term "Asian Tigers," as these countries were called in the West, but they recognized their tremendous growth rates. All these countries were opponents of communism in general and the Soviet Union in particular. Moscow had no diplomatic ties with Taipei or with Seoul. Relations with Singapore were rocky, particularly after Moscow established its military base in Vietnam's Cam Ranh Bay. And Hong Kong remained a British colony, a symbol of imperialism which, at least in theory, the Soviet Union deplored.

Nevertheless, these countries' economic success made an impression on Soviet observers. Soviet analysts watched as the Asian Tigers started exporting textiles and footwear, adopting new technology, and entering new markets. This was the Japanese model of export-led growth, and it was likely to produce the same spectacular results for the Asian Tigers, remaking the world economy in the process. "The Pacific region has become the center of world development," academic Yevgeny Primakov observed, viewing Asia's economic future with a rose-tinted lens reminiscent of Sergei Witte's optimism about access to Asian markets a century earlier. Another Soviet economist perceived "a radical restructuring of the world capitalist economy" in which "the Asian-Pacific region will set the tone." "The twenty-first century," wrote a third Soviet analyst, "promises to become the century of the Pacific."[14]

"WE CANNOT GO ON LIVING LIKE THIS"

Many of the foreign policy analysts and Communist Party apparatchiks who dreamed of recasting Soviet diplomacy served in high positions under Brezhnev and his conservative successors. But they kept their critiques of Soviet diplomacy mostly to themselves, and they never made public their eroding faith in the Soviet system itself. To most outsiders, it seemed as though the Soviet elite was united in its conservative approach to politics at home and abroad, as well as its commitment to the sclerotic status quo. After the death of Soviet leader Konstantin Chernenko in 1985, the Politburo selected Mikhail Gorbachev as his successor, a move that was not generally interpreted as a vote for change. Gorbachev was a product of the system, widely seen as a protégé of former general secretary Yuri Andropov, a bureaucrat whose main distinguishing feature was not his unique beliefs or skill set—neither of these appeared noteworthy—but rather his age. This is probably why his fellow Soviet leaders selected him: they believed he would continue the policies of the Brezhnev-Andropov-Chernenko era, but implement them with youthful vigor.

A child of peasants from Ukraine and Southern Russia, Gorbachev came from the agricultural region of Stavropol Krai, about as far from the Pacific Ocean as any point in the USSR. After attending university in the early 1950s, he moved up through the Communist Party hierarchy. Launching his party career around the time of Stalin's death, Gorbachev never experienced the brutality of the purges, though his parents had suffered from Stalin's collectivization of agriculture and his assault on the peasantry. Gorbachev was somewhat unique among Soviet leaders in remaining a true believer in some of the more humanistic claims of Soviet socialism even as he made many moral compromises in his rise to power. Naively, he did not see the contradiction at the center of his career, as he led one of the world's greatest autocracies but remained relatively liberal-minded in comparison with almost all his colleagues.[15]

Upon becoming general secretary in 1985, Gorbachev faced a dilemma. The sense of stagnation was impossible to deny. Unlike the gerontocrats who appointed him, Gorbachev found the status quo unacceptable. Yet the political system remained dominated by old-school cadres who resisted change. The economy had stopped growing and was falling behind technologically. Marxist-Leninist ideology bore ever less resemblance to the reality of Soviet life. At least Lenin and Stalin could tell an optimistic story of socialism's future. By the time Gorbachev took power, the Soviets had governed Russia for nearly seventy years. Promising that things would become better in the future was no longer enough. Unless life improved now, the country would face a crisis of legitimacy. "We cannot go on living like this," Gorbachev told his wife. "We must change."[16]

The demand for change was widespread in the Soviet Union, but there was no consensus on what must be done. Everyone agreed that the economy must be reinvigorated, but how? Many of the most inefficient parts of the economy—the heavy industries, the steel mills, the vast factories, and the collective farms—had been held up as examples of socialism's successes since Stalin. The Kremlin could not simply declare that they had become part of the problem without undermining the foundations on which Soviet socialism had been built. The Soviet defense-industrial complex consumed a vast share of the country's production—estimated at around 15 percent of GDP—but elevated levels of military spending were crucial if the country was to wage simultaneous Cold Wars with the United States and the People's Republic of China. In the United States, arch-conservative Ronald Reagan had just won reelection in 1984 on a viciously anticommunist agenda. He had famously branded the Soviet Union an "evil empire," and was spending billions to expand the US Navy and to build a new generation of weapons in outer space. It was far easier to imagine relations with the United States getting worse rather than better.

Gorbachev turned, therefore, to Asia. He had only a cursory understanding of the region and had spent barely any time studying countries like Japan or China. Yet the advisers that he surrounded himself with were the people who, during the early 1980s, had advocated a new foreign policy in the region. Some, such as Karen Brutents and Yevgeny Primakov, wanted the Kremlin to see foreign policy questions through the lens of power politics rather than ideology. The country must learn to play rivals off each other, forging a more multipolar world, they believed. Others, such as Alexander Yakovlev, were more idealistic, seeing Soviet militarism as the primary cause of the country's foreign policy problems and advocating disarmament as the solution. All these advisers told Gorbachev that, though Soviet propaganda was correct in describing Reagan as an inveterate anticommunist, it was wrong to see Japan as militaristic or to claim that China coveted Soviet territory.[17] Influenced by these aides, Gorbachev came to believe not only that he could resolve some of the USSR's disputes in Asia, but that the region could be the centerpiece of a new diplomacy focused on nonideological assessments, mutual disarmament, negotiations, and peace.

Gorbachev's efforts to improve ties with the West are well known. Less frequently recognized is his simultaneous drive to reestablish Soviet influence in Asia. He transformed the USSR's strategy in the region, downplaying the importance of military power and instead seeking to build diplomatic and economic influence—a return to soft power, Soviet-style. He was not the first Russian ruler to sense such an opportunity. Prince Esper Ukhtomsky had believed that the peoples of Asia looked to Russia as a ruler, while Khrushchev had seen a continent ripe for the USSR's socialist ideals. Gorbachev believed that the Asia-Pacific region would be receptive to the "new thinking" that underlay his foreign policy, and set out a new Asian agenda for the Soviet Union, promising disarmament, friendship, and trade. These were the tactics, he believed, that could expand the Soviet Union's influence in Asia, and make Moscow a major player in the region again.

Looking back, many historians view Gorbachev's foreign policy as primarily about retrenchment, a recognition that the Soviet Empire was overextended.[18] The Kremlin had indeed made too many enemies. Yet is wrong to view Gorbachev's foreign policy as intended only to row back Soviet commitments. Gorbachev sought policies that would increase the USSR's international influence, especially in Asia. He put forth a positive vision—a promise of peace and disarmament, a rejection of ideology, and an idealistic hope of resolving security dilemmas. His proposal of a "Common European Home" attracted most of the West's attention. But Gorbachev believed that his policies might be just as powerful in Asia. In summer 1986, he traveled to the Far Eastern city of Vladivostok to explain his vision.

"CIVILIZATION IS MOVING TOWARD THE PACIFIC OCEAN"

Gorbachev was not, of course, the first Russian leader to visit Vladivostok. Before ascending to the throne, a young Nicholas II had visited the city for a ceremony to launch the construction of the Trans-Siberian Railway. When Khrushchev visited Vladivostok in 1959, he declared it the "San Francisco of the East," and provided funds to modernize the city.[19] Yet because of its large military facilities and deeply ingrained Soviet paranoia, the city remained closed to foreign visitors and cut off from the outside world. It was geographically far to the east of Beijing, but its only major connection with Asia was via the Pacific Fleet, headquartered in Vladivostok's port, which stared down the Soviet Union's rivals in China, the United States, and Japan.

For a general secretary looking to reassert his country's role in Asia, therefore, Vladivostok presented an opportunity. Brezhnev had not visited the Soviet Far East until 1978, his fourteenth year in power.[20] Gorbachev decided to travel to the city almost immediately after being selected as general secretary, underscoring the importance he placed on the region. He believed that it was time for a change of strategy. Rather than continuing the military buildup, Gorbachev wanted disarmament agreements. Where bilateral relationships were frozen due to Soviet belligerence, Gorbachev wanted conciliation to reopen ties. New trade, investment, and cultural exchanges could strengthen ties between nations. Gorbachev's policy of perestroika—restructuring Soviet society and politics—needed to have Asian angle. He could resolve the country's conflicts with its Far Eastern neighbors, he believed, and advance Soviet influence in the rapidly growing region. "Everything is in movement on this continent," Gorbachev told his top aides only months after taking power in 1985. "Civilization is moving toward the Pacific Ocean." It was time for the Soviet Union to take advantage.[21]

To mark his visit to Vladivostok, Gorbachev prepared a speech that would outline a new policy of engagement with Asia, offer an olive branch to all the neighbors that Soviet militarization had frightened, and propose initiatives to connect the USSR to Asia's fast-growing economies. The logic was straightforward: Soviet ties with the West were frozen, but perhaps relations with East Asia—the region that would shape the future of the world economy—might be reopened. Reinvigorating the Soviet Union's position in Asia would therefore be a focus. As Gorbachev explained to his colleagues in April 1986 while preparing the speech: "The development of civilization is moving in that direction. We are also moving, in Siberia, in the Soviet Far East. There is an objective interest in questions about Asia-Pacific Cooperation. . . . The Asian-Pacific region is one of our most important orientations." The Soviet Union, he declared on a different occasion, was "one of the greatest Asian powers." Thus, the significance of Moscow's "Asian and Pacific Ocean orientation is increasing."

As he planned his speech in Vladivostok, Gorbachev had these grand ambitions in mind. "The speech in Vladivostok should be large-scale," Gorbachev told his speechwriters in July 1986, as they drafted the address. It is "for the country, and for the world, and not only about regional problems." Asia "is an enormous continent, where dozens of new governments have entered the arena. They are searching for their path. How those processes turn out, especially in the big countries . . . will define the fate of the world," Gorbachev noted. The speech must emphasize that "the Soviet Union is a European and at the same time an Asian country, so it is closer to Asian problems."[22]

Gorbachev's Vladivostok speech set off a slow-moving diplomatic revolution. The Soviet Union was a military power, but it would no longer place threats of force at the center of its Asian diplomacy. "I am not inclined to believe that the military industrial complex is omnipotent," Gorbachev declared in his speech. Instead, he said, the Soviet Far East would begin exporting to Asia and integrating with the region's fast-growing economics. "Many major states of the world, including the USSR, the United States, India, China, Japan, Vietnam, Mexico and Indonesia," border the Pacific Ocean. "Here are situated states which are considered to be medium-sized ones, but are rather big by European standards—Canada, the Philippines, Australia, and New Zealand. . . . This colossal human and socio-political massif calls for close attention, study and respect."[23]

Asia's economic vitality had caught Soviet attention. Asia has "woken up to a new life in the twentieth century," Gorbachev declared, citing a "whirlwind of changes—social, scientific, and technological . . . a renaissance of world history." The USSR's economic future, too, looked Asian. "The laws of growing interdependence and the need for economic integration urge one to look for ways leading to agreement and to the establishment of open ties between states." To increase trade with Asia, and to forge the interdependence that Gorbachev saw as desirable and inevitable, the Soviet Union must shift from a war footing toward peace. "Why not support each other? Why not cooperate?" Gorbachev asked in his speech. "Some of the major problems of cooperation are literally knocking at our door."[24]

AFGHANISTAN

It was one thing for Gorbachev to call for better relations with Asia, as his aged predecessors had all done, with varying degrees of sincerity. Actually changing Soviet policy required substantive steps. The Vladivostok speech signaled to the Soviet bureaucracy that change was inevitable, and that the old foreign policy line, which had guaranteed the militarization of Soviet diplomacy in Asia, was no longer acceptable. The old guard must either give in or be swept aside. Hawkish defense minister Dmitry Ustinov, who had long blocked better ties with Beijing, had died in December 1984, right before Gorbachev took power, opening space for change in that ministry. Gorbachev sidelined long-serving foreign minister Andrei Gromyko in 1985, in addition to influential diplomat Andrei Aleksandrov-Agentov and Communist Party officials Boris Ponomarev and Konstantin Rusakov, each of whom advocated a hawkish policy on China and an aggressive, ideological, and militarized policy across the region.[25]

These old-guard officials were replaced by advisers who were in most cases a half-generation younger. This new set of foreign policy experts shaped Gorbachev's thinking about international politics and advocated a new role for the Soviet Union in Asia. Soviet foreign policy, they believed, had become overly militarized, exaggerating threats and making unnecessary enemies. Withdrawal from Afghanistan, which had become a hopeless quagmire, was a priority. "Our military presence in Afghanistan," argued one of Gorbachev's aides, "places an enormous financial burden on the USSR . . . damages our reputation with the Muslim world, and gives the Americans an ideal opportunity to exhaust us. . . . The faster we leave that mousetrap, the better."[26]

From his earliest days in office, Gorbachev realized he needed to address Afghanistan. The Soviet invasion of the country had created tension with countries across Asia; even North Korea opposed the invasion. Japan tightened its relationship with the United States, describing ties as a "military alliance" and promising to help the United States defend sea lanes in the Pacific Ocean, from Vladivostok to Taiwan.[27] There were few countries in the Asia-Pacific region that welcomed the Soviet military presence in Afghanistan.

Moreover, by the mid-1980s, the invasion had become a quagmire, with thousands of Soviet soldiers killed or wounded and no victory in sight. *Pravda*, the most prominent Soviet newspaper, received "literally a torrent of letters about Afghanistan," one Gorbachev aide recorded in his diary. "Unlike before, there are very few anonymous anti-Soviet letters. Almost all of them are signed. The main message: why do we need this, and when will it end?!" After over five years of war, the Kremlin had no real answer. The outpouring of anger against a core foreign policy decision had little precedent in Soviet history. "Women are writing, pitying the young men who are dying and suffering mentally there. They are writing that if 'this is so necessary,' then send volunteers . . . but not the recruits; because being there and doing what they must do mutilates their souls," this Gorbachev aide noted.[28]

Even the military—whose top leaders had opposed the intervention in Afghanistan in the first place—complained about the war. "Soldiers are writing, sincerely and simply reporting that they do not understand 'why we are here.' Officers, and even one general, who signed his name, are writing that they are unable to explain to their soldiers, subordinates, 'why they are here,' and that only from the outside it can seem that they are 'fulfilling the international duty,' but being there it is impossible to believe."[29] Gorbachev and his aides also struggled to explain 'why are we here?' The war seemed to serve no purpose; it caused horrible losses for the Soviet military and antagonized the USSR's neighbors. It was obviously going to be lost; the only question was when.

As early as 1985, Gorbachev made up his mind: the USSR must leave Afghanistan. In a meeting a month after taking power, Gorbachev told an adviser who urged a drawdown from Afghanistan that he was "thinking it over." Two months after that, he reiterated that Afghanistan was a "paramount issue" in his effort to reorient Soviet foreign policy.[30] When he met with Afghanistan's president Babrak Karmal that autumn, he demanded that "the Afghans learn to defend themselves" and that Afghanistan's government back down from its revolutionary aims. "There is no popular base," Gorbachev admonished Karmal. "Without that any kind of revolution has no chances." Afghanistan's government needed "to make a sharp turn back," he declared, "to free capitalism, to the Afghani and Islamic values, to sharing power with oppositional and even the currently hostile forces." He was even advised "to seek compromises even with rebel leaders"—the very rebels that were waging guerrilla war against Soviet forces, too.

Gorbachev told his Soviet colleagues that it was time to leave Afghanistan. "With or without Karmal, we will follow this line firmly," he declared, "which must in a minimally short amount of time lead to our withdrawal from Afghanistan."[31] In the end, the withdrawal would take half a decade to implement, in part because Gorbachev was distracted by other issues, in part because he and most of his colleagues wanted to withdraw in a manner that didn't look like a complete defeat. But by 1985, it was clear that the Soviet Union would eventually pull out, if necessary in a humiliating fashion. The militarization of Soviet foreign policy in Asia—the core of Brezhnev's strategy to assert Soviet interests in the region—was being unwound.

GORBACHEV'S "TRIANGLE" DIPLOMACY

The decision to withdraw from Afghanistan also made possible an improvement in relations with China. Mao was gone, but Beijing's demands persisted, namely that the USSR leave Afghanistan, reduce support for Vietnam's invasion of Cambodia, and cut Soviet military forces in the Far East. Given how isolated the Kremlin was from most other powers, Chinese leaders believed that they were in the stronger position. Beijing was unwilling to yield and was prepared to wait. Improved relations with China would only come if the Soviet Union changed its strategy in Asia and offered concessions to Beijing.

Gorbachev had put China at the center of his Vladivostok speech to signal to Beijing that he was shifting course, and not only on the question of Afghanistan. Vietnam's war in Cambodia served no obvious Soviet interest, either. And reducing Soviet military forces in the Far East fit the goal of the new diplomacy, shifting emphasis from military means to economic and diplomatic tools. What the old guard saw as "concessions" to China, Gorbachev's new advisers perceived as steps that suited the Soviet Union's own interests. If these foreign policy changes improved relations with Beijing, too, so much the better.

Gorbachev's most important promise in his Vladivostok speech was that "the question of withdrawing a large part of the Soviet troops in Mongolia is being considered." Any change to Soviet force posture in the Far East would represent a remarkable shift in strategy, a reversal of Soviet policy in Asia since the days of Stalin. Gorbachev's logic, as he explained to his colleagues in the Politburo before the speech, was that the "two divisions" of the Soviet army in Mongolia are not "saving the USSR! Better to bring them home." They were "hostages" sitting merely a "two days' march from Beijing. . . . When the forces were sent to Mongolia, the idea was to make China, Japan, and the USA appear to us and to the Mongols like enemies." If the forces were withdrawn, he suggested, perhaps these countries could now be friends.[32]

Even as Gorbachev announced preparations to draw down forces, reducing China's perception that the Soviet Union posed an urgent military threat, he also changed his diplomatic strategy, ending the effort to contain China. The withdrawal from Afghanistan was part of this shift, symbolizing a change in tack on the USSR's willingness to use force in Asia. More substantive was India, a country that had long leaned to the Soviet Union's side in the Cold War, which saw China as its main security threat, and which had been relatively tolerant of the USSR's invasion of Afghanistan. A new prime minister, Rajiv Gandhi, took power in India in 1984. Like Gorbachev, the youthful Gandhi was seen as representing an energetic new generation of political leaders. "It is just amazing how much we have in common," Gandhi exclaimed in one meeting with Gorbachev. Like his predecessors, Gorbachev showered aid on India, providing the country advanced military equipment. After visiting India in 1986, Gorbachev told his Politburo colleagues, "We cannot say aloud the world 'ally' with regard to India but we should take matters in that direction."[33]

Gorbachev did not use his relationship with Gandhi to push for an antiChina line, however. Where Brezhnev had pressured India to join a system of "collective security" against China, Gorbachev took a different tack. The effort to contain China was set aside. Collective security against China was replaced by proposals for an "all-Asia forum" that would promote "united efforts of Asian governments to develop a comprehensive approach to security in Asia"—an idea intended to include China. The USSR, India, and China could work together in a "triangle in Asia," Gorbachev declared, and could collectively shape the continent's politics and guarantee its security.[34]

Gorbachev's new diplomatic strategy vis-à-vis Beijing was coupled with a shift in the tone of Soviet debate about China. The vicious attacks on Maoism that had marked the Brezhnev era began to disappear, in part because the Kremlin discouraged them, in part because they were increasingly at odds with reality, as China moved ever farther from Mao's radicalism. Rather than dispute the meaning of Marxism-Leninism, many of Gorbachev's top foreign policy aides celebrated "diversity" within the socialist community. "The time when such diversity was viewed with dogmatic, sectarian suspicion . . . is now past," Gorbachev adviser Vadim Medvedev argued. Deputy Foreign Minister Anatoly Adamishin declared that "injecting ideology into foreign policy" was "dangerous" because it "is the direct path to foisting one's views, scale of values and ideals [and] hence one step to the imposition of one's convictions by force."[35]

Gorbachev's foreign policy aides had their own domestic reasons to attack ideological foreign policies, which they saw as the root of many of the ill-advised foreign adventures of the Brezhnev era. Such an approach also smoothed ties with Beijing by setting aside the question of which socialist power would play the leading role in interpreting Marx and Engels. Moreover, it was clear that Chinese "socialism" was shifting dramatically—in the same direction that Gorbachev was pushing Soviet politics. Central planning and state ownership were being slowly replaced by de facto private property, all in the name of boosting economic growth. China served as a "laboratory" for reformed socialism, one Soviet scholar said. Another Soviet analyst recounted looking at China's reforms as if they were "our own personal business." At the time, a Soviet journalist walked the streets of Moscow and asked what ideas came to mind upon mention of China. "They thought of the Great Wall and China's capital, Beijing. They named well-known Chinese goods . . . but almost every one of those questioned mentioned the word 'reform.'"[36] As the USSR and China both transformed their concepts of socialism, the old disputes about the meaning of Marxism melted away.

As a result of these changes, the Chinese soon realized that Gorbachev was promising something substantively different from what Brezhnev and his successors had offered. The pledge to withdraw from Afghanistan, the draw-down in troops from the Far East, the end to efforts to pressure India into joining an anti-Beijing alliance—these were major Soviet concessions. By 1989, the Chinese were ready to host Gorbachev in Beijing in recognition of his change of tack.

Gorbachev arrived in the Chinese capital on May 15, 1989, just as protestors were beginning to assemble on Tiananmen Square, angry at their govern-ment's slow pace of political opening and an array of economic problems. Like Gorbachev, China's liberal-minded Communist Party general secretary, Zhao Ziyang, was facing intense opposition from hardline party cadres that opposed change. Gorbachev had expected to celebrate "socialist brother-hood" in Beijing, but even as he visited he found the idea of socialism itself under debate. Chinese students chanted "Let's change Deng for Gorbachev," referring to hardline authoritarian Deng Xiaoping, whom they wanted to oust. Protestors held placards welcoming Gorbachev that declared, "We Sa-lute the Ambassador of Democracy." Chinese students took trains from the provinces just to glimpse the USSR's leader, while protesters studied Gor-bachev's book *Perestroika: New Thinking for Our Country and the World.*[37]

The 200,000 protesters on Tiananmen Square only slightly obstructed Gor-bachev's visit, forcing his Chinese hosts to reshuffle the schedule of meet-ings between the general secretary and Chinese officials. Yet the Soviet leader struggled to balance the need to forge new relations with China's reactionary leaders and his desire to promote the new, liberalized socialism that he be-lieved he represented. Gorbachev's meeting with Deng focused on geopo-litical matters, stressing the importance of their relations "as great powers." The two sides agreed on a joint communique that de facto ended the Sino-Soviet split after decades of vitriol. But in a public speech in Beijing, Gor-bachev declared that "economic reform will not work unless supported by a radical transformation of the political system." The Chinese declined to broadcast these comments to their people. And Deng invited three US war-ships to visit Shanghai, arriving in the city's port one day after Gorbachev.[38] Deng wanted to the Soviets to remember that China had options, so Gor-bachev should choose his words and actions carefully.

Just after Gorbachev left China, Deng toppled General Secretary Zhao and sent in tanks to crush the protestors on Tiananmen Square. Many parts of Soviet society condemned Deng and his fellow Chinese reactionaries. Influential Soviet foreign policy experts penned essays denouncing the massacre. When a top Chinese Communist Party official later sought to visit St. Petersburg, the newly elected mayor refused to meet with him. But Gorbachev stuck close to China's leaders. He would not imperil Sino-Soviet rapprochement, whatever the domestic backlash against Beijing—or against him. In the Soviet Union's legislature, famed dissident Andrey Sakharov sought to condemn the Chinese leadership, to "protest the inhuman cruelty of the Chinese authorities and express our solidarity. . . . We appeal to the Chinese government to . . . stop immediately . . . executions and the persecution of dissidents." But when Sakharov stood up to deliver his rebuke of the Chinese Communist Party, Gorbachev had Sakharov's microphone turned off.[39]

Ultimately Gorbachev declined to criticize China over the massacre. Meeting with Rajiv Gandhi two months after the Tiananmen killings, he told the Indian prime minister that condemning Beijing's hardline response "would be interference in the internal affairs of a country." Gorbachev grumbled to Gandhi that, on a visit to Paris, French intellectuals had asked him to condemn China, "a country," he told Gandhi, "with a population higher than one billion people. This is a whole civilization!" Gorbachev would not put this relationship at risk over China's killing of perhaps several thousand protestors. Instead, he reiterated his view to Gandhi that Moscow, Beijing, and New Delhi should create a "triangle" of partnership to jointly manage international politics in Asia.[40] Rebalancing the Soviet Union's position in Asia, and trying to place Moscow at the center of Asian diplomacy, remained Gorbachev's focus. Criticism of China, whether for being too radical under Mao Zedong, or too authoritarian under Deng Xiaoping, was seen as counterproductive and even dangerous. The Brezhnev era had demonstrated the dangers of picking fights with Beijing. Gorbachev was focused relentlessly on befriending the Chinese government instead.

COMPROMISE IN KOREA

China was not the only ostensible socialist ally with which Gorbachev had inherited a history of complicated and conflictual relations. Unlike Mao Zedong, North Korean leader Kim Il Sung never sent his armies across the border to fight his Soviet big brother. But Pyongyang had never been a perfectly pliable client, either. When Sino-Soviet relations had collapsed during the 1960s during the Cold War, North Korea skillfully played the two communist superpowers off each other, winning concessions from both Beijing and Moscow as each socialist superpower feared that Pyongyang was leaning toward the other side. North Korea's greatest fear, meanwhile, remained its rival in South Korea and the American military forces that backed it. In much of the Brezhnev era, one Soviet diplomat remembered, the Kremlin "perceived [North Korea] as a strategic ally, a Far Eastern outpost," crucial to the struggle against both China and the United States.[41]

By the time Gorbachev took power, however, Soviet diplomacy in the 1960s and 1970s looked to many Soviet analysts like a costly failure. Such foreign policy experts urged a new approach to North Korea, just as they advocated a new line toward China. But like Soviet relations with Beijing, the old guard long obstructed efforts at change. In a 1984 meeting of the USSR's International Department, for example, one expert suggested improving ties with Seoul. At the time, the Soviet Union had no diplomatic relations with South Korea at all. "It is high time that the tail stops telling the dog what to do," this analyst suggested. "Why should we look at South Korea through Pyongyang's eyes? It is obvious that South Korea is a successful and respected country which is genuinely interested in being our friend."

Hardliners long rejected such an approach. "Accepting South Korean moves will not only undermine our cooperation with an ally, the DPRK [Democratic People's Republic of Korea], it will undermine the unity of the whole Socialist Commonwealth," one retorted. A second official noted that North Korea was a "bastion in the Far East of our struggle against American and Japanese imperialism and Chinese revisionism. It is politically irresponsible to advocate betrayal of the Soviet ally for the sake of an utterly pro-American and repressive regime in the South." And anyway, as then–foreign minister Andrey Gromyko pointed out on a different occasion, South Korea was nothing more than "a huge [American] base, more precisely a complex of bases of nuclear weapons." Before Gorbachev took power, in other words, the trend in Soviet foreign policy was toward closer relations with Pyongyang, symbolized by a summit with Kim Il Sung in Moscow in 1984, the North Korean leader's first visit to Moscow in seventeen years.[42]

When Gorbachev took power in 1985, this began to change. He had no desire to imperil relations with Pyongyang. In meetings with North Korean leaders he parroted long-standing Soviet warnings about "ominous plans to create a Washington-Tokyo-Seoul military block . . . a kind of Eastern NATO." Yet the same foreign policy advisers that were devising foreign policy toward China applied their new thinking to the Korean Peninsula as well, drawing several conclusions. First, Moscow had become a "hostage" of Pyongyang, as Soviet official Karen Brutents put it, fearing to establish normal relations with Seoul. Second, South Korea was not simply a tool of Washington but "a factor of global, military-strategic balance," as the Politburo concluded in a May 1986 discussion. Third, as the USSR de-emphasized ideology in its foreign policy, it had new space "for contacts and exchanges between socialist countries and South Korea," as Yakovlev wrote. Finally, as the Soviet Union looked to reinvigorate its economy, Seoul was "the most promising partner in the Far East," as an official put it in an August 1988 meeting. This view was echoed by officials working in industries from finance to oil and gas, all of whom perceived opportunities to trade with South Korea.[43]

South Korea itself was newly interested in relations with the Soviet Union. As early as the 1970s, Seoul had declared its willingness to open relations with the Soviet Union, albeit with unrealistic conditions such as a complete cessation of Soviet aid to Pyongyang. Efforts at diplomacy between the USSR and South Korea accelerated after the Kremlin decided to send athletes to the 1988 Olympic Games in Seoul. Expanded media freedom in the USSR reduced the popularity of North Korea, as Pyongyang was subjected to a torrent of criticism for being totalitarian, repressive, and an economic failure. When North Korean diplomats complained to pro-perestroika journalist Alexsandr Bovin about his critical articles in the late 1980s, he told them to "go to hell"—not the attitude that Soviet journalists had been previously known for.[44]

Soviet journalists also levied a second line of criticism: that their country's relations with Pyongyang had proven a bad deal for the USSR. "For a long time," the newspaper *Izvestia* declared in September 1989, "we had no policy of our own, we merely automatically supported the course of our ally . . . [and] we stubbornly rejected economic contacts with the South which were beneficial to the Soviet Union." By contrast, in the Soviet public sphere, discussion of South Korea grew only more optimistic. One of Gorbachev's aides told him that "there is definitely no other place on earth where people so heartily welcome Soviets," and to expect "tremendous opportunities" in relations with Seoul. The key opportunity that Soviet leaders perceived was trade and investment. The South Koreans' main interest was in opening ties with Moscow, but in the Kremlin, one leading foreign policymaker told a South Korean interlocutor, "Giving priority to economic exchange is Soviet policy."[45]

In theory, there was plenty of scope for increased economic exchange between the two countries. South Korea had technology and consumer goods, while the USSR had commodities. South Korean business was interested in timber and natural gas, for example, and Samsung considered building factories for color TVs in the USSR. But South Korea already had access to the world's biggest markets, including the United States, Japan, and Europe. It saw relations with the USSR primarily as a political question and offered a loan of $3 billion if the Kremlin would agree to open diplomatic relations. Moscow promptly agreed. Gorbachev and South Korean president Roh Tae Woo planned a secret meeting in mid-1990 and agreed on the terms of the loan. Three months later, formal diplomatic relations between the two countries were established, a previously unthinkable repudiation of Soviet policy toward South Korea since the days of Stalin.[46]

THE LAWS OF INTERDEPENDENCE

As Gorbachev celebrated his fifth year in office in 1990, the political agenda of perestroika in the Pacific was progressing nicely. The Soviet Union had cast off its pariah status, renewing its relationship with most of the region's powers. Vietnam and North Korea were frustrated by Gorbachev's rapprochement with their rivals, of course. But with the most powerful countries in the Asia-Pacific region the Kremlin had vastly better relations in 1990 than five years earlier. The Afghanistan War had finally been wound down, as had Vietnam's occupation of Cambodia. Most importantly, the Soviet Union had signaled that it was no longer a military threat by beginning to draw down forces from the Far East. In late 1988, Gorbachev announced plans to pull three-quarters of Soviet troops from Mongolia, a reduction of 50,000 soldiers. The Kremlin also began redeploying its planes at the Vietnamese military base of Cam Ranh Bay back to the Soviet Union.[47] Within the USSR, discussion turned to the question of converting military factories to civilian production, an effort to overcome the militarization that had contributed to Soviet economic stagnation. The only outlier in this landscape of improving relations was the Soviet Union's ties with Japan, which as late as 1990 remained relatively frozen, especially in comparison with the transformation of Moscow's relations with other regional players, from Seoul to Beijing.

In the process of transforming the Soviet presence in Asia, however, Gorbachev came to realize that his predecessors overemphasized military tools in part because the military was one of the few levers that the Kremlin could reliably pull. In his 1986 Vladivostok speech, Gorbachev had declared that "growing interdependence" was a "law." He advocated "economic integration." But despite his speeches, the Soviet Union developed little new interdependence and even less integration. The natural law of interconnectedness that Gorbachev had hypothesized was not as inevitable as he had hoped. The rest of Asia was plugging into new supply chains that crisscrossed the region, from Seoul to Singapore to Shenzhen. But almost all this integration passed by the Soviet Union.

There was some increase in trade between the USSR and its neighbors. Trade with China grew from $1.8 billion in 1988 to $5.2 billion two years later, a promising trend. But in the context of what the Soviet Union needed— or in comparison to the depth of the trade that linked Japan, the Asian Tigers, and increasingly China, too—this was far smaller than Gorbachev had hoped. Trade with South Korea increased, too, but the country's powerhouse firms invested only one-eighth the amount in the USSR as they did in China.[48]

The Soviet Union tried to encourage trade by creating special economic zones for foreign investors of the type that China had used to attract substantial funds to its manufacturing sector. In a 1988 speech, Gorbachev backed "the establishment of special joint enterprise zones in the Far East," noting "the possibilities of developing Chinese-Soviet-Japanese trilateral economic activity." The city of Nakhodka, a port not far from the Chinese and North Korean borders, created a free enterprise zone. Its port already handled most of the USSR's trade by sea with Asia. Yet the zone never took off, with local officials blaming the Kremlin, despite Moscow having supportive legislation. Foreigners continued to complain, as one Japanese official put it, that "for an entrepreneur to play an active role, a minimum of two factors are needed: a good infrastructure and settled legislation. At present these do not exist."[49]

The deeper problem was that Gorbachev, like many Russian leaders before him, had overestimated the scope for integrating Russia with East Asia's economies. "We are only at the beginning of the path to the future of the world's great Asian and Pacific region," he declared in 1988, but he was wrong to assume that this Asia-Pacific future would include the Soviet Union. There was no obvious fit between the Soviet Union and its Asian neighbors. In 1988, a Japanese embassy official asked several Soviet economists, "What is the most important goal of development of the Far East?" Was it "creating a great technological base for developing connections with the Pacific" or a focus on "traditional branches" such as fish and timber? "An orientation toward natural resources would be incorrect," the Soviet official declared. "We are striving for a transition to modern production, including in machine construction."[50]

Yet where to find the foreigners willing to invest in such production, none could say. The South Koreans had just lent the USSR $3 billion, but were neither interested nor capable of bankrolling the renovation of the Soviet industrial base in the Far East. The Chinese, having just escaped the horrors of Maoism, had no money. Gorbachev's enthusiasm on its own was not enough to convince international firms to set up shop. Five years of perestroika proved that Gorbachev's optimism about economic integration in the Asia-Pacific region had been misplaced.

"POLITICAL SUICIDE"

By 1991, perestroika's Asian agenda had left Gorbachev weaker rather than stronger. He had succeeded in transforming Soviet foreign policy in the region, reducing its reliance on military force. Withdrawing from Afghanistan ended the stream of body bags and cut costs, too. Drawing down forces from the Far East was probably also beneficial for the Soviet economy, at least in the long term. But few of the positive changes that Gorbachev had expected came to pass. Ties with China remained, but the post-Tiananmen "butchers of Beijing" seemed like much less attractive partners to perestroika-era liberals. With South Korea, the Kremlin had opened relations—no small accomplishment—but it had no subsequent agenda for relations beyond hoping that South Korean firms might start building factories in the Russian Far East. This never materialized.

Longtime partners such as India, meanwhile, soon lost their interest in perestroika. Indian prime minister Rajiv Gandhi had at first established a strong relationship with Gorbachev, seeing in him a similarly young, energetic, and reform-minded leader. Yet Gorbachev's perception of "huge potential" in relations between "the USSR, India, and China" struck New Delhi as misguided. The Americans are "literally shaking over the signs of improvement in Sino-Soviet relations and rapprochement between the USSR and India," Gorbachev claimed on one occasion. But New Delhi looked on warily as the USSR improved ties with India's archrival in Beijing. Gorbachev grumbled that India was pursuing a "great power policy," which sat poorly with his desire to play the leadership role in Asia. Meanwhile, Gandhi, who had established a solid working relationship with Gorbachev, was assassinated in 1989. The economic interconnections that perestroika promised disappointed in India, too, as the country's trade with the USSR fell rather than increased.[51]

As late as 1990, however, there was one other Asian superpower that perestroika had thus far ignored. Gorbachev finally turned his attention toward Japan in 1990, preparing for a visit in 1991. Relations between Tokyo and Moscow had long been obstructed by a territorial dispute over the four southernmost Kuril Islands, which the Soviet Union occupied after World War II, but which Japan continued to claim as its own. The islands themselves were small and sparsely populated, but the Soviet military argued that they were important in controlling entrance into the Sea of Okhotsk, and thus crucial for the defense of the Far East. Throughout the Cold War, Japan conditioned relations with the Soviet Union on a resolution of the island dispute. Because little progress was made, ties between the two countries remained frozen.

As perestroika began, some Soviet foreign policy experts had urged a change of tack on the islands. Georgy Arbatov, who had advised Gorbachev to wind town tensions with China, also urged him in 1985 to "give up two, if not all four, islands to the Japanese because otherwise we will not get anywhere." Gorbachev at first resisted the idea of surrendering islands to Japan. But as his efforts in other regions failed, and the Soviet economy slowed, he began to reconsider. The Japanese promised up to $22 billion, far more than the meager $3 billion that the USSR had charged Seoul as the price of reestablishing relations.[52] By the time of Gorbachev's visit to Japan in April 1991, at the peak of Tokyo's cherry blossom season, he was willing at least to consider such a trade.

Gorbachev's declining popularity at home obstructed his ability to pursue new ideas abroad, however. Japan's demand that the USSR turn over territory, meanwhile, was hard to describe as anything other than a humiliating concession. Gorbachev was able to change Soviet policies when they appeared win-win, benefiting the Soviet people by ending useless wars or shifting spending from defense to domestic production. But handing over territory was something different. The head of the KGB and the defense minister sent Gorbachev a terse one-page letter in early 1991 warning him that the islands were too militarily important to surrender, and that the Soviet people would not support such a move.

Gorbachev, meanwhile, was losing influence to Boris Yeltsin, the leader of the Russian Republic within the Soviet Union. In January 1990, Yeltsin had visited Japan and considered ways that the dispute might be resolved. But by August of that year, Yeltsin sensed that the political winds were shifting. Visiting the contested island of Kunashir, he declared his opposition to Gorbachev's plan to "sell Russian territory." Polls from the period found that most residents of the Russian Far East—up to 90 percent in some regions—opposed territorial concessions to Japan. Any compromise with Japan that exchanged territory for cash would be "political suicide," one Soviet provincial governor declared. It might even lead to a military coup, others worried.[53]

By 1991, it was not only with Japan that perestroika in the Pacific had failed. Anti-China feelings were rising across the Soviet Far East, with one Soviet newspaper declaring in April 1991 that "the love of things Chinese has passed." Dreams of economic interconnectedness had not materialized. Rather than bolstering his popularity, Gorbachev's Pacific strategy was now seen as requiring embarrassing concessions to Russia's rivals. Across Asia Gorbachev had succeeded in making the Soviet Union seem less threatening, but he could not make it more appealing. The leadership role he so desired proved impossible to obtain. Perestroika in the Pacific had produced as many risks as it had rewards, with foreign powers like Japan trying even to coerce the Kremlin into surrendering territory that it had controlled for decades.

There had been a moment in the late 1980s when the optimistic vision of perestroika in the Pacific seemed to be working. The Soviet Union resolved long-standing conflicts and ideological clashes with China and South Korea. Trade and investment increased, if only slightly. But the aggregate effects of Gorbachev's Asia policies proved far more limited than he expected. The re-

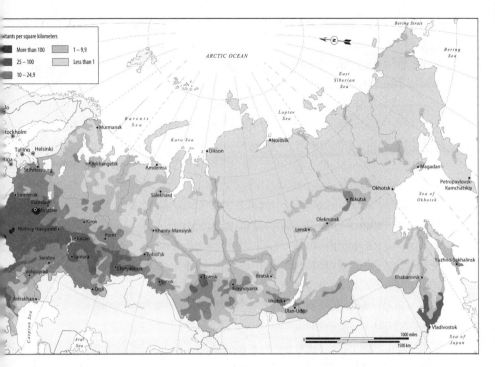

Population density of Soviet Russia

establishment of diplomatic relations with South Korea and the eventual settlement of the border dispute with China were two enduring legacies of Gorbachev's Asian pivot. Yet the broader agenda of disarmament, economic exchange, and mutual security soon petered out. The Soviet Union's Asian neighbors were happy to pocket concessions but were uninterested in offering their own.

Many of the region's most intractable disputes, from the Korean Peninsula to the Kuril Islands, remained unsolved. The promise that Russian cities such as Vladivostok or the port of Nakhodka might become Asian metropolises was unfulfilled. Asia boomed, as Gorbachev had predicted, but it left Russia behind. Trade barely increased, and foreign investment into the Russian Far East remained limited. Gorbachev's program of perestroika was not the first time that Russian leaders had perceived the opportunity to build a "New Canaan" along the Pacific Coast. He was right in thinking that "civilization was moving toward the Pacific." But the Soviet Union, despite Gorbachev's exhortations, was not.

Soon Gorbachev himself was cast out of power, first by a hardliner coup against him, then by Yeltsin, who dissolved the Soviet Union and took leadership of a new Russian state. Yeltsin had dabbled in Asian affairs during the time of perestroika, most notably by supporting, and then, after a flip-flop, opposing a deal with Japan. But as Russia's president in the 1990s, Yeltsin declined to prioritize Asia. He held occasional summits with Asian leaders but failed to articulate any positive agenda. His focus was on winning aid and recognition from the Western powers. The Russian Far East, meanwhile, suffered a painful decline, with military-industrial factories closing and the population shrinking, as 9 percent of the region's residents moved west in search of better living standards.[54] The perestroika pivot had ended.

Gorbachev may have been lucky to have been cast out of power in late 1991, before the painful decline of the Russian Far East and the final collapse of his optimistic Asian vision. There were risks lurking everywhere. Hardline factions of the KGB and military who saw Gorbachev's policy as a strategy of surrender were mobilizing against him. On Gorbachev's visit to Tokyo in April 1991, Japanese police arrested a man wearing a kimono and carrying an eleven-inch-long knife. He planned to commit suicide, police reported.[55] Gorbachev was lucky here, too. His predecessor Tsar Nicholas II had barely survived a knife attack in Japan 100 years earlier, also amid the April cherry blossom season. Like Nicholas, Gorbachev had imagined Asia as a land of opportunities, but few of these materialized. Unlike the Asian expansionism of Nicholas's day, however, Gorbachev's perestroika pivot ended not with a bloody war, but simply by petering out.

"HEIR TO THE EMPIRE OF GENGHIS KHAN"

Vladimir Putin's Pivot to Asia

"GOOD AFTERNOON friends, ladies, and gentlemen. Let me welcome you to Vladivostok." So began Russian president Vladimir Putin's address to the Far Eastern Economic Forum, a conference organized by Russia's government, in September 2015. Putin had traveled to Russia's Far East with the aim of highlighting the "great interest," "great potential," and "radical changes" in the region. Russia was pursuing a policy of "fast-track development" in the Far East, Putin declared. Why? Because Asia is the future of the global economy, "a major production center, an established world workshop . . . [with] engineering centers and high technology production."[1]

Because of Asia's economic growth, Putin declared, Russia's government was prioritizing it like never before. "State authorities are investing 13.8 billion rubles in infrastructure development," he promised, which "will enable us to attract private investment totaling 126.5 billion rubles." There would be a new bridge, a new investment fund, tax breaks, a free port at Vladivostok, subsidized loans, streamlined visas, and even a revitalized railroad. "I am convinced that the Asia-Pacific countries," Putin continued, "will clearly remain the locomotive of the global economy." "With its colossal resources, Russia can ensure the enhanced growth of the economies of the Asia-Pacific region."[2]

Putin has made many promises to many Russian cities over the course of twenty years as the country's paramount leader. Bridges, railroads, tax breaks—all this was standard fare. Yet Putin's visit to Vladivostok was about far more than port infrastructure or subsidized loans. It was about reasserting Russia's status as a major player in Asia, and convincing Russians that their future was not with the West, but in the East.

The twelve months before Putin's speech in Vladivostok had been traumatic for Russian leaders. In 2014, amid a political crisis in Kyiv, the Kremlin had decided to invade Ukraine, first seizing the Crimean Peninsula, then setting up a puppet government in part of Eastern Ukraine. Russian troops defeated Ukrainian forces on the battlefield, but caused Europe and the United States to impose painful economic sanctions, slashing the level of foreign investment into Russia. At the same time, the price of oil, Russia's primary export, plunged by half, from over $100 per barrel to less than $50, dragging Russia's economy down with it. Suddenly Russia's deep economic and political ties with Europe looked less like an opportunity than a weapon that Western powers would use against it. Hence Putin traveled to Vladivostok in 2015, promising not only new investment in Russia's Far Eastern province, but also declaring that "strengthening relations" with Asia-Pacific countries is a matter of "strategic importance for Russia." Locked out of the West, the Kremlin decided to turn east instead.[3] In the years since 2014, Russia has deepened its relationship with China and declared that its foreign policy would focus on the "Greater Eurasia" region.

YELTSIN AND CHINA

Putin's pivot to Asia over the past decade came after twenty years in which Asia has played only a minor role in Russian foreign policy. Boris Yeltsin, who took power as president of Russia at the end of 1991 after outmaneuvering Mikhail Gorbachev and abolishing the Soviet Union, had mostly ignored Asia. Inheriting a country broken by decades of Soviet misrule, Yeltsin's government barely had the capacity to consider foreign policy as his country lurched between domestic crises. The economy was in a deep depression for much of the 1990s. The Soviet Union had bequeathed to independent Russia a backward industrial sector careening toward bankruptcy.

Galloping inflation destroyed the life savings of nearly every Russian family. And Russia's bureaucratic apparatus, inherited from the Soviet Union, remained incapable of basic government functions such as tax collection or law enforcement.

The Soviet state had dissolved during the final days of Gorbachev's rule, but the Soviet-era Communist Party elite remained, often rebranded as nationalists or conservatives. Regional leaders, managers of major firms, law enforcement personnel, and government bureaucrats—all of these cadres changed far less than the image of the Soviet collapse suggested. Yeltsin's inheritance, in other words, was as challenging as could be imagined: the state had collapsed, but the pathologies of the Soviet Communist Party persisted.

Political infighting, regional separatism, hyperinflation, and a very brief civil war were the result. Political clashes erupted not only between Yeltsin and the Duma, now controlled by the Communist Party of the Russian Federation, but also between the Kremlin and regional elites. Yeltsin had famously told regional leaders to "take as much sovereignty as they could swallow," and Russia's governors soon began treating tax payment as optional. Large corporations like Gazprom, the government-owned gas monopoly, did the same. Unable to collect much tax revenue, the government ran massive budget deficits throughout the 1990s, mostly funded by printing money, causing a surge of hyperinflation. Social unrest exploded in 1993 amid a standoff between Yeltsin and the Duma. Yeltsin ordered the army to fire on parliament before both sides agreed to back down from the brink of civil war. Several hundred people were killed. Bloodier still was the civil war in the province of Chechnya, along Russia's southern border, which fought a failed but vicious war for independence from Moscow during the 1990s and into the early 2000s.

Amid these crises, the scope for thinking about foreign policy was limited. The Kremlin's main aim was managing relations with the United States, its former Cold War rival. Upon taking power, Yeltsin and Foreign Minister Andrei Kozyrev saw their main goal not as standing up to the West but extracting aid from Western powers. Kozyrev had been a perestroika liberal in the Gorbachev period, denouncing the Marxist-Leninist theory of class struggle in international politics and advocating a more cooperative relationship with the West. Yeltsin backed Kozyrev's conciliatory policy because he saw no other option. Russia needed Western cash to stabilize the economy;

it needed Western investment to rebuild the country's businesses; it needed arms control with the United States to justify reducing military expenditures; it needed Western backing for its territorial integrity if it was to halt the centrifugal forces pulling apart the country's far-flung provinces. Moscow had no choice but to tolerate American demands.[4]

Kozyrev's conciliatory policy toward the United States made him many enemies in Moscow. They argued that he was sacrificing Russia's core interests for the sake of cooperation with the West. Yet what was the alternative given Russia's broken and bankrupt government? In Asia, too, Yeltsin's foreign policy was defined by conciliation and problem solving. He continued Gorbachev's efforts to restore relations with China, visiting Beijing in December 1992 to sign a series of agreements with Chinese Communist Party leaders. Yeltsin was partially responsible for the dissolution of the Soviet Union's Communist Party, but he got along well with China's communists, selling them advanced weaponry, and receiving credit in exchange to buy foodstuffs from China, including grain and peanuts. Both countries promised to "regard each other as friends" and to reject alliances directed at the other. "I had considered the Chinese people to be extremely regimented under the [Communist] Party yoke, who march to work singing songs and march home without singing songs," Yeltsin mused to journalists. "I'm now convinced that first there is no such regimentation."[5]

Whatever the quality of Yeltsin's analysis of Chinese society, Beijing and Moscow continued to improve ties. Two years after Yeltsin's visit to Beijing in 1992, Chinese president Jiang Zemin traveled to Russia, becoming the first Chinese leader to do so since Mao Zedong visited Khrushchev in 1957. The two leaders finally settled their countries' long-lasting border dispute, resolving the questions over ownership of the islands in the Ussuri River that had led to clashes in 1969. China and Russia's relationship was a "constructive partnership," they declared. Two years later, they agreed to upgrade their relationship to a "strategic partnership."[6]

What did this mean in practice? Yevgeny Primakov, who was appointed foreign minister in early 1996, was tasked with providing substance to the Russia-China relationship. Primakov had been named foreign minister after Kozyrev was sacked amid a conservative turn in Yeltsin's politics and growing domestic opposition to rapprochement with the West. Russia was scarcely stronger in 1996 than it had been in 1991, facing conflict in Chechnya, unsettled relations with Russia's regions, and an ongoing economic crisis. Yet Russians were fed up with Kozyrev's concessions and wanted a more assertive foreign policy in accordance with what they saw as Russia's rightful place on the world stage. The United States and Western European powers were redrawing the map of Europe without Moscow's consent, letting Eastern European countries join NATO and deepening Europe's economic and political integration, including Eastern Europe but excluding Russia.

As an adviser to Gorbachev in the mid-1980s, Yevgeny Primakov had urged the Kremlin to abandon the Brezhnev-era ideologically driven confrontation with China and the United States and adopt a "multipolar strategy." As foreign minister in the mid-1990s, he wanted to abandon what he saw as Kozyrev's excessive trust in the West and replace it with a "multipolar strategy," which like during the Gorbachev era would seek to balance against the United States by improving ties with China. In April 1997, Yeltsin and Chinese Communist Party general secretary Jiang Zemin promised to build a "multipolar world," condemning the "Cold War thinking" and "policy of blocs" that they accused the United States of pursuing. "We want multipolarity," Yeltsin declared. "There must be several pillars on which the present world order should rest." One Russian analyst explained Yeltsin's statement as an effort "to somehow demonstrate to the West that Russia is not isolated . . . [that Russia] may always find some partners in the East."[7]

Despite Primakov's grandiose designs, the effort to play China off the West had little substance and even less impact. Yeltsin's relations with East Asia in general were hamstrung by the reality that there was little business to be done amid the Kremlin's desperate need to focus on domestic affairs. Yeltsin held a series of summits with Japanese leaders, but Japanese firms remained wary of investing in Russia outside of a small number of state-backed projects, notably gas development on the island of Sakhalin. Japan's government, meanwhile, was only interested in investments that might lead to a resolution of the two countries' disagreement about control of the disputed islands—yet no progress was made.[8] There was also ongoing hope that South Korea would be a major source of investment, but little materialized. As Yeltsin declared in 1992, the two countries "now have nothing that separates them."[9] But they had little that united them, either. Yeltsin signed a friendship treaty with Seoul and agreed to investigate the downing of a South Korean airliner, KAL 007, which the Soviet military had shot down in 1983.[10] Even though Russia tacked away from North Korea in an effort to boost ties with the South, Pyongyang's nuclear program encouraged Seoul to lean more heavily on the United States, its main source of security. By comparison, Russia had hardly anything to offer.

The Kremlin was therefore largely locked out of Asian affairs, as much by its own lack of relevance or focus as by any other country's design. The United States remained the world's superpower in Asia. China was relentlessly focused on its internal economic development. Russia was beset by economic crises that required Western financial aid to resolve. In 1998, the year after Russian and Chinese leaders demanded multipolarity, the value of Russia's currency collapsed and the country careened toward debt default, requiring a bailout by the International Monetary Fund and more support from the West. Foreign Minister Primakov could visit Beijing and issue statements advocating multipolarity as often as he would like. So long as Russia's solvency required regular disbursements of Western cash, Asia would remain an afterthought.

CHINA RISES, THE RUSSIAN FAR EAST STAGNATES

Even as Russia struggled to engage in the Asia-Pacific region during the 1990s, it benefited hugely from the remarkable growth in East Asia's economy. China's economy grew by 10 percent annually for much of the 1990s and 2000s, and its consumption of raw materials increased rapidly. The growth of low-cost, high-efficiency manufacturing in China and elsewhere in Asia had bankrupted Russia's high-cost industrial sector during the 1990s, but Asia's rapacious demand for commodities was good news for Russian firms. Oil and gas, iron and steel, aluminum and copper, timber and fish—prices of all these resources were driven upward by Asian demand. Dollars flowed into Russia's resource sector, and commodities poured back into China. The few remaining internationally competitive segments of Russia's manufacturing sector benefited too, including nuclear power and military aircraft, both of which found customers in China.

Chinese demand was good news for Russia. But even when these commodities were produced in the Russian Far East, most of the benefits flowed to corporate headquarters and the central government's coffers in Moscow.

For the Russian Far East, the two decades after the Soviet collapse were a time of extended decline. In the Soviet period, life in the Far East had been heavily subsidized because the cost of living was higher than in other parts of Russia. The demise of the USSR caused many of these subsidies to be cut. Inflation-adjusted wages fell by 30 percent over the 1990s, according to the best estimates. The military industry, which for decades had been the backbone of the Russian Far East's industrial base, faced severe budget cuts, factory closures, and layoffs. With fewer jobs and lower salaries, over 2 million people—a quarter of the population of the Russian Far East—left for other parts of the country.[11]

As the population of Russia's territories along the Pacific declined, those Russians who remained looked worriedly over the long border with China. Fear of China was suddenly reawakened, whipped up by local leaders and exacerbated by a deep-seated sense among Russians in the region that their country's hold on its Far Eastern territories was weaker than it appeared. Russians again looked worriedly at the population differentials between Northern China and the Russian Far East, and focused on anecdotes about Chinese migration into Russia. The specter of a "Yellow Peril," which had driven Russian politics in the Far East during the late tsarist period, was resurrected. Khabarovsk governor Viktor Ishaev warned in 1994 of a "hidden expansion of China in the Russian Far East" and predicted several years later that "all the land in Russia's Far East will be bought up by the Chinese." Yevgeny Nazdratenko, governor of the Far Eastern region, warned in 1999 that because of Chinese migration, Russia's territory risked becoming an "Asian Balkans." In fact, few Chinese were moving to Russian Far East because of the region's deep economic crisis, but the issue proved politically evocative and was frequently aired throughout the 1990s and 2000s.[12]

In part because of this, it was not Asian but Western countries that remained among the biggest investors in the Far East, largely in commodity sectors. Japan was only the tenth largest investor in Russia in 2000, despite being the world's second largest economy and sharing a maritime border with Russia. South Korea continued to promise investment in Russia, but there was far less substance than the press releases suggested. Seoul instead remained focused on winning Russian support for its efforts to pressure North Korea—something that Russia had little interest in.[13]

As to the Russian Far East itself, the Kremlin has put forth numerous plans to resuscitate the province. In 2006, it created a State Commission for the Far

East to support the development of the region. The next year, it launched a program promising to spend 567 billion rubles on the Far Eastern and Trans-Baikal regions, hoping to revitalize the economy. In 2009, the government issued a new strategy for developing the region. Then, in 2012, a cabinet-level Ministry for the Development of the Far East and the Arctic was formed, with Putin describing the region's development as Russia's "most important geopolitical task."[14] But although the population exodus from the Russian Far East has been halted, and the central government's spending on the region increased, the provinces on Russia's Pacific coast remain far poorer than elsewhere in the country, lacking economic dynamism, and relying on support from Moscow.

"WE'VE GOTTEN EVERYTHING WE NEED FROM THE WEST"

Even before the 2014 war with Ukraine, some Russian analysts proposed that "the globalization of Russia" required rebalancing Russia's foreign relations away from Europe and toward Asia.[15] Yet it took a war to reorient the Kremlin's perspective. After 2014, the West was no longer seen as a credible partner, given the standoff over Ukraine. Nor was it sensible to bet on economic ties with the West because Europe and the United States were restricting investment in Russia. Locked out of the West in political and economic terms, it made sense for Russia to consider its neighbors to the east. Russia could not be a great power in Europe, so it turned to Asia to achieve its geopolitical goals.

Yet as with previous periods of Russian interest in Asia, Putin's pivot was not only about practical matters. It was conceived in more abstract terms too. One Russian analyst described the move not "as pragmatic economics" but as a decision that "has taken on geopolitical and civilizational traits." Another report written by authors close to the Kremlin declared that Russia's turn toward Asia "implies moral and political independence from the West, and the strengthening of positions in relations with the West." The shift in Russia's orientation has been interpreted in moral and ideological terms as often as it has been seen through a practical lens.

Start with the practical side: what is new in Russia's relations with Asia? Energy diversification is one thing. Russia has built a new gas pipeline to

China, called "Power of Siberia," which connects East Siberian gas fields with China. Russia is also shipping more oil to Asia than ever before and has become one of the largest suppliers of oil to China. More recently, Asian investors have begun to finance development of Arctic and Siberian oil and gas production. Indian firms invested in the vast Siberian Vankor oil field, for example. China and Japan, meanwhile, are major investors in liquified natural gas production, both in Sakhalin, where gas has been produced for some time, and in new gas fields in the Arctic. Some of the Russian energy sector's shift toward Asia would have happened naturally, driven by rising demand in Asian markets. Yet politics has pushed this forward, as the Kremlin pressured Russian energy companies to strike deals with Chinese, Japanese, and Indian firms.[16]

A second facet of Russia's new pivot toward Asia is an enhanced military and political presence, partially in coordination with China. In 2019, for example, Russia and China conducted a joint air patrol in the airspace between Japan and South Korea. This prompted both Tokyo and Seoul to scramble jets in response, alleging that the Russian and Chinese planes violated their airspace, with the South Korean planes firing hundreds of warning shots. This is just one of a series of joint Russia-China military patrols and exercises that have taken place in Russia as part of the country's 2018 Vostok military exercises, as well as in the disputed waters of the South China Sea. Russia is losing its technological edge over China's rapidly improving military equipment, but it is nevertheless selling Beijing some of its most high-tech gear, from anti-aircraft missile systems to advanced jet engines to military helicopters. In the 2000s, Russia tried to balance its desire to sell arms with its interest in limiting China's military modernization. Now Russia has gone all-in on the China market. Beijing has been delighted to reciprocate, or at least to say it is doing so. "Russia is the country that I have visited the most times," China's president Xi Jinping proudly delcared, "and Putin is my best friend."[17]

A third part of Russia's pivot to Asia since 2014 has been an effort to deepen ties with countries beyond China. The Eurasian Economic Union, which unites Russia, Belarus, Armenia, Kazakhstan, and Kyrgyzstan, was initially conceived of as competing with the European Union. Since 2014, however, it has been repurposed as a vehicle by which Russia can solidify Russia's role in Central Asia amid rising Chinese investment and political activity. The bloc has signed trade deals with countries from Vietnam to Iran.[18] In addition to the Eurasian Economic Union, Russia has embraced the Shanghai Cooperation Organization, a group that includes China, Russia, and other countries in the region, though it has also supported the entry of India into the organization, which many analysts interpreted as part of an effort to balance against Chinese dominance.

What is the result of this surge diplomatic, economic, and military activity in Asia? Many Russian analysts, especially those who are close to the government, celebrate the success of this turn to the east. The Kremlin has found a "Eurasian exit from the European crisis," Russian analyst Sergei Karaganov has written. No longer would Russia accept a subsidiary role in relations with the West, nor did it need to learn any longer from Europe. "We've already gotten everything we need from the West. . . . During the long 'Period of Peter the Great,' we received technology, military organization, and created a magnificent high culture," Karaganov wrote. "By the beginning of the current millennium, we had almost exhausted everything that could and should have been taken from Europe." As a result, the time had come to embrace Russia's Asian orientation. It was not only that "Russia is the heir to the empire of Genghis Khan," leaving a legacy of ties to Asia, Karaganov continued. The crisis in relations with the West coupled with China's economic rise were also "pushing us now further towards the East."[19]

THE LIMITS TO PUTIN'S PIVOT

Will Russia's current pivot last? It faces two risks, one economic and the other geopolitical.[20] Russia's past turns toward Asia have often been sparked by promises of rich Asian markets, but this commerce has rarely brought the benefits that boosters promised. One challenge for Russia is that trade with Asia has always been costly and complicated, given the distances involved, requiring massive investments that often failed to recoup their costs. In the past, the recognition that Russia had overestimated the economic benefits of devoting attention to Asia often led to a reassessment of the country's Asian role.

Does Russia's current pivot to Asia rest on stronger economic foundations? Russia has found a large market for oil and gas in China, but Beijing has many other potential energy suppliers, so it will not be reliant on Russia. Russia has failed, meanwhile, to make much of its proximity to Japan or South Korea, two economic powerhouses. Nor is it clear that there is much scope for growth in trade with other Asian countries, especially outside of energy. Russia's investment in liquified natural gas will make it possible to sell more to some Asian markets. Existing liquified natural gas infrastructure in Sakhalin Island already supplies Japan with gas.[21] But investing more funds in liquification is expensive, especially at a time when pipelines can already transport gas to Europe. Australia, Qatar, and the United States, meanwhile, continue to bring more gas online, driving down Asian prices. Thus, even though Asian demand for gas will grow, new supply will keep a lid on prices.

No country has been more important for Russian economic development over the past two decades than China. Russia's southern neighbor voraciously consumes the oil, gas, and minerals that Russia produces in abundance, and Chinese consumption has propped up commodity prices over the past quarter century. Yet though China's economic growth has helped Russia, direct trade between Eurasia's two giants remains surprisingly small and one-sided. China only accounts for about 11 percent of Russian exports. By contrast, half of Russian sales abroad go to Europe. Yet while Europe's trade with Russia is more balanced—half of Russia's imports come from Europe—Russo-Chinese trade remains marked by significant imbalances and a Russian trade deficit. As Russia's trade with China grows, moreover, so too does its exposure to a potential Chinese economic slowdown.

Even if Chinese commodity consumption growth slows, some Russian policymakers hope that Beijing can be induced to invest its newfound wealth in Russian companies, thereby boosting Russian growth. Thus far, however, Chinese investment in Russia has disappointed the Kremlin's expectations. Outside of major deals in the energy sector, Chinese investors approach Russia cautiously, largely for the same reasons that warming ties between Japan and Russia have not unlocked significant Japanese capital inflows: foreign firms doubt they can make money in Russia given the business climate. Russia, meanwhile, is growing frustrated that its attempt to work with Chinese initiatives such as the Asian Infrastructure Investment Bank and the Belt and Road Initiative have not produced major new inflows of Chinese money. The economic foundations of Russia's Asian pivot today look weak, as they so often have historically. If China's growth trajectory slows faster than expected, these foundations will look weaker still. It would not be the first time that overly optimistic dreams about Asian markets were disappointed.

A second challenge to the durability of Putin's turn toward Asia is geopolitical. Will Russia's foreign policy goals and geopolitical position continue to support an Asian orientation? The key dynamic driving Russian interest in Asia is the Kremlin's isolation from Europe. Today Russia has locked itself out of Europe by its annexation of Crimea and its broader war on Ukraine. Its only European partners are third-tier players like Hungary's Viktor Orbán or Belarus's Alexander Lukashenko. Russia has been ejected from powerful forums such as the G7 and is widely condemned by Europeans for its foreign policy. Hence Russia turned toward Asia—a policy that the Kremlin had dabbled with in the years before 2014, but which leaped forward as relations with the West deteriorated.

Multiple factors are uniting Russia's and China's current visions of politics across Eurasia. One is a desire to create a safe space for authoritarian rule. Today, Russia partners with China to promote a set of political ideas, including opposition to democracy and human rights. Both countries feel threatened by demands for political changes and believe that the international order should bolster existing regimes, regardless of their political tint. Given these shared beliefs, the two countries have cooperated to oppose recognition of universal rights and norms in international organizations, to share internet censorship technology, and to support the extradition of political dissidents across Eurasia.

Will the glue of ideological similarity continue to focus Russia's attention on its relationship with Beijing and other Central Asian autocrats? Perhaps. But Russia has swung historically between periods of openness and reaction. In recent years, Putin has presided over a crackdown. His successor could well tack in the other direction. Similarly, while Xi Jinping has consolidated his power and abolished term limits, it is difficult to predict the course of Chinese politics over the next several decades. There is no guarantee that the two countries' authoritarian alignment will persist indefinitely. An even bigger risk to Russia's Asian pivot is that Russia eventually decides to improve ties with Europe, undermining the primary purpose of its turn toward Asia.

A HISTORY OF GRAND PLANS

Putin is far from the first Russian leader to have visited Vladivostok or to have hatched grand plans for expanding Russia's role in Asia. Today most of Russia's Asian border disputes have been settled, though Japan and Russia still disagree about ownership of several small islands in the Kurile chain. The advent of nuclear weapons, meanwhile, and their spread to China and North Korea, plus the US nuclear umbrella that defends South Korea and Japan, make border changes in East Asia hard to imagine. But Putin's vision that Russia can be a great power in Asia is nothing new. Nor is hope that projecting Russian influence in Asia will boost Russia's weight on the world stage.

Putin's 2015 speech in Vladivostok, after all, sounded surprisingly similar to the Soviet leader whom he most detests. Putin has described the collapse of the Soviet Union as the "greatest geopolitical catastrophe of the twentieth century," and Russian state-controlled media regularly denigrate Mikhail Gorbachev for presiding over its dissolution.[22] Yet Gorbachev, too, had also traveled to Vladivostok to declare a new dawn in relations between Russia and Asia, and to announce a new set of tactics to assert Russian influence in the region. Gorbachev had embraced cooperation with China and Japan, spoke of the importance of "economic diplomacy," of joint enterprises, even of a new railroad. Asia "woke up to a new life" thanks to a "whirlwind of changes—social, scientific, and technological . . . a renaissance of world history." The result would be an expansion of Soviet influence in Asia, Gorbachev promised, driven by "the laws of growing interdependence and the need for economic integration."[23]

Gorbachev's optimistic vision of Russia's role in Asia, underpinned by growing trade and by promises of demilitarization, did not pan out as he expected. Yet it is difficult to blame Gorbachev's tactics, because the opposite methods have a track record that is scarcely better. Consider, for example, Brezhnev's militarized containment of China during the 1970s, which alienated almost all the USSR's neighbors. Or Stalin's efforts to boost the Soviet Union's presence in Asia during the decade after World War II. Stalin's goal after 1945 was to reverse the legacy of the 1904–1905 Russo-Japanese War. As he declared in 1945, "The Russian defeat in the Russo-Japanese War left a painful memory ... [and] a black mark on our history. ... We the old generation have waited for forty years to remove this mark."[24]

Yet despite the opening provided by the defeat of the Japanese Empire and the implosion of Chiang Kai-shek's nationalist government in China, Stalin's coupling of expansionary ideology with military force proved no more effective at increasing Soviet influence in Asia than Gorbachev's promises of trade and disarmament. Stalin's legacy was a dysfunctional relationship with ostensible ideological allies in Pyongyang and Beijing coupled with a fearsome US military presence along the Pacific Coast, which his expansionism had provoked. It was hard to describe Stalin's postwar tactics as a success, which is why his successors promptly changed course after he died.

Stalin had turned to force in Asia in part because his earlier strategy of waiting for communist revolutions to take power in Asian countries had also failed. In the 1920s, Stalin had gambled the Soviet position in Asia on the progress of socialism in China, seeing the region as ripe for revolution. Stalin led the Soviet Union in taking rhetoric about Russia's Asian role and dressing it in communist garb. One Bolshevik journal created for the study of "Eastern" countries declared that Soviet Russia has not only "the right to participate in charting the destiny of the Asian countries ... [but also] the moral duty ... of assisting in the political development and education of the Asian peoples."[25] The Soviet Union tried teaching communism to the masses in China, studying the class structure of Chinese society, shipping weapons to revolutionary partners in Wuhan, even organizing the furniture budget of the revolutionaries in Canton. But no amount of aid or ideological instruction could convince the Chinese to submit to Moscow. As soon as Chiang Kai-shek took power, he cast out the Soviet Union's advisers and treated Moscow as no better than any other European imperialist.

No one would have mistaken the Bolsheviks' predecessors for being anything other than ordinary European imperialists. Tsar Nicholas II's plans in Asia were distinguished by their territorial ambition, especially when compared to other European powers' desire only for ports, not whole provinces. Count Sergei Witte, Nicholas's finance minister, prioritized economic interests and tactics, using railroads and trade to pave the way for political influence. Nicholas found this inadequate, envisioning his empire not as a trading company but as a great military power, a competitor to the empires of Britain,

France, and Germany. Promises of market access, of commercial profits, or of banking networks would not produce the glory that Nicholas believed his empire deserved. The tsar equated success with territory: first a naval base at Port Arthur, then de facto control over Manchuria, and finally, he dreamed, predominance in Korea. By carelessly driving Russia toward war with Japan, however, Nicholas squandered his country's position and was forced to beat a humiliating retreat.

Russia's leaders had been more cautious three decades earlier, when hotheaded explorer Nicholas Przhevalsky urged St. Petersburg to wage war on China over the tiny valley of Yili, along the borders of the Russian and Chinese Empires. Then, it seemed that Central Asia was the key to imperial success, and that the passes of the Pamirs and the trade routes to Tibet would shape the future of Asia and of world power. Przhevalsky had spearheaded Russia's expansion in the region, and he had as much respect for the Chinese as Nicholas II would later have for the Japanese, telling his superiors that "few of the officers"—to say nothing of the average Chinese soldiers—even "know how to shoot."[26]

Amid the crisis over the Yili Valley, war was the only way that Russia could have remained on the offensive in Central Asia, and the only way for adventurous military officers to take more territory for the tsar. Yet officials in St. Petersburg realized then what Nicholas would struggle to understand in 1904: that Asia could bring vast costs to Russia compared to meager tangible benefits. The Yili Valley, over which Przhevalsky urged war, was of "no strategic value," one diplomat declared. An influential Russian commentator concluded that "our history is played out in Europe and not in Asia," an argument that was used against those who urged taking large risks on Russia's Asian frontiers.[27] Russia's period of rapid expansion along China's Central Asian borderlands was short-lived, and quickly forgotten, but St. Petersburg managed to pull back before embroiling itself in a disastrous war.

Przhevalsky had started his career as an explorer not in Central Asia, but along the Pacific Coast. For the two centuries before his arrival in the 1850s, the Amur and Ussuri Rivers and the far-off Pacific Coast had been terra incognita for all but the most adventurous Russian fur trappers. As railroads began to crisscross the world's continents, and as steamships plodded up and down the great rivers, Russians began to worry that another imperial power might succeed in opening the Amur River and the Pacific Coast to exploration and even to settlement. "A holy location will not remain empty," warned one of the scholars who advised Nikolai Muravev, the governor-general who ruled Eastern Siberia for Nicholas I and Alexander II. "When the country is populated it will prosper quickly . . . creating an unescapable flow of hardworking, skillful, and sober people from these two empires into all parts of Eastern Siberia." Hence Muravev drove the Russian Empire's expansion into the Far East, risking war with Qing China to acquire a vast swath of land along the Pacific Coast. Holy land this may have been, but prosper it did not. Muravev's predictions of railroads and steamships sailing along the Amur did not materialize for decades. The prosperity of which he dreamed has yet to arrive. The region remains reliant on handouts from richer provinces. More accurate was the prediction of Muravev's ally Gennady Nevelskoy, the ship captain who foresaw that the region was "fated to live like an army camp." After it was conquered, it was ignored for the remainder of the 1800s, sparsely inhabited by a motley mix of foreigners, military officials, and prisoners.[28]

Russia's other colonies in the Pacific—Alaska, California, and the island of Kauai—did not remain Russian at all. Nikolai Rezanov, the nobleman and explorer, had tried to connect the Russian lands along the Pacific Ocean's coasts, promising Tsar Alexander I that California was a land of wine, chocolate, and grain that could feed the scurvy-ridden settlements in Alaska. Georg Schaffer, meanwhile, told officials in St. Petersburg that Hawaii could become a "Russian West India and a second Gibraltar," if only he was provided some military support, perhaps a frigate, with which to wage war on Hawaii's king. Yet lacking even the ability to feed its colonies, Russia's provision of substantial military support was impossible. That is not to say that Rezanov's transpacific vision lacked logic. By the end of the 1800s, Hawaii, San Francisco, and Alaska had been knit together in a Pacific Ocean empire that traded with Japan and China. But this new empire was headquartered not in St. Petersburg, but in Washington, DC.

"MAKING CASTLES IN THE AIR"?

Nikolai Rezanov's contemporaries ascribed his California dreams to his "hot temper" and his inclination to "making castles in the air."[29] Yet Rezanov is far from the only Russian to have had grand plans about his country's advancement in Asia. It was "a holy land," in the view of Muravev's adviser Aleksandr Balasoglo. "'Russia and the Orient' as a concept are one," Prince Esper Ukhtomsky declared. It was only a small jump to today's declaration by influential foreign policy analyst Sergei Karaganov that, through Putin's pivot to Asia, Russia has "returned to its familiar role as a strong state and recovered its confidence." For nearly three centuries, Russian leaders have had a persistent soft spot for mystical declarations about their relations with Asia.

Why have Russia's rulers repeatedly sought opportunity in Asia? The vast market in China and Japan. The proximity to Siberia's riches. The outlet to the Pacific. The space—or so it has often seemed—for geopolitical expansion and even territorial aggrandizement. And perhaps most importantly, the hope of finding "Eurasian exits" from "European crises," as Karaganov has described Russia's Asian pivot today. For centuries, Russia's border with Asia has seemed to provide an open door for all sorts of grandiose schemes.

This explains why the notion of Russia's "Eurasian" identity has been so persistent. A country torn between two continents; a country with one foot in Europe and a second in Asia; a country influenced by European civilization and by the legacy of the Mongols—such tropes are useful to anyone looking to mobilize resources or to muster support for a focus on Asia. Yet whenever Russia has placed one of its metaphorical feet in Asia, the other has stayed firmly ensconced in Europe. "Eurasianism" has proven a useful theme in Russian domestic politics for forces looking to stir up discontent with European powers. Asserting that Russia has its own unique Eurasian identity is a time-tested way to get published in op-ed pages or even to win an audience in the Kremlin. But assertions of Eurasian identity are as cyclical as Russia's foreign policy engagement with Asia. This is a trope that is rolled out when useful and put to bed when not.

As an outlet for what Ukhtomsky called Russia's "creative energies," Asia has been less a holy land than a graveyard of grand ambitions. The pattern of pivots to Asia, of promises of progress in the Far East, of expansionary designs in Manchuria, the Mongol lands, the Korean Peninsula, or along the Pacific Coast, are repetitive, even mechanical. Once a generation, some Russian leader hauls out the Asian idea and promises great successes in ties with China or along the vast Pacific Coast. Yet these Asian pivots have repeatedly disappointed, often exploding spectacularly, and rarely persisting for more than a handful of years. One enduring dilemma is that few Russians live in country's Far East. Historically the region was populated as much by forced labor as by voluntary settlement, first by the exile of prisoners in the tsarist era, then by the creation of vast Gulags under Stalin. Even during the late Soviet period, the country struggled to convince people to move to the region. Since 1991 the population has declined sharply. It is difficult to convince most Russians, who live tightly clustered along the border with Europe, that far-off Asia matters much to them.

It has been more difficult still to get supplies to the Far East, especially during a crisis. Gone are the days of scurvy-ridden Pacific outposts, but the dilemmas of transport remain. Even today, Kamchatka can only be supplied by sea or air—there are no road or rail links. The quality of Siberian roads has improved somewhat since Rezanov was thrown off his horse into an icy river, but even major thoroughfares in the region turn into gravel paths with little warning. Russia completed its first transcontinental railroad almost half a century after the United States and Canada built railways traversing North America. As late as the 1980s, the construction of the Baikal-Amur Mainline railway, a second rail track connecting Siberia to the Pacific Coast, was a difficult and chaotic endeavor. It is no coincidence that when speaking in Vladivostok in 2015, Putin highlighted his commitment to building roads and bridges in the Far East. China's relentless construction of infrastructure across its vast territory in recent decades provides a painful contrast to the sorry state of transport in the Russian Far East today.

Because Russia's population is clustered on its western border, and because infrastructure connecting these lands with Asia has long been dysfunctional, trade with Asia has repeatedly disappointed. Talk of vast markets in China and Japan have been a feature of Russian discussion for centuries. East Asia has always had a vast population, and Russia has always traded little with it, so the potential for growth has always been present in theory. But this trade has rarely materialized, notwithstanding the conquest of the Amur or the construction of the Trans-Siberian Railway. China's economic growth today means that trade between Russia and China is on a cyclical upswing. But the long history of unfulfilled promises about the Asian market suggests reason for caution.

Some historians have perceived an "overarching vision" motiving Russian policy toward Asia.[30] Yet rather than "enduring interests," the primary factor governing Russia's approach to the region has been spasms of enthusiasm. At times Russia has devoted immense resources to expansion in Asia, only to turn its back just years later. This is the "perpetual swinging of the pendulum," that historian Lobanov-Rostovsky perceived.[31] Yet it is driven not by clockwork or by the laws of physics, but by emotion, ideology, and optimism.

Chinese president Xi Jinping recently declared that Vladimir Putin is his "best friend." Yet Russian leaders sense that their current Asian pivot rests on shaky grounds.[32] In his speech in Vladivostok in 2015, Putin compared his Asian visions to those of "statesmen such as Sergei Witte" and the "Soviet leaders" who "had grand plans for developing the Far East," such as "the Trans-Siberian and the Baikal-Amur Mainline railways." Many people close to the Kremlin insist, as did Putin in his Vladivostok speech, that these projects "advanced not just the Far East region but practically the entire country."[33] But it is difficult to paint either the Witte system or Soviet socialism in the Far East as a resounding success. Even more obvious is the failure of Mikhail Gorbachev's Asian pivot, which the Kremlin's current promise of increased trade and diplomatic attention toward Asia most resembles.

What Putin desires above all is to be compared with Peter the Great, the leader he says he most admires.[34] The comparison is apt. From Peter's first meeting with the mysterious captive Dembei, the great tsar was fascinated by the lands of the east, striking up friendship with Europe's greatest experts on Asian geography. One of Peter's advisers urged him to use Kamchatka as a springboard to influence in Japan and India. Even on his deathbed, Peter had visions of a new Arctic passage to the Chinese seas. But Peter is remembered for his relations with Amsterdam and London, his wars along the Black and Baltic Seas, his adoption of European culture, and his imitation of Western politics. His deathbed dreams of influence in Asia, meanwhile, are today all but forgotten.

ABBREVIATIONS

CWIHP   *Cold War International History Project Bulletin*

DVP   *Dokumenty Vneshnei Politiki SSSR* (Moscow: Izdatelstvo Politicheskoi Literaturoi), multiple volumes

FRUS   *Foreign Relations of the United States* (Washington, DC: Government Printing Office), multiple volumes (https:// history.state.gov/historicaldocuments)

GARF   State Archive of the Russian Federation, Moscow

KA   *Krasny Arkhiv*, multiple volumes

KiK   *VKP(b), Komintern, i Natsional'no Revoliutsionnoe Dvizhenie v Kitae: Dokumenty* (Moscow: AO Buklet), multiple volumes

LOC   Library of Congress, Washington, DC

OS   Old Style dates, per the calendar used in Russia before 1918

PRO FO   British Foreign Office Papers, National Archives, Kew

RGANI   Russian State Archive of Contemporary History, Moscow

RKO   *Russko-Kitaiskie Otnosheniia v XX Veke* (Moscow: Pamiatni Istoricheskoi Mysli), multiple volumes

SDFP   Jane Degras, ed., *Soviet Documents on Foreign Policy,* 3 vols. (London: Oxford University Press, 1951–1953)

SRE   Xenia Joukoff Eudin and Robert C. North, eds., *Soviet Russia and the East, 1920–1927: A Documentary Survey* (Stanford, CA: Stanford University Press, 1957)

VPR   *Vneshniaia Politika Rossii XIX i Nachala XX Veka: Dokumenty Rossiiskogo Ministerstva Innostrannikh Del* (Moscow: Gos. Izd-vo polit. lit-ry), multiple volumes

WP CUA Witte Papers, Columbia University Archive, New York

NOTES

Introduction

1. George Alexander Lensen, *The Russian Push toward Japan* (London: Forgotten Books, 2017), 26–30; W. Bruce Lincoln, *The Conquest of a Continent: Siberia and the Russians* (Ithaca, NY: Cornell University Press, 1994), 100–102.

2. Arthur MacGregor, "The Tsar in England: Peter the Great's Visit to London in 1698," *The Seventeenth Century* 19, no. 1 (January 2013): 118.

3. Ian Grey, *Peter the Great* (Boston: New Word City, 2015), 99; Vladimir Matveev, "Summit Diplomacy of the Seventeenth Century: William III and Peter I in Utrecht and London, 1697–98," *Diplomacy & Statecraft* 11, no. 3 (2000): 29–48; Robert K. Massie, *Peter the Great: His Life and World* (New York: Random House, 2011), 211.211.

4. On tobacco, see Massie, *Peter the Great*, 211.

5. K. E. Cherevko, *Rossiia na Rubezhakh Iaponii, Kitai i SShA* (Moscow: Institut Russkoi Tsivilizatsii, 2010), 86.

6. Marion Peters, *De wijze koopman: Het wereldwijde onderzoek van Nicolaes Witsen (1641–1717), burgemeester en VOC-bewindhebber van Amsterdam* (Amsterdam: Bert Bakker, 2010), 99–127.

7. On Peter's wife, see Massie, *Peter the Great*, 372. On Peter's politics, see Paul Bushkovitch, *Peter the Great: The Struggle for Power, 1671–1725* (Cambridge: Cambridge University Press, 2001).

8. Lensen, *The Russian Push toward Japan*, 26–30.

9. Gaston Cahen, *Histoire des relations de la Russie avec la Chine sous Pierre le Grand* (Paris: Librairie Felix Alcan, 1912), 205.

10. On Peter's policy toward Asia, see Cahen, *Histoire des relations de la Russie avec la Chine*, 189–226. On Preobrazhenskoe, see James Cracraft, *The Petrine Revolution in Russian Architecture* (Chicago: University of Chicago Press, 1988), 114–115; Earnest A. Zitser, *The Transfigured Kingdom: Sacred Parody and Charismatic Authority at the Court of Peter the Great* (Ithaca, NY: Cornell University Press, 2004), 51–53, 143; Massie, *Peter the Great*, 67–69.

11. Cherevko, *Rossiia na Rubezhakh Iaponii*, 86–88; Lincoln, *The Conquest of a Continent*, 101–102.

12. On cycles of expansion and containment, see John P. LeDonne, *The Russian Empire and the World, 1700–1917: The Geopolitics of Expansion and Containment* (New York: Oxford University Press, 1997).

13. William C. Fuller Jr., *Strategy and Power in Russia, 1600–1914* (New York: Free Press, 1992); Patricia Kennedy Grimsted, *The Foreign Ministers of Alexander I: Political Attitudes and the Conduct of Russian Diplomacy, 1801–1825* (Berkeley: University of California Press, 1969); Barbara Jelavich, *St. Petersburg and Moscow: Tsarist and Russian Foreign Policy, 1814–1974* (Bloomington: Indiana University Press, 1974).

14. Johannes Keuning Nicolaas, "Witsen as a Cartographer," *Imago Mundi* 11 (1954): 103.

15. G. F. Kim and P. M. Shastitko, *Istoriia Otechestvennogo Vostokovedeniia do serediny XIX Veka* (Moscow: Nauka, 1990), 151–152; Aida Ipatova, "Deyetel'nost' Rossiiskoi Dukhovnoi Missii v Kitae," *Otechestvennye Zapiski* 42, no. 3 (2008): 320–331.

16. Fyodor Dostoyevsky, "Geok-Tepe: What Does Asia Mean to Us?," in *A Writer's Diary*, vol. 2, *1877–1881*, trans. Kenneth Lantz (Evanston, IL: Northwestern University Press, 1994).

17. On "urge to the sea," see Stephen Kotkin, "Robert Kerner and the Northeast Asia Seminar," *Acta Slavica Iaponica* 15 (1993): 100. For "enduring interest" interpretations of Russian policy in the Pacific, see David J. Dallin, *The Rise of Russia in Asia* (Hamden, CT: Archon Books, 1971), v–viii; Barbara Jelavich, *A Century of Russian Foreign Policy, 1814–1914* (Philadelphia: Lippincott, 1964), v–vii; John Le Donne, "Russia's Eastern Theater, 1650–1850: Springboard or Strategic Backyard?," *Cahiers du Monde Russe* 49, no. 1 (2008): 17–45.

18. Alfred Thayer Mahan, *The Problem of Asia: Its Effect upon International Politics* (New York: Routledge, 2017), 55–56, 117.

19. Dostoyevsky, *A Writer's Diary*, 2:1374.

20. Andrei Lobanov Rostovsky, "Russia at the Crossroads: Europe or Asia," *Slavonic and East European Review* 6, no. 18 (March 1928): 496–504.

21. Gerald Brown, "Andrei A Lobanov Rostovsky," Faculty History Project, University of Michigan, http://faculty-history.dc.umich.edu/faculty/andrei-lobanov-rostovsky/memorial.

22. Lobanov Rostovsky, "Russia at the Crossroads," 496.

23. John Le Donne, "Building an Infrastructure of Empire in Russia's Eastern Theater 1650s–1840s," *Cahiers du Monde Russe* 47, no. 3 (2006): 586.

1. Lord of Alaska

1. I. G. Kokh (commandant of Okhotsk) to Baranov, August 14, 1790, in Petr A. Tikhmenev, *A History of the Russian American Company*, vol. 2, *Documents*, ed. and trans. Richard A. Pierce and Alton S. Donnelly (Kingston, ON: Limestone Press, 1979), 23–24 (hereafter cited as Tikhmenev, *Documents*).

2. Important scholarly histories of Russia in Alaska include Andrei Val'terovich Grinëv, *Russian Colonization of Alaska: Preconditions, Discovery, and Initial Development, 1741–*

1799, trans. Richard L. Bland (Lincoln: University of Nebraska Press, 2018); Grinëv, *Russian Colonization of Alaska: Baranov's Era, 1799–1818*, trans. Richard L. Bland (Lincoln: University of Nebraska Press, 2020); Ilya Vinkovetsky, *Russian America: An Overseas Colony of a Continental Empire, 1804–1867* (Oxford: Oxford University Press, 2011); Alexander Yu. Petrov, *Obrazovanie Rossiisko-Amerikansoi Kompanii* (Moscow: Nauka, 2000); Kenneth N. Owens with Alexander Yu. Petrov, *Empire Maker: Aleksandr Baranov and Russian Colonial Expansion into Alaska and Northern California* (Seattle: University of Washington Press, 2015); Alexander Iu. Petrov, *Rossiisko-amerikanskaia Kompaniia: Deiatelnost' na otechestvennom i zarubezhnom rynkakh* (Moscow: Russian Academy of Sciences, 2006).

3. Richard Pierce, "Shelikhov, Grigorii Ivanovich," *American National Biography*, https://doi.org/10.1093/anb/9780198606697.article.0200286.

4. Owens, *Empire Maker*, 21, 32, 38; "Dogovor mezhdu G. I. Shelikhovym i A. A. Baranovym," August 15, 1790, in Alexander Iu. Petrov, *Natalia Shelikhova i istokov Russkoi Ameriki* (Moscow: Ves Mir, 2012), 227–232. On loose morals, see Hubert Howe Bancroft, *History of Alaska, 1730–1885* (San Francisco: A. L. Bancroft and Company, 1886), 316.

5. Ryan Tucker Jones, *Empire of Extinction: Russians and the North Pacific's Strange Beasts of the Sea, 1741–1867* (New York: Oxford University Press, 2014), 72.

6. Owen Matthews, *Glorious Misadventures: Nikolai Rezanov and the Dream of a Russian America* (London: Bloomsbury, 2014), 59; Semen B. Okun, *The Russian-American Company*, trans. Carl Ginsberg (Cambridge, MA: Harvard University Press, 1951), 22; Richard A. Pierce, "Introduction," in Grigorii I. Shelikhov, *A Voyage to America, 1783–1786*, trans. Marina Ramsay (Kingston, ON: Limestone Press, 1981), 10, 12, 15. The number of men on Shelikhov's voyage is from his ship's logbook.

7. Shelikhov, *A Voyage to America*, 52–53.

8. Shelikhov, *A Voyage to America*, 53–56.

9. W. Michael Mathes, *The Russian-Mexican Frontier: Mexican Documents regarding the Russian Establishments in California 1808–1842* (Jenner, CA: Fort Ross Interpretive Association, 2008), 12; Warren L. Cook, "The Clash at Nootka, 1789," and "To the Brink of War," in *Flood Tide of Empire: Spain and the Pacific Northwest 1543–1819* (New Haven, CT: Yale University Press, 1973), 146–250.

10. Svetlana G. Fedorova, *The Russian Population in Alaska and California, Late 18th Century–1867*, trans. and ed. Richard A. Pierce and Anton S. Donnelly (Kingston, ON: Limestone Press, 1973), 108; "Ukaz of Catherine the Great," December 22, 1786, in *To Siberia and Russian America: Three Centuries of Russian Eastward Expansion*, ed. and trans. Basil Dmytryshyn, E. A. P. Crownhart-Vaughan, and Thomas Vaughan, vol. 2, *Russian Penetration of the North Pacific Ocean, 1700–1797* (Portland: Oregon Historical Society Press, 1988), 325 (hereafter Dmytryshyn et al., *Russian Penetration*); Okun, *The Russian-American Company*, 13–14.

11. Yakoby to Shelikhov, Samoilov, and Delarov, June 21, 1787, in Dmytryshyn et al., *Russian Penetration*, 334; Okun, *The Russian-American Company*, 22–25.

12. Okun, *The Russian-American Company*, 26, 28–29; Nikolai N. Bolkhovitinov, *The Beginnings of Russian-American Relations, 1775–1815*, trans. Elena Levin (Cambridge, MA: Harvard University Press, 1975), 165; translation modified.

13. Owens, *Empire Maker,* 55, 59, 63.

14. Okun, *The Russian-American Company,* 53; Petr A. Tikhmenev, *A History of the Russia-American Company,* trans. Richard A. Pierce and Alton S. Donnelly (Seattle: University of Washington Press, 1978), 61, 68 (hereafter cited as Tikhmenev, *History*).

15. On "the Bostonians," see Mary E. Wheeler, "Empires in Conflict and Cooperation: The 'Bostonians' and the Russian-American Company," *Pacific Historical Review* 40, no. 4 (November 1971): 421.

16. Ilya Vinkovetsky, *Russian America: An Overseas Colony of a Continental Empire, 1804–1867* (New York: Oxford University Press, 2011), 82; Tikhmenev, *History,* 63.

17. For the number of employees, see Tikhmenev, *History,* 82; James R. Gibson, *Feeding the Russian Fur Trade: Provisionment of the Okhotsk Seaboard and the Kamchatka Peninsula 1639–1856* (Madison: University of Wisconsin Press, 1969). For travel times, see Gavriil I. Davydov, *Two Voyages to Russian America, 1802–1807,* ed. and trans. Richard A. Pierce (Kingston, ON: Limestone Press, 1979), chaps. 1–2; Nikoklai A. Khvostov, "Report by Imperial Russian Navy Lieutenant Nikoklai A. Khvostov," 1804, in *To Siberia and Russian America: Three Centuries of Russian Eastward Expansion,* ed. and trans. Basil Dmytryshyn, E. A. P. Crownhart-Vaughan, and Thomas Vaughan, vol. 3, *The Russian American Colonies, 1798–1867* (Portland: Oregon Historical Society Press, 1989), 52 (hereafter Dmytryshyn et al., *The Russian American Colonies*).

18. On tides, see "Report by Imperial Russian Navy Lieutenant Nikoklai A. Khvostov," 1804, in Dmytryshyn et al., *The Russian American Colonies,* 52; Owens, *Empire Maker,* 56. On Okhotsk, see G. A. Sarychev to N. S. Mordvinov, February 18, 1802 (OS), in A. E. Ioffe and L. I. Spiridonova, comps., *Rossiisko-Amerikanskaia Kompaniia i izuchenie Tikhookeanskogo Severa, 1799–1815* (Moscow: Nauka, 1994), 33. On Russian-American prices, see Pavel N. Golovin, "Last Report," in *The End of Russian America: Captain P.N. Golovin's Last Report, 1862,* trans. Basil Dmytryshyn and E. A. P. Crownhart-Vaughan (Portland: Oregon Historical Society Press, 1979), 35; on Moscow and St. Petersburg prices, see Global Price and Income History Group, "Prices and Wages in Russia, 1590s–1871," http://gpih.ucdavis.edu/files/Russia_p_w_1590s-1871.xls, and "Silver and Gold Content of the Russian Ruble, 1535–1913," http://gpih.ucdavis.edu/files/Russia_Ag_content_ruble_1535-1913.xls; and Thomas C. Owen, "A Standard Ruble of Account for Russian Business History, 1769–1914: A Note," *Journal of Economic History* 49, no. 3 (September 1989): 699–706.

19. On the *Enterprise,* see Kiril T. Khlebnikov, *Baranov: Chief Manager of the Russian Colonies in America,* ed. Richard A. Pierce and trans. Colin Bearne (Kingston, ON: Limestone Press, 1973), 35; Tikhmenev, *History,* 64.

20. Kuskov to Baranov, July 1, 1802, in Tikhmenev, *Documents,* 139–140; Tikhmenev, *History,* 61; Vinkovetsky, *Russian America,* 82.

21. Vinkovetsky, *Russian America,* 82; Okun, *The Russian-American Company,* 53; Tikhmenev, *History,* 68–69, 95, 110.

22. Tikhmenev, *History,* 111–112.

23. Jennifer Milam, "Toying with China: Cosmopolitanism and Chinoiserie in Russian Garden Design and Building Projects under Catherine the Great," *Eighteenth-Century Fiction* 25, no. 1 (Fall 2012): 115–138.

24. John P. LeDonne, "Proconsular Ambitions on the Chinese Border: Governor General Iakobi's Proposal of War on China," *Cahiers de Monde Russe* 45, nos. 1–2 (2004): 31–60.

25. Clifford M. Foust, *Muscovite and Mandarin: Russia's Trade with China and Its Setting, 1727–1805* (Chapel Hill: University of North Carolina Press, 1969), 323.

26. Okun, *The Russian-American Company*, 46.

27. "Dokladnaia zapiska glavnogo pravleniia rossiisko-amerikanskoi kompanii Aleksandru I," August 10, 1802, *VPR*, 1:266–269; Rumiantsev to Rezanov, July 22, 1803, *VPR*, 1:491; Rumiantsev to A. R. Vorontsov, November 15, 1803, *VPR*, 1:544; "Dokladnaia Zapiska Ministra Kommertsii N. P. Rumiantsev Aleksandru I," March 4, 1803, *VPR*, 1:386–387; Rumiantsev to Alexander, April 1, 1803, *VPR*, 1:403–405; Alexander I to the Emperor of Japan, July 12, 1803, *VPR*, 1:474–475; Rumiantsev to Alexander, January 28, 1805, *VPR*, 1:297; *VPR*, 2:472, 476, 480. On lobbying for trade with Japan, see G. A. Sarychev to N. S. Mordvinov, February 18, 1802 (OS), in Ioffe and Spiridonova, *Rossiisko-Amerikanskaia Kompaniia*, 34. On Richelieu, see Jean Potocki quoted in Daniel Beauvois, "Le 'System Asiatique' de Jean Potocki ou le reve oriental dans les Empires d'Alexandre I et de Napoleon, 1806–1808," *Cahiers du Monde Russe et Sovietique* 20, no. 3 (July–December 1979): 467.

28. Matthews, *Glorious Misadventures*, 1.

29. Urey Lisiansky, *A Voyage Round the World, in the Years 1803, 4, 5, & 6* (London: John Booth, 1814), 24.

30. Matthews, *Glorious Misadventures*, 115; Okun, *The Russian-American Company*, 15–16; Vinkovetsky, *Russian America*, 60.

31. Okun, *The Russian-American Company*, 51.

32. Okun, *The Russian-American Company*, 51, 66–67.

33. Lisiansky, *A Voyage Round the World*, 24, 128; Tikhmenev, *History*, 73.

34. Tikhmenev, *History*, 74–75, 89.

35. "A Report to the Holy Governing Synod of the Russian Orthodox Church from Missionaries in Russian America Detailing Complaints against Aleksandr A. Baranov," August 1, 1804, and Rezanov to the Directors of the Russian-American Company, November 6, 1805, in Dmytryshyn et al, *The Russian American Colonies*, 63–64, 102.

36. "Letter from Rezanov to the Directors of the Russian-American Company," November 6, 1805, in Dmytryshyn et al., *The Russian American Colonies*, 105, 108.

37. Rezanov to Alexander I, August 16, 1804, in Dmytryshyn et al., *The Russian American Colonies*, 70; Rezanov to the Emperor, from Unalashka Island, July 18, 1805, and Rezanov to the Directors of the Russian-American Company from New Archangel, November 6, 1805, in Tikhmenev, *Documents*, 149–150, 157.

38. Okun, *The Russian-American Company*, 119.

39. Georg Heinrich von Langsdorff, *Langsdorff's Narrative of the Rezanov Voyage to Nueva California in 1806*, trans. Thomas C. Russell (San Francisco: Private Press of T. C. Russell, 1927), 17–18; Tikhmenev, *History*, 96.

40. Conversation of Portola "con un amigo," Madrid, September 4, 1773, in *Documentos secretos de la expedicion de Portola a California: Juntas de Guerra*, ed. Fernando Boneu Companys (Lleida: Instituto de Estudios Ilerdenses de la Excma. Diputación Provincial de Lérida, 1973), 163; Okun, *The Russian-American Company*, 118.

41. Matthews, *Glorious Misadventures*, 256–258.

42. Rezanov to N. P. Rumyantsev, June 17, 1806, in *Rezanov Reconnoiters California, 1806*, ed. Richard A. Pierce (San Francisco: The Book Club of California, 1972), 2–3; Okun, *The Russian-American Company*, 120.

43. Rezanov to N. P. Rumyantsev, June 17, 1806, in Pierce, *Rezanov Reconnoiters California*, 7; Langsdorff, *Langsdorff's Narrative of the Rezanov Voyage*, 53, 84–85; James R. Gibson, ed. and trans., *California through Russian Eyes, 1806–1848* (Norman, OK: Arthur H. Clark, 2013), 30; James R. Gibson and Alexei A. Istomin, eds., *Russian California, 1806–1860: A History in Documents*, 2 vols. (London: Published by Ashgate for the Hakluyt Society, 2014), 1:185.

44. Rezanov to N. P. Rumyantsev, June 17, 1806, in Pierce, *Rezanov Reconnoiters California*, 16; Matthews, *Glorious Misadventures*, 136.

45. Langsdorff, *Langsdorff's Narrative of the Rezanov Voyage*, 85; Rezanov to N. P. Rumyantsev, June 17, 1806, in Pierce, *Rezanov Reconnoiters California*, 16.

46. Langsdorff, *Langsdorff's Narrative of the Rezanov Voyage*, 53, 86, 88; Rezanov to Rumyantsev, June 17, 1806, in Gibson and Istomin, *Russian California*, 1:196; Tikhmenev, *History*, 96–99.

47. Tikhmenev, *History*, 99.

48. Rezanov, "Report about a Voyage to Alta California," 1806, in Gibson, *California through Russian Eyes*, 39.

49. Rezanov, "Report about a Voyage to Alta California," 55–56; translation modified.

50. On trade, see Langsdorff, *Langsdorff's Narrative of the Rezanov Voyage*, 53, 87–88 (quotations adjusted for clarity); Rezanov to Alexander I, May 5, 1806, in Gibson and Istomin, *Russian California*, 1:179.

51. On Rezanov's heart, see Rezanov to Mikhail Buldakov, January 24, 1807, in *Komandor: Stranytsy Zhizni I deitalnosti Dvora ego imperatorskogo velichestva deistvitelnogo kamergera, ruovoditelia pervoi russkoi krugosvetnoi ekspeditsii Nikolaia Petrovicha Rezanova*, ed. Yuri P. Avdyukhov et al. (Krasnoyarsk: Ofset, 1995), 646. Baranov to Commandant Arguello, no later than May 1808, in Gibson and Istomin, *Russian California*, 1:255; Owens, *Empire Maker*, 216; Tikhmenev, *History*, 106; Dawn Lea Black and Alexander Yu. Petrov, eds. and trans., *Natalia Shelikhova: Russian Oligarch of Alaska Commerce* (Fairbanks: University of Alaska, 2010), xlviii.

52. Baranov to Kuskov, October 14, 1808, in Dmtryshyn et al., *The Russian American Colonies*, 166; Okun, *The Russian-American Company*, 121.

53. Okun, *The Russian-American Company*, 124.

54. Jose Manuel Ruiz to Arrillaga, March 16, 1813, in Mathes, *The Russian-Mexican Frontier*, 66; Okun, *The Russian-American Company*, 135.

55. "Report from Mikhail M. Buldakov, Principal Director of the Russian American Company, to Emperor Alexander I," January 28, 1808, and "Instructions from N. P. Rumiantsev, Minister of Commerce and Foreign Affairs, to G. A. Stroganov, Russian Minister in Madrid," April 20, 1808, in Dmytryshyn et al., *The Russian American Colonies*, 153, 157.

56. "Report to Emperor Alexander I from the Russian American Company Council, concerning Trade with California and the Establishment of Fort Ross," after December 16, 1813, in Dmytryshyn et al., *The Russian American Colonies*, 207–208.

57. Georg Heinrich von Langsdorff, *Voyages and Travels in Various Parts of the World, during the Years 1803, 1804, 1805, 1806, and 1807* (London: H. Colburn, 1813), 163–164; Klaus Mehnert, *The Russians in Hawaii: 1804–1819* (Honolulu: University of Hawaii Press, 1939), 4.

58. Gavan Daws, *Shoal of Time: A History of the Hawaiian Islands* (Honolulu: University of Hawaii Press, 1968), 7, chaps. 2–3.

59. La Harpe to Alexander, December 31, 1801, in *Correspondance de Frederic-Cesar de la Harpe et Alexandre 1er: Suivie de la correspondence de F.-C. de La Harpe avec les membres de la famille imperiale de Russie*, vol. 1, ed. Jean Charles Biaudet and Francoise Nicod (Neuchatel: Editions de la Baconniere, 1978), 386; Rezanov to Rumiantsev, July 29, 1806, *VPR*, 3:209.

60. Interior Minister O. P. Kozodavlev to the Council of Ministers, October 25, 1814, *VPR*, 8:119. On agriculture, see "Report from Count Nikolai P. Rumiantsev, Foreign Minister, to Emperor Alexander I," November 12, 1809, in Dmytryshyn et al., *The Russian American Colonies*, 186–187.

61. On Kamehameha's letter, see Dymytryshyn et al., *The Russian American Colonies*, 44–45.

62. On Schaffer, see N. Bolkhovitinov, "Avantyura Doktora Sheffera na Gavayyakh v 1815–1819 Godakh," *Novaya i Noveyshaya Istoriya*, no. 1 (1972): 121–137; English translation: Igor V. Vorobyoff, trans., "Adventures of Doctor Schäffer in Hawaii, 1815–1819," *Hawaiian Journal of History* 7 (1973): 55–78; Tikhmenev, *History*, 109; Leo Tolstoy, *War and Peace*, trans. Constance Garnett (New York: Random House, 2002), 858; Alexander Tarsaidze, "The Air Blitz of 1812," *The Russian Review* 2, no. 1 (Autumn 1942): 93, 98; Okun, *The Russian-American Company*, 156.

63. Baranov to Schaffer, October 1, 1815; Baranov to Kamehameha, October 1, 1816; and Schaffer to Russian-American Company Main Office, January 1, 1816, in Richard A. Pierce, *Russia's Hawaiian Adventure* (Berkeley: University of California Press, 1965), 41–44, 45, 60; Bolkhovitinov, "Avantyura Doktora Sheffera," 59; Richard A. Pierce, "Georg Anton Schaffer, Russia's Man in Hawaii, 1815–1817," *Pacific Historical Review* 32, no. 4 (November 1963): 398–399.

64. Baranov to I. A. Podushkin, February 15, 1816; "Act of Allegiance of King Kaumuali'i to Emperor Alexander I of Russia," May, 21 1816; "Award of Honorary Naval Rank to King Kaumuali'i," May 21, 1816; "Contract between King Kaumuali'i and Schaffer," May 21, 1816; Georg A. Schaffer, "Award of Medal to Prince Kaukari Tautuno of Kauai," May 21, 1816; and "Secret Treaty between King Kaumuali'i and Schaffer," July 1, 1816, in Pierce, *Russia's Hawaiian Adventure*, 49, 63–65, 72; Bolkhovitinov, "Avantyura Doktora Sheffera," 59–60.

65. "Report, Schaffer to Main Office," August 1816, in Pierce, *Russia's Hawaiian Adventure*, 74; Bolkhovitinov, "Avantyura Doktora Sheffera," 61.

66. Mehnert, *The Russians in Hawaii*, 28–29.

67. Russian-American Company to Minister of Foreign Affairs Nesselrode, August 17, 1817, in Dmytryshyn et al., *The Russian American Colonies*, 291; Bolkhovitinov, "Avantyura Doktora Sheffera," 63–64.

68. Shaffer to Alexander I, February 1, 1819, and Shaffer to Alexander I, March 2, 1819, in "Tsarskaia Rossiia i Gavaiskie ostrova," *KA* 78, no. 5 (1936): 176, 182; Pierce, "Russia's Man in Hawaii," 402; Bolkhovitinov, "Avantyura," 62; Okun, *The Russian-American Company*, 163.

69. "Report from the Main Administration of Russian American Company to Nesselrode," January 19, 1818, in Dmytryshyn et al., *The Russian American Colonies*, 299; Nesselrolde to Osip P. Kozodavlev, Minister of Internal Affairs, February 24, 1818, in Dmytryshyn et al., *The Russian American Colonies*, 303; Bolkhovitinov, "Avantyura Doktora Sheffera," 64–65.

70. Ministry of Interior to the Main Office of the Russian-American Company (quoting communication from Nesselrode), July 15, 1819, in Pierce, *Russia's Hawaiian Adventure*, 139–141; Hagemeister to the Main Office, April 6, 1818, in *The Russian-American Company: Correspondence of the Governors, Communications Sent, 1818*, ed. and trans. Richard A. Pierce (Kingston, ON: Limestone Press, 1984), 72–73; Russian-American Company to Chief Administrator Leontii A Hagemeister, August 12, 1819, in Dmytryshyn et al., *The Russian American Colonies*, 311–312; "Board of Directors of the RAC to Governor Muravev," February 28, 1822, in Gibson and Istomin, *Russian California*, 1:481; Bolkhovitinov, "Avantyura," 63; Pierce, "Russia's Man in Hawaii," 402.

71. Angela de Castro Gomes, ed., *Historias de Imigrantes e de Imigracao no Rio de Janeiro* (Rio de Janeiro: 7 Letras, 2000), 20. The German and Dutch versions of Schaffer's book are Georg Anton von Schäffer, *Brasilien als unabhängiges Reich in historischer, mercantilistischer und politischer Beziehung* (Altona: Hammerich, 1824), and Georg Anton Schäffer, *Brazilië, als onafhankelijk rijk, uit een geschied-koop-handel- en staatkundig oogpunt* (Amsterdam: C. L. Schleijer, 1825). Pierce, *Russia's Hawaiian Adventure*, 32; Enrico Schaeffer, "De Velhas Cronicas de Familias: Cavalheiro George Antonio de Schaeffer (1779–1836)," *Revista Genealogica Latina* 11 (1959): 157–160.

72. Mathes, *The Russian-Mexican Frontier*, 98, 108; Okun, *The Russian-American Company*, 135; Tatishchev to Nesselrode, March 14, 1817, in Gibson and Istomin, *Russian California*, 1:311–312; Cea Bermudez, Spanish Minister in St. Petersburg, to Nesselrode, April 15 / 27, 1817, and "Explanatory Note from the Board of Directors of the RAC to Minister of Foreign Affairs Nesselrode," August 13, 1817, in Gibson and Istomin, *Russian California*, 1:314, 318, 320.

73. Okun, *The Russian-American Company*, 128–129.

74. "A Report from the Board of Directors of the RAC to Minister of Foreign Affairs Nesselrode," January 29, 1820, in Gibson and Istomin, *Russian California*, 1:410–411.

75. On pigs and rum, see Hagemeister to Baranov, January 17, 1818; Hagemeister to Baranov, April 18, 1818; and Hagemeister to Kuskov, July 8, 1818, in Pierce, *The Russian-American Company*, 3, 83, 118. On Baranov's tears, see Owens, *Empire Maker*, 257, 267–268. Cf. Pierce, *The Russian-American Company*, x. On Baranov's death, see K. T. Khlebnikov, *Baranov: Chief Manager of the Russian Colonies in America*, ed. Richard A. Pierce and trans. Colin Bearne (Kingston, ON: Limestone Press, 1973), 99.

76. "Statement from the Directors of the Russian American Company," April 21, 1808, and "A Report from the Main Administration of the RAC," December 23, 1816, in Dmytryshyn et al., *The Russian American Colonies*, 160, 223.

77. Romanzoff [Foreign Minister Rumiantsev] to Harris, May 17, 1808, in *American State Papers: Foreign Relations*, vol. 5 (Washington, DC: Gales & Seaton, 1858), 439; "Report from

Count Nikolai P. Rumiantsev, Foreign Minister, to Emperor Alexander I," November 12, 1809, in Dmytryshyn et al., *The Russian American Colonies*, 188.

78. "Report by Lieutenant Nikolai Khvostov," likely early 1804, in Dmytryshyn et al., *The Russian American Colonies*, 49; Gibson, *California through Russian Eyes*, 220.

79. Adams (St. Petersburg) to Smith (Secretary of State), September 5, 1810, in *American State Papers*, 442.

80. Dashkov to Smith, January 4, 1810, in *American State Papers*, 439; Howard I. Kushner, *Conflict on the Northwest Coast: American-Russian Rivalry in the Pacific Northwest, 1790–1867* (Westport, CT: Greenwood Press, 1975), 12–13, 16–17.

81. Kushner, *Conflict on the Northwest Coast*, 29–31, 34–35.

82. "Imperial Ukaz Prohibiting Ships," September 4, 1821, in Dmytryshyn et al., *The Russian American Colonies*, 342; Okun, *The Russian-American Company*, 68.

83. Directors of the Russian-America Company to Count Mordvinov, May 5, 1824, in *Arkhiv Grafov Mordvinovikh*, ed. V. A. Bil'bassov, vol. 6 (St. Petersburg: Tipografiia I. N. Skorokhodov, 1902), 660; Wheeler, "Empires in Conflict and Cooperation," 436; Okun, *The Russian-American Company*, 68–69.

84. Kushner, *Conflict on the Northwest Coast*, 31, 35, 37, 39–40.

85. Adams to Middleton, July 22, 1823, in *American State Papers*, 436–437 (emphasis in original); Kushner, *Conflict on the Northwest Coast*, 48–51.

86. Nesselrode to Tuyll, September 1, 1823, *VPR*, 13:206–207; Nesselrode to Middleton, April 6, 1824, *VPR*, 13:403; Kushner, *Conflict on the Northwest Coast*, 51–52; Charles Frances Adams, ed., *The Memoirs of John Quincy Adams*, vol. 6 (Philadelphia: Lippincott, 1874–1877).

87. "Convention between the United States and Russia," in *American State Papers*, 433–434; James Monroe, "Seventh Annual Message," December 2, 1823, in The American Presidency Project, ed. Gerhard Peters and John T. Woolley, http://www.presidency.ucsb.edu /ws/?pid=29465; Kushner, *Conflict on the Northwest Coast*, 59; Ernest May, *Making of the Monroe Doctrine* (Cambridge, MA: Harvard University Press, 1975); Vinkovetsky, *Russian America*, 85.

88. "Protocol of the Talks between Governor De Sola of Alta California and Manager Kuskov and Lieutenant Kotzebue about the Demand of the Spanish Authorities to Abandon the Russian Settlement in California," October 28, 1816, in Gibson and Istomin, *Russian California*, 1:310–311; "Board of Directors of the RAC to Governor Kupreyanov," March 24, 1838, in Gibson and Istomin, *Russian California*, 2:434; Okun, *The Russian-American Company*, 134.

89. Nesselrode to Minister of Finance Kankrin, January 3, 1838; Nesselrode to Wrangel, late 1834; Governor Tebenkov to Novo-Arkhangelsk, December 20, 1848; Nesslerode to Minister of Finance Kankrin, April 17, 1839; Minutes of a Meeting of the Board of Directors of the Russia America Company, November 16, 1838; and "Anonymous Survey of the Activities of the Managers of Ross Counter," no earlier than 1839, in Gibson and Istomin, *Russian California*, 2:304–305, 429, 471, 475, 481, 553. On visions of expansion that were overruled, see Anatole G. Mazour, "Dimitry Zavalishin: Dreamer of a Russian-American

Empire," *Pacific Historical Review* 5, no. 1 (March 1936): 26–37; Okun, *The Russian-American Company*, 145.

90. A. Rotchev, Letter of November 10, 1851, in Frederick C. Cordes and A. Rotchev, "Letters of A. Rotchev, Last Commandant at Fort Ross: And the Resume of the Report of the Russian-American Company for the Year 1850–51," *California Historical Society Quarterly* 39, no. 2 (June 1960): 102. F. P. Wrangell, *Russian America: Statistical and Ethnographic Information*, ed. Richard A. Pierce (Kingston, ON: Limestone Press, 1980), 5.

91. On Muravev, see Oleh W. Gerus, "Russian Withdrawal from Alaska: The Decision to Sell," *Revista de Historia de América* 75 / 76 (January–December 1973): 162. James Gibson, "The Sale of Russian America to the United States," in *Russia's American Colony*, ed. Frederick Starr (Durham, NC: Duke University Press, 1987), 271–285; Nikolay N. Bolkhovitinov, "The Crimean War and the Emergence of Proposals for the Sale of Russian America, 1853–1861," *Pacific Historical Review* 59, no. 1 (February 1990): 4.

2. "Russian Control Will Be Guaranteed Forever"

1. Muravev to the Interior Minister, September 14, 1848, in *Nikolai Nikolaevich Muravev-Amurskii po ego pismam, offitsialnym dokumentam, razkazam sovremnnikov i pechatnym istochnikam*, ed. Ivan Barsukov, vol. 2 (Moscow: Sinodalnaya Tipografiya, 1891), 35; translated liberally. The chapter title is Muravev quoted in S. C. M. Paine, *Imperial Rivals: China, Russia, and Their Disputed Frontier* (London: Routledge, 2015), 37. On the etymology of the Amur, see Jerry Norman, "The Manchus and Their Language," *Journal of the American Oriental Society* 123, no. 3 (2003): 484.

2. James R. Gibson, *Feeding the Russian Fur Trade: Provisionment of the Okhotsk Seaboard and the Kamchatka Peninsula, 1636–1856* (Madison: University of Wisconsin Press, 1969).

3. These explorers were Vasili Poiarkov and Yerofey Khabarov. Peter Simon Pallas, "Puteshestviye po sibiri k vostoku lezhashchey dazhe i do samoy daurii 1772 goda," in *Puteshestviye po raznym provintsiyam rossiyskogo gosudarstva*, trans. Vasili Zuev (St. Petersburg, 1788), 259. On food supplies and alleged cannibalism, see W. Bruce Lincoln, *The Conquest of a Continent: Siberia and the Russians* (Ithaca, NY: Cornell University Press, 1994), 64–65; Mark Mancall, "War along the Amur" and "The Treaty of Nerchinsk," in *Russia and China: Their Diplomatic Relations to 1728* (Cambridge, MA: Harvard University Press, 1971).

4. John P. LeDonne, "Proconsular Ambitions on the Chinese Border: Governor General Iakobi's Proposal of War on China," *Cahiers du Monde Russe* 45, nos. 1–2 (January–July 2004): 47–48.

5. Important works on Russia's push into the Amur region include: Paine, *Imperial Rivals;* Mark Bassin, *Imperial Visions: Nationalist Imagination and Geographical Expansion in the Russian Far East, 1840–1865* (Cambridge: Cambridge University Press, 1999), 52; R. K. I. Quested, *The Expansion of Russia in East Asia, 1857–1860* (Kuala Lumpur: University of Malaya Press, 1968); Gregory Afinogenov, *Spies and Scholars: Chinese Secrets and Imperial Russia's Quest for World Power* (Cambridge, MA: Harvard University Press, 2020).

6. Muravev received news of British goods in China from Russia's Ecclesiastical Mission (and de facto embassy) in Beijing; see Arkhimandrite Palladia to Muravev, June 1, 1850

(OS), in "Perepiska nachal'nika Pekinskoi missii arkhimandrita Palladiia s Generalom-Gubernatorom Vostochnoi Sibiri Gr. N. N. Murav'evym-Amurskim," ed. V. Kryzhanov-skii, *Russkii Arkhiv,* no. 8 (1914): 493–494; Peter Ivanovich Kabanov, *Amurskii Vopros* (Blagoveshchensk: Amurskoye Knizhnoye Izdatelstvo, 1959), 64–65.

7. On Kiakhta, see Berngard Vasilyevich Struve, *Vospominaniya o Sibiri 1848–1854* (St. Petersburg: Obshchestvennaia pol'za, 1889), 11; Paine, *Imperial Rivals, 33–34.*

8. Gennady Nevelskoy, *Podvigi russkikh morskikh ofitserov na krainem vostoke Rossii, 1849–55* (St. Petersburg, 1878), 44–45; George Alexander Lensen, *The Russian Push toward Japan* (London: Forgotten Books, 2017), 263–264. On Nesselrode and Vronchenko's skepticism of eastern expansion, see Struve, *Vospominaniya o Sibiri 1848–1854,* 8–10; Mark Bassin, "A Russian Mississippi? A Political-Geographical Inquiry into the Vision of Russia on the Pacific, 1840–1865" (PhD diss., University of California, Berkley, 1983), 80, 112; P. V. Schumaker, "K istorii priobreteniya Amura: Nashi snosheniya s Kitayem (1848–1860), po neizdannym istochnikam," *Russkii Arkhiv,* no. 11 (1878): 267.

9. Bassin, "A Russian Mississippi?," 15, 92, 185.

10. Perry McDonough Collins, *Siberian Journey down the Amur to the Pacific 1856–1857,* ed. Charles Vevier (Madison: University of Wisconsin Press, 2011), 93; Bassin, "A Russian Mississippi?," 78. Muravev was said to have "discussed the chances of creating the United States of Siberia, federated across the Pacific Ocean with the United States of America"; see Joseph Lewis Sullivan, "Count N. N. Muraviev-Amursky" (PhD diss., Harvard University, 1955), 300.

11. Galen Blaine Ritchie, "The Asiatic Department during the Reign of Alexander II, 1855–1881," (PhD diss., Columbia University, 1970), 27.

12. Ritchie, "The Asiatic Department," 27; Patricia Kennedy Grimsted, *The Foreign Ministers of Alexander I* (Berkeley: University of California Press, 1969), chaps. 6 and 8. On Nesselrode, see Grimsted, *The Foreign Ministers of Alexander I,* 194–226, 269–286.

13. Karl Nesselrode, *Lettres et Papiers du Chancelier Comte de Nesselrode 1760–1850,* 10 vols. (Paris: Lahure, 1904), 9:63, 81, 92, 104, 237, 284; Nesselrode, *Lettres et Papiers,* 10:5. China is mentioned briefly in Nesselrode, *Lettres et Papiers,* 10:121; Bassin, "A Russian Mississippi?," 110; translation modified.

14. Paine, *Imperial Rivals, 36–37;* Sullivan, "Count N. N. Muraviev-Amursky," chaps. 1–3.

15. Sullivan, "Count N. N. Muraviev-Amursky," 11, 102–107, 293, and chap. 8; Alfred J. Rieber, *Merchants and Entrepreneurs in Imperial Russia* (Chapel Hill: University of Carolina Press, 1982), 71–73.

16. Nicholas I, "Vysochayshiy Manifest," March 14, 1848, in Boris Tarasov, *Nikolay Pervyy: Rytsar samoderzhaviya* (Moscow: Olma Press, 2006), 143.

17. Bassin, *Imperial Visions,* 91. This and the subsequent paragraphs draw heavily from this work.

18. Bassin, *Imperial Visions,* 52.

19. Bassin, *Imperial Visions,* 89.

20. A. P. Balasoglo, "Ispoved," in P. E. Shchegeleva, *Petrashevtsy: Sbornik Materialov* (Moscow: Gosudarstvennoe Izdatelstvo, 1927), 251; Aleksandr P. Balasoglo, "Vostochnaia Sibir: Zapiska c kommandirovke na ostrov Sakhalin kapitan-leitenanta Posdushkina,"

Chteniia v imp. obshchestve istorii i drevnostei Rossiiskikh pri Moskovskom Universitete 2 (April–June 1875): 183–184; Bassin, *Imperial Visions,* 86, 90.

21. Lensen, *The Russian Push toward Japan,* 289; Barsukov, *Nikolai Nikolaevich Muravev-Amurskii,* 51.

22. Muravev to Tsar Nicholas I, March 18, 1850 (OS), in Barsukov, *Nikolai Nikolaevich Muravev-Amurskii,* 56; Bassin, "A Russian Mississippi?," 141–143; Quested, *The Expansion of Russia in East Asia,* 42.

23. Sullivan, "Count N. N. Muraviev-Amursky," 246, 250, 260; Barsukov, *Nikolai Nikolaevich Muravev-Amurskii,* 23.

24. Muravev to Vronchenko, May 19, 1848 (OS), April 27, 1849 (OS), and July 25, 1848 (OS), all in Barsukov, *Nikolai Nikolaevich Muravev-Amurskii,* 28–29, 44; Sullivan, "Count N. N. Muraviev-Amursky," 245.

25. Muravev to the Minister of Internal Affairs, September 14, 1848 (OS), in Barsukov, *Nikolai Nikolaevich Muravev-Amurskii,* 35–36; Paine, *Imperial Rivals,* 37.

26. Nevelskoy, *Podvigi russkikh morskikh ofitserov,* 51–52, 57, quoting a document that he says was held in the Ministry of Foreign Affairs Archive.

27. Nevelskoy, *Podvigi russkikh morskikh ofitserov,* 40.

28. Nevelskoy, *Podvigi russkikh morskikh ofitserov,* 36, 40, 98; Instructions to Nevelskoy, November 12, 1848 (OS), in Barsukov, *Nikolai Nikolaevich Muravev-Amurskii,* 36–38. This account follows Afinogenov, *Spies and Scholars,* 234–256. On Nesselrode's desire to avoid conflict with China, see Schumaker, "K istorii priobreteniya Amura," 258.

29. Lensen, *The Russian Push toward Japan,* 275; Schumaker, "K istorii priobreteniya Amura," 260. On Nesselrode, see Nevelskoy, *Podvigi russkikh morskikh ofitserov,* 66, 79, 111.

30. Nevelskoy, *Podvigi russkikh morskikh ofitserov,* 109–110, 120. See also Afinogenov, *Spies and Scholars,* 235–256.

31. Nevelskoy, *Podvigi russkikh morskikh ofitserov,* 106; Schumaker, "K istorii priobreteniya Amura," 260–261, 263.

32. Nevelskoy, *Podvigi russkikh morskikh ofitserov,* 111, 166; Barsukov, *Nikolai Nikolaevich Muravev-Amurskii,* 73, 78. On disinformation, see Afinogenov, *Spies and Scholars,* 234–256.

33. Barsukov, *Nikolai Nikolaevich Muravev-Amurskii,* 47–49.

34. Schumaker "K istorii priobreteniya Amura," 273; Sullivan, "Count N. N. Muraviev-Amursky," 223; Muravev to the Emperor, November 27, 1850 (OS), in Barsukov, *Nikolai Nikolaevich Muravev-Amurskii,* 70; Nevelskoy, *Podvigi russkikh morskikh ofitserov,* 114.

35. Archmandrite Palladia to Muravev, June 6, 1852 (OS), in Kryzhanovskii, "Perepiska nachal'nika Pekinskoi missii," 510–511; Paine, *Imperial Rivals,* 39; T. C. Lin, "The Amur Frontier Question between China and Russia, 1850–1860," *Pacific Historical Review* 3, no. 1 (March 1934): 8; Schumaker "K istorii priobreteniya Amura," 272; Nevelskoy, *Podvigi russkikh morskikh ofitserov,* 115, 161–162, 184.

36. Archmandrite Palladia to Muravev, June 6, 1852 (OS), in Kryzhanovskii, "Perepiska nachal'nika Pekinskoi missii," 502; Muravev to Lev Grigorievich Seniavin, July 27, 1850 (OS), in Barsukov, *Nikolai Nikolaevich Muravev-Amurskii,* 61; Sullivan, "Count N. N. Muraviev-Amursky," 177; Jonathan D. Spence, "The Crisis Within: The Taiping," in *The Search for Modern China* (New York: Norton, 1990), 165–193.

37. Lensen, *The Russian Push toward Japan,* 300.

38. Copy of Report from a Special Committee on the Expedition of the United States to Japan, May 7, 1852 (OS), in Russian State Archives of the Navy, St. Petersburg, 296 f. 75a, l. 12. I was directed to this set of documents by Edgar Franz, *Philipp Franz von Siebold and Russian Policy and Action on Opening Japan to the West in the Middle of the Nineteenth Century* (Munich: Indicium, 2005).

39. On Russia's response to Perry's mission, see Russian State Archives of the Navy, St. Petersburg, 296 f. 75 a, ll. 1–270; Nevelskoy, *Podvigi russkikh morskikh ofitserov,* 210; Lensen, *The Russian Push toward Japan,* 279–280.

40. Lensen, *The Russian Push toward Japan,* 3, 8.

41. Lensen, *The Russian Push toward Japan,* 252.

42. Lensen, *The Russian Push toward Japan,* 263; Franz, *Philipp Franz von Siebold,* 75.

43. Lensen, *The Russian Push toward Japan,* 280, 289, 299–300.

44. Lensen, *The Russian Push toward Japan,* 280; Francis L. Hawks, *Narrative of the Expedition to the China Seas and Japan Performed in the Years 1852, 1853, and 1854, under the Command of Commodore M. C. Perry, United States Navy* (Washington, DC: A. O. P. Nicholson, 1856), 44–45, 75.

45. Untitled Report, Warsaw, May 18, 1852 (OS), in Russian State Archives of the Navy, St. Petersburg, 296 f. 75a, ll. 21–22.

46. "Instructions from the Russian Ministry of Foreign Affairs to Vice-Admiral Putiatin," August 23, 1852 (OS); Nesselrode to Senior Council of Japan, February 27, 1853 (OS); both in Franz, *Philipp Franz von Siebold,* 147–148, 206–207, 219.

47. Lensen, *The Russian Push toward Japan,* 312–314; William McOmie, *The Opening of Japan, 1853–1855* (Folkestone, UK: Global Oriental, 2006), 139.

48. Ivan Goncharov, *The Frigate Pallada,* trans. Klaus Goetze (New York: St. Martin's Press, 1987), 265, 303; Voin Andreevich Rimsky-Korsakov quoted in McOmie, *The Opening of Japan,* 143–144.

49. Lensen, *The Russian Push toward Japan,* 323–329; McOmie, *The Opening of Japan,* 154.

50. Lensen, *The Russian Push toward Japan,* 329–330.

51. Andrew C. Rath, "The Global Dimensions of Britain and France's Crimean War Naval Campaigns against Russia, 1854–1856" (PhD diss., McGill University, 2011), 201; John Stephan, "The Crimean War in the Far East," *Modern Asian Studies* 3, no. 3 (1969): 257–277; Bassin, "A Russian Mississippi?," 157.

52. Petition from Military Governor of Kirin Province to the Chinese Government, July 1854, in Ian Nish, *The History of Manchuria, 1840–1948: A Sino-Russo-Japanese Triangle,* vol. 2 (Folkestone, UK: Renaissance, 2016), 1; Schumaker, "K istorii priobreteniya Amura," 277–279; Quested, *The Expansion of Russia in East Asia,* 45; Lensen, *The Russian Push toward Japan,* 330.

53. Governor of Kamchatka, R. K. Villie, to the Hawaiian King, June 12, 1854, in "Arkhivnie materialiy k istorii sobytii na Dalnem Vostoke Rossii s 1847 po 1855 god, izvelchennie iz del Vladivostokoskogo portovogo arkhiva," ed A. P. Silnitskii, *Voprosy Istorii Kamchatki* 4 (2009): 36, 73; Stephan, "The Crimean War in the Far East."

54. Lensen, *The Russian Push toward Japan,* 330–331, 337. On UK-Japan talks, see W. G. Beasley, *Great Britain and the Opening of Japan 1834–1858* (New York: Routledge, 1995).

55. W. Bruce Lincoln, *The Great Reforms: Autocracy, Bureaucracy, and the Politics of Change in Imperial Russia* (DeKalb: Northern Illinois University Press, 1990).

56. Bassin, "A Russian Mississippi?," 96, 160. On Russian forces in the Amur, see Nevelskoy, *Podvigi russkikh morskikh ofitserov*, 324.

57. Steve Tsang, *A Modern History of Hong Kong* (London: I. B. Tauris, 2007), 32; Paine, *Imperial Rivals*, 41–42; Quested, *The Expansion of Russia in East Asia*, 65.

58. N. P. Ignatiev, *Materialy, otnosyashchiyesya do prebyvaniya v Kitaye N. P. Ignat'yeva v 1859–60 godakh* (St. Petersburg: Tipografiia V. V. Komarova, 1895), 8; A. N. Khokhlov, "Voennaia pomoshch rossii kitaiiu v kontse 50-x–nachale 60-x godov XIX v.," in *Strany dal'nego vostoka v iugo-vostochnoi azii*, ed. I. S. Kazakevich (Moscow: Izdatelstvo Nauka, 1967), 121–130; Schumaker, "K istorii priobreteniya Amura," 301; Quested, *The Expansion of Russia in East Asia*, 80; Lin, "The Amur Frontier Question," 15.

59. Schumaker, "K istorii priobreteniya Amura," 281; Paine, *Imperial Rivals*, 60; Nevelskoy, *Podvigi russkikh morskikh ofitserov*, 384; Lin, "The Amur Frontier Question," 12–13; Quested, *The Expansion of Russia in East Asia*, 60–61.

60. Ignatiev, *Materialy otnosyashchiyesya do prebyvaniya v Kitaye N. P. Ignat'yeva*, 3; Charles Vevier, "Introduction," in Collins, *Siberian Journey down the Amur*, 27; Collins, *Siberian Journey down the Amur*, 216.

61. Paine, *Imperial Rivals*, 42, 58, 67–68; Nevelskoy, *Podvigi russkikh morskikh ofitserov*, 402, 420; Lin, "The Amur Frontier Question," 18–19. On future destiny, see Tsar Alexander to Bariatinsky, August 30, 1858 (OS), in *Politics of Autocracy: Letters of Alexander II to Prince A. I. Bariatinskii, 1857–1864*, ed. Alfred Rieber (Paris: Mouton & Co., 1966), 121–122.

62. Paine, *Imperial Rivals*, 65, 79–80.

63. Mark Mancall, "Major-General Ignatiev's Mission to Peking 1859–1860," *Papers on China* 10 (1956): 60; Paine, *Imperial Rivals*, 58; Humphrey Marshall to the Secretary of State, July 10, 1853, in *FRUS*, 40:204.

64. Ignatiev to Father, May 9, 1859 (OS), and Ignatiev to Father, June 26, 1859 (OS), both in Ignatiev, *Materialy otnosyashchiyesya do prebyvaniya v Kitaye N. P. Ignat'yeva*, 29, 46, 51, 53, 212–213; Schumaker, "K istorii priobreteniya Amura," 321; Paine, *Imperial Rivals*, 100n34.

65. Ignatiev, *Materialy otnosyashchiyesya do prebyvaniya v Kitaye N. P. Ignat'yeva*, 104; Lin, "The Amur Frontier Question," 25; Schumaker, "K istorii priobreteniya Amura," 307, 313–314.

66. Paine, *Imperial Rivals*, 88–89; Schumaker, "K istorii priobreteniya Amura," 341.

67. Bassin, "A Russian Mississippi?," 167–168; Collins to Secretary of State Lewis Cass, March 6, 1858, quoted in Collins, *Siberian Journey down the Amur*, 301.

68. Frederick Engels, "Russia's Successes in the Far East," *New-York Daily Tribune*, November 18, 1858, http://marxengels.public-archive.net/en/ME1094en.html.

69. Takahiro Yamamoto, "The End of the 'Dual Possession' of Sakhalin as Multilateral Diplomacy, 1867–73," *Institute of Historical Research* 89, no. 244 (March 2016): 340, 346; Sharyl Corrado, "The 'End of the Earth': Sakhalin Island in the Russian Imperial Imagination, 1849–1906," (PhD diss., University of Illinois at Urbana-Champaign, 2010), 34–36; Yamamoto, "The End of the 'Dual Possession,'" 340. For a critique of the 1860s and 1870s as "lost decades," see Kimitaka Matsuzato, "The Creation of the Priamur Governor-Generalship

in 1884 and the Reconfiguration of Asiatic Russia," *Russian Review* 71, no. 3 (July 2012): 365–367.

70. Rosemary Neering, *Continental Dash: The Russian-American Telegraph* (Ganges, BC: Horsdal and Schubart, 1989), 196.

71. S. Maksimov, *Na Vostoke: Poezdka na Amur* (St. Petersburg: Izdanie Knigoprodavtsa, 1871), 180–181. Data from Dietrich Geyer, *Russian Imperialism: The Interaction of Domestic and Foreign Policy, 1860–1914*, trans. Bruce Little (New Haven, CT: Yale University Press, 1987), 37.

72. Bassin, "A Russian Mississippi?," 275; Steven G. Marks, *Road to Power: The Trans-Siberian Railroad and the Colonization of Asian Russia, 1850–1917* (Ithaca, NY: Cornell University Press, 1991), 17. "Soldiers and military officials" here includes Cossack settlers.

73. Nikolai Przhevalsky, "Ussuriiskii Krai: Novaia territoria rossii," *Vestnik Evropy* 6 (1870): 551, 553, 556–571, 576; Bassin, "A Russian Mississippi?," 279.

74. Corrado, "The 'End of the Earth,'" 41; Bassin, "A Russian Mississippi?," 285; Anton P. Chekhov, *Ostrov Sakhalin: Iz putevykh zapisk* (Moscow: Russkaia mysl, 1895), chap. 18.

75. Sullivan, "Count N. N. Muraviev-Amursky," 305–320; Nevelskoy, *Podvigi russkikh morskikh ofitserov*, 357; Bassin, "A Russian Mississippi?," 286.

3. "We Can Still Repeat the Exploits of Cortez"

1. Mark Bassin, "A Russian Mississippi? A Political-Geographical Inquiry into the Vision of Russia on the Pacific 1840–1865" (PhD diss., University of California, Berkley, 1983), 279; Alexandre Andreyev, Mikhail Baskhanov, and Tatiana Yusupova, *The Quest for Forbidden Lands: Nikolai Przhevalskii and His Followers on Inner Asian Tracks* (London: Brill, 2018), 77.

2. For pathbreaking work on Nikolai Przhevalsky as an advocate of "conquistador imperialism," see David Schimmelpenninck van der Oye, *Toward the Rising Sun: Russian Ideologies of Empire and the Path to War with Japan* (DeKalb: Northern Illinois University Press, 2006), 24–41. Important histories of Russia's push into China's Central Asian borderlands include Evgeny Sergeev, *The Great Game, 1856–1907: Russo-British Relations in Central and East Asia* (Washington, DC: Woodrow Wilson Center Press, 2014); Alexander Morrison, *Russian Rule in Samarkand* (Oxford: Oxford University Press, 2008); Morrison's exceptional series of articles on the subject, including "Killing the Cotton Canard and Getting Rid of the Great Game: Rewriting the Russian Conquest of Central Asia, 1814–1895," *Central Asia Survey* 33, no. 2 (2014): 131–142, and "Camels and Colonial Armies: The Logistics of Warfare in Central Asia in the Early 19th Century," *Journal of the Economic and Social History of the Orient* 57, no. 4 (2014): 443–485; Svetlana Gorshenina, *Asie Centrale: L'invention des Frontières et l'Héritage Russo-Soviétique* (Paris: CNRS Editions, 2012); S. C. M. Paine, *Imperial Rivals: China, Russia, and Their Disputed Frontier* (London: Routledge, 2015); Immanuel Hsu, *The Ili Crisis: A Study of Sino-Russian Diplomacy, 1871–1881* (Oxford: Clarendon Press, 1965); Hodong Kim, *Holy War in China: The Muslim Rebellion and State in Chinese Central Asia, 1864–1877* (Stanford, CA: Stanford University Press, 2004); and Alex Marshall, *The Russian General Staff and Asia, 1860–1917* (New York: Routledge, 2006).

3. Paine, *Imperial Rivals*, 112, 123.

4. Paine, *Imperial Rivals*, 112.

5. Ian W. Campell, "Information Revolution and Administrative Reform, ca. 1845–1868," in *Knowledge and the Ends of Empire* (Ithaca, NY: Cornell University Press, 2017), chap. 2; Willard Sunderland, *Taming the Wild Field* (Ithaca, NY: Cornell University Press, 2004); Michael Khodarkovsky, *Russia's Steppe Frontier* (Bloomington: Indiana University Press, 2002).

6. Andreyev, Baskhanov, and Yusupova, *The Quest for Forbidden Lands*, 87; Marshall, *The Russian General Staff and Asia*, 3; David Mackenzie, "Expansion in Central Asia: St. Petersburg vs. the Turkestan Generals (1863–1866)," *Canadian-American Slavic Studies* 3, no. 2 (1969): 299; Sergeev, *The Great Game*, 34.

7. Victor Dubovitskii with Khaydarbek Bababekov, "The Rise and Fall of the Kokand Khanate," in *Ferghana Valley: The Heart of Central Asia*, ed. Frederick Starr (Armonk, NY: M. E. Sharpe, 2011), 29–68; Morrison, *Russian Rule in Samarkand*, 13–15; "realm of civilized peoples": Przhevalsky quoted in Daniel Brower, *Turkestan and the Fate of the Russian Empire* (London: Routledge, 2003), 50.

8. Morrison, *Russian Rule in Samarkand*, 12–13.

9. Dubovitskii, "The Rise and Fall of the Kokand Khanate," 29–68; Morrison, *Russian Rule in Samarkand*, 13–15.

10. Paine, *Imperial Rivals*, 118.

11. Sergeev, *The Great Game*, 16, 63, 78–79.

12. Paine, *Imperial Rivals*, 113, 118; Hsu, *The Ili Crisis*, 21, 26. On patronage and taxation, see Mikhail Terentev, *Russia and England in Central Asia*, vol. 1, trans. F. C. Daukes (Calcutta: Foreign Department Press, 1876), 229. On Qing rule, see L. J. Newby, *The Empire and the Khanate: A Political History of Qing Relations with Khoqand c. 1760–1860* (Leiden: Brill, 2005), esp. chap. 5; James Millward, *Beyond the Pass: Economy, Ethnicity, and Empire in Qing Central Asia, 1759–1864* (Stanford, CA: Stanford University Press, 1998), 235–241; Kim, *Holy War in China*, 3.

13. V. C. Kadnikov, "Iz istorii kuldzhinskogo voprosa," *Istoricheskii Vestnik*, no. 6 (1911): 894; Terentev, *Russia and England*, 233, 237–238; Paine, *Imperial Rivals*, 119–120.

14. Kim, *Holy War in China*, 79–81.

15. "Zhurnal voen: Proischestvii na pogranichnom prostranstve, prilegaiushchem k zapadnomu kitaiu, za iul mesiats 1866 g.," in *Turkestanskii Krai: Sbornik Materialov dlia istorii ego zavoevaniia 1866*, pt. 2 (St. Petersburg, 1915), 3–8, 50–56; Hsu, *The Ili Crisis*, 30; Valeriy Tumaikin, "Osnovnyye napravleniya voyenno-politicheskoy i administrativnoy deyatel'nosti G.A. Kolpakovskogo" (PhD diss., Altai University, 2010), 78–79, 94; Terentev, *Russia and England*, 230–231, 242; Paine, *Imperial Rivals*, 119; Aleksandr K. Geins, "O vosstanii musul'manskogo naseleniya ili dungeney v zapadnom Kitaye," *Voennyi Sbornik*, no. 1 (August 1866): 208.

16. Gerasim A. Kolpakovskii, "Doneseniye Kolpakovskogo o zanyatii Kul'dzhinskom rayone v 1871," *Russkii Turkestan*, no. 3 (1872): 218, in *Turkestanskii Sbornik*, vol. 58; "O nastoiashem polozhenii musulmanskoi insurrektsii v Kitae," and "Otnosheniia nashi k dun-

ganam, Kashgaru, i Kuldzhe," in *Turkestanskii Sbornik,* vol. 60, 165, 170, 173; Dinara V. Dubrovskaya, *Sudba Sintszyana* (Moscow: IVRAN, 1998), 144.

17. Kadnikov, "Iz istorii kuldzhinskogo voprosa," 894; Sergei Tikhvinskii, *Dokumenty Oprovergayut: Protiv falsifikatsii istorii russko-kitayskikh otnosheniy* (Moscow: Mysl, 1982), 436; Eugene Schuyler, *Turkistan: Notes of a Journey in Russian Turkistan, Kokand, Bukhara, Kuldja,* vol. 2 (London: Sampson Low, Marston, Searle, and Rivington, 1876), 157. On the perceived threat to Semirechinsk Krai, see Dubrovskaya, *Sudba Sintszyana,* 139.

18. Dmitry Miliutin, "Zapiska Voen. Ministra," December 12, 1866 (OS), and "Ministr Finansov Voennomu Ministru," December 29, 1866 (OS), in *Turkestanskii Krai,* 230–231, 244–245. On the War Ministry, see Peter Morris, "The Russians in Central Asia, 1870–1887," *Slavonic and East European Review* 53, no. 133 (October 1975): 521–538; Mackenzie, "Expansion in Central Asia," 298–290, 299; Alexander Morrison, "'Nechto eroticheskoe', 'courir après l'ombre'? Logistical Imperatives and the Fall of Tashkent," *Central Asian Survey* 33, no. 2 (2014): 163–165.

19. V. A. Moiseev, *Rossiia i Kitai v Tsentralnoi Azii* (Barnaul: Az Buka, 2003), 105; Dubrovsky, *Sudba Sintszyana,* 144–147; Terentev, *Russia and England,* 251; Paine, *Imperial Rivals,* 121.

20. Kadnikov, "Iz istorii kuldzhinskogo voprosa," 897; N. N. Pantusov, *Svedeniia o Kul'djinskom Raione za 1871–1877 gody* (Kazan: Universitetskaia Tipografiia, 1881); Terentev, *Russia and England,* 235; Marshall, *The Russian General Staff and Asia,* 58; Paine, *Imperial Rivals,* 114.

21. Andreyev, Baskhanov, and Yusupova, *The Quest for Forbidden Lands,* 34; Terentev, *Russia and England,* 253; Paine, *Imperial Rivals,* 121–122; Hsu, *The Ili Crisis,* 33; Dubrovskaya, *Sudba Sintszyana,* 147; Schuyler, *Turkistan,* 198.

22. Marshall, *The Russian General Staff and Asia,* 75.

23. Donald Rayfield, *The Dream of Lhasa* (London: Faber and Faber, 2013), 150.

24. Schimmelpenninck van der Oye, *Toward the Rising Sun,* 25, 39.

25. On Przhevalsky's education, see Andreyev, Baskhanov, and Yusupova, *The Quest for Forbidden Lands,* 22. On the War Ministry: Peter Morris, "The Russians in Central Asia," *The Slavonic and East European Review* 53, no. 133 (October 1975): 521–538; Dmitry Miliutin, "Zapiska Voen. Ministra," December 12, 1866 (OS), in *Turkestanskii Krai,* 230–231; Rayfield, *The Dream of Lhasa,* 111–112. Not all of Russia's military leaders were keen on expansion, with Governor-General Konstantin von Kaufman often urging restraint.

26. "O nastoiashem polozhenii musulmanskoi insurrektsii v kitae," November 4, 1870, in *Turkestanskii Sbornik,* 60:158, 161.

27. Andreyev, Baskhanov, and Yusupova, *The Quest for Forbidden Lands,* 131.

28. *Turkestanskii Vedomosti,* 1872, no. 28, 3.

29. Kemal Karpat, "Yakub Beg's Relations with the Ottoman Sultans: A Reinterpretation," *Cahiers du Monde russe et sovietique* 32, no. 1 (January–March 1991): 20, 24; Sergeev, *The Great Game,* 141; *Turkestanskii Vedomosti,* 1872, no. 28, 3; Kim, *Holy War in China,* 144–145, 152. On supplies of British goods, see Wellesley (in St. Petersburg) to Loftus (London), September 22, 1876, PRO FO 65 / 940, no. 22.

30. On Yakub Beg's imperial diplomacy, see Fedor Radetsky to General von Kaufman, 1878, in Kadnikov, "Iz istorii kuldzhinskogo voprosa," 901; Dubrovskaya, *Sudba Sintszyana*, 149; "Otnosheniia nashi k dunganam, Kashgaru, i Kuldje," in *Turkestanskii Sbornik*, 60:181; Sergeev, *The Great Game*, 141–142. On Russians' fear of Yakub Beg's "immense" following, see *Journal de St Petersbourg*, no. 219, August 19 / 31, 1876, PRO FO 65 / 940; Ram Lakhan Shukha, *Britain, India, and the Turkish Empire, 1853–1882* (New Delhi: People's Publishing House, 1973), 131, citing *Russkii Mir*, July 17, 1877; *Turkestanskii Sbornik*, 60: 260–268.

31. March 8, 1974 (OS), in D. A. *Miliutin: Dnevnik, 1873–1875* (Moscow: Rosspen, 2008), 107.

32. Przhevalsky to Main Staff, June 6, 1877, in Nikolai F. Dubrovin, *Nikolai Mikhailovich Przhevalskii: Biograficheskii ocherk* (St. Petersburg: Voennaia Tipografiia, 1890), 571–573; Sergeev, *The Great Game*, 48.

33. Sergeev, *The Great Game*, 162.

34. Przhevalsky to Main Staff, June 6, 1877, and Przhevalsky to the Imperial Russian Geographic Society, January 14, 1876, in Dubrovin, *Nikolai Mikhailovich Przhevalskii*, 560, 573. International law scholar Fedor Martens also argued that "international law does not apply to savages", see Schimmelpenninck van der Oye, *Toward the Rising Sun*, 34; Sergeev, *The Great Game*, 48.

35. Kuropatkin to Przhevalsky, January 15, 1877, in Dubrovin, *Nikolai Mikhailovich Przhevalskii*, 566; Nikolai M. Przhevalsky, *From Kulja, across the Tian Shan to Lob Nor*, trans. E. Delmar Morgan (London: Sampson Low, Marston, Searle, & Rivington, 1879), 126–129; Immanuel Hsu, "British Mediation of China's War with Yakub Beg," *Central Asiatic Journal* 9, no. 2 (June 1964): 147; Kim, *Holy War in China*, 168.

36. Przhevalsky to Main Staff, June 6, 1877, in Dubrovin, *Nikolai Mikhailovich Przhevalskii*, 575–576.

37. Barbara Jelavich, *A Century of Russian Foreign Policy* (Philadelphia: Lippincott, 1964), 181; Byron Farwell, *The Encyclopedia of Nineteenth-Century Land Warfare* (New York: W. W. Norton, 2001), 714; Quintin Barry, *War in the East: A Military History of the Russo-Turkish War 1877–78* (West Midlands, UK: Helion and Company, 2012), 9, 415; Timothy C. Dowling, ed., *Russia at War* (Santa Barbara, CA: ABC-CLIO, 2015), 643, 750.

38. V. A. Frankini to Sviatpolk Mirskii, March 26, 1878 (OS), and A. K. Geins memo, April 3, 1878, in *"Bolshaia Igra" v Tsentralnoi Azii*, ed. T. N. Zagorodnikova (Moscow: IVRAN, 2005), 45, 70.

39. June 20, 1878, in *Dnevnik D. A. Miliutina, 1878–1880*, vol. 3, ed. P. A. Zaionchkovskii (Moscow: Biblioteka SSSR imeni V. I. Lenina, 1950), 73; Hsu, *The Ili Crisis*, 154. On Russia's pullback, see Telegram from the War Ministry to Kaufman, July 18, 1878 (OS), in Zagorodnikova, *"Bolshaia Igra,"* 129.

40. Paine, *Imperial Rivals*, 123, 135; Hsu, *The Ili Crisis*, 44.

41. Kaufman, March 10, 1878 (OS), in Kadnikov, "Iz istorii kuldzhinskogo voprosa," 902–903.

42. Meeting of Giers, Greig, Zhomini, Biutzov, Melnikov, Miliutin, Gens. Geiden, Obruchev, Kaznakov (Governor-General of Western Siberia), Colonels Kuropatkin and Kaulbars, March 4, 1879 (OS), in Zaionchkovskii, *Dnevnik D. A. Miliutina*, 124; Zhomini to Giers,

August 21 and August 31, 1879 (OS), in *Russia in the East 1876–1880: The Russo-Turkish War and the Kuldja Crisis as Seen through the Letters of A. G. Jomini to N. K. Giers*, ed. Charles Jelavich and Barbara Jelavich (Leiden: E. J. Brill, 1959), 92, 94.

43. Hsu, *The Ili Crisis*, 58; Paine, *Imperial Rivals*, 133–135.

44. Sergeev, *The Great Game*, 195.

45. Graf Geiden to Alexander II, "Iz doklada glavnogo shtaba aleksandru II o prisoedinenii akhal-teke k Rossii i Administrativnogo ustroistva Zakaspiia," April 23, 1881 (OS), in *Prisoedinenii Turkmenii k Rossii*, ed. A. Ilyasov (Ashgabat: Izdatelsctvo akademicheski nauk Turkmenskoi SSR, 1960), 496; Fyodor Dostoyevsky, *A Writer's Diary*, vol. 2, *1877–1881*, trans. Kenneth Lantz (Evanston, IL: Northwestern University Press, 1994), 1374–1375.

46. Paine, *Imperial Rivals*, 141; Hsu, *The Ili Crisis*, 49.

47. Paine, *Imperial Rivals*, 141–144, 151; Hsu, *The Ili Crisis*, 49, 71.

48. Paine, *Imperial Rivals*, 155; Hsu, *The Ili Crisis*, 95–96, 98.

49. Roman Romanovic Baron Rosen, *Forty Years of Diplomacy*, vol. 1 (Abingdon: Routledge, 2018), 45; Michael Share, "The Bear Yawns? Russian and Soviet Relations with Macao," *Journal of the Royal Asiatic Society 16*, 3rd ser., no. 1 (April 2006): 45; Hsu, *The Ili Crisis*, 95–96, 98, 110–111, 122; Immanuel C. Y. Hsu, "Gordon in China, 1880," *Pacific Historical Review 33*, no. 2 (May 1964): 147–166; Sergeev, *The Great Game*, 166.

50. Nikolai Przhevalsky, "O vozmozhnoi voine c Kitaem," *Sbornik geograficheskikh, topograficheskikh, i statisticheskikh materialov po azii*, no. 1 (1883): 293–303.

51. Don C. Price, *Russia and the Roots of the Chinese Revolution, 1896–1911* (Cambridge, MA: Harvard University Press, 1974), 172.

52. Przhevalsky, "O vozmozhnoi voine c Kitaem," 294.

53. "Veroiatna li voina Kitaia c Rosiiei," *Golos*, nos. 198 and 200 (1889), in *Turkestanskii Sbornik*, vol. 319; Mikhail Veniukov, "Pozemelynye priobreteniya i ustupki Rossii za poslednie tridsaty let," *Russkaia Mysl* (January 1880), 20, 22–23; Marshall, *The Russian General Staff and Asia*, 68–70.

54. Hsu, *The Ili Crisis*, 100, 157; Marshall, *The Russian General Staff and Asia*, 75, 78. On British support for China in Russian calculations, see Aleksei Voskresenskii, *Diplomaticheskaya istoriia russko-kitaiskogo Sankt-Peterburgskogo dogovora 1881 goda* (Moscow: Pamiatniki istoricheskoi mysli, 1995), 272.

55. Thanks to Dong Yan for pointing this out.

56. October 18 (OS), 1880, in Zaionchkovskii, *Dnevnik D. A. Miliutina*, 276; Marshall, *The Russian General Staff and Asia*, 75, 78–79; Edwin Bilof, "China in Imperial Russian Military Planning, 1881–1887," *Military Affairs 42*, no. 2 (April 1982): 71. On General Staff thinking, though written slightly after the crisis, see G. Butakov, *Sbornik Geograficheskikh, Topograficheskikh, i Statisticheskikh Materialov po Azii* (St. Peterburg: Voen. tp., 1888), 24.

57. Miliutin Diary, April 4, August 13, October 18 and 25, and December 1, 1880 (OS), in Zaionchkovskii, *Dnevnik D. A. Miliutina*, 239, 267, 276, 280, 283; Zhomini to Giers, August 27 and 29, and September 22, 1880 (OS), in Jelavich and Jelavich, *Russia in the East*, 102–103, 111; Paine, *Imperial Rivals*, 160.

58. Zhomini to Giers, September 22, 1880 (OS), in Jelavich and Jelavich, *Russia in the East*, 111.

59. December 1 and 9, 1880, in Zaionchkovskii, *Dnevnik D. A. Miliutina*, 283, 285; Zhomini to Giers, September 22, October 1, 3, 12, 21, and 22, 1880 (OS), in Jelavich and Jelavich, *Russia in the East*, 112-128.

60. Giers to Zhomini, September 6, 23, 25, and 27, 1880 (OS), in Jelavich and Jelavich, *Russia in the East*, 138, 149-151; Hsu, *The Ili Crisis*, 187; Paine, *Imperial Rivals*, 161-162, 171; January 10, 1881 (OS), in Dmitry A. Miliutin, *Dnevnik, 1879-1881* (Moscow: Rossiiskaia politicheskaia entsiklopediia, 2010), 257.

61. Katkov in *Russkie Vedomosti*, March 2, 1865 (OS), in Geyer, *Russian Imperialism*, 94; Charles Marvin, *Russian Advance toward India* (London: Sampson Low, Marston, Searle, and Rivington, 1882), 306-307; Peter A. Zaionchkovsky, *The Russian Autocracy in Crisis*, ed. and trans. Gary M. Hamburg (Gulf Breeze, FL: Academic International Press, 1979), chap. 5.

62. March 27, 1895 (OS), in A. Polovtsov, *Dnevnik Gosudarstvennogo Sekretarya A.A. Polovtsova*, vol. 1 (Moscow: Nauka, 1966), 304-305; Sergeev, *The Great Game*, 206-207; Morris, "The Russians in Central Asia," 529.

63. In *The Great Game*, Sergeev argues that "Eastern Turkestan . . . had ceased to be one of major 'playfields' of the Great Game after the end of the Yili Crisis." On subsequent sparring, see Jennifer Siegel, *Endgame: Britain, Russia and the Final Struggle for Central Asia* (London: I. B. Tauris, 2002).

64. N. M. Przhevalsky, *Ot Kiakhti na istoki Zheltyi Reki* (Moscow: OGIS, Gosudarstvennoe izdatelstvo geograficheskoi literatury, 1948), 328; Andreyev, Baskhanov, and Yusupova, *The Quest for Forbidden Lands*, 139; Rayfield, *The Dream of Lhasa*, 203-204.

65. Price, *Russia and the Roots of the Chinese Revolution*, 31.

66. Hsu, *The Ili Crisis*, 55; Dostoyevsky, *A Writer's Diary*, 1374.

4. "Tightening the Bonds between Us"

1. Esper Ukhtomsky, *Travels in the East of Nicholas II, Emperor of Russia when Cesarewitch 1890-1891*, vol. 1, ed. G. Birdwood, trans. R. Goodlet (London: A. Constable & Company, 1896), 1-8, 293, 369; Ukhtomsky, *Travels in the East of Nicholas II, Emperor of Russia when Cesarewitch 1890-1891*, vol. 2, ed. G. Birdwood, trans. R. Goodlet (London: A. Constable & Company, 1900), 329; Grand Duke Alexander of Russia, *Once a Grand Duke* (New York: Farrar & Rinehart, 1932), 167. Nicholas "personally revised" Ukhtomsky's text before publication; see V. I. Gurko, *Features and Figures of the Past*, ed. J. E. Sterling, Xenia Eudin, and H. Fisher, trans. Laura Matveev (New York: Russell & Russell, 1970), 257. On Nicholas's Asian journey as a European Grand Tour, see David Schimmelpenninck van der Oye, *Toward the Rising Sun: Russian Ideologies of Empire and the Path to War with Japan* (DeKalb: Northern Illinois University Press, 2006), chap. 1, which shaped my thinking about Nicholas's Asian vision.

2. Schimmelpenninck van der Oye, *Toward the Rising Sun*, 17.

3. Schimmelpenninck van der Oye, *Toward the Rising Sun*, 50-51.

4. In recounting Russia's path to war with Japan, this chapter draws heavily on Schimmelpenninck van der Oye, *Toward the Rising Sun*. On the Trans-Siberian Railway, I have relied on Steven G. Marks, *Road to Power: The Trans-Siberian Railroad and the Colonization*

of Asian Russia, 1850–1917 (Ithaca, NY: Cornell University Press, 1991). On international politics in East Asia more broadly, see George A. Lensen, *Balance of Intrigue: International Rivalry in Korea & Manchuria, 1884–1899*, vol. 2 (Tallassee: University Presses of Florida, 1982); David MacLaren McDonald, *United Government and Foreign Policy in Russia, 1900–1914* (Cambridge, MA: Harvard University Press, 1992); and Alex Marshall, *The Russian General Staff and Asia, 1860–1917* (New York: Routledge, 2006). Useful older works include Andrew Malozemoff, *Russian Far Eastern Policy: 1881–1904* (Berkeley: University of California Press, 1958); B. A. Romanov, *Russia in Manchuria, 1892–1906*, trans. Susan Wilbur Jones (New York: Octagon Books, 1974).

5. Stephen R. Halsey, *Quest for Power* (Cambridge, MA: Harvard University Press, 2015); Schimmelpenninck van der Oye, *Toward the Rising Sun*, 50.

6. Clarence B. Davis, Kenneth E. Wilburn, and Ronald E. Robinson, eds., *Railway Imperialism* (Westport, CT: Greenwood Press, 1991).

7. Roman R. Rosen, *Forty Years of Diplomacy*, vol. 1 (New York: A. A. Knopf, 1922), 190. On "monarchical power," see Don C. Price, *Russia and the Roots of the Chinese Revolution, 1896–1911* (Cambridge, MA: Harvard University Press, 1974), 33.

8. Schimmelpenninck van der Oye, *Toward the Rising Sun*, 44.

9. The figure of 6–10 million is in R. K. I. Quested, *"Matey" Imperialists: The Tsarist Russians in Manchuria 1895–1917* (Hong Kong: University of Hong Kong, 1982), 8–9. Marks, *Road to Power*, 37, cites "fewer than 100,000" in Russia's Maritime Oblast. Malozemoff, *Russian Far Eastern Policy*, 22, says there were thirty times more Chinese in the region than Russians. Seung Kwon Synn, *Russo-Japanese Rivalry over Korea, 1876–1904* (Seoul: Yuk Phub Sa, 1981), 43.

10. Famed Sinologist V. P. Vasilev, in Malozemoff, *Russian Far Eastern Policy*, 43.

11. Ukhtomsky, *Travels in the East*, 2:451–455. Witte quoted in S. C. M. Paine, *The Sino-Japanese War of 1894–1895* (Cambridge: Cambridge University Press, 2002), 62.

12. Gurko, *Features and Figures of the Past*, 256; Ukhtomsky, *Travels in the East*, 2:474.

13. Chekhov to A. S. Suvorin, May 20, 1890, in Anton Chekhov, *A Journey to the End of the Russian Empire*, trans. Rosamund Bartlett, Anthony Phillips, Luba Terpak, and Michael Terpak (New York: Penguin, 2007), 1–5.

14. Captain P. H. Colomb, "Memorandum on the Russian Settlement of Vladivostok," August 14, 1875, in *British Documents on Foreign Affairs: Reports and Papers from the Foreign Office Confidential Print*, vol. 1, pt. 1, ser. A, ed. Kenneth Bourne and D. Cameron Watt (Frederick, MD: University Publications of America, 1983), 27; Schimmelpenninck van der Oye, *Toward the Rising Sun*, 48; Malozemoff, *Russian Far Eastern Policy*, 3.

15. Colomb, "Memorandum on the Russian Settlement," 271; Marks, *Road to Power*, 13–14, 30; Schimmelpenninck van der Oye, *Toward the Rising Sun*, 48.

16. Malozemoff, *Russian Far Eastern Policy*, 15, 33; Synn, *Russo-Japanese Rivalry over Korea*, 46.

17. Aleksei Kuropatkin, *The Russian Army and the Japanese War*, vol. 1, ed. E. D. Swinton, trans. A. B. Lindsay (New York: E. P. Dutton, 1909), 71.

18. T. H. Von Laue, "A Secret Memorandum of Sergei Witte on the Industrialization of Imperial Russia," *Journal of Modern History* 26, no. 1 (March 1954): 72; Marks, *Road to Power*,

52, 154; Victor Zatsepine, *Beyond the Amur* (Vancouver: UBC Press, 2017), 85; Malozemoff, *Russian Far Eastern Policy,* 24; Synn, *Russo-Japanese Rivalry over Korea,* 6.

19. Romanov, *Russia in Manchuria,* 39; Marshall, *The Russian General Staff and Asia,* 44; Marks, *Road to Power,* 38, 41–42; Malozemoff, *Russian Far Eastern Policy,* 48.

20. Donald W. Treadgold, *The Great Siberian Migration* (Princeton, NJ: Princeton University Press, 2015), 107; Romanov, *Russia in Manchuria,* 39–40.

21. Sergei Witte, "Vsepoddanneishii doklad upravliaiushchego ministerstvom finansov o sposobakh sooruzheniia velikogo sibirskogo zheleznodorozhnogo puti i o naznachenii soveshchaniia dlia obsuzhdeniia sego dela," November 6, 1892, in Witte, *Sobranie Sochinenii i Dokumentalnikh Materialov,* vol. 1, bk. 2, pt. 1 (Moscow: Nauka, 2006), 159.

22. Frank Wcislo, *Tales of Imperial Russia: The Life and Times of Sergei Witte, 1849–1915* (Oxford: Oxford University Press, 2011), 25; Sidney Harcave, *Count Sergei Witte and the Twilight of Imperial Russia* (Armonk, NY: M. E. Sharpe, 2004), 15, 21.

23. Sergei Witte, *The Memoirs of Count Witte,* ed. and trans. Abraham Yarmolinksy (Garden City, NY: Double, Page, & Company, 1921), 142, 224.

24. Witte, *The Memoirs of Count Witte,* 209–210.

25. Alexander Izvolsky, *Recollections of a Foreign Minister,* trans. Charles L. Seeger (Garden City, NY: Doubleday, Page, & Company, 1921), 114. On Witte's marriage, see Wcislo, *Tales of Imperial Russia;* Harcave, *Count Sergei Witte,* 46–47.

26. Izvolsky, *Recollections of a Foreign Minister,* 118; Gurko, *Features and Figures of the Past,* 52.

27. E. J. Dillon, *The Eclipse of Russia* (New York: George H. Doran, 1918), 187.

28. Witte, "Po povodu natsionalizma," in *Sobranie Sochinenii i Dokumentalnikh Materialov,* 41, 42, 46, 48, 51, 53, 54, 67; Witte, *The Memoirs of Count Witte,* 41. On Russian industrialists' thinking, see Thomas Owen, *Capitalism and Politics in Russia* (Cambridge: Cambridge University Press, 1981), 34–35.

29. Witte, "Vsepoddanneishii doklad upravliaiushchego ministerstvom finansov," 169; Malozemoff, *Russian Far Eastern Policy,* 47; Izvolsky, *Recollections of a Foreign Minister,* 123; Treadgold, *The Great Siberian Migration,* 128; Romanov, *Russia in Manchuria,* 43; Marks, *Road to Power,* 126.

30. Romanov, *Russia in Manchuria,* 39–40; Gurko, *Features and Figures of the Past,* 256; Ukhtomsky, *Travels in the East,* 2:474; K. Korol'kov, *Zhizn' i tsarstvovanie Imperatora Aleksandra III, 1881–1894* (Kiev: I. I. Chokolov, 1901), 193–196.

31. On "peaceful penetration," see Shimmelpennick van der Oye, *Toward the Rising Sun,* 61–81.

32. Malozemoff, *Russian Far Eastern Policy,* 47; Romanov, *Russia in Manchuria,* 38, 41. On Witte's strategy as "penetration pacifique," see Schimmelpennick van Der Oye, *Toward the Rising Sun,* chap. 4.

33. Marks, *Road to Power,* 172; Romanov, *Russia in Manchuria,* 40, 48, 62; Rosen, *Forty Years of Diplomacy,* 135; Paine, *The Sino-Japanese War of 1894–1895,* 127.

34. Romanov, *Russia in Manchuria,* 50; K. I. Vogak, "Iz raporta Polkovnika Vogaka upravliaiushchemu voenno-uchenogo komiteta Glavnogo shtaba," February 14, 1897, in *Port-Artur i Dalnii, 1894–1904 gg: Poslednii Kolonialnii proekt Rossiiskoi imperii; Sbornik Doku-*

mentov, ed. Igor Lukoyanov and Dmitry Pavlov (Moscow: Institut rossiiskoi istorii RAN, 2018), 53–54; Paine, *The Sino-Japanese War of 1894–1895*, 104; Yoshihisa Tak Matsusaka, *The Making of Japanese Manchuria, 1904–1932* (Cambridge, MA: Harvard University Press, 2003), 24.

35. Frank W. Ikle, "The Triple Intervention: Japan's Lesson in the Diplomacy of Imperialism," *Monumenta Nipponica* 22, nos. 1 / 2 (1967): 122–130; R. K. I. Quested, *The Russo-Chinese Bank: A Multinational Financial Base of Tsarism in China* (Birmingham: University of Birmingham, 1977); Romanov, *Russia in Manchuria*, 50–51, 67–68.

36. On the "Yellow Peril" in Russian thinking, see Schimmelpenninck van der Oye, *Toward the Rising Sun*, chap. 5.

37. Tsar Nicholas to his mother, Marie, August 7, 1896, in *Letters of Tsar Nicholas and Empress Marie*, ed. Edward J. Bing (London: Nicholson and Watson, 1937), 116–117; Witte, *The Memoirs of Count Witte*, 189; Grand Duke Alexander of Russia, *Once a Grand Duke*, 169, 177; Zachary Adam Hoffman, "Orienting the Empire: Russian Identity and East Asian Imperialism in the Conservative Press, 1894–1905" (PhD diss., University of Virginia, 2017), 122.

38. Paine, *The Sino-Japanese War of 1894–1895*, 282.

39. "Kopia Doklada kn. Lobanov, ot 25 Marta 1895," WP CUA, d. 22, in folder "Dokumenty Kasaiushchiesa Vziatiia Port Artura"; cf. "Zhurnal osobago soveshchaniia 30 Marta 1895," in "Dokumenty Kasaiushchiesa Vziatiia Port Artura"; Malozemoff, *Russian Far Eastern Policy*, 60; Paine, *The Sino-Japanese War of 1894–1895*, 283.

40. "Zhurnal osobago soveshchaniia 30 Marta 1895." "Versts" translated as "kilometers."

41. Dominic C. B. Lieven, *Nicholas II: The Emperor of All the Russias* (London: John Murray, 1993), 65; Richard Wortman, *Scenarios of Power: From Alexander II to the Abdication of Nicholas II*, vol. 2 (Princeton, NJ: Princeton University Press, 1995), 345–351.

42. Witte, *The Memoirs of Count Witte*, 85–88.

43. Witte, *The Memoirs of Count Witte*, 86.

44. Russia-China Treaty of 1896, Article I; "Doklad Ministra Finansov, o zakliuchenii Kitaiskim Pravitelstvom i Russko-Kitaiskim Bankom dogovora na postroiku dorogi v Manchzhurii," WP CUA, d. 22, in "Dokumenty Kasaiushchiesa vziatiia Port Artura," 2, 3; Witte, *The Memoirs of Count Witte*, 89, 190.

45. Witte, *The Memoirs of Count Witte*, 91; Romanov, *Russia in Manchuria*, 83–84; Paine, *The Sino-Japanese War of 1894–1895*, 308.

46. Lensen, *Balance of Intrigue*, 531, 538–541.

47. "Protokol po Koreiskim Delam, Podpisannii v Moskve 28-go Maia 1896 mezhdu Russkim i Iaponskim Pravitelstvami," in *Recueil de traités et documents diplomatiques concernant l'Extrême Orient, 1895–1905* (St. Petersburg: Impr. A. Mendelewitch, 1906), 159–160; Lensen, *Balance of Intrigue*, 634; Romanov, *Russia in Manchuria*, 113, 116. Sources differ on the crucial question of where a partition line was to be. Japanese sources say along the Yalu river; see Yosaburo Takekoshi, *Prince Saionji* (Kyoto: Ritsumeikan University, 1933), 142. Romanov, by contrast, says Yamagata proposed the 38th parallel: Romanov, *Russia in Manchuria*, 104.

48. Romanov, *Russia in Manchuria*, 132–138.

49. Sergei Witte, "Zapiska ministra finansov o zasedanii po povodu zapiski M-ra Inostr. Del. o zaniatii Talianvania," WP CUA, d. 22, in "Dokumenty Kasaiushchiesa vziatiia Port Artura," 2; Romanov, *Russia in Manchuria,* 137.

50. Witte, "Zapiska ministra finansov," 3–5; Rosen, *Forty Years of Diplomacy,* 156–157.

51. George F. Kennan, *The Fateful Alliance: France, Russia, and the Coming of the First World War* (New York: Pantheon Books, 1985); Izvolsky, *Recollections of a Foreign Minister,* 44–45; William II, *Letters from the Kaiser to the Czar* (New York: Frederick A. Stokes, 1920), 10–13.

52. "Kopia telegramma nadv. sov. Pokotilova," March 16, 1898, and "Vypiska iz Pravitel-stvennago Vestnika," March 17, 1898, WP CUA, d. 22, in "Dokumenty Kasaiushchiesa vzi-atiia Port Artura," 4; Kuropatkin to Muravev, March 10, 1898, in *Port-Artur i Dalnii,* 96; William II, *Letters from the Kaiser to the Czar,* 52.

53. "Kopia pisma Ministra Inostrannikh Del k Ministru Finansov, ot 13 Ianvaria 1898 g, c telegrammoiu d. t. s. Staalia iz Londona," January 12, 1898, WP CUA, d. 22, in "Doku-menty Kasaiushchiesa vziatiia Port Artura"; Rosen, *Forty Years of Diplomacy,* 156–157.

54. Lensen, *Balance of Intrigue,* 627, 807; Rosen, *Forty Years of Diplomacy,* 158–159.

55. Quested, *"Matey" Imperialists,* 24.

56. Izvolsky, *Recollections of a Foreign Minister,* 125; Paine, *The Sino-Japanese War of 1894–1895,* 9.

57. Kerbedz to I. P. Shipov, May 30, 1899, and Witte to Kuropatkin, September 1, 1899, in *Port-Artur i Dalnii,* 281–282, 284–286; Kuropatkin to Witte, April 24, 1898; "Vypiska iz Zhurnala Komiteta Sibirskoi zheleznoi dorogi," January 27, 1899; and "Pechatnaia Za-piska," March 1–7, 1899; in WP CUA, d. 22. On religion, see Witte to Pobedonostsev, 1897, in *KA,* vol. 30 (1928): 99.

58. "Telegramma Suboticha Nachalniku Glavnogo Shtaba," February 8, 1899, in *Port-Artur i Dalnii,* 322–323, 388–389; Quested, *"Matey" Imperialists,* 39, 101, 110–111.

59. Marks, *Road to Power,* 155; Zatsepine, *Beyond the Amur,* 43; Quested, *"Matey" Impe-rialists,* 26; David Wolff, *To the Harbin Station* (Stanford, CA: Stanford University Press, 1999), 33.

60. "Kopia pisma M-ra Finansov na imia Grafa V. N. Lamzdorfa," October 30, 1898, WP CUA, d. 22, 457–458; Wolff, *To the Harbin Station,* 9, 43–44; spelling adjusted; Gurko, *Features and Figures of the Past,* 259; Quested, *"Matey" Imperialists,* 81–82, 112.

61. "Depesha poslannika v Pekine," April 18, 1900, Giers to St. Petersburg, June 7, 1900, and Lamsdorf Memo, July 13, 1900, in *KA,* vol. 14 (1926): 8, 12, 18; Witte, *The Memoirs of Count Witte,* 107–108.

62. Lamzdorf memo, July 13, 1900, and Lamzdorf to Alekseev, June 28, 1900, in *KA,* vol. 14 (1926): 16, 19.

63. Tsar Nicholas to his mother, Marie, August 11, 1900, in *The Letters of Tsar Nicholas and Empress Marie,* ed. Edward J. Bing (London: Nicholson and Watson, 1937), 144; Giers to Beijing, October 11, 1900, and Lamzdorf to Kuropatkin, December 16, 1900, in *KA,* vol. 14 (1926), 37, 41; Witte, *The Memoirs of Count Witte,* 113–114; Schimmelpenninck van der Oye, *Toward the Rising Sun,* chap. 11.

64. Grand Duke Alexander of Russia, *Once a Grand Duke,* 211.

65. Tsar Nicholas to his mother, Marie, July 23, 1897, in Bing, *The Letters of Tsar Nicholas and Empress Marie*, 128; Kaiser to Tsar, September 2, 1902, September 19, 1903, and December 4, 1903, in Isaac Don Levine, ed. *Letters from the Kaiser to the Tsar* (New York: Stokes, 1920), 86, 93, 96; spelling adjusted; A. Savinsky, *Recollections of a Russian Diplomat* (London: Hutchinson & Co., 1992), 73.

66. Gurko, *Features and Figures of the Past*, 276; Marshall, *The Russian General Staff and Asia*, 86–87, 93; Lieven, *Nicholas II*, 95; Mikhail Alekseev, *Voennaia razvedka Rossii*, vol. 1 (Moscow: Izdatelskii Dom "Russkaia Razvedka," 1998), 77.

67. On the backlash against Witte, see Memo to Landsdowne, March 14, 1903, PRO FO, 65 / 1659, 141–142; "Extract from Novoe Vremya," March 5, 1903, PRO FO, 65 / 1659, 20; Memo to Landsdowne on Russian Budget, March 17, 1903, PRO FO, 65 / 1659, 209; Gurko, *Features and Figures of the Past*, 270; Schimmelpenninck van der Oye, *Toward the Rising Sun*, 101, 205; McDonald, *United Government and Foreign Policy in Russia*, 173–175; Malozemoff, *Russian Far Eastern Policy*, 189.

68. Cecil Spring Rice to Lansdowne, October 29, 1903, PRO FO, 65 / 1662, 31; Gurko, *Features and Figures of the Past*, 264; Lieven, *Nicholas II*, 98; Igor V. Lukoianov, "The Bezobrazovtsy," in *The Russo-Japanese War in Global Perspective: World War Zero*, ed. David Wolff et al. (Leiden: Brill, 2005), 67.

69. Gurko, *Features and Figures of the Past*, 274; Kuropatkin, *The Russian Army and the Japanese War*, 181–182; A. M. Bezobrazov, "Les premières causes de l'effondrement de la Russie: Le conflit russo-japonais," *Le Correspondant*, May 25, 1923, 585; Vonliarliarskii, "Why Russia Went to War with Japan: The Story of the Yalu Concession," *Fortnightly Review* 86 (June 1910): 1033.

70. A. Savinsky, *Recollections of a Russian Diplomat*, 45; McDonald, *United Government and Foreign Policy in Russia*, 31.

71. Scott to Lansdowne, August 20, 1903, and Memo to Lansdowne, September 3, 1903, in PRO FO, 65 / 1661, 87, 130; McDonald, *United Government and Foreign Policy in Russia*, 35 and passim; Savinsky, *Recollections of a Russian Diplomat*, 44; Vasili Vonliarliarskii, *Moi Vospominaniia, 1852–1939 gg.* (Berlin: Russkoe natsionalnoye izdatelstvo, 1939), 13; Evgeny Sergeev, *Russian Military Intelligence in the War with Japan, 1904–05* (London: Routledge, 2007), 35; Schimmelpenninck van der Oye, *Toward the Rising Sun*, 199; Wolff, *To the Harbin Station*, 54. On "yids and Poles," see Lukoianov, "The Bezobrazovtsy," 65–86, esp. 75 (translation modified).

72. Memo to Lansdowne, August 20, 1903, PRO FO, 65 / 1661, 83; Memo to Lansdowne, December 9, 1903, PRO FO, 65 / 1662, 298; Scott to Lansdowne, January 6, 1904, PRO FO, 65 / 1678, 16; Savinsky, *Recollections of a Russian Diplomat*, 79; Wolff, *To the Harbin Station*, 7.

73. McDonald, *United Government and Foreign Policy in Russia*, 72; Dillon, *The Eclipse of Russia*, 284; Lukoianov, "The Bezobrazovtsy," 85; Gurko, *Features and Figures of the Past*, 285–286.

74. Felix Patrikeeff and Harold Shukman, *Railways and the Russo-Japanese War* (New York: Routledge, 2007), 1–2; Abraham Ascher, *Revolution of 1905: A Short History* (Stanford, CA: Stanford University Press, 2004), 15; Sergeev, *Russian Military Intelligence*, 33–34.

75. Marks, *Road to Power*, 205; Sergeev, *Russian Military Intelligence*, 46; Patrikeeff and Shukman, *Railways and the Russo-Japanese War*, 80; Peter Gatrell, *Government Industry and Rearmament in Russia* (Cambridge: Cambridge University Press, 2010), 67–68; Zatsepine, *Beyond the Amur*, 131.

76. Ascher, *Revolution of 1905*, 48, 88; John Bushnell, *Mutiny amid Repression* (Bloomington: Indiana University Press, 1985).

77. Dillon, *The Eclipse of Russia*, 294–295; W. Bruce Lincoln, *The Great Reforms: Autocracy, Bureaucracy, and the Politics of Change in Imperial Russia* (DeKalb: Northern Illinois University Press, 1990), 199; Lieven, *Nicholas II*, 89.

78. Peter Berton, *Russo-Japanese Relations, 1905–1917: From Enemies to Allies* (London: Routledge, 2012), 2; John Albert White, *The Diplomacy of the Russo-Japanese War* (Princeton, NJ: Princeton University Press, 1964).

79. Olga Crisp, "The Russian Liberals and the 1906 Anglo-French Loan to Russia," *The Slavonic and East European Review* 39, no. 92 (June 1961): 497–511.

80. Tsar Nicholas to his mother, Marie, January 12, 1906, in *The Secret Letters of the Last Tsar*, ed. Edward J. Bing (New York: Longmans, 1938), 211.

81. Witte, *The Memoirs of Count Witte*, 83, 183

82. Witte to Kuropatkin, May 26, 1905 (OS), in *KA*, vol. 19 (1926), 80; Donald W. Mitchell, *A History of Russian and Soviet Seapower* (New York: Macmillan, 1974), 269.

83. Bronevskii to Sazonov, March 3, 1912, in *Mezhdunarodnie Otnosheniia v Epokhu Imperializma*, vol. 19, pt. 2, ed. L.A. Telesheva (Moscow: Gosudarstvennoe izdatelstvo politicheskoi literatury, 1939), 227–229; Izvolsky, November 21, 1909, in Edward H. Zabriskie, *American-Russian Rivalry in the Far East* (Philadelphia: University of Pennsylvania Press, 1946), 155–157, 160; Berton, *Russo-Japanese Relations*, 4–5.

84. Neratov to Korostovts, November 22, 1911, and Sazanov to Nicholas II, January 23, 1912, in *Mezhdunarodnie Otnosheniia v Epokhu Imperializma*, vol. 19, pt. 1, ed. L.A. Telesheva (Moscow: Gosudarstvennoe izdatelstvo politicheskoi literatury, 1939), 56, 84; Michael M. Walker, *The 1929 Sino-Soviet War: The War Nobody Knew* (Lawrence: University Press of Kansas, 2017), 41–42.

85. Peter S. H. Tang, *Russian and Soviet Policy in Manchuria and Outer Mongolia, 1911–1931* (Durham, NC: Duke University Press, 1959), 291–292, 357–358; Thomas E. Ewing, "Russia, China, and the Origins of the Mongolian People's Republic, 1911–1921: A Reappraisal," *The Slavonic and East European Review* 58, no. 3 (July 1980): 399–421.

86. "Notes by Lieutenant Binstead on the Position and Policy of Russia in Northern Manchuria, April 3, 1914," in Ian Nish, *The History of Manchuria, 1840–1948: A Sino-Russo-Japanese Triangle*, vol. 2 (Folkestone, UK: Renaissance, 2016), 67–69.

87. Kuropatkin, *The Russian Army and the Japanese War*, 185–186; Marshall, *The Russian General Staff and Asia*, 91; Dietrich Geyer, *Russian Imperialism: The Interaction of Domestic and Foreign Policy, 1860–1914*, trans. Bruce Little (New Haven, CT: Yale University Press, 1987), 202–203; Berton, *Russo-Japanese Relations*, 6.

88. Izvolskii to Beckendorff, January 9, 1907, Izvolskii to Beckendorff, August 21, 1906, and Izvolskii to Giers, February 9, 1907, in Alexandre Iswolsky, *Au service de la Russie: Alexandre Iswolsky, Correspondance Diplomatique* (Paris: Les Éditions Internationales, 1937), 226, 352, 418.

5. "A New Mecca for the East"

1. Karl Marx and Friedrich Engels, "Karl Marx and Friedrich Engels: Preface to the Second Russian edition of the *Manifesto of the Communist Party,*" in *Late Marx and the Russian Road: Marx and the "Peripheries of Capitalism,"* ed. Teodor Shanin (New York: Monthly Review Press, 1983), 139; "Draft of an Article on Friedrich List's book: *Das Nationale System der Politischen Oekonomie,*" https://marxists.catbull.com/archive/marx/works/1845/03/list.htm; Xenia Joukoff Eudin and Robert C. North, *Soviet Russia and the East* (Stanford, CA: Stanford University Press, 1957), 155.

2. Theodore H. von Laue, *Sergei Witte and the Industrialization of Russia* (New York: Columbia University Press, 1965); Abraham Ascher, *P. A. Stolypin: The Search for Stability in Late Imperial Russia* (Stanford, CA: Stanford University Press, 2002); Dominic Lieven, *Russia and the Origins of the First World War* (London: Palgrave Macmillan, 1983).

3. Jonathan Haslam, *Near and Distant Neighbors* (New York: Farrar, Straus and Giroux, 2015), 9.

4. Robert C. Tucker, *Stalin in Power: The Revolution from Above, 1928–1941* (New York: Norton, 1990), 89; translation modified; Edvard Radzinsky, *The Last Tsar: The Life and Death of Nicholas II* (New York: Anchor Books, 1993), 1–2.

5. Charles S. Maier, *Recasting Bourgeois Europe* (Princeton, NJ: Princeton University Press, 1975); Karl Marx and Frederick Engels, *Manifesto of the Communist Party,* Marxists Internet Archive, https://www.marxists.org/archive/marx/works/download/pdf/Manifesto.pdf.

6. "Greetings from the All-Russian Central Executive Committee," April 9, 1919, in *SDFP,* 1:150; "Radiograma Narodnogo Komisariata inostrannikh del RSFSR," January 10, 1919, in *DVP,* 2:20, 39; "Radiogramma Narodnogo Kmissara inostrannikh del RSFSR," March 30, 1919, in *DVP,* 2:109; "Nota narodnogo komissara inostrannikh del RSFSR," May 25, 1919, in *DVP,* 2:173; Georgy Chicherin, "Obrashenia narodnogo komissariata inostrannikh del RSFSR," July 17, 1919, in *DVP,* 2:208.

7. Erez Manela, *The Wilsonian Moment* (Oxford: Oxford University Press, 2009); Arno J. Mayer, *Wilson vs. Lenin* (New York: Meridian Books, 1969); "Wilson's War Message to Congress," April 2, 1917, World War I Document Archive, https://wwi.lib.byu.edu/index.php/Wilson%27s_War_Message_to_Congress.

8. Haslam, *Near and Distant Neighbors,* 9.

9. Zara Steiner, *The Lights That Failed: European International History, 1919–1933* (New York: Oxford University Press, 2005), 131.

10. On British encirclement, see Chicherin to Karakhan, December 21, 1924, in *Perepiska I. V. Stalina i G. V. Chicherina s polpredom SSSR v Kitae L. M. Karakhanom,* ed. A. I. Kartunov (Moscow: Natalis, 2008), 401 (hereafter Kartunov, *Perepiska*).

11. *SRE,* 51, 66; Lars-Erik Nyman, *Great Britain and Chinese, Russia, and Japanese Interests in Sinkiang, 1918–1934* (Stockholm: Esselte Stadium, 1977), 42. On raw materials, see Robert C. North, *Moscow and Chinese Communists* (Stanford, CA: Stanford University Press, 1953), 80.

12. Stephen White, "Communism and the East: The Baku Congress, 1920," *Slavic Review* 33, no. 3 (September 1974): 492.

13. "Appeal of the Council of People's Commissars to the Moslems of Russia and the East," December 1917, in *SDFP*, 1:16; White, "Communism and the East," 492; Grigory Zinoviev, "Manifesto the Peoples of the East," *Komunisticheskii Internatsional*, no. 15 (December 1920); *To See the Dawn: Baku, 1920; First Congress of the Peoples of the East*, ed. John Riddell (New York: Pathfinder Press, 1993), 231.

14. Maring quoted in *SRE*, 41; Jon Jacobson, *When the Soviet Union Entered World Politics* (Berkeley: University of California Press, 1994), 116.

15. "Declaration Signed by Karakhan to the Chinese People," July 25, 1919, in *SDFP*, 1:158; Alexander Pantsov, *The Bolsheviks and the Chinese Revolution, 1919–1927* (New York: Routledge, 2000), 27, 33; James E. Sheridan, *Chinese Warlord: The Career of Feng Yu-Hsiang* (Stanford, CA: Stanford University Press, 1966), 142; Paul V. Reilly, "Lev Karakhan and the Development of Early Soviet Foreign Policy" (PhD diss., New York University, 1980), 44.

16. Jeremy Friedman, *Shadow Cold War* (Chapel Hill: University of North Carolina Press, 2015); Bruce A. Elleman, *Diplomacy and Deception: The Secret History of Sino-Soviet Diplomatic Relations, 1917–1927* (Armonk, NY: M. E. Sharpe, 1997), chap. 2; Don C. Price, *Russia and the Roots of the Chinese Revolution, 1896–1911* (Cambridge, MA: Harvard University Press, 1974), 88. Evidence of the Borodin–Sun Chicago encounter comes entirely from Borodin; Sun never mentioned it. We cannot exclude the possibility that Borodin exaggerated his closeness to Sun; see Dan Jacobs, *Borodin: Stalin's Man in China* (Cambridge, MA: Harvard University Press, 1981), 113.

17. Jacobs, *Borodin*, 3, 24; Chicherin to Sun Yat-Sen, August 1, 1918, in *SDFP*, 1:92.

18. "Doklad M. M. Borodina," February 15–17, 1926, in *KiK*, vol. 2, pt. 1, *1926–1927*, 85; A. C. Potapov to Chicherin, December 12, 1920; "Doklad K. N. Sokolova-Strakhova," April 21, 1921; Lenin to Chicherin, November 7, 1921; and Ioffe to Sun Yat-sen, August 1922, in *KiK*, vol. 1, *1920–1925*, 46, 56, 65, 98; *Izvestiya*, March 9, 1919, in *SRE*, 141.

19. Pantsov, *The Bolsheviks and the Chinese Revolution*, 62; "Soobrazheniia A. A. Ioffe," Shanghai, January 26, 1923, in *KiK*, vol. 1, *1920–1925*, 199; "First Congress of the Toilers of the Far East," January 21, 1922, in *Congress of Toilers of Far East* (London: The Hammersmith Bookshop, 1970), 4, 7; *SRE*, 226. On Russia's effect on China's revolutionaries, see Price, *Russia and the Roots of the Chinese Revolution*.

20. North, *Moscow and Chinese Communists*, 76; Marie-Claire Bergere, *Sun Yat-Sen* (Stanford, CA: Stanford University Press, 1998), 315. On Borodin in China, see N. L. Mamaeva, *Komintern i Gomindan, 1919–1929* (Moscow: Rosspen, 1999), 153–171. On the Soviets in Canton, see Viktor Usov, *Sovetskaia Razvedka v Kitae: 20-e gody XX Veka* (Moscow: Olma, 2002), 207–230. Dong Yan pointed out to me Borodin's impact on the Nationalist Party.

21. Yueh Sheng, *Sun Yat-sen University in Moscow and the Chinese Revolution: A Personal Account* (Lawrence: Center for East Asian Studies, University of Kansas, 1971). On Chinese revolutionaries' infatuation with Soviet Russia, see Elizabeth McGuire, *Red at Heart: How Chinese Communists Fell in Love with the Russian Revolution* (New York: Oxford University Press, 2017); North, *Moscow and Chinese Communists*, 76; James C. Bowden, "Soviet Military Aid to Nationalist China, 1923–1941," in *Sino-Soviet Relations*, ed. Raymond L. Garthoff (New York: Praeger, 1966), 46, 50; A. V. Blagodatov, *Zapiski o Kitaiskoi Revoliutsii, 1925–1927 gg.* (Moscow: Nauka, 1979); "Zapiski M. M. Borodina," December 10, 1923, in *KiK*,

vol. 1, *1920–1925,* 341; On Sun's financial woes, see Maring to Comintern, May 31, 1923, and Maring, "Schemes for Reorganization of the KMT," in Tony Saich, *The Origins of the First United Front in China,* 2 vols. (Leiden: Brill, 1991), 2:535, 561.

22. "Extracts from Lenin's Speech," March 7, 1918, in *SDFP,* 1:57.

23. Haslam, *Near and Distant Neighbors,* 8, citing Viacheslav Nikonov, *Molotov: Molodost'* (Moscow: Vagrius, 2005), 704–705. I was unable to find the quote in the source that Nikonov cites.

24. Stephen Kotkin, *Stalin,* vol. 1, *Paradoxes of Power, 1878–1928* (New York: Penguin, 2014), 509–511, 514–517, 525–526. On postwar stabilization, see Maier, *Recasting Bourgeois Europe.*

25. "Doklad L. M. Karakhana," Beijing, February 11, 1926, in *KiK,* vol. 2, pt. 1, *1926–1927,* 75; Jonathan Haslam, *The Soviet Union and the Threat from the East, 1933–41: Moscow, Tokyo, and the Prelude to the Pacific War* (Pittsburgh: University of Pittsburgh Press, 1992), 1, 3.

26. "Rech V I Lenina," November 20, 1922, in *DVP,* 6:9; Sergey Grishachev and Vladimir Datsyshen, "Allied Intervention in Russian Civil War and Japanese Troops in Russia's Far East, 1918–1922," in *A History of Russo-Japanese Relations: Over Two Centuries of Cooperation and Competition,* ed. Dmitry Streltsov and Nobuo Shimotomai (London: Brill, 2019), 137–154.

27. "Extracts from a Report by Chicherin," March 4, 1925, in *SDFP,* 2:16; Ian Nish, *Japanese Foreign Policy in the Interwar Period* (Westport, CT: Praeger, 2002), 49; Chicherin to Karakhan, April 20, 1925, in Kartunov, *Perepiska,* 495. On Soviet analysis of Japanese politics, see "Otvety G. N. Voitinskogo na Voprosy I. V. Stalina," Moscow, February 16, 1926, in *KiK,* vol. 2, pt. 1, *1926–1927,* 83.

28. Stalin to Karakhan, June 16, 1924, in Kartunov, *Perepiska,* 237. On threats to Soviet power in Asia, see Haslam, *The Soviet Union and the Threat from the East.*

29. Reilly, "Lev Karakhan," 66.

30. Sheridan, *Chinese Warlord,* 10.

31. "Declaration signed by Karakhan," July 25, 1919, in *SDFP,* 1:159–160. Rolling back this promise: "Nota predstavitelia RSFSR [Ioffe] v Kitae," September 19, 1923, in *DVP,* 5:587; "Note from Chicherin to the Foreign Ministers," December 8, 1921, in *SDFP,* 1:283; "Notes from Joffe to the Chinese government," September 21, 1922, in *SDFP,* 1:333. Karakhan claimed to Chicherin, his boss, that the original 1919 declaration was a mistake by one of his colleagues; see Karakhan to Chicherin, October 13, 1923, in Kartunov, *Perepiska,* 88; Elleman, *Diplomacy and Deception,* chap. 4; A. A. Ioffe to Politburo, July 22, 1922, in A. V. Kvashonkin, *Bolshevistskoe rukovodostvo: Perepiska, 1912–1927* (Moscow: Rosspen, 1996), 260–262; Sun Yat-sen to Lenin, December 6, 1922, in *KiK,* vol. 1, *1920–1925,* 151. On Soviet public relations, see "Extracts from an interview by Chicherin," October 25, 1922, in *SDFP,* 1:342.

32. Stalin to Karakhan, January 29, 1924, in Kartunov, *Perepiska,* 165–166; Peter S. H. Tang, *Russian and Soviet Policy in Manchuria and Outer Mongolia, 1911–1931* (Durham, NC: Duke University Press, 1959), 149, 152–153.

33. Chicherin to Karakhan, April 20, 1925, in Kartunov, *Perepiska,* 495; Bruce A. Elleman, *Moscow and the Emergence of Communist Power in China* (London: Routledge, 2009), 21; Tang, *Russian and Soviet Policy in Manchuria,* 187, 194.

34. Sheridan, *Chinese Warlord*, 13; Michael M. Walker, *The 1929 Sino-Soviet War: The War Nobody Knew* (Lawrence: University Press of Kansas, 2017), 104–105.

35. Chicherin, December 6, 1926, in Elleman, *Moscow and the Emergence of Communist Power*, 55. "Guomindang" changed to "Nationalist Party."

36. Stalin to Karakhan, March 6, 1925, in Kartunov, *Perepiska*, 474.

37. Stalin in *Izvestiia*, February 22, 1919, in *SRE*, 45; Jacobs, *Borodin*, 170. On two camps, see *SRE*, 59.

38. "Joint Statement by Sun-Yat Sen and Joffe," January 26, 1923, in *SDFP*, 1:370; Saich, *The Origins of the First United Front in China*, 1:82.

39. Stalin to Karakhan, June 16, 1924, in Kartunov, *Perepiska*, 237; Lenin, "Dve taktiki sotsial-demoratii v democratkicheskoi revoliutsii," 1905, in *SRE*, 36–38; Maring, Report to Comintern, July 11, 1922, and Karl Radek, "The Tasks of the Chinese Communist Party," probably late 1922, in Saich, *The Origins of the First United Front in China*, 1:308, 377.

40. "Dokladnaia Zapiska M. M. Borodina," April 6, 1925, in *KiK*, vol. 1, *1920–1925*, 544; Pantsov, *The Bolsheviks and the Chinese Revolution*, 93; translation modified; Elleman, *Moscow and the Emergence of Communist Power*, 17; punctuation modified.

41. Zinoviev, "Stenograficheskii otchet o zasedanii ispolkoma," November 26, 1923, in *KiK*, vol. 1, *1920–1925*, 303; "Directive of Policy to the Third Congress," May 1923, and "Theses on the Chinese Question," February 17– March 25, 1926, in *SRE*, 344, 349; Chen Duxiu, "The Immediate Tactics of the Communist Party of China," November 1922, in Saich, *The Origins of the First United Front in China*, 1:363; Pantsov, *The Bolsheviks and the Chinese Revolution*, 54, 104; Alexander Pantsov and Gregor Benton, "Did Trotsky Oppose Entering the Guomindang 'From the First?,'" *Republican China* 19, no. 2 (1994): 52–66; Elleman, *Moscow and the Emergence of Communist Power*, 16. "Guomindang" changed to "Nationalist Party."

42. Elleman, *Moscow and the Emergence of Communist Power*, 17; Pantsov, *The Bolsheviks and the Chinese Revolution*, 86–87. On the death toll in Shanghai, see Hung-Ting Su, "Urban Mass Movement: The May Thirtieth Movement in Shanghai," *Modern Asian Studies* 13, no. 2 (1979): 208; Phoebe Chow, *Britain's Imperial Retreat from China, 1900–1931* (London: Routledge, 2016), 148. On strikes in Manchuria, see Chong-Sik Lee, *Revolutionary Struggle in Manchuria* (Berkeley: University of California Press, 1983), 44. On strikes in Hong Kong, see Ming K. Chan, "Hong Kong in Sino-British Conflict: Mass Mobilization and the Crisis of Legitimacy, 1912–1926," in *Precarious Balance: Hong Kong between China and Britain, 1842–1992*, ed. Ming K. Chan and John D. Young (Armonk, NY: M. E. Sharpe, 1994), 49; David J. Dallin, *The Rise of Russia in Asia* (New Haven, CT: Yale University Press, 1949), 201.

43. Gill Bennett, *The Zinoviev Letter: The Conspiracy That Never Dies* (Oxford: Oxford University Press, 2018); Jacobson, *When the Soviet Union Entered World Politics*, 174.

44. Jacobson, *When the Soviet Union Entered World Politics*, 175.

45. "Extract from a Speech by Stalin," January 19, 1925, in *SDFP*, 2:1–2.

46. "Extracts from a Press Interview by Chicherin," January 22, 1925; "Extracts from a Speech by Chicherin," May 14, 1925; "Article by Stalin on the International Situation," March 22, 1925; and "Extracts from a Report by Stalin," May 9, 1925, in *SDFP*, 2:5–6, 20,

25–28, 43. On economic shifts, see Dmitry Manuilsky, "Excerpts from a Report to the Seventh Enlarged Plenum, November 22–December 16, 1925," in *SRE*, 389.

47. "Extracts from an Address by Stalin," May 18, 1925, in *SDFP*, 2:49; Futse, correspondent of the *Nichi-Nichi* newspaper, interview with Stalin, June or July 1925, in *SRE*, 336; J. V. Stalin, "The October Revolution and the National Question," November 6 and 19, 1918, Marxists Internet Archive, https://www.marxists.org/reference/archive/stalin/works/1918/11/19.htm.

48. D. Anuchin, "Aziia kak prarodina i uchitelnitsa chelovechestva; ee nastoiashchee i budushchee," *Novy Vostok*, no. 1 (1922), 249; *SRE*, 89.

49. Jacobs, *Borodin*, 186; "Zapiski M. M. Borodina," December 10, 1923, in *KiK*, vol. 1, *1920–1925*, 329; Tang Leang-li, The *Foundations of Modern China* (London: Noel Douglas, 1928), 168; "Report on the National Revolutionary Army and the Guomindang," early 1926, in C. Martin Wilbur and Julie Lien-ying How, *Missionaries of Revolution: Soviet Advisers and Nationalist China, 1920–1927* (Cambridge, MA: Harvard University Press, 1989), 614. "Guomindang" changed to "Nationalist Party."

50. "Pismo N. V. Kuibysheva i I. Ia. Razgona v TsIK KPK," Canton, January 13, 1926; Tovarish Semar, responding to "Doklad Tov. Voitinskogo Na Zasedanii Presidiuma IKKI," February 10, 1926; and "Doklad L. M. Karakhana," Beijing, February 11, 1926, in *KiK*, vol. 2, pt. 1, *1926–1927*, 21, 43, 51, 61; North, *Moscow and Chinese Communists*, 85.

51. "Iz protokola No 5 (Osoby no 3) zasedaniia politbiuro TsK VKP(b)," Moscow, January 21, 1926, in *KiK*, vol. 2, pt. 1, *1926–1927*, 25–26; Chicherin to Karakhan, March 23, 1926, in Kartunov, *Perepiska*, 615–616.

52. Jay Taylor, *The Generalissimo: Chiang Kai-shek and the Struggle for Modern China* (Cambridge, MA: Harvard University Press, 2009); North, *Moscow and Chinese Communists*, 86.

53. Stalin to Molotov, June 3, 1926, in *Stalin's Letters to Molotov*, ed. Lars T. Lih, Oleg V. Naumov, and Oleg V. Khlevniuk (New Haven, CT: Yale University Press, 1995), 111; Taylor, *The Generalissimo*, 57; Bowden, "Soviet Military Aid to Nationalist China," 52; "Tezisy K. B. Radeka 'ob osnovakh kommuniisticheskoi politiki v kitae,'" Moscow, June 22, 1926, in *KiK*, vol. 2, pt. 1, *1926–1927*, 262; Elleman, *Moscow and the Emergence of Communist Power*, 43, 88, quoting Trotsky in 1926 and 1927; M. N. Roy, *My Experience in China* (Calcutta: Renaissance Publishers, 1945), 69–70; "Iz protokola no 18 (osoby no 13) Zasedaniia politbiuro TsK VKP(b)," Moscow, April 1, 1926, and "Itogi i vyvody komissii dalbiuro," Shanghai, September 12, 1926, in *KiK*, vol. 2, pt. 1, *1926–1927*, 166, 401–402, 408; M. N. Roy quoted in North, *Moscow and Chinese Communists*, 104, 109. Trotsky himself prevaricated; see Trotsky, "Problems of Our Policy with Respect to China and Japan," March 25, 1926; Trotsky to Radek, August 30, 1926; and "The Chinese Communist Party and the Guomindang," September 27, 1926, in Peng Shu-tse, ed., *Leon Trotsky on China* (New York: Monad Press, 1976), 102–120.

54. Stalin to Molotov, September 23, 1926, in *KiK*, vol. 2, pt. 1, *1926–1927*, 445; S. A. Dalin, *Kitaiskie Memuary, 1921–1927* (Moscow: Nauka, 1975), 311–317; Walter E. Weyl, "The Chicago of China," *Harper's*, October 1918.

55. Chow, *Britain's Imperial Retreat from China*, 150; *North China Herald*, January 11, 1927; Elleman, *Moscow and the Emergence of Communist Power*, 87; Pantsov, *The Bolsheviks and the Chinese Revolution*, 127.

56. "Dokladnaia zapiska T. G. Mandalian, A. E. Albrekht, N. M. Nasonov i N. A. Fokin o vtorom shankhaiskom vostannii," March 4, 1927, in *KiK*, vol. 2, pt. 1, *1926–1927*, 634–635; Elleman, *Moscow and the Emergence of Communist Power*, 55.

57. "Doklad N. I. Bukharina," March 30, 1927, in *KiK*, vol. 2, pt. 1, *1926–1927*, 65; Stalin to Radek, April 6, 1927, in Elleman, *Moscow and the Emergence of Communist Power*, 73; Kotkin, *Stalin*, 1:629.

58. S. A. Smith, *A Road Is Made: Communism in Shanghai, 1920–1927* (Honolulu: University of Hawaii Press, 2000), 190–205; Elleman, *Moscow and the Emergence of Communist Power in China*, 75–76; Patricia Stranahan, *Underground: The Shanghai Communist Party and the Politics of Survival* (Lanham, MD: Rowman & Littlefield, 1998), 11.

59. "Peking Gets Proof Reds Incited Mobs," *New York Times*, April 9, 1927; Elleman, *Moscow and the Emergence of Communist Power in China*, 75; N. Mitarevsky, *World Wide Soviet Plots* (Tientsin: Tientsin Press, 1927).

60. Sir Austen Chamberlain to M. Rosengolz, May 26, 1927, in *Russia No. 3 (1927): A Selection of Papers Dealing with the Relations between His Majesty's Government and the Soviet Government, 1921–1927* (London: His Majesty's Stationery Office, 1927); *Russia No. 2 (1927): Documents Illustrating the Hostile Activities of the Soviet Government and Third International against Great Britain* (London: His Majesty's Stationery Office, 1927), 69–70; Elleman, *Moscow and the Emergence of Communist Power*, 95; Anglo-Russian Parliamentary Committee, *Raid on Arcos Ltd. and the Trade Delegation of the U.S.S.R.: Facts and Documents* (London: Anglo-Russian Parliamentary Committee, 1927), 31.

61. "Soobshchenie M. M. Borodina," Hankou, early May 1927, in *KiK*, vol. 2, pt. 1, *1926–1927*, 703; Stalin to Molotov, June 27, 1927, in Lih, Naumoy, and Khlevniuk, *Stalin's Letters to Molotov*, 137; *Pravda*, April 15, 1927; *SRE*, 365. On the embassy raid, see William J. Oudendyck, *Ways and By-ways in Diplomacy* (London: Peter Davies, 1939), 350–351.

62. Comintern, "Resolution on the Chinese Question," May 8–30, 1927, in *SRE*, 369–371. On Red Square, see Kotkin, *Stalin*, 1:631.

63. Stalin to Molotov, June 27, 1927, in Lih, Naumoy, and Khlevniuk, *Stalin's Letters to Molotov*, 137; Kotkin, *Stalin*, 1:633; Stalin to Molotov, July 11, 1927, in Pantsov, *The Bolsheviks and the Chinese Revolution*, 152.

64. Jacobs, *Borodin*, 287–305; Stalin in *Pravda*, July 29, 1927, in *SRE*, 305.

65. "Telegramma G Noimana v Politbiuro Ts VKP(b)," Canton, November 29, 1927, in *KiK*, vol. 3, pt. 1, *1927–1931*, 164–165.

66. "Extracts from Stalin's Report," December 3, 1927, in *SDFP*, 2:287; Stalin, Speech at the Fifteenth Congress of the Russian Communist Party, December 3, 1927, in *SRE*, 396; "Telegramma O. Iu. Pliche L. M. Karakhanu," Hankou, December 3, 1927; "Pismo O. A. Mitkevich v IKKI," Shanghai, no earlier than December 5, 1927;and Stalin, "Iz protokola no 139," December 10, 1927, in *KiK*, vol. 3, pt. 1, *1927–1931*, 174, 180, 181, 191.

67. *SRE*, 309; Tang, *Russian and Soviet Policy in Manchuria*, 199; "Rech i zakliuchitelnoe slovo N I Bukharina," January 31, 1928, in *KiK*, vol. 3, pt. 1, *1927–1931*, 252.

68. Pantsov, *The Bolsheviks and the Chinese Revolution*, 81–82.

69. Ante Ciliga, *The Russian Enigma* (London: Routledge, 1940), 85; Haslam, *Near and Distant Neighbors*, 9. This quote appears to be Molotov around 1929. On the Mongols, see

R. W. Davies, *Soviet History in the Gorbachev Revolution* (Bloomington: Indiana University Press, 1989), 60; transliteration adjusted.

70. Willard Sunderland, *The Baron's Cloak: A History of the Russian Empire in War and Revolution* (Ithaca, NY: Cornell University Press, 2014); Tang, *Russian and Soviet Policy in Manchuria*.

71. Bruce A. Elleman, "Sino-Soviet Relations on Outer Mongolia, 1918–1925," *Pacific Affairs* 66, no. 4 (Winter 1993): 559–560.

72. James Forsyth, *A History of the Peoples of Siberia: Russia's North Asian Colony, 1581–1990* (Cambridge: Cambridge University Press, 1992), 281; Alfred J. Rieber, *Stalin and the Struggle for Supremacy in Eurasia* (Cambridge: Cambridge University Press, 2015), 143–148.

73. Forsyth, *A History of the Peoples of Siberia*, 281; Rieber, *Stalin and the Struggle for Supremacy in Eurasia*, 143–148.

74. The assassination of Zhang Zuolin is traditionally ascribed to the Japanese, but new evidence points to Soviet complicity; see Hiroaki Kuromiya, "The Battle of Lake Khasan Reconsidered," *Journal of Slavic Military Studies* 24, no. 2 (2011): 99n2. On Zhang Xueliang's vices, see Taylor, *The Generalissimo*, 100.

75. On Soviet stoves, see "Stoves in the Summer," in *Documents with Reference to the Sino-Russian Dispute* (Nanking: Far Eastern Information Bureau, 1929), 18; Ian Nish, *The History of Manchuria, 1840–1948: A Sino-Russo-Japanese Triangle*, vol. 1 (Folkestone, UK: Renaissance Publishers, 2016), 129–131; "Nota upravliaiushchego generalnym konsulstvom SSSR," February 2, 1929; Karakhan to A. A. Troianovksy, January 31, 1929; and "Nota generalnogo konsula SSSR," February 19, 1929, in *DVP*, 7:54–55, 58, 85; Tang, *Russian and Soviet Policy in Manchuria*, 195, 201, 218, 243; Walker, *The 1929 Sino-Soviet War*.

76. Karakhan to Voroshilov, August 10, 1929, in *Sovetskoe rukovodstvo: Perepiska, 1928–1941*, comp. A. V. Kvashonkin (Moscow: Political Encyclopedia Publishers, 1999), 87; Stalin to Molotov, August 29 and October 7, 1929, in Lih, Naumoy, and Khlevniuk, *Stalin's Letters to Molotov*, 174, 182; Tang, *Russian and Soviet Policy in Manchuria*, 232; Nish, *The History of Manchuria*, 1: 131.

77. Kotkin, *Stalin*, 1:661–740; Stalin to Molotov, probably late August 1930, in Lih, Naumoy, and Khlevniuk, *Stalin's Letters to Molotov*, 203; Jonathan Haslam, *Soviet Foreign Policy 1930–33: The Impact of the Depression* (London: Macmillan, 1983), 4–9.

78. Stalin to Molotov, September 1, 1930, in Lih, Naumoy, and Khlevniuk, *Stalin's Letters to Molotov*, 208; Haslam, *Soviet Foreign Policy*, 29.

79. Walker, *The 1929 Sino-Soviet War*, 290–291; Haslam, *Soviet Foreign Policy*, 22.

80. Kaganovich to Stalin, August 20, 1931, and Stalin to Kaganovich, September 14, 1931, in *Stalin-Kaganovich Correspondence, 1931–36*, ed. R. W. Davies et. al., trans. Steven Shabad (New Haven, CT: Yale University Press, 2003), 61, 89; Elleman, *Moscow and the Emergence of Communist Power*, 200–203.

81. "Statement by Karakhan," April 16, 1933; "Extracts from a Speech by Molotov," November 6, 1933; and "Statement by the Vice-Commissar for Foreign Affairs," May 31, 1933, in *SDFP*, 3:12–14, 19, 35; Lee, *Revolutionary Struggle in Manchuria*, 93.

82. On grumbling, see Karakhan to Yenukidze, June 4, 1932, in *Sovetskoe rukovdostvo*, 235; Haslam, *The Soviet Union and the Threat from the East*, 18–19, 31; "Extracts from a Speech by Molotov," December 28, 1933, in *SDFP*, 3:47.

6. "We Must Have Our Hands Free"

1. Molotov quoted in "Extracts from a Speech by Molotov at a Conference of Collective Farm Workers," February 18, 1933, in *SDFP*, 3:5–7.

2. On the Japanese statement, see Ben David Dorfman, "The Manchurian 'Incident' of 1931," *Harper's*, September 1934.

3. Robert H. Ferrell, "The Mukden Incident: September 18–19, 1931," *Journal of Modern History* 27, no. 1 (March 1955): 67.

4. "Manchuria: What This Is All About," *Popular Mechanics*, February 1932, 210–215.

5. Ferrell, "The Mukden Incident," 66.

6. Sha Qingqing, "Reinterpreting the Soviet Policy toward Japan before and after the Mukden Incident," *Social Sciences in China* 36, no. 4 (2015): 197.

7. Ferrell, "The Mukden Incident," 67; Dorfman, "The Manchurian 'Incident' of 1931."

8. On China's expectations of a Soviet intervention and Soviet threats, see Sha, "Reinterpreting the Soviet Policy toward Japan," 194, 204. Stalin rules out intervention: Stalin to Kaganovich and Molotov, September 23, 1931, in *KiK*, vol. 4, pt. 1, *1931–1937*, 70. A "cautious" step: "TASS Statement on Soviet-Japanese Negotiations," January 17, 1933, in *SDFP*, 2:552; "Extracts from a Report by Molotov," January 23, 1933, in *SDFP*, 3:5.

9. "Within a few hours": Aitchen Wu, *China and the Soviet Union* (London: Methuen & Co., 1950), 224. On international law: Arthur K. Kuhn, "The Lytton Report on the Manchurian Crisis," *American Journal of International Law* 27, no. 1 (January 1933): 96–100; Ferrell, "The Mukden Incident," 67.

10. Stalin to Voroshilov, November 27, 1931, in *Sovetskoe rukovodstvo: Perepiska, 1928–1941*, comp. A. V. Kvashonkin (Moscow: Political Encyclopedia Publishers, 1999), 162–163; "Postanovlenie PB TsK VKP(b) o Kitae," September 20, 1931, and Stalin to Kaganovich and Molotov, September 23, 1931, in *RKO*, vol. 3, *1931–1937*, 31, 34; Voroshilov to J. B. Gamarnik, January 13, 1932, in *Sovetskoe rukovodstvo*, 168. From 1931 to 1933, Moscow invested intensely in Far Eastern defense, creating Far Eastern naval forces in late 1931 and the Soviet Pacific Fleet in April 1933, and testing submarines shortly thereafter; see Jonathan Haslam, *Soviet Foreign Policy 1930–33: The Impact of the Depression* (London: Macmillan, 1983), 83.

11. Kaganovich to Stalin, June 2, 1932, and Stalin to Kaganovich, sometime before June 12, 1932, in *Stalin-Kaganovich Correspondence, 1931–36*, ed. R. W. Davies et al., trans. Steven Shabad (New Haven, CT: Yale University Press, 2003), 114, 125–126.

12. Ferrell, "The Mukden Incident," 67.

13. "Extracts from Molotov's Report," December 22, 1931, in *SDFP*, 2:519, 529, 532; "Extracts from a Report by Molotov."

14. See, for example, Steven Levine, *Anvil of Victory: The Communist Revolution in Manchuria, 1945–1948* (New York: Columbia University Press, 1987), 28.

15. "Extracts from a Speech by Molotov at a Conference of Collective Farm Workers."

16. On Soviet military support, see forthcoming research by Ian Johnson of the University of Notre Dame.

17. Ivan Maisky to Moscow, October 2, 1938, in *God Krizisa, 1938–1939: Dokumenty i Materialy v Dvukh Tomakh*, 2 vols. (Moscow: Politizdat, 1990), 1:41.

18. Stephen Kotkin, *Stalin,* vol. 2, *Waiting for Hitler, 1929–1941* (New York: Penguin, 2017), 590, 601.

19. "Extracts from a Speech by Molotov at a Conference of Collective Farm Workers."

20. Jonathan Haslam, "On the Popular Front: The Comintern and the Origins of the Popular Front, 1934–1935," *The Historical Journal* 22, no. 3 (September 1979): 673–691.

21. Scholars such as Hiroaki Kuromiya have begun excavating Soviet special operations in China in the 1920s and 1930s, which were more extensive than realized at the time; see Hiroaki Kuromiya, "The Battle of Lake Khasan Reconsidered," *Journal of Slavic Military Studies* 24, no. 2 (2011): 659–677.

22. For the Nevelskoy quote, see Mark Bassin, "A Russian Mississippi? A Political-Geographical Inquiry into the Vision of Russia on the Pacific, 1840–1865" (PhD diss., University of California, Berkley, 1983), 285; cf. David R. Stone, *Hammer and Rifle: The Militarization of the Soviet Union, 1926–1933* (Lawrence: University Press of Kansas, 2000), 187–188; Jonathan Haslam, *The Soviet Union and the Threat from the East, 1933–41: Moscow, Tokyo, and the Prelude to the Pacific War* (Pittsburgh: University of Pittsburgh Press, 1992), 112.

23. Haslam, *The Soviet Union and the Threat from the East,* 112.

24. Beckmann and Okubo, *The Japanese Communist Party, 1922–1945* (Stanford, CA: Stanford University Press, 1969), 215, 219, 253, 275. On Japanese Communist Party weakness after the war, see A. Rozanov, "Raskol Profsoiuznovo Dvizheniia v Iaponii," April 11, 1950, RGANI, f. 17, o. 37, d. 412, esp. l. 53. On pressuring Chinese communists, see Dieter Heinzig, *The Soviet Union and Communist China, 1945–1950: The Arduous Road to the Alliance* (Armonk, NY: M. E. Sharpe, 2004), 21. One exception was in China's Xinjiang province, where the Soviet Union backed the warlord who ran the province, deploying troops to support him. Yet Stalin did not take additional territory and discouraged Xinjiang leadership from rapidly adopting communism. The Kremlin focused instead on the perceived Japanese threat in Xinjiang. For Soviet intelligence reports on Japanese influence in Xinjiang, see "Dokladnaia Zapiska Nachalnika Piatogo Upravleniia RKKA . . . ," July 31, 1939, in *Voennaia Razvedka Informiruet: Dokumenty Razvedupravleniia Krasnoi Armii* (Moscow: Mezdunarodnoi Fond Demokratii, 2008), 162. An excellent overview of Soviet policy is Jamil Gasanli, *Sintszian v Orbite Sovetskoi Politike: Stalin i Musulmanskoe Dvizhenie v Vostochnom Turkestane* (Moscow: Nauka, 2015).

25. Vinogradov to Voroshilov, 1933, in *Pisma vo Vlast, 1928–1939* (Moscow: Rosspen, 2002), 228–230; John J. Stephan, "'Cleansing' the Soviet Far East, 1937–1938," *Acta Slavica Iaponica* 10 (1992): 47; M. Gelb, "An Early Soviet Ethnic Deportation: The Far Eastern Koreans," *Russian Review* 54, no. 3 (July 1995): 390–391; Jon Chang, *Burnt by the Sun: The Koreans of the Russian Far East* (Honolulu: University of Hawai'i Press, 2018).

26. Haslam, *Soviet Foreign Policy 1930–33,* 72, 77; John J. Stephan, *The Russian Fascists: Tragedy and Farce in Exile, 1925–1945* (New York: Harper and Row, 1978), 60–90. On the White Russians and Japan in Manchuria, see N. E. Ablova, *KVZhD i Rossiiskaia Emigratsiia v Kitae* (Moscow: Russkaia Panorama, 2005), 295–305; Stephan, "'Cleansing' the Soviet Far East," 44, 50.

27. Lavrentiy Beria to Stalin, August 16, 1941, Volkogonov Papers, LOC, container 6, reel 4.

28. *The Maisky Diaries: Red Ambassador to the Court of St James, 1932–1943,* ed. Gabriel Gorodetsky, trans. Tatiana Sorokina and Oliver Ready (New Haven, CT: Yale University Press, 2015), March 15, 1935, and March 23, 1938, 1:102, 282. The 17th Comintern Congress in July–August 1935 formally named Japan an enemy; see H. Ikuhiko, "The Japanese-Soviet Confrontation, 1935–1939," in *Deterrent Diplomacy: Japan, Germany, and the USSR,* ed. J. W. Morley (New York: Columbia University Press, 1976), 132.

29. "Protest against the Violation of the Soviet Frontier by Japanese-Manchurian Forces," November 4, 1935, in *SDFP,* 3:147; "Extracts from a Report by Molotov to the Central Executive Committee," January 10, 1936, in *SDFP,* 3:152, 155–156; "Note from Litvinov to the Chinese Charge in Moscow," April 8, 1936, in *SDFP,* 3:187; Alvin D. Coox, *Nomonhan: Japan against Russia, 1939* (Stanford, CA: Stanford University Press, 1985), 93–95; Ikuhiko, "The Japanese Soviet Confrontation," 135–137; *Pogranichnye Voiska SSSR, 1939–1941: Sbornik Dokymentov i Materialov,* ed. P. I. Zyrianov (Moscow: Nauka, 1970), 563–748.

30. Coox, *Nomonhan,* 100; Haslam, *Soviet Foreign Policy 1930–33,* 79.

31. Doc. 1.4, January 21, 1939, and Doc. 1.6, January 25, 1939, in *Voennaia Razvedka Informiruet,* 25, 59.

32. Litvinov to the Peoples Commissariat of Foreign Affairs, October 2, 1938, in *God Krizisa, 1938–1939,* 1:39–40; Kotkin, *Stalin,* 2:621.

33. Kotkin, *Stalin,* 2:657.

34. Kotkin, *Stalin,* 2:695.

35. Coox, *Nomonhan,* 136 and chaps. 9–10; "Prikaz Narodnogo Komissara Oborony Soiuza SSR," September 4, 1938, Volkogonov Papers, LOC, container 6, reel 4.

36. Alvin D. Coox, *The Anatomy of a Small War: The Soviet-Japanese Struggle for Changkufeng-Khasan, 1938* (Westport, CT: Greenwood Press, 1977), xix. Traditionally Japan has been seen as the aggressor, but the Soviets may have provoked the battle. Either way, Moscow's strategic aim was defensive. For the revisionist view, see Hiroaki Kuromiya, "The Mystery of Nomonhan, 1939," *Journal of Slavic Military Studies* 24, no. 4 (2011): 659–677; *Pravda,* September 1, 1939, in *God Krizisa, 1938–1939,* 2:355–356. On Japanese losses, see Boris Slavinsky, *The Japanese-Soviet Neutrality Pact: A Diplomatic History, 1941–1945* (New York: Routledge, 2004), 18. On Japan's "panic," see Doc. 2.33, October 26, 1939, in *Voennaia Razvedka Informiruet,* 170; David Stone, *A Military History of Russia* (Westport, CT: Praeger, 2006), 190; Coox, *Nomonhan,* 993, 1000.

37. Coox, *Nomonhan,* 986.

38. On China's war, see Rana Mitter, *China's War with Japan, 1937–1945* (London: Penguin, 2013). On Soviet intelligence, see Docs. 2.9 and 5.32, October 2, 1940, in *Voennaia Razvedka Informiruet,* 393; I. T. Luganets-Orelskii to People's Commissariat for Foreign Affairs (hereafter NKID), January 2 and 16, 1939, in *RKO,* vol. 4, no. 1, 1937–1944, 378–380, 389.

39. Doc. 2.21, July 31, 1939, and Doc. 2.25, September 1, 1939, in *Voennaia Razvedka Informiruet,* 161, 165; "Narodnomu Kommisaru Oboronu SSSR Marshalu Sovietskogo Soiuza tov. Voroshilovu," May 4, 1936, Volkogonov Papers, LOC, container 6, reel 4.

40. On changing the equilibrium, see Kotkin, *Stalin,* 2:698. On the Red Army's difficulties in Poland and Finland, see Mary Habeck, "Dress Rehearsals, 1937–1941," in *The Mili-*

tary History of the Soviet Union, ed. Robin Higham and Frederick Kagan (New York: Palgrave, 2002), 102–107.

41. Kotkin, *Stalin,* 2:793.

42. On showing respect to the Japanese, see *Molotov Remembers: Inside Kremlin Politics; Conversations with Felix Chuev,* ed. Albert Resis (Chicago: Ivan R. Dee, 1993), 21.

43. Slavinsky, *The Japanese-Soviet Neutrality Pact,* 76–77.

44. Solomon Lozovsky to Stalin, December 26, 1941, in *Istochnik,* no. 4 (1995): 114–115.

45. On US airbase requests, see "Poslanie Prededatelia Soveta Ministrov SSSR Presidentu SShA," January 5, 1943, in *Russkii Arkhiv: Velikaia Otechestvennaia,* vol. 18, no. 7, part 1, ed. V. A. Zolotarev (Moscow: Terra, 1997), 283. Stalin eventually offered the US bases in 1944; see Averill Harriman to Franklin D. Roosevelt, October 17, 1944, in *FRUS: The Conferences at Malta and Yalta, 1945,* 370–374; George Lensen, *The Strange Neutrality: Soviet-Japanese Relations during the Second World War, 1941–1945* (Tallahassee, FL: The Diplomatic Press, 1972), 14, 19, 30, 33, 41, 45, 50, 57, 79; Slavinsky, *The Japanese-Soviet Neutrality Pact,* 71–73.

46. Jenifer Van Vleck, *Empire of the Air: Aviation and the American Ascendancy* (Cambridge, MA: Harvard University Press, 2013), 135.

47. On portraits, see Milovan Djilas, *Conversations with Stalin* (New York: Harcourt, Brace and World, 1962), 60. On Alexander I, see Vladislav Zubok and Constantine Pleshakov, *Inside the Kremlin's Cold War: From Stalin to Krushchev* (Cambridge, MA: Harvard University Press, 1996), 27.

48. On Sakhalin's oil industry, see John J. Stephan, *Sakhalin: A History* (Oxford: Oxford University Press, 1971), 131–141.

49. David Dallin, *The Rise of Russia in Asia* (New Haven, CT: Yale University Press, 1949), 137.

50. On the end of the war in Asia, see C. A. Bayly and Tim Harper, *Forgotten Wars: The End of Britain's Asian Empire* (London: Allen Lane, 2007).

51. Zubok and Pleshakov, *Inside the Kremlin's Cold War,* 38.

52. Maiskii to Molotov, January 11, 1944, in *Istochnik* 4 (1995): 125, 133; Slavinsky, *The Japanese-Soviet Neutrality Pact,* 136–137; Averill Harriman to Franklin D. Roosevelt, December 15, 1944, in *FRUS: The Conferences at Malta and Yalta, 1945,* 378. On spheres of influence, see Voitech Mastny, *The Cold War and Soviet Insecurity* (New York: Oxford University Press, 1996), 16.

53. Djilas, *Conversations with Stalin,* 114.

54. "Bohlen Minutes: Voice of Smaller Powers in Postwar Peace Organization," Yalta, February 4, 1945, Office of the Historian, https://history.state.gov/historicaldocuments/frus1945Malta/d331.

55. "Bohlen Minutes: Voice of Smaller Powers in Postwar Peace Organization."

56. "Bohlen Minutes: Air Bases in the Far East," Leningrad, February 8, 1948, Office of the Historian, https://history.state.gov/historicaldocuments/frus1945Malta/d393; S. M. Plokhy, *Yalta: The Price of Peace* (New York: Viking, 2010), 216–228.

57. Y. A. Malik to NKID, June 7, 1945, in *Vestnik Ministerstva Innostrannikh Del* 19, no. 77 (October 15, 1990): 49.

58. Y. A. Malik to NKID, June 28, 1945, in *Vestnik Ministerstva Innostrannikh Del* 19, no. 77 (October 15, 1990): 49–50; Harriman to Franklin D. Roosevelt, October 17, 1944, and Deane to the Joint Chiefs of Staff, October 17, 1944, in *FRUS: The Conferences at Malta and Yalta, 1945*, 370–375; Tsuyoshi Hasegawa, *Racing the Enemy: Stalin, Truman, and the Surrender of Japan* (Cambridge, MA: Harvard University Press, 2005), 29; Slavinsky, *The Japanese-Soviet Neutrality Pact*, 150.

59. "Prikaz Komanduiushchego Voiskami 2-go dalnevostochnogoo fronta . . . ," August 10, 1945, and "Prikaz glavnokomanduiushchego sovetskimi voiskami . . . ," August 18, 1945, in *Russkii Arkhiv: Velikaia Otechestvennaia*, vol. 18, no. 7, part 2, ed. V. A. Zolotarev (Moscow: Terra, 2000), 7, 35; Slavinsky, *The Japanese-Soviet Neutrality Pact*, 181; Hasegawa, *Racing the Enemy*, 45–48, 187–190; Odd Arne Westad, *Cold War and Revolution: Soviet-American Rivalry and the Origins of the Chinese Civil War, 1944–1946* (New York: Columbia University Press, 1993), 78.

60. "Prikaz glavnokomanduiushchego sovetskimi voiskami . . . ," 7, 35; Slavinsky, *The Japanese-Soviet Neutrality Pact*, 153–154, 181; Hasegawa, *Racing the Enemy*, 46, 187–190, 289; Boris Slavinsky and Ljubica Erickson, "The Soviet Occupation of the Kuril Islands and Plans for the Capture of Northern Hokkaido," *Japan Forum* 5, no. 1 (1993): 98; Westad, *Cold War and Revolution*, 78. On naval bases, see "Donesenie komanduiushchego voiskami 2-go dalnevostochnogo fronta . . . ," August 24, 1945, in *Russkii Arkhiv: Velikaia Otechestvennaia*, vol. 18, no. 7, part 2, 145–146. On dividing Korea, see William Stueck, *Rethinking the Korean War: A New Diplomatic and Strategic History* (Princeton, NJ: Princeton University Press, 2004), 22–23.

61. "Donesenie zamestitelia nachalnika shtaba tikhookeanskogo flota," September 5, 1945, in *Russkii Arkhiv: Velikaia Otechesvennaia*, vol. 18, no. 7, part 2, 249.

62. The classic statement of this thesis is Gar Alperowitz, *Atomic Diplomacy: Hiroshima and Potsdam* (New York: Simon and Schuster, 1965).

63. Hasegawa, *Racing the Enemy*, 286.

64. Hasegawa, *Racing the Enemy*, 115–116; I. V. Shikin to Molotov, February 21, 1964, in *RKO*, vol. 5, no. 1, *1946–1948*, 65; "Vopros Mid'a SSSR," November 1947, GARF, f. 5446, o. 48a, d. 3346, l. 1; "Rasopriazhenie no. 4483pc," GARF, f. 5446, o. 48a, d. 2218, l. 7–8; "Ob utverzhdenie otchetov . . . ," May 1947, GARF, f. 5446, o. 49a, d. 558, l. 41; Stalin memo of November 1948, GARF, f. 5446, o. 50, d. 618, l. 8; GARF, f. 5446, o. 48a, d. 408. Some historians argue that Stalin's Asian aims were limited because he only sought to reestablish Nicholas's sphere of influence; see Ilya Gaiduk, "The Second Front of the Cold War: Asia in the System of Moscow's Foreign Policy Priorities," in *Cold War in East Asia*, ed. Tsuyoshi Hasegawa (Washington, DC: Woodrow Wilson Center Press, 2011), 63–80. Yet the Kremlin's aims were expansive compared to Stalin's own goals just a decade earlier. On Chinese schoolchildren, see *Posledniye pisma Stalinu: 1952–1953 gg*, ed. G. V. Gorskaia (Moscow: Rosspen, 2015), 32.

65. Feliks Chuev, *Sto Sorok Besed s Molotvym: Iz dnevnika F. Chueva* (Moscow: Terra, 1991), entries for May 1 and June 3, 1981.

66. Zubok and Pleshakov, *Inside the Kremlin's Cold War*, 38; Resis, *Molotov Remembers*, 8.

67. Westad, *Cold War and Revolution*, 4, 37–38, 53; Hasegawa, *Racing the Enemy*, 129. "No contradictions," see A. A. Petrov and Chen Lifu, "Zapis Besedy," June 14, 1946, in *RKO*, vol. 5, no. 1, *1946–1948*, 120.

68. On Molotov's views, see George Kennan, *Memoirs: 1925–1950* (New York: Pantheon Books, 1983), 236; Heinzig, *The Soviet Union and Communist China*, 23, 33, 34. On radishes, see Sergei Radchenko, *Two Suns in the Heavens: The Sino-Soviet Struggle for Supremacy, 1962–1967* (Washington, DC: Woodrow Wilson Center Press, 2009), 5.

69. Henzig, *The Soviet Union and Communist China*, 21, 27, 53; Westad, *Cold War and Revolution*, 62.

70. Stalin to Antonov, August 18, 1945, Volkogonov Papers, LOC, container 8, reel 5; Westad, *Cold War and Revolution*, 38; Steven I. Levine, *Anvil of Victory: The Communist Revolution in Manchuria, 1945–1948* (New York: Columbia University Press, 1987), 62. On Nazi guns, see Yevgen Sautin, "China's Last Warlord: Gao Gang and the Northeast People's Government, 1948–1954" (PhD diss., University of Cambridge, 2020), 45.

71. Westad, *Cold War and Revolution*, 169; Levine, *Anvil of Victory*, 90, 104; Heinzig, *The Soviet Union and Communist China*, 121. On the debate over Mao's quote about China standing up: "The Famous Mao Slogan, That He Never Even Used," *South China Morning Post*, September 25, 2009.

72. On the dangers of haste, see Sergei Goncharov, "The Stalin-Mao Dialogue," *Far Eastern Affairs*, no. 1 (1992): 102, 105; Li Haiwan and Wang Xi, "A Distortion of History: An Interview with Shi Zhe," *Chinese Historians* 5 (Fall 1992): 61. On Mao's shoes and the grain harvest, see Andrei Ledovsky, "Mikoyan's Secret Mission to China," *Far Eastern Affairs*, no. 2 (1995): 76, 77.

73. On Tito, see Heinzig, *The Soviet Union and Communist China*, 123. On Stalin's support for moderation, see Stalin to Chen Yun, March 15, 1949, in Goncharov, "The Stalin-Mao Dialogue," 99–100. On Stalin's hesitation over aid, see Stalin to Mao, April 1994, in Sergei N. Goncharov, John W. Lewis, and Litai Xue, *Uncertain Partners: Stalin, Mao, and the Korean War* (Stanford, CA: Stanford University Press, 1993), 231. On Soviet nuclear policy, see Viktor M. Gobarev, "Soviet Policy toward China: Developing Nuclear Weapons 1949–1969," *Journal of Slavic Military Studies* 12, no. 4 (1999): 2–3; Goncharov, "The Stalin-Mao Dialogue," 97, 103. On the Soviet refusal to provide military aid, see Heinzig, *The Soviet Union and Communist China*, 119.

74. David Holloway, *Stalin and the Bomb: The Soviet Union and Atomic Energy, 1939–1956* (New Haven, CT: Yale University Press, 1994), 268.

75. "Solid and intelligent communists": Heinzig, *The Soviet Union and Communist China*, 306.

76. "Countries of East Asia": Goncharov, "The Stalin-Mao Dialogue," 95; "peoples of Asia": Goncharov, Lewis, and Xue, *Uncertain Partners*, 71.

77. Heinzig, *The Soviet Union and Communist China*, 268–307; Sergey Radchenko and David Wolff, "To the Summit via Proxy-Summits: New Evidence from Soviet and Chinese Archives on Mao's Long March to Moscow, 1949," *CWIHP*, no. 16 (Fall 2007–Winter 2008): 111. On the Communist Party of China's submission to the Communist Party of the

Soviet Union, see Andrei Ledovsky, ed., "Report of the CPC Central Committee Delegation," July 4, 1949, in "The Moscow Visit of a Delegation of the Communist Party of China in June to August 1949," *Far Eastern Affairs*, no. 4 (1996): 84. Mao's Farewell Speech at the Moscow Railway Station, February 17, 1950: Goncharov, Lewis, and Xue, *Uncertain Partners*, 267–268; Heinzig, *The Soviet Union and Communist China*, 320–322, 341–342.

78. Forty-eight telegrams: Kathryn Weathersby, "New Findings on the Korean War," *CWIHP*, no. 3 (Fall 1993): 14. On Stalin's birthday, see Shtykov to Grigorian, February 4, 1950, Russian State Archive of Social and Political History, Moscow, f. 17, o. 37, d. 409, ll. 4–18. Shtykov to Vyshinsky, September 3, 1949; Gromyko to Tunkin, September 11, 1949; Tunkin to Moscow, September 14, 1949; and "Politburo Decision to Confirm the Following Directive to the Soviet Ambassador in Korea, September 24, 1949, in Kathryn Weathersby, "Korea, 1949–1950: To Attack, or Not to Attack?," *CWIHP*, no. 5 (Spring 1995): 6–8.

79. Stueck, *Rethinking the Korean War*, 73. On Soviet assessments of the risk of US intervention in Korea, see Kathryn Weathersby, "'Should We Fear This?' Stalin and the Danger of War with America," Cold War International History Project, working paper no. 39, July 2002; Haruki Wada, *The Korean War: An International History* (Lanham, MD: Rowman & Littlefield, 2018), 71.

80. Shtykov to Vyshinsky, January 19, 1950, *CWIHP*, no. 5 (Spring 1995): vi; Stueck, *Rethinking the Korean War*, 29; Chen Jian, *China's Road to the Korean War: The Making of the Sino-American Confrontation* (New York: Columbia University Press, 1994), 64, 86, 112; Stalin to Mao, May 1950, in Kathryn Weathersby, "The Soviet Role in the Early Phase of the Korean War," *Journal of American-East Asian Relations* 2, no. 4 (1993): 430.

81. Fyn Si to Shtykov, October 1, 1950, in Wada, *The Korean War*, 119.

82. Katheryn Weathersby, "Stalin, Mao, and the End of the Korean War," in *Brothers in Arms: The Rise and Fall of the Sino-Soviet Alliance, 1945–1963*, ed. Odd Arne Westad (Washington, DC: Woodrow Wilson Center Press, 1998), 94; William Stueck, *The Korean War: An International History* (Princeton, NJ: Princeton University Press, 1997), 65.

83. Kathryn Weathersby, "Stalin, Mao, and the End of the Korean War," in Westad, *Brothers in Arms*, 103–105; translation modified.

84. Wada, *The Korean War*, 133.

85. Mastny, *The Cold War and Soviet Insecurity*, 151; Odd Arne Westad, "Introduction," in Westad, *Brothers in Arms*, 14.

86. A. V. Torkunov, *Zagadochnaia Voina: Koreiskii Konflikt 1950–1953 godov* (Moscow: Rosspen, 2000), 272–273; Elizabeth A. Stanley, "Ending the Korean War," *International Security* 34, no. 1 (2009): 76.

87. Khrushchev, Speech to Factory No. 23, August 11, 1955, in *Nikita Sergeevich Khrushchev: Dva Tsveta Vremeni*, vol. 1 (Moscow: Mezhdunarodny Fond Demokratii, 2009), 549–551; Elizabeth A. Stanley, *Paths to Peace: Domestic Coalition Shifts, War Termination and the Korean War* (Stanford, CA: Stanford University Press, 2009), 113; Zubok and Pleshakov, *Inside the Kremlin's Cold War*, 155. On Japanese anti-communism, see "Kratkii Obzor Raboty 8-I Vneocherednoi Sessii Parlamenta," Russian State Archive of Social and Political History, Moscow, f. 17, o. 137, d. 412, ll. 158–161, 179–181.

88. On Khrushchev's critique of Molotov, see Benjamin Aldrich-Moodie's translation of the July 1955 Plenum of the Communist Party of the Soviet Union in *CWIPH*, no. 10 (March 1998): 6. This quote is after the decision to end the war but representative of a broader shift in Soviet foreign policy. On Kim Il Sung, see Wada, *The Korean War*, 260.

7. "The Great Hope of Humankind"

1. Vojtech Mastny, "The Soviet Union's Partnership with India," *Journal of Cold War Studies* 12, no. 3 (Summer 2010): 54.

2. Nikita Khrushchev, *The Memoirs of Nikita Khrushchev*, vol. 3, *Statesman, 1953–1964*, ed. Sergei Khrushchev (University Park: Pennsylvania State University Press, 2007), 728.

3. "Information on Khrushchev and Bulganin's November–December 1955 trip to India, Burma, and Afghanistan," January 11, 1956, obtained by David Wolff, trans. Stephan Kieninger, Wilson Center History and Public Policy Program Digital Archive, https://digital archive.wilsoncenter.org/document/119273; transcript of a Meeting between Soviet Prime Minister (Nikolai Bulganin) and Indian Prime Minister (Jawaharlal Nehru), June 8, 1955, RGANI, f. 5, o. 30, d. 116, l. 73–84, http://www.php.isn.ethz.ch/lory1.ethz.ch/collections/colltopic5de3.html?lng=en&id=93135&navinfo=56154; Welles Hangen, "Khrushchev Attacks Eisenhower, Rejects His Air Inspection Plan," *New York Times*, December 30, 1955; "Soviet Chieftains Off to South Asia," *New York Times*, November 17, 1955; A. M. Rosenthal, "American Argues with Soviet Chief," *New York Times*, November 22, 1955; "Khrushchev Talks Held Irking Nehru," *New York Times*, December 23, 1955; Nikita Khrushchev, *Khrushchev Remembers* (Boston: Little, Brown, 1970), 561; David C. Engerman, "Learning from the East: Soviet Experts and India in the Era of Competitive Coexistence," *Comparative Studies of South Asia, Africa, and the Middle East* 33, no. 2 (2013): 228; Khrushchev, *The Memoirs of Nikita Khrushchev*, 3:729, 738.

4. Aleksandr Fursenko and Timothy Naftali, *Khrushchev's Cold War: The Inside Story of an American Adversary* (New York: Norton, 2006), 81.

5. Mikoyan speech in GARF, f. 5446, o. 120, d. 1249, l. 2, 14, 16, 18.

6. On MacMillan and Gaitskell, see William Taubman, *Khrushchev: The Man and His Era* (New York: W. W. Norton, 2003), 352, 357; Bohlen quoted in Furskeno and Naftali, *Khrushchev's Cold War*, 25.

7. Khrushchev, *Khrushchev Remembers*, 4.

8. Taubman, *Khrushchev*, 332.

9. Taubman, *Khrushchev*, 347. On changing nuclear thinking, see Campbell Craig and Sergey Radchenko, "MAD, Not Marx: Khrushchev and the Nuclear Revolution," *Journal of Strategic Studies* 41, nos. 1–2 (2018): 212–215.

10. Fursenko and Naftali, *Khrushchev's Cold War*, 28–29. On defining peaceful coexistence, see Taubman, *Khrushchev*, 348.

11. On "socialism without kolkhozes," see Chris Miller, "Georgii Mirskii and Soviet Theories of Authoritarian Modernization," *International History Review* 41, no. 2 (2019): 304–322.

12. On Brutents, see Engerman, "Learning from the East," 234.

13. Andreas Hilger, "The Soviet Union and India: The Khrushchev Era and Its Aftermath until 1966," Parallel History Project on Cooperative Security, February 2009, http://www.php.isn.ethz.ch/lory1.ethz.ch/collections/coll_india/documents/IntroII _final_001.pdf, 2, 5, 7.

14. "Khrushchev's 'We Will Bury You,'" n.d., CIA CREST Archive, https://www.cia .gov/library/readingroom/docs/CIA-RDP73B00296R000200040087-1.pdf.

15. "From the Journal of Pavel F. Yudin: Record of Conversation with Mao Zedong," December 21, 1955, Wilson Center History and Public Policy Program Digital Archive, Archive of Foreign Policy of the Russian Federation (AVPRF), f. 0100, o. 49, p. 410, d. 9, ll. 11–19, trans. Gary Goldberg, http://digitalarchive.wilsoncenter.org/document/117834; "From the Journal of Ambassador Pavel Yudin: Memorandum of Conversation with Mao Zedong," May 30, 1955, Wilson Center History and Public Policy Program Digital Archive, AVPRF, f. 0100 o. 48, p. 393, d. 9, obtained by Paul Wingrove, trans. Gary Goldberg, http://digitalarchive.wilsoncenter.org/document/111373.

16. Odd Arne Westad, "The Sino-Soviet Alliance and the United States," in *Brothers in Arms: The Rise and Fall of the Sino-Soviet Alliance, 1945–1963*, ed. Odd Arne Westad (Washington, DC: Woodrow Wilson Center Press, 1998), 152. On tech transfer, see William Kirby cited in Taubman, *Khrushchev*, 337. On Mao's translator and 203 factories, see Taubman, *Khrushchev*, 336–337; On Mao to Yudin, see "From the Journal of Ambassador Pavel Yudin: Memorandum of Conversation with Mao Zedong," May 30, 1955; translation modified. On the "great friendship," see Austin Jersild, *The Sino-Soviet Alliance: An International History* (Chapel Hill: University of North Carolina Press, 2014), ix.

17. "From the Journal of Pavel F. Yudin: Record of Conversation with Mao Zedong," December 21, 1955.

18. "Zamechaniia Gosplana . . . po proektu pervogo piatiletnego plana razvitiia narodnogo khoziastva KNR," no later than May 19, 1955, in *Prezidium TsK KPSS 1954–1964: Chernovyye protokolnyye zapisi zasedaniy. Stenogrammy*, vol. 2 (Moscow: Rosspen, 2003), 71; Zhihua Shen and Yafeng Xia, "The Great Leap Forward, the People's Commune and the Sino-Soviet Split," *Journal of Contemporary China* 20, no. 72 (2011): 861–880; B. Ponomarev, "Spravka o Polozhenii v KNDR," April 1955, RGANI, f. 5, o. 28, d. 314, ll. 35–59; Ponomarev, Memo on North Korea, RGANI, f. 5, o. 28, d. 314, ll. 212–214. On the Sino-Soviet split, see Lorenz Luthi, *The Sino-Soviet Split: Cold War in the Communist World* (Princeton, NJ: Princeton University Press, 2008); Sergey Radchenko, *Two Suns in the Heavens: The Sino-Soviet Struggle for Supremacy, 1962–1967* (Washington, DC: Woodrow Wilson Center, 2009).

19. "Khrushchev's Secret Speech, 'On the Cult of Personality and Its Consequences,' Delivered at the Twentieth Party Congress of the Communist Party of the Soviet Union," February 25, 1956, Wilson Center History and Public Policy Program Digital Archive, from the Congressional Record: Proceedings and Debates of the 84th Congress, 2nd Session (May 22, 1956–June 11, 1956), C11, Part 7 (June 4, 1956), 9389–9403, http://digitalarchive .wilsoncenter.org/document/115995.

20. Odd Arne Westad, "Introduction," in Westad, *Brothers in Arms*, 18; Taubman, *Khrushchev*, 338–339; "From the Journal of Ambassador P. F. Yudin, Record of Conversation with Mao Zedong, 31 March 1956," April 5, 1956, Wilson Center History and Public Policy

Program Digital Archive, AVPRF, f. 0100, o. 49, p. 410, d. 9, ll. 87–98; also RGANI, f. 5, o. 30, d. 163, ll. 88–99, trans. Mark Doctoroff, http://digitalarchive.wilsoncenter.org/document/116977.

21. Mikoyan speech in GARF, f. 5446, o. 120, d. 1249, l. 26; "Zapis Besedy," March 8 and October 2, 1958, RGANI, f. 5, o. 49, d. 128, ll. 22, 241; "First Conversation between N.S. Khrushchev and Mao Zedong, Hall of Huaizhentan [Beijing]," July 31, 1958, Wilson Center History and Public Policy Program Digital Archive, Archive of the President of the Russian Federation (APRF), f. 52, o. 1, d. 498, ll. 44–477, copy in Dmitry Volkogonov Collection, Manuscript Division, LOC, Washington, DC, trans. Vladislav M. Zubok, http://digitalarchive.wilsoncenter.org/document/112080.

22. Heinzig, 393; Khrushchev, *Khrushchev Remembers*, 513.

23. Vladislav M. Zubok, "First Conversation of N.S. Khrushchev with Mao Zedong, Hall of Huaizhentan [Beijing]," July 31, 1958, *CWIHP*, no. 12–13 (Fall / Winter 2001): 251, 254; Charles Kraus, "Creating a Soviet 'Semi-Colony'? Sino-Soviet Cooperation and Its Demise in Xinjiang, 1949–1955," *Chinese Historical Review* 17, no. 2 (2010): 132.

24. "Minutes of Conversation, Mao Zedong and Ambassador Yudin," July 22, 1958, in Wilson Center History and Public Policy Program Digital Archive, *Mao Zedong waijiao wenxuan* [Selected works of Mao Zedong on diplomacy] (Beijing: Zhongyang wenxian chubanshe, 1994), 322–333, trans. Zhang Shu Guang and Chen Jian, http://digitalarchive.wilsoncenter.org/document/116982.

25. On Khrushchev's shift in orientation, see Radchenko, *Two Suns in the Heavens*, 80.

26. Westad, "The Sino-Soviet Alliance," 158.

27. "Conversation of Mao Zedong with Soviet Ambassador Pavel Yudin," March 28, 1958, Wilson Center History and Public Policy Program Digital Archive, *Dang de wenxian* [Party historical documents], no. 3 (1994): 15, trans. Neil Silver, http://digitalarchive.wilson center.org/document/114342; "half of humanity": Taubman, *Khrushchev*, 341.

28. Khrushchev, *Khrushchev Remembers*, 518–519.

29. Chen Jian, *Mao's China and the Cold War* (Chapel Hill: University of North Carolina Press, 2001), 163, 183, 187.

30. "Discussion between N.S. Khrushchev and Mao Zedong," October 2, 1959, Wilson Center History and Public Policy Program Digital Archive, APRF, f. 52, o. 1, d. 499, ll. 1–33, copy in Volkogonov Collection, LOC, trans. Vladislav M. Zubok, http://digitalarchive.wilsoncenter.org/document/112088; Westad, "The Sino-Soviet Alliance," 150–151.

31. "Attacking China means attacking the Soviet Union": Westad, "The Sino-Soviet Alliance," 151; "Discussion between N.S. Khrushchev and Mao Zedong," October 2, 1959, Wilson Center History and Public Policy Program Digital Archive, APRF, f. 52, o. 1, d. 499, ll. 1–33, copy in Volkogonov Collection, LOC, Washington, DC, trans. Vladislav M. Zubok, http://digitalarchive.wilsoncenter.org/document/112088; Chen, *Mao's China and the Cold War*, 189. On swimming pool summits, see Khrushchev, *Khrushchev Remembers*, 518; *CWIHP*, no. 12–13 (Fall / Winter 2001): 263–264.

32. Mastny, "The Soviet Union's Partnership with India," 58.

33. Westad, "The Sino-Soviet Alliance," 177; "Otchet Posolstva SSSR v Kitaiskoi Narodnoi Respublike za 1958 god," RGANI, f. 5, o. 49, d. 134, l. 237.

34. "One cannot mechanistically repeat": Westad, "The Sino-Soviet Alliance," 25; Vladimir M. Zubok, *A Failed Empire: The Soviet Union in the Cold War from Stalin to Gorbachev* (Chapel Hill: University of North Carolina Press, 2007), 137.

35. Mao Zedong, "On Khrushchov's Phoney Communism and Its Historical Lessons for the World," Marxists Internet Archive, July 1964, https://www.marxists.org/reference/archive/mao/works/1964/phnycom.htm.

36. On the collapse of Sino-Soviet friendship, see Chen, *Mao's China and the Cold War*, 49–84; Luthi, *The Sino-Soviet Split*; Radchenko, *Two Suns in the Heavens*.

37. On the Cuban Missile Crisis, see Enrico Maria Fardella, "Mao Zedong and the 1962 Cuban Missile Crisis," *Cold War History* 15, no. 1 (2015): 81. On Hong Kong and Russian imperialism, see Elizabeth Wishnick, *Mending Fences: The Evolution of Moscow's China Policy from Brezhnev to Yeltsin* (Seattle: University of Washington Press, 2001), 28.

38. Wishnick, *Mending Fences*, 24, 31.

39. Paul Du Quenoy, "The Role of Foreign Affairs in the Fall of Nikita Khrushchev in October 1964," *International History Review* 25, no. 2 (June 2003): 335.

40. "Minutes from a Conversation between A.N. Kosygin and Mao Zedong," February 11, 1965, Wilson Center History and Public Policy Program Digital Archive, AAN, KC PZPR, XI A / 10, 517, 524, obtained by Douglas Selvage, trans. Malgorzata Gnoinska, http://digitalarchive.wilsoncenter.org/document/118039.

41. "Minutes from a Conversation between A.N. Kosygin and Mao Zedong," February 11, 1965.

42. "Minutes from a Conversation between A.N. Kosygin and Mao Zedong," February 11, 1965.

43. Wishnick, *Mending Fences*, 28.

44. On US-Soviet discussions, see William Stearman, Memcon, August 18, 1969, National Security Archive, https://nsarchive2.gwu.edu/NSAEBB/NSAEBB49/sino.sov.10.pdf; Y. Kuisong, "The Sino-Soviet Border Clash of 1969: From Zhenbao Island to Sino-American Rapprochement," *Cold War History* 1, no. 1 (2000): 21–52; Lyle Goldstein, "Return to Zhenbao Island: Who Started Shooting and Why It Matters," *China Quarterly* 168 (December 2001): 985–997. On Soviet fears of Chinese irrationality, see Wishnick, *Mending Fences*, 30, 35.

45. Gennady Nevelskoy, *Podvigi russkikh morskikh ofitserov na krainem vostoke Rossii, 1849–55* (St. Petersburg, 1878), 114.

46. On Brezhnev's humor, see Sergey Radchenko, *Unwanted Visionaries: The Soviet Failure in Asia at the End of the Cold War* (Oxford: Oxford University Press, 2013), 13. On changing names, see Wishnick, *Mending Fences*, 55.

47. *The Military Balance, 1984–1985* (London: International Institute for Strategic Studies, 1985), 21; Charles E. Ziegler, *Foreign Policy and East Asia: Learning and Adaptation in the Gorbachev Era* (Cambridge: Cambridge University Press, 1993), 131; Donald S. Zagoria, "The Soviet Quandary in Asia," *Foreign Affairs* 56, no. 2 (January 1978), 318; Henry Gelman, "Andropov's Policy toward Asia," *Journal of Northeast Asian Studies* 2 (June 1983): 3–11; Wishnick, *Mending Fences*, 24, 30, 43.

48. Ezra Vogel, *China and Japan: Facing History* (Cambridge, MA: Harvard University Press, 2019), 327–355.

49. Excerpts from the "Protocol Transcript of the Moscow Meeting," May 16–18, 1973, trans. Malgorzata K. Gnoiska, in James Hershberg, Sergey Radchenko, Péter Vámos, and David Wolff, "The Interkit Story: A Window into the Final Decades of the Sino-Soviet Relationship," Cold War International History Project, working paper no. 63, February 2011, 92–94.

50. Arnold L. Horelick, "The Soviet Union's Asian Collective Security Proposal: A Club in Search of Members," *Pacific Affairs* 47, no. 3 (Autumn 1974): 269.

51. Nehru quoted in Ramesh Thacker and Carlyle Thayer, *Soviet Relations with India and Vietnam* (Houndmills, UK: Macmillan, 1992), 34, 64; Wishnick, *Mending Fences*, 51.

52. Thacker and Thayer, *Soviet Relations with India and Vietnam*, 36, 95; Radchenko, *Unwanted Visionaries*, 100.

53. On the USSR's aid to North Korea, see Zagoria, "The Soviet Quandary in Asia," 313; On "unparalleled" friction, see Balazs Szalontai, *Kim Il Sung in the Khrushchev Era: Soviet-DPRK Relations and the Roots of North Korean Despotism, 1953–1964* (Washington, DC: Woodrow Wilson Center Press, 2005), 174.

54. On Hanoi's radical views and pro-Chinese orientation, see Ilya Gaiduk, "The Vietnam War and Soviet-American Relations, 1964–1973," *CWIHP*, nos. 6–7 (Winter 1995): 250; Nicholas Khoo, *Collateral Damage: Sino-Soviet Rivalry and the Termination of the Sino-Vietnamese Alliance* (New York: Columbia University Press, 2011). On Soviet aid to Vietnam in 1979, see Radchenko, *Unwanted Visionaries*, 126; Gelman, "Andropov's Policy toward Asia," 4–5. On Soviet bases in Vietnam, see Robert Horn, "Soviet Policy in Southeast Asia in the Gorbachev Era," in *The Soviet Union and the Asia-Pacific Region*, ed. Pushpa Thambipillai and Daniel C. Matuszewski (New York: Praeger, 1989), 63. On debates over Soviet aid to Vietnam, see Balazs Szalontai, "The Diplomacy of Economic Reform in Vietnam: The Genesis of Doi Moi, 1986–1989," *Journal of Asiatic Studies* 51, no. 2 (2008): 199–252; Thacker and Thayer, *Soviet Relations with India and Vietnam*, 125.

55. "CPSU CC Politburo Decision," January 28, 1980, trans. Mark Kramer, *CWIHP*, nos. 8–9 (Winter 1996): 163.

56. "Personal Memorandum, Andropov to Brezhnev," early December 1979, obtained by Odd Arne Westad, trans. Daniel Rozas, *CWIHP*, nos. 8–9 (Winter 1996): 159.

57. Thacker and Thayer, *Soviet Relations with India and Vietnam*, 3; Gelman, "Andropov's Policy toward Asia," 6; Zagoria, "The Soviet Quandary," 315.

58. On "imperialist circles," see "CPSU CC Directive to Soviet Ambassadors," March 4, 1980, trans. Elizabeth Wishnick, *CWIHP*, nos. 6–7 (Winter 1995): 201–202. On American imperialism, see "CPSU CC Politburo Directive to Soviet Ambassadors," October 2, 1980, *CWIHP*, nos. 6–7 (Winter 1995): 203–204; cf. Ponomarev, "Polish Record of Soviet Alliance Meeting in Moscow," February 1980, trans. Malgorzata Gnoiska, in Hershberg et al., "The Interkit Story," 110. "Anti-Sovietism" quoted in Radchenko, *Unwanted Visionaries*, 14; Wishnick, *Mending Fences*, 60.

59. "Unbridled and aggressive": Radchenko, *Unwanted Visionaries*, 24. On Eastern Europe, see Radchenko, *Unwanted Visionaries*, 18, 20; Wishnick, *Mending Fences*, 41.

60. East German record of talk with Soviet Communist Party official Boris Kulik, January 26, 1977, in Hershberg et al., "The Interkit Story," 100.

61. On preparing for war, see "Directive to Soviet Ambassadors and Representatives," October 2, 1980, RGANI, f. 89, per. 34, doc. 10, in Elizabeth Wishnick, "Sino-Soviet Tensions, 1980," *CWIHP*, nos. 6–7 (Winter 1995): 202; Alexander Lukin, *The Bear Watches the Dragon: Russia's Perceptions of China and the Evolution of Russian-Chinese Relations since the Eighteenth Century* (Armonk, NY: M. E. Sharpe, 2003), 144; Mikhail Kapitsa, *Na Raznykh Paralleliakh: Zapiski Diplomala* (Moscow: AO Kniga I biznes, 1996); Anatoly Chernayev Diary, May 29, 1982, http://www2.gwu.edu/~nsarchiv/rus/text_files/Chernyaev/1982 .pdf. Evgeny Bazhanov quoted in Lukin, *The Bear Watches the Dragon*, 145; Gil Rozman, "Moscow's China-Watchers in the Post-Mao Era: The Response to a Changing China," *China Quarterly* 94 (June 1983): 215–241; R. Neronov and G. Stepanova, "CPC: Certain Tendencies of Development," *Far Eastern Affairs*, no. 2 (1982): 44; Alexander Lukin, "Kitaievedenie i Politika," *Vostok*, no. 2 (1991): 218.

62. Brezhnev in "President Brezhnev's Speech, Tashkent 24 Mar 1982," *Survival* 24, no. 4 (1982): 186. On the Cultural Revolution, see Fedor Burlatsky, "Nasledniki Mao," *Novy Mir* 9 (1978): 217. On the propaganda war, see Ziegler, *Foreign Policy and East Asia*, 62. On Brezhnev's policy changes, see Rozman, "Moscow's China-Watchers in the Post-Mao Era," 215, 217; Radchenko, *Unwanted Visionaries*, 17.

63. On Southeast Asia, see Khoo, *Collateral Damage*. On China's demands, see Wishnick, *Mending Fences*, 99. On Beijing's interpretation of Brezhnev's Tashkent speech, see Radchenko, *Unwanted Visionaries*, 25.

64. "Faulty assessment": Georgy Arbatov quoted in Wishnick, *Mending Fences*, 40. On US-China difficulties, see Radchenko, *Unwanted Visionaries*, 30–33.

65. On Brezhnev, see Hershberg et al., "The Interkit Story," 29; Wishnick, *Mending Fences*, 75, 77, 82.

66. On China hawks, see Lukin, *The Bear Watches the Dragon*, 144–145; Wishnick, *Mending Fences*, 85. On Ustinov, see Radchenko, *Unwanted Visionaries*, 38. On Soviet military placements, see Wishnick, *Mending Fences*, 79.

67. On Zionist conspiracy, see Evgeny Bazhanov, *Aktualnye Problemy Mezhdunarodnikh Otnoshenii* (Moscow: Nauchniaia Kniga, 2002), 313; Lukin, *The Bear Watches the Dragon*, 150. On geopolitical enemies, see Eugene Bazhanov, "Policy by Fiat," *Far Eastern Economic Review*, June 11, 1992, 16.

68. Bazhanov, "Policy by Fiat," 16.

69. "Polish Report on Meeting in Moscow with Oleg Rakhmanin," February 1985, trans. Malgorzata Gnoinska, in Hershberg et al., "The Interkit Story," 135.

8. Perestroika and the Pacific

1. The best survey of Gorbachev's Asian diplomacy is Sergey Radchenko's *Unwanted Visionaries: The Soviet Failure in Asia at the End of the Cold War* (Oxford: Oxford University Press, 2013), from which this chapter draws heavily. An excellent survey of Sino-Soviet rapprochement is Vladislav Zubok, "The Soviet Union and China in the 1980s: Reconciliation and Divorce," *Cold War History* 17, no. 2 (2017): 121–141. On shifting views of Asia, see Chris Miller, *The Struggle to Save the Soviet Economy: Mikhail Gorbachev and the Collapse of the*

USSR (Chapel Hill: University of North Carolina Press, 2016). On Gorbachev's politics and relations with the West, see William Taubman, *Gorbachev: His Life and Times* (New York: Norton, 2017); Archie Brown, *The Gorbachev Factor* (Oxford: Oxford University Press, 1996).

2. On the 1986 exercise, see Clyde Haberman, "Challenge in the Pacific," *New York Times,* September 7, 1986. On "bastion defense," see Narushige Michishita, Peter M. Swartz, and David F. Winkler, "Lessons of the Cold War in the Pacific: U.S. Maritime Strategy, Crisis Prevention, and Japan's Role (Washington, DC: Woodrow Wilson Center, 2016), https://www.wilsoncenter.org/sites/default/files/lessons_of_the_cold_war_in_the _pacific_one_page.pdf; On subsurface ballistic nuclear submarine vulnerabilities, see Eugene Miasnikov, "Can Russian Strategic Submarines Survive at Sea? The Fundamental Limits of Passive Acoustics," *Science & Global Security* 4, no. 2 (1994): 213–251.

3. On ship counts, see Clyde Haberman, "Challenge in the Pacific," *New York Times,* September 7, 1986.

4. Historians such as Sergey Radchenko and Vladimir Lukin have noted that efforts to improve ties with China began during the early 1980s. But these efforts were obstructed by hawks until Gorbachev's ascent tipped the internal balance in favor of rapprochement.

5. On the "uncultivated," see Evgeny Bazhanov's judgment of Boris Ponomarev in Bazhanov, "Soviet Policy towards South Korea under Gorbachev," in *Korea and Russia: Toward the 21st Century,* ed. Il Yung Chung (Seoul: Sejong Institute, 1992), 67.

6. Shevardnadze quoted in Charles E. Ziegler, *Foreign Policy and East Asia: Learning and Adaptation in the Gorbachev Era* (Cambridge: Cambridge University Press, 1993), 58. On "balanced trade," see "Spravka ob Ekonomicheskom Sotrudnichestve SSSR c Sotsialisticheskoi Respublike Vietnam," n.d., Hoover Institution Library and Archives, Stanford, CA, Kataev Papers, box 12, p. 8. On the cost of aiding Vietnam, see M. S. Krapivin and D. V. Mosiakov, "Otnosheniia Sovetskogo Soiuza s Vetnamom (60–90-e gg. XX veka)," *Vostok,* no. 3 (2006): 45; Radchenko, *Unwanted Visionaries,* 133; Balazs Szalontai, "The Diplomacy of Economic Reform in Vietnam: The Genesis of Doi Moi, 1986–1989," *Journal of Asiatic Studies* 51, no. 2 (2008): 229–230.

7. Primakov also mentioned Western Europe as a candidate for a "multipolar strategy"; see Viktor Kuzminov and Viktor Pavlyatenko, "Soviet-Japanese Relations from 1960–1985: An Era of Ups and Downs," in *A History of Russo-Japanese Relations: Over Two Centuries of Cooperation and Competition,* ed. Dmitry Streltsov and Nobuo Shimotomai (London: Brill, 2019), 460; "Multi-polar strategy": Yakovlev quoted in Seung-Ho Joo, *Gorbachev's Foreign Policy toward the Korean Peninsula, 1985–1991* (Lewiston, NY: Edwin Mellen Press, 2000), 25. On Yakovlev, see "Tezisy k Vystupleniiu A. N. Iakovleva na Soveshchaniii v TsK KPSS," December 6, 1985, in *Aleksandr Iakovlev: Perestroika, 1985–1991; Dokumenty* (Moscow: Mezhdunarodnii Fond Demokratiia, 2008), 19.

8. On ideology in Soviet foreign policy, see Vladislav Zubok and Constantine Pleshakov, *Inside the Kremlin's Cold War: From Stalin to Krushchev* (Cambridge, MA: Harvard University Press, 1996).

9. David M. Levy and Sandra J. Peart, "Soviet Growth and American Textbooks," *Journal of Economic Behavior and Organization* 78, no. 1–2 (2001): 110–125.

10. Aleksandr Yakovlev, "Keystones of the New Thinking," *Far Eastern Affairs*, no. 1 (1989): 75.

11. The subsequent paragraphs draw from Miller, *The Struggle to Save the Soviet Economy*, chap. 2. On Japanese capitalism, see A. I. Bykova, "SShA I ikh konkurenty na mirovkh rynkakh naukoemokoi produktsii," 1985, data annex, Archive of the Academy of Sciences, Moscow, f. 2021, o. 2, d. 16, ll. 44–59; "Amerikansko-iaponskoe ekonomicheskoe protivorechie," 1986, Archive of the Academy of Sciences, Moscow, f. 2021, o. 2, d. 19, ll. 2–17.

12. Gilbert Rozman, "Moscow's Japan-Watchers in the First Years of the Gorbachev Era: The Struggle for Realism and Respect in Foreign Affairs," *Pacific Review* 1 (1988): 261, 269; V. Khlynov, "Iaponskie plany i prognozy razvitiia na 80-e gody," *Mirovaya ekonomika i mezhdunarodnyye otnosheniya* (1981): 128.

13. S. I. Verbitskii, "Evoliutsia vzgliadov na iaponiu v period perestroika," in *Znakomtes Iaponiia: K visitu B.N. Eltsina*, ed. V. B. Ramzes (Moscow: Nauka, 1992), 38–39.

14. Primakov quoted in Scott Atkinson, "The USSR and the Pacific Century," *Asian Survey* 30, no. 7 (July 1990): 636; I. Tselishchev, "High Technologies and the Economics of the Asian-Pacific Region," *Mirovaya ekonomika i mezhdunarodnyye otnosheniya* (1989): 91, quoted in Atkinson, "The USSR and the Pacific Century," 636; Vladimir Klyuchnikov, "How Do We Answer the Call? The Soviet Far East on the World Map," *Sotsialisticheskaya Industriya*, September 11, 1988, 1, quoted in Atkinson, "The USSR and the Pacific Century," 629.

15. On Gorbachev, see Taubman, *Gorbachev;* Brown, *The Gorbachev Factor.*

16. Brown, *The Gorbachev Factor*, 336.

17. Miller, *The Struggle to Save the Soviet Economy*, chaps. 1–2.

18. On Gorbachev's Asia policy retrenchment, see William Wohlforth, "Defying Expectations: Russia's Missing Asian Revisionism," in *The United States and Northeast Asia: Debates, Issues, and New Order*, ed. G. John Ikenberry and Chung-in Moon (Lanham, MD: Rowman & Littlefield, 2008), 99. Gorbachev may have retrenched the Soviet military, but he tried to expand the Kremlin's political influence. When this failed, Moscow's relevance in Asia by the mid-1990s returned to its level of the mid-1980s: it had many nuclear weapons and few other levers of influence.

19. On Vladivostok, see William Richardson, "Vladivostok: City of Three Eras," *Planning Perspectives* 10, no. 1 (1995): 43–65.

20. On Brezhnev's visit to the Far East, see "Zasedanii Politbiuro TsK KPSS," April 13, 1978, Volkogonov Papers, LOC, reel 16; Joachim Glaubitz, *Between Tokyo and Moscow: The History of an Uneasy Relationship* (Honolulu: University of Hawaii Press, 1995), 174–175.

21. "Na soveshchanii u Gorbacheva v svyazi s poesdkoi na Dalnii Vostok," July 16, 1986, in *Otvechaia na Vyzov Vremeni: Veshniaia Politika Perestroiki: Dokumentalnie Svidetel'stva* (Moscow: Ves Mir, 2010), 799.

22. "Iz Zaiavleniia Generalnogo Sekretaria TsK KPSS," January 15, 1986; "Na politburo. O mezhdunarodnyi situatsii," April 3, 1986; "Iz Politicheskogo Doklada TsK KPSS XXVII sezdu KPSS," February 25, 1986; and "Na soveshchanii u Gorbacheva v svyazi s poesdkoi na Dalnii Vostok," July 16, 1986, in *Otvechaia na Vyzov Veka Vremeni*, 795–799.

23. "Gorbachev Accents Soviet Role in Asia," *Current Digest of the Soviet Press* 38, no. 30 (August 27, 1986): 5; Mikhail Gorbachev, *Speech by Mikhail Gorbachev in Vladivostok, July 28, 1986* (Moscow: Novosti Press Agency Publishing House, 1986), 9.

24. Gorbachev, *Speech by Mikhail Gorbachev in Vladivostok*, 24, 26, 29.

25. David Wolff, "Interkit: Soviet Sinology and the Sino-Soviet Rift," *Russian History* 30, no. 4 (Winter 2003): 453; Elizabeth Wishnick, *Mending Fences: The Evolution of Moscow's China Policy from Brezhnev to Yeltsin* (Seattle: University of Washington Press, 2001), 99–100; Alexander Lukin, *The Bear Watches the Dragon: Russia's Perceptions of China and the Evolution of Russian-Chinese Relations since the Eighteenth Century* (Armonk, NY: M. E. Sharpe, 2003), 150.

26. On generational change, see Lukin, *The Bear Watches the Dragon*, 150–151. The best account of the withdrawal from Afghanistan is Artemy Kalinovsky, *The Long Goodbye: The Soviet Withdrawal from Afghanistan* (Cambridge, MA: Harvard University Press, 2011), 178.

27. On North Korea, see Joo, *Gorbachev's Foreign Policy toward the Korean Peninsula*, 99–100. On Japan, see Tsuyoshi Hasegawa, *The Northern Territories Dispute and Russo-Japanese Relations*, 2 vols. (Berkeley: University of California Press, 1998), 1:167.

28. *The Diary of Anatoly Chernyaev, 1985*, ed. Svetlana Savranskaya, trans. Anna Melyakova, April 4, 1985, National Security Archive, https://nsarchive2.gwu.edu/NSAEBB/NSAEBB192/Chernyaev_Diary_translation_1985.pdf.

29. *The Diary of Anatoly Chernyaev*, April 4, 1985.

30. *The Diary of Anatoly Chernyaev*, April 11 and June 20, 1985.

31. *The Diary of Anatoly Chernyaev*, October 16–17, 1985.

32. For Gorbachev on Mongolia, see "Gorbachev Accents Soviet Role in Asia," 6. On Cambodia, see Leszek Buszynski, *Gorbachev and Southeast Asia* (London: Routledge, 1992), 121–146. On withdrawal from Mongolia, see "Notes from Politburo Meeting on July 24, 1986," in *V Politburo TsK KPSS: Po zapisyam Anatoliya Chernyaeva, Vadima Medvedeva, Georgiya Shakhnazarova (1985–1991)*, ed. Anatoly Chernyaev, Vadim Medvedev, and Georgy Shakhnazarov (Moscow: Gorbachev Foundation, 2008), 75. The best analysis is Sergey Radchenko, "Soviet Withdrawal from Mongolia, 1986–1992: A Reassessment," *Journal of Slavic Military Studies* 25, no. 2 (2012): 183–203.

33. "How much we have in common": Vojtech Mastny, "The Soviet Union's Partnership with India," *Journal of Cold War Studies* 12, no. 3 (Summer 2010): 77; "We cannot say aloud": Radchenko, *Unwanted Visionaries*, 95, 98; translation modified.

34. Mastny, "The Soviet Union's Partnership with India," 78; Buszynski, *Gorbachev and Southeast Asia*, 60. On Gorbachev's triangle concept, see Radchenko, *Unwanted Visionaries*, 100–102.

35. Wishnick, *Mending Fences*, 113–114.

36. "Personal business": Mark D'Anastasio, "Soviets Now Hail China as a Source of Ideas for Reviving Socialism," *Wall Street Journal*, September 18, 1987; I. Nekrasov, "Open Windows—the Future of Soviet-Chinese Relations," *Sovietskaya Rossiya*, July 9, 1988, trans. in Joint Publications Research Service: Soviet Union, International Affairs, September 15, 1988, 74.

37. On socialist brotherhood, see Lukin, *The Bear Watches the Dragon*, 153, 154. On Gorbachev's visit, see Ezra F. Vogel, *Deng Xiaoping and the Transformation of China* (Cambridge, MA: Harvard University Press, 2011), 612; Andrew J. Nathan and Perry Link, eds., *The Tiananmen Papers* (New York: PublicAffairs, 2001), 144; "Other Reports on Early Part of Visit; Reactions from People in Peking," *BBC Summary of World Broadcasts*, May 17, 1989.

38. "Iz Vystupleniia Gorbacheva na Vstreche s Kitaiskoi Obshchestvennostiu," May 17, 1989, in *Otvechaia na Vyzov Vremeni*, 882–883; Andrew Higgins and Rupert Cornwell, "Students Spoil Gorbachev's Party," *Independent*, May 16, 1989, 16; Michael Dobbs, "Gorbachev, in China, Calls for Democracy," *Washington Post*, May 17, 1989, A1; Wishnick, *Mending Fences*, 104.

39. Lukin, *The Bear Watches the Dragon*, 156–162.

40. "Excerpts from the Conversation between Mikhail Gorbachev and Rajiv Gandhi," July 15, 1989, Wilson Center History and Public Policy Program Digital Archive and Archive of the Gorbachev Foundation, trans. Sergey Radchenko, https://digitalarchive.wilsoncenter.org/document/119291.pdf?v=6a44a2603e0ef9559df45d0b2d1d461a; Radchenko, *Unwanted Visionaries*, 101.

41. Joo, *Gorbachev's Foreign Policy toward the Korean Peninsula*, 97; Bazhanov, "Soviet Policy towards South Korea under Gorbachev," 63.

42. Bazhanov, "Soviet Policy towards South Korea under Gorbachev," 65; Gromyko quoted in Joo, *Gorbachev's Foreign Policy toward the Korean Peninsula*, 94. On the 1984 Summit, see Mikhail Kapitsa, *Na Raznikh Parallelakh: Zapiski Diplomala* (Moscow: AO Kniga I biznes, 1996), 240–243; Ziegler, *Foreign Policy and East Asia*, 112–113.

43. On an "Eastern NATO," see Bazhanov, "Soviet Policy towards South Korea under Gorbachev," 71. On Moscow as a "hostage," see Karen Brutents, *Nesbyvsheesya: Neravnodushnye zametki o perestroike* (Moscow: Mezhdunarodnye otnosheniya, 1995), 217. On the Politburo's thinking, see Evgeny Bazhanov, "Soviet Policy toward the Asia-Pacific Region: The 1980s," in *Russian Strategic Thought toward Asia*, ed. Gibert Rozman, Kazuhiko Togo, and J. Ferguson (New York: Palgrave, 2006), 48. On changing views of South Korea, see Oleg Davydov, "Seoul: In Search of New Horizons," *Far Eastern Affairs*, no. 3 (1990): 35–49. Yakovlev quoted in Joo, *Gorbachev's Foreign Policy toward the Korean Peninsula*, 112. On Yakovlev and South Korea, see Brutents, *Nesbyvsheesya*, 216. On Seoul as a promising partner, see Bazhanov, "Soviet Policy towards South Korea under Gorbachev," 94.

44. Joo, *Gorbachev's Foreign Policy toward the Korean Peninsula*, 60, 71–72, 142–143. On the Olympics, see the fascinating research from the International Olympic Committee archives in Radchenko, *Unwanted Visionaries*, 198–248. On Bovin, see Bazhanov, "Soviet Policy towards South Korea under Gorbachev," 87.

45. *Izvestiya* in Joo, *Gorbachev's Foreign Policy toward the Korean Peninsula*, 144. On "tremendous opportunities," see Bazhanov, "Soviet Policy towards South Korea under Gorbachev," 96. On prioritizing economics, see Radchenko, *Unwanted Visionaries*, 199, 219; Joo, *Gorbachev's Foreign Policy toward the Korean Peninsula*, 154.

46. Joo, *Gorbachev's Foreign Policy toward the Korean Peninsula*, 67, 73, 115, 191, 194, 196; Brutents, *Nesbyvsheesia*, 219; Kim Hakjoon, "The Process Leading to the Establishment of

Diplomatic Relations between South Korea and the Soviet Union," *Asian Survey* 37, no. 7 (July 1997): 650.

47. Xiaoming Zhang, *Deng Xiaoping's Long War* (Chapel Hill: University of North Carolina Press, 2015), 198.

48. Wishnick, *Mending Fences*, 103; Joo, *Gorbachev's Foreign Policy toward the Korean Peninsula*, 69.

49. Gorbachev, Speech in Krasnoyarsk, September 19, 1988, Foreign Broadcast Information Service: Soviet Union, FBIS-SOV-88-191; On legislation, see "Postanovlenie Verkhovnogo Soveta RSFSR . . . ," July 14, 1990, GARF, f. 10026, o. 4, d. 2637, ll. 1–3. On the zones, see Miller, *The Struggle to Save the Soviet Economy*, chap. 5; I. Latyshev, in *Pravda*, January 24, 1991, trans. in Joint Publications Research Service: Soviet Union, International Affairs, February 5, 1991, 2.

50. Gorbachev, Speech in Krasnoyarsk, September 19, 1988; Meeting of Iamada E. and F. V. Diakonov, November 30, 1988, in Russian State Archive of the Economy, Moscow, f. 399, o. 1, d. 2205, ll. 85–86.

51. Radchenko, *Unwanted Visionaries*, 100, 117, 121.

52. On the Japanese promise of $22 billion, see Yakovlev and H. Kumagi, "Zapis Besedy," January 9, 1991, in *Aleksandr Iakovlev*, 596. On Arbatov, see Radchenko, *Unwanted Visionaries*, 71.

53. Lisbeth Tarlow Bernstein, "On the Rocks: Gorbachev and the Kurile Islands" (PhD diss., The Fletcher School, 1997), 250 (mentioning the army's opposition), 259, 271; Tsuyoshi Hasegawa, "Gorbachev's Visit to Japan and Soviet-Japanese Relations," *Acta Slavica Iaponica* 10 (1992): 74; Hasegawa, *The Northern Territories Dispute and Russo-Japanese Relations*, 2:358.

54. On population decline, see Vladimir Kontorovich, "Can Russia Resettle the Far East?," *Post-Communist Economies* 12, no. 3 (2000): 365.

55. On anti-Chinese sentiment, see Lukin, *The Bear Watches the Dragon*, 165–166. On the man with the knife, see Radchenko, *Unwanted Visionaries*, 294.

Conclusion

1. Vladimir Putin, speech at the First Far Eastern Economic Forum, September 4, 2015, http://en.kremlin.ru/events/president/news/50232.

2. Putin, speech at the First Far Eastern Economic Forum.

3. Putin, speech at the First Far Eastern Economic Forum.

4. On early Yeltsin foreign policy toward Asia, see Alexey Bogaturov, "Russia's Strategic Thought toward Asia: The Early Yeltsin Years," in *Russian Strategic Thought toward Asia*, ed. Gilbert Rozman, Kazuhito Togo, and Joseph P. Ferguson (New York: Palgrave, 2006), 57–74.

5. Lena H. Sun, "Russia, China Set Closest Ties in Years," *Washington Post*, December 19, 1992; Elizabeth Wishnick, "Russia and China," *Asian Survey* 41, no. 5 (September–October 2001): 799.

6. Richard Boudreaux, "China, Russia Settle Final Land Border," *Los Angeles Times*, September 4, 1994.

7. On "multipolar strategy," see Viktor Kuzminov and Viktor Pavlyatenko, "Soviet-Japanese Relations from 1960–1985: An Era of Ups and Downs," in *A History of Russo-Japanese Relations: Over Two Centuries of Cooperation and Competition,* ed. Dmitry V. Streltsov and Shimotomai Nobuo (Leiden: Brill, 2019), 460; Wishnick, "Russia and China"; "Russia: Chinese President Jiang Zemin Meets President Boris Yeltsin," Associated Press, April 23, 1997.

8. Alexey Zagorsky, "Russian-Japan Relations: Back to the Deadlock," in *Russia and Asia: The Emerging Security Agenda,* ed. Gennady Chufrin (Oxford: Oxford University Press, 1999), 337–352.

9. "Yeltsin v Iuzhnoi Koree," *Kommersant,* November 21, 1992, https://www.kommersant.ru/doc/30695.

10. James Kim, "Yeltsin Ends Three Day Visit to South Korea," UPI, November 20, 1992, https://www.upi.com/Archives/1992/11/20/Yeltsin-ends-three-day-visit-to-South-Korea/8897722235600/.

11. On the fall in wages in the 1990s, see Viktor B. Supian and Mikhail G. Nosov, "Reintegration of an Abandoned Fortress: Economic Security of the Russian Far East," in *Russia and East Asia: The 21st Century Security Environment,* ed. Gilbert Rozman, Mikhail B. Nosov, and Koji Watanabe (Armonk, NY: M. E. Sharpe, 1999), 76; cf. Rensselaer Lee, "The Far East between Russia, China, and America," Foreign Policy Research Institute E-note, July 27, 2012, https://www.fpri.org/article/2012/07/the-far-east-between-russia-china-and-america/.

12. On Ishaev, see Yin Jian Ping, "Kitaitsy na Rossiiskom Dalnom Vostoke," Hokkaido University, http://src-h.slav.hokudai.ac.jp/pdf_seminar/050228yin.pdf, 3; Harley Balzer and Maria Repnikova, "Chinese Migration to Russia: Missed Opportunities," Kennan Institute and Comparative Urban Studies Eurasian Migration Paper no. 3 (Washington, DC: Woodrow Wilson International Center for Scholars, 2009), 9. On "Asian Balkans," see Mikhail Alekseev, "Chinese Migration in the Russian Far East: Security Threats and Incentives for Cooperation in Primorskii Krai," in *Russia's Far East: A Region at Risk,* ed. Judith Thornton and Charles E. Ziegler (Seattle: University of Washington Press, 2002), 319. On migration data, see Harley Balzer and Maria Repnikova, "Migration between China and Russia," *Post-Soviet Affairs* 26, no. 1 (2010): 1–37.

13. On Japanese foreign investment, see Kunio Okada, "The Japanese Economic Presence in the Russian Far East," in Thornton and Ziegler, *Russia's Far East,* 430; Lee, "The Far East between Russia, China, and America." On South Korea, see Andrew Salmon, "4-Day Meeting Begins with Closed Visit at Russian's Dacha," *New York Times,* September 22, 2004.

14. This paragraph draws extensively from Lee, "The Far East between Russia, China, and America."

15. Anton Barabashin and Alexander Graef, "Thinking Foreign Policy in Russia: Think Tanks and Grand Narratives," Atlantic Council, November 12, 2019, https://www.atlanticcouncil.org/in-depth-research-reports/report/thinking-foreign-policy-in-russia-think-tanks-and-grand-narratives, chap. 6.

16. Erica Downs et al., "The Emerging Russia-Asia Energy Nexus" (Washington, DC: National Bureau of Asian Research, Special Report no. 74, December 2018), esp. 10; Nich-

olas Trickett, *Russia's Long Pivot East* (Philadelphia: Foreign Policy Research Institute, 2019).

17. "The Junior Partner: How Vladimir Putin's Embrace of China Weakens Russia," *Economist*, July 25, 2019, https://www.economist.com/briefing/2019/07/25/how-vladimir -putins-embrace-of-china-weakens-russia.

18. Rilka Dragneva, *The Eurasian Economic Union: Putin's Geopolitical Project* (Philadelphia: Foreign Policy Research Institute, 2018).

19. David Lewis, "The Evolution of Greater Eurasia," *Europe-Asia Studies* 70, no. 10 (2018): 1617; Barabashin and Graef, "Thinking Foreign Policy in Russia," chap. 6; Sergey Karaganov, "Avtoritarizm Rossii ne Naviazan Sverhu," Russian Council on International Affairs, October 12, 2018, https://russiancouncil.ru/analytics-and-comments/comments/av toritarizm-rossii-ne-navyazan-sverkhu/?sphrase_id=32847771.

20. This section draws extensively from Chris Miller, "Will Russia's Pivot to Asia Last?," *Orbis* 64, no. 1 (2020): 43–57.

21. A useful survey is James Henderson, *Energy Relations between Russia and China: Playing Chess with the Dragon* (Oxford: Oxford Institute for Energy Studies, 2016), https:// www.oxfordenergy.org/wpcms/wp-content/uploads/2016/08/Energy-Relations -between-Russia-and-China-Playing-Chess-with-the-Dragon-WPM-67.pdf.

22. On the instrumentalization of the Soviet collapse, see Shaun Walker, *The Long Hangover: Putin's New Russia and the Ghosts of the Past* (Oxford: Oxford University Press), chap. 1.

23. Mikhail Gorbachev, *Speech by Mikhail Gorbachev in Vladivostok, July 28, 1986* (Moscow: Novosti Press Agency Publishing House, 1986), 26.

24. Tsuyoshi Hasegawa, *Racing the Enemy: Stalin, Truman, and the Surrender of Japan* (Cambridge, MA: Harvard University Press, 2005), 286.

25. D. Anuchin, "Aziia kak prarodina i uchitelnitsa chelovechestva; ee nastoiashchee i budushchee," *Novy Vostok*, no. 1 (1922), 249; *SRE*, 89.

26. Nikolai Przhevalsky, "O vozmozhnoi voine c Kitaem," *Sbornik geograficheskikh, topograficheskikh, i statisticheskikh materialov po azii*, no. 1 (1883): 293–303.

27. Katkov in *Russkie Vedomosti*, March 2, 1865 (OS), in Dietrich Geyer, *Russian Imperialism: The Interaction of Domestic and Foreign Policy, 1860–1914*, trans. Bruce Little (New Haven, CT: Yale University Press, 1987), 94; Charles Marvin, *Russian Advance toward India* (London: Sampson Low, Marston, Searle, and Rivington, 1882), 306–307; Peter A. Zaionchkovsky, *The Russian Autocracy in Crisis*, ed. and trans. Gary M. Hamburg (Gulf Breeze, FL: Academic International Press, 1979), chap. 5.

28. Mark Bassin, *Imperial Visions: Nationalist Imagination and Geographical Expansion in the Russian Far East, 1840–1865* (Cambridge: Cambridge University Press, 1999), 86, 90; A. P. Balasoglo, "Ispoved," in *Petrashevtsy: Sbornik Materialov*, ed. P. E. Shchegelev (Moscow: Gosudarstvennoe Izdatelstvo, 1927), 251; Aleksandr P. Balasoglo, "Vostochnaia Sibir. Zapiska c kommandirovke na ostrov Sakhalin kapitan-leitenanta Posdushkina," *Chteniia v imp. obshchestve istorii i drevnostei Rossiiskikh pri Moskovskom Universitete* 2 (April–June 1875): 183–184; Mark Bassin, "A Russia Mississippi? A Political-Geographical Inquiry into the Vision of Russia on the Pacific, 1840–1865" (PhD diss., University of California, Berkeley, 1983), 87, 284.

29. Owen Matthews, *Glorious Misadventures: Nikolai Rezanov and the Dream of a Russian America* (New York: Bloomsbury, 2013), 1.

30. John Le Donne, "Russia's Eastern Theater, 1650–1850: Springboard or Strategic Backyard?," *Cahiers du Monde Russe* 49, no. 1 (2008): 17–46; Barbara Jelavich, *A Century of Russian Foreign Policy, 1814–1914* (Philadelphia: Lippincott, 1964), v–vii.

31. Andrei Lobanov Rostovsky, "Russia at the Crossroads: Europe or Asia," *Slavonic and East European Review* 6, no. 18 (March 1928).

32. "China's Xi Praises 'Best Friend' Putin during Russia Visit," BBC, June 6, 2019, https://www.bbc.com/news/world-europe-48537663.

33. Putin, "Speech at the First Far Eastern Forum," translation adjusted.

34. Lionel Barber and Henry Foy, "Transcript of Interview with Vladimir Putin," *Financial Times*, June 27, 2019, https://www.ft.com/content/878d2344-98f0-11e9-9573-ee5cbb98ed36.

ACKNOWLEDGMENTS

This book was completed with the support of many colleagues over five years of research and writing. Any book that examines over 300 years of history relies heavily on the discoveries of other scholars. The historians whose work I read and drew on are acknowledged in the notes, but I also benefited from the opportunity to exchange ideas with many scholars. Sergey Radchenko and Lis Tarlow helped me to understand Gorbachev's policies toward Asia and in particular toward Japan. Sulmaan Khan saved me from many misinterpretations of Chinese foreign policy. Dong Yan helped me understand Qing history and the Russian architectural legacy in Harbin. Greg Afinogenov clarified Russia's seizure of the Pacific Coast. Arne Westad and Yevgen Sautin shaped my thinking on the Soviet approach to the Chinese Civil War. Stephen Kotkin was a helpful sounding board for interpreting Stalin's diplomacy. John Gaddis helped me to see the global importance of Li Hongzhang and the Trans-Siberian Railroad. Hiroaki Kuromiya pointed out the uncertainty over who assassinated Zhang Zuolin. A workshop at Yale on Russian foreign policy organized by Ian Johnson was crucial in helping shape my arguments, and I thank all the participants of that workshop for stimulating debate.

I conducted research for this book in a variety of archives in Russia, the United States, and the United Kingdom. In Russia I thank the archivists at the Archive of the Foreign Policy of the Russian Federation, the Gorbachev Foundation Archive, the Russian Academy of Sciences Archive, the Russian State Archive of Contemporary History, the Russian State Archive of the Economy, the Russian State Archive of the Navy, the Russian State Archive of Social and Political History, and the State Archive of the Russian Federation. In the United States I thank the archivists at the Bakhmeteff Archive at Columbia University Library and the Hoover Institution. In the United Kingdom I thank the archivists at the National Archives.

Stephanie Petrella has been an extraordinary colleague over the past several years, shaping my understanding of the history described in these pages and helping me chase documents across multiple continents. Jacob Clemente read and commented on the entire manuscript and also helped me make sense of Soviet policy toward Xinjiang. Anastasiia Posnova and Roksana Gabidullina also helped me gather relevant documents.

My colleagues and students at the Fletcher School have provided a supportive audience as I refined the ideas presented in this book in classes, conferences, and conversations. Special thanks are due to my colleagues at the Fletcher School's Russia and Eurasia Program, Dan Drezner and Arik Burakovsky, for tolerating my absence for a writing sabbatical. The Fletcher School's exchanges with MGIMO University, meanwhile, have shaped my thinking about Russian foreign policy today. The Fletcher School's librarians, meanwhile, patiently handled a never-ending flood of requests for obscure books and microfilms.

Alan Luxenberg of the Foreign Policy Research Institute (FPRI) was an early believer in this project, and in me. This book would not have gotten off the ground without him. Thanks also to Maia Otarashvili and the entire team at FPRI for their support in assembling an extensive research agenda that helped me understand contemporary Russian foreign policy and its historical roots. Al Song played a crucial role in helping me refine the book's framing in the earliest stage; it would have been a very different and less interesting book without his advice. Kathleen McDermott of Harvard University Press has been a pleasure to work with and a helpful guide.

Liya and Anton have tolerated this history intruding into all aspects of family life—mornings, evenings, weekends, holidays. I dedicate this book to them.

INDEX